Haganai²

I don't have many friends

VOLUME 1

art by Itachi
story by Yomi Hirasaka
Character Design Buriki

STAFF CREDITS

translation
adaptation
lettering   Roland Amago
layout   Bambi Eloriaga-Amago

cove
co

HAGANAI: I DON'T HAVE MANY FRIENDS VOL. 1
Copyright © 2010 Itachi, © 2010 Yomi Hirasaka
First published in Japan in 2010 by MEDIA FACTORY, Inc.
English translation rights reserved by Seven Seas Entertainment, LLC.
under the license from MEDIA FACTORY, Inc., Tokyo, Japan.
No portion of this book may be reproduced or transmitted in any form
without written permission from the copyright holders.

This is a work of fiction. Names, characters, places, and incidents are the
products of the author's imagination or are used fictitiously. Any resemblance
to actual events, locales, or persons, living or dead, is entirely coincidental.

Seven Seas and the Seven Seas logo are trademarks of
Seven Seas Entertainment, LLC.

ISBN: 978-1-937867-12-6

Printed in Canada

First Printing: November 2012

10 9 8 7 6 5 4 3

Seven Seas

FOLLOW US ONLINE: www.gomanga.com

READING DIRECTIONS

This book reads from *right to left*, Japanese style.
your first time reading manga, you start
from the top right panel o
from there. If you get los
ed diagram here. It may
but you'll get the hang of

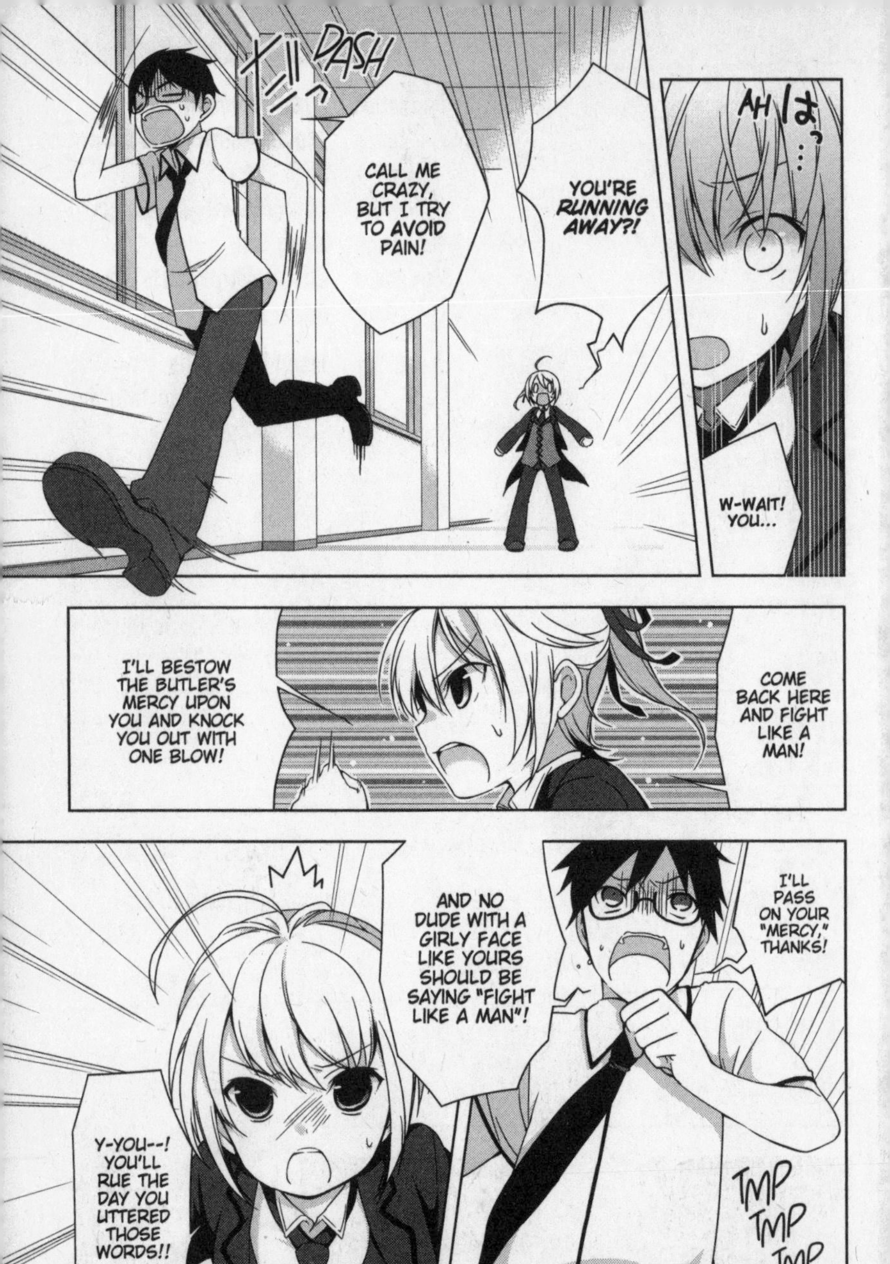
AH は っ…
W-WAIT! YOU...
YOU'RE RUNNING AWAY?!
CALL ME CRAZY, BUT I TRY TO AVOID PAIN!
DASH
COME BACK HERE AND FIGHT LIKE A MAN!
I'LL BESTOW THE BUTLER'S MERCY UPON YOU AND KNOCK YOU OUT WITH ONE BLOW!
I'LL PASS ON YOUR "MERCY," THANKS!
AND NO DUDE WITH A GIRLY FACE LIKE YOURS SHOULD BE SAYING "FIGHT LIKE A MAN"!
TMP TMP TMP
Y-YOU--! YOU'LL RUE THE DAY YOU UTTERED THOSE WORDS!!

Continued in *Mayo Chiki!* Vol. 1

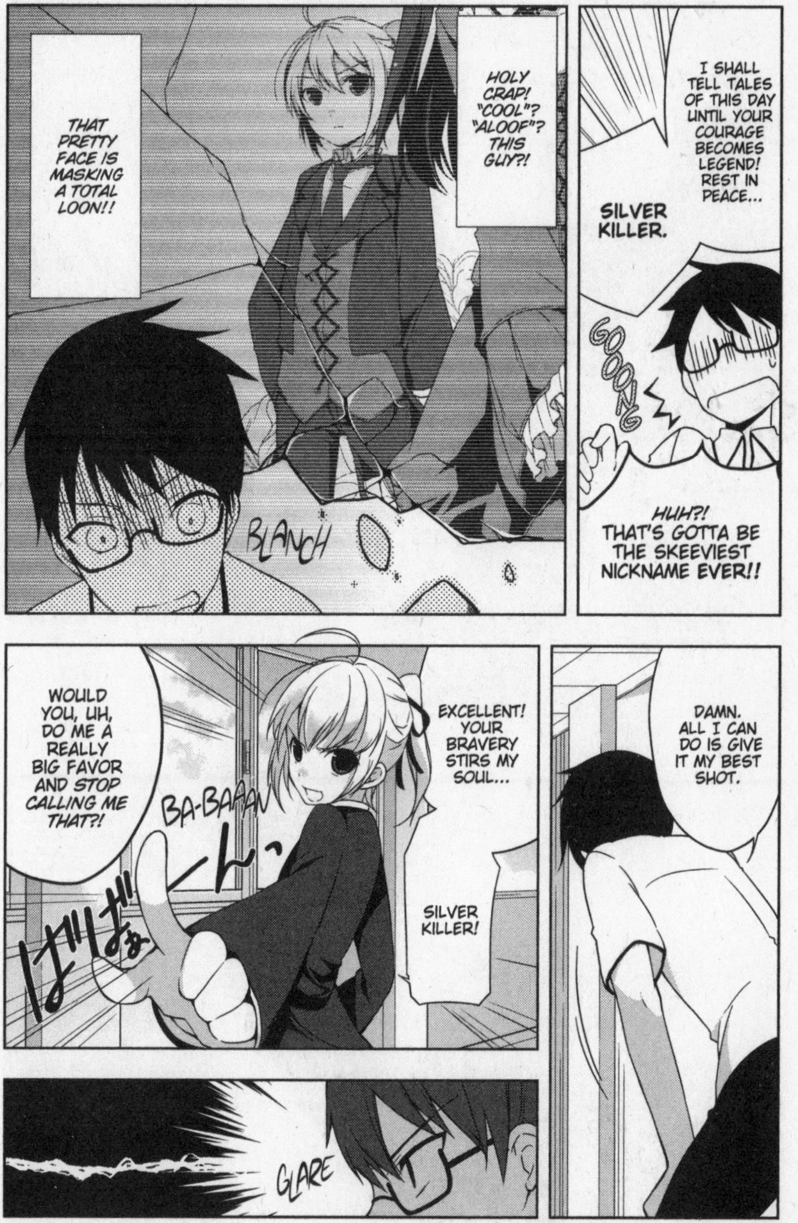
I SHALL TELL TALES OF THIS DAY UNTIL YOUR COURAGE BECOMES LEGEND! REST IN PEACE...
SILVER KILLER.
GOOONG
HUH?! THAT'S GOTTA BE THE SKEEVIEST NICKNAME EVER!!
HOLY CRAP! "COOL"? "ALOOF"? THIS GUY?!
THAT PRETTY FACE IS MASKING A TOTAL LOON!!
BLANCH
DAMN. ALL I CAN DO IS GIVE IT MY BEST SHOT.
EXCELLENT! YOUR BRAVERY STIRS MY SOUL...
SILVER KILLER!
BA-BAAAN
WOULD YOU, UH, DO ME A REALLY BIG FAVOR AND STOP CALLING ME THAT?!
GLARE

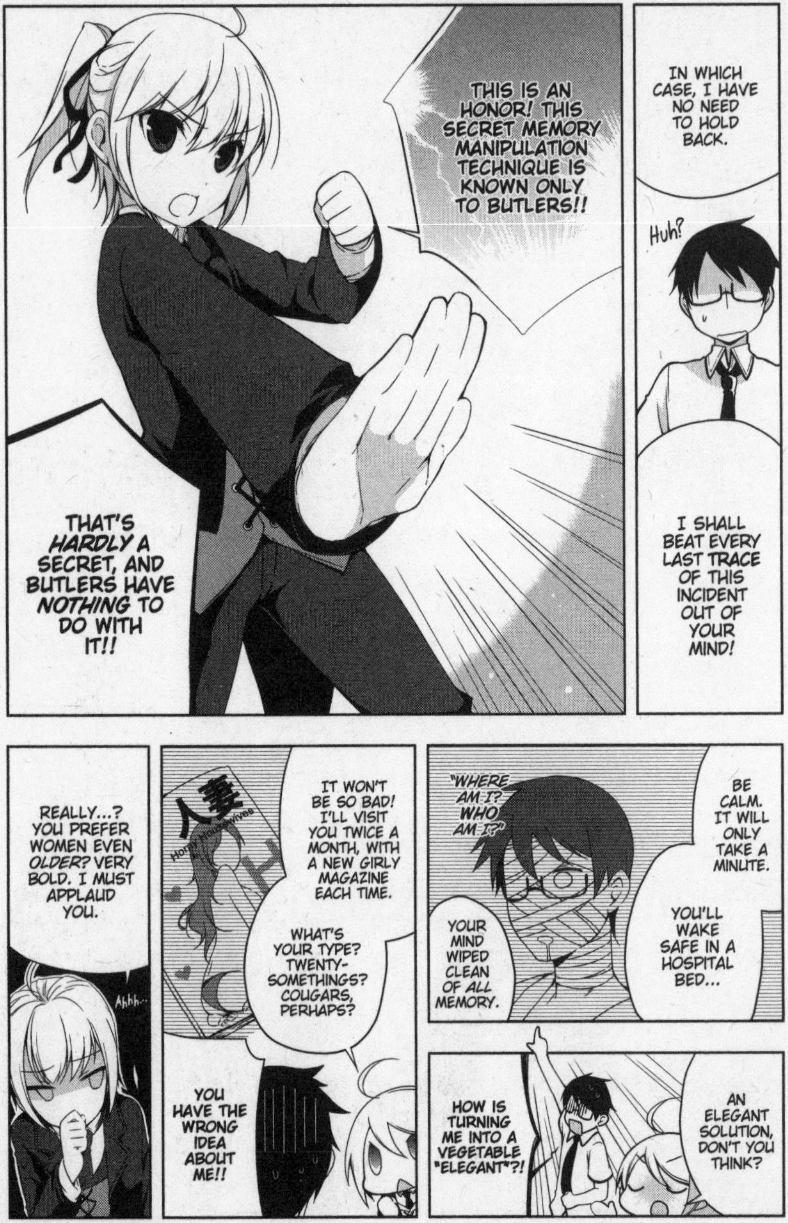
IN WHICH CASE, I HAVE NO NEED TO HOLD BACK.
Huh?
I SHALL BEAT EVERY LAST TRACE OF THIS INCIDENT OUT OF YOUR MIND!
THIS IS AN HONOR! THIS SECRET MEMORY MANIPULATION TECHNIQUE IS KNOWN ONLY TO BUTLERS!!
THAT'S *HARDLY* A SECRET, AND BUTLERS HAVE *NOTHING* TO DO WITH IT!!
BE CALM. IT WILL ONLY TAKE A MINUTE.
"*WHERE AM I? WHO AM I?*"
YOU'LL WAKE SAFE IN A HOSPITAL BED...
YOUR MIND WIPED CLEAN OF *ALL* MEMORY.
AN ELEGANT SOLUTION, DON'T YOU THINK?
HOW IS TURNING ME INTO A VEGETABLE "ELEGANT"?!
IT WON'T BE SO BAD! I'LL VISIT YOU TWICE A MONTH, WITH A NEW GIRLY MAGAZINE EACH TIME.
人妻
Horny Housewives
WHAT'S YOUR TYPE? TWENTY-SOMETHINGS? COUGARS, PERHAPS?
YOU HAVE THE WRONG IDEA ABOUT ME!!
REALLY...? YOU PREFER WOMEN EVEN *OLDER*? VERY BOLD. I MUST APPLAUD YOU.
Ahhh...

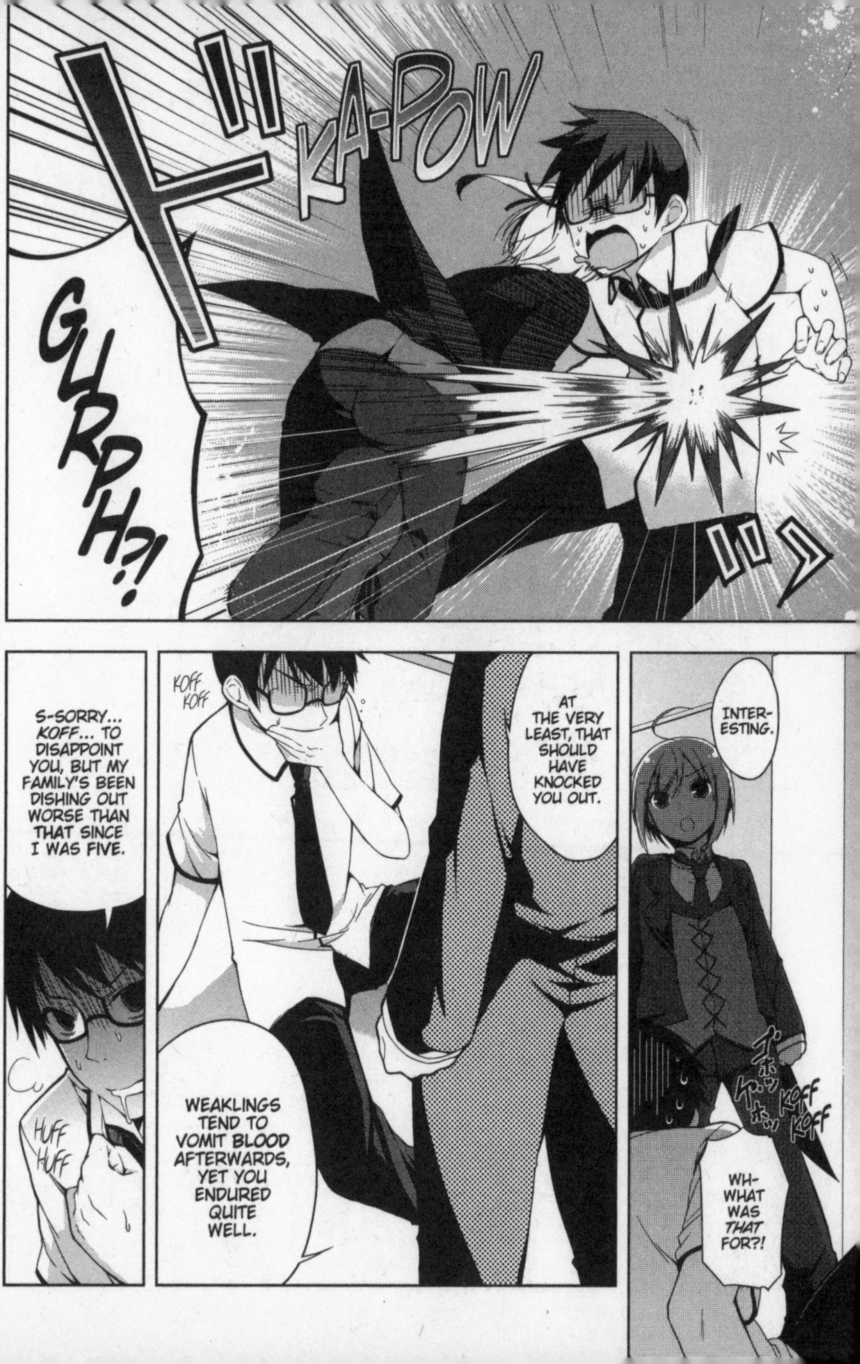
KA-POW
GURPH?!
INTER-ESTING.
KOFF KOFF
WH-WHAT WAS THAT FOR?!
AT THE VERY LEAST, THAT SHOULD HAVE KNOCKED YOU OUT.
KOFF KOFF
WEAKLINGS TEND TO VOMIT BLOOD AFTERWARDS, YET YOU ENDURED QUITE WELL.
S-SORRY... KOFF... TO DISAPPOINT YOU, BUT MY FAMILY'S BEEN DISHING OUT WORSE THAN THAT SINCE I WAS FIVE.
HUFF HUFF

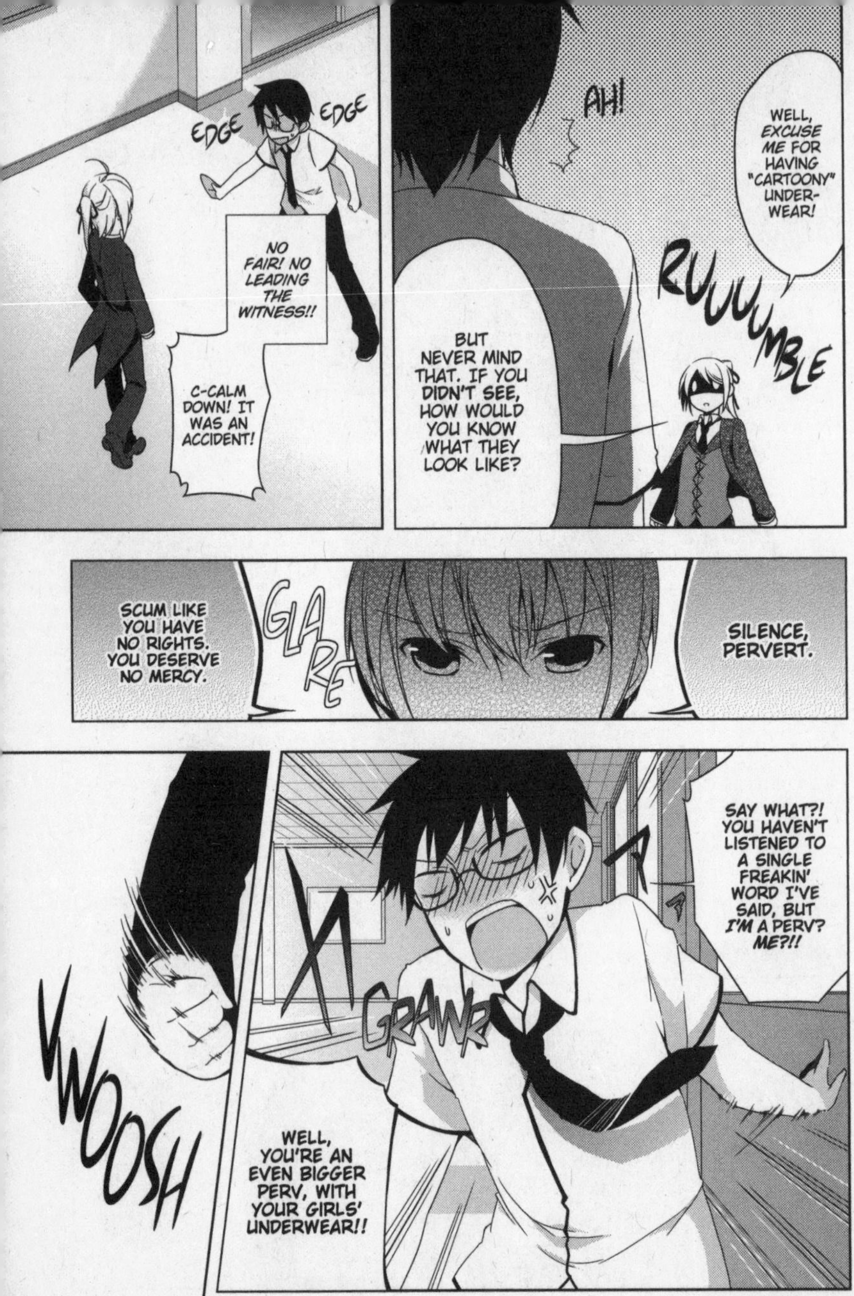
WELL, EXCUSE ME FOR HAVING "CARTOONY" UNDER-WEAR!
AH!
RUUUUMBLE
BUT NEVER MIND THAT. IF YOU DIDN'T SEE, HOW WOULD YOU KNOW WHAT THEY LOOK LIKE?
EDGE
EDGE
NO FAIR! NO LEADING THE WITNESS!!
C-CALM DOWN! IT WAS AN ACCIDENT!
SILENCE, PERVERT.
GLARE
SCUM LIKE YOU HAVE NO RIGHTS. YOU DESERVE NO MERCY.
SAY WHAT?! YOU HAVEN'T LISTENED TO A SINGLE FREAKIN' WORD I'VE SAID, BUT I'M A PERV? ME?!!
GRAWR
WELL, YOU'RE AN EVEN BIGGER PERV, WITH YOUR GIRLS' UNDERWEAR!!
VWOOSH

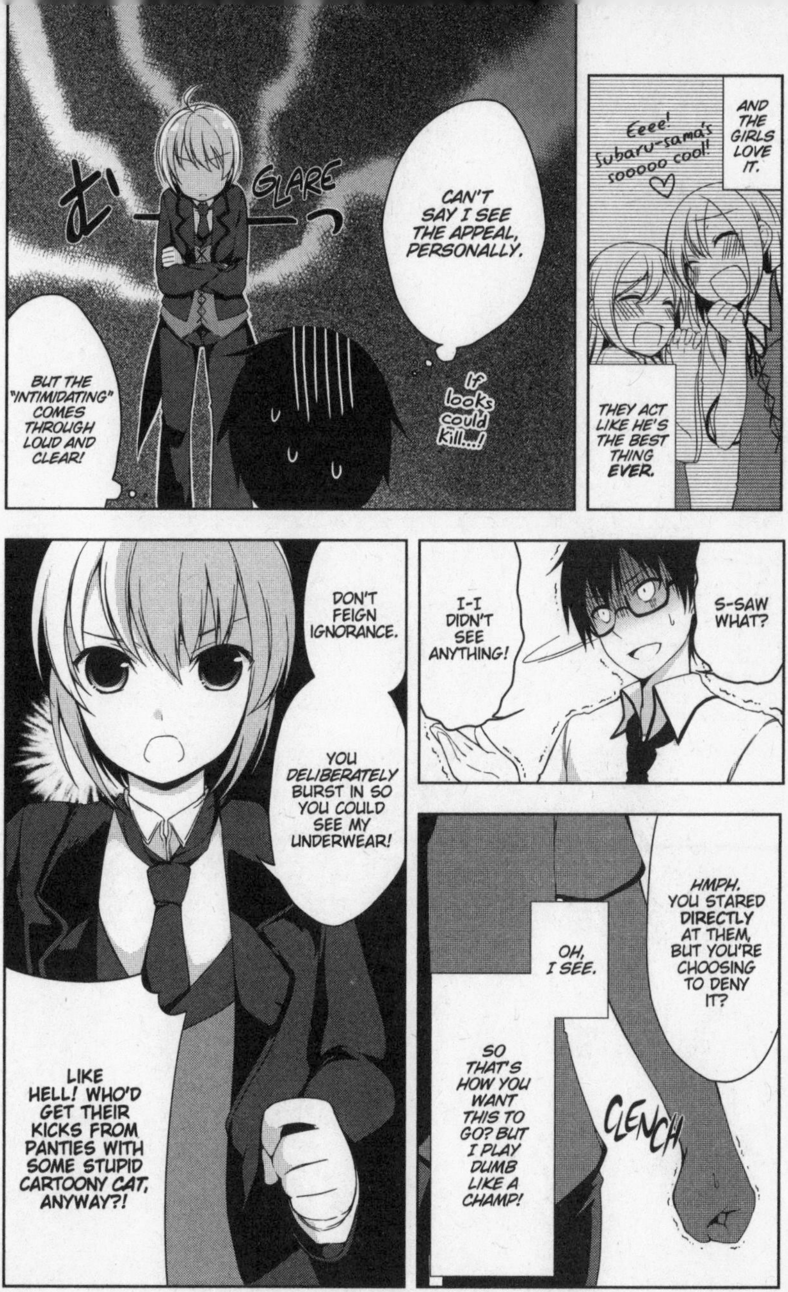
AND THE GIRLS LOVE IT.
Eeee! Subaru-sama's sooooo cool! ♥
THEY ACT LIKE HE'S THE BEST THING EVER.
CAN'T SAY I SEE THE APPEAL, PERSONALLY.
GLARE
If looks could kill...!
BUT THE "INTIMIDATING" COMES THROUGH LOUD AND CLEAR!
S-SAW WHAT?
I-I DIDN'T SEE ANYTHING!
HMPH. YOU STARED DIRECTLY AT THEM, BUT YOU'RE CHOOSING TO DENY IT?
OH, I SEE.
SO THAT'S HOW YOU WANT THIS TO GO? BUT I PLAY DUMB LIKE A CHAMP!
CLENCH
DON'T FEIGN IGNORANCE.
YOU DELIBERATELY BURST IN SO YOU COULD SEE MY UNDERWEAR!
LIKE HELL! WHO'D GET THEIR KICKS FROM PANTIES WITH SOME STUPID CARTOONY CAT, ANYWAY?!

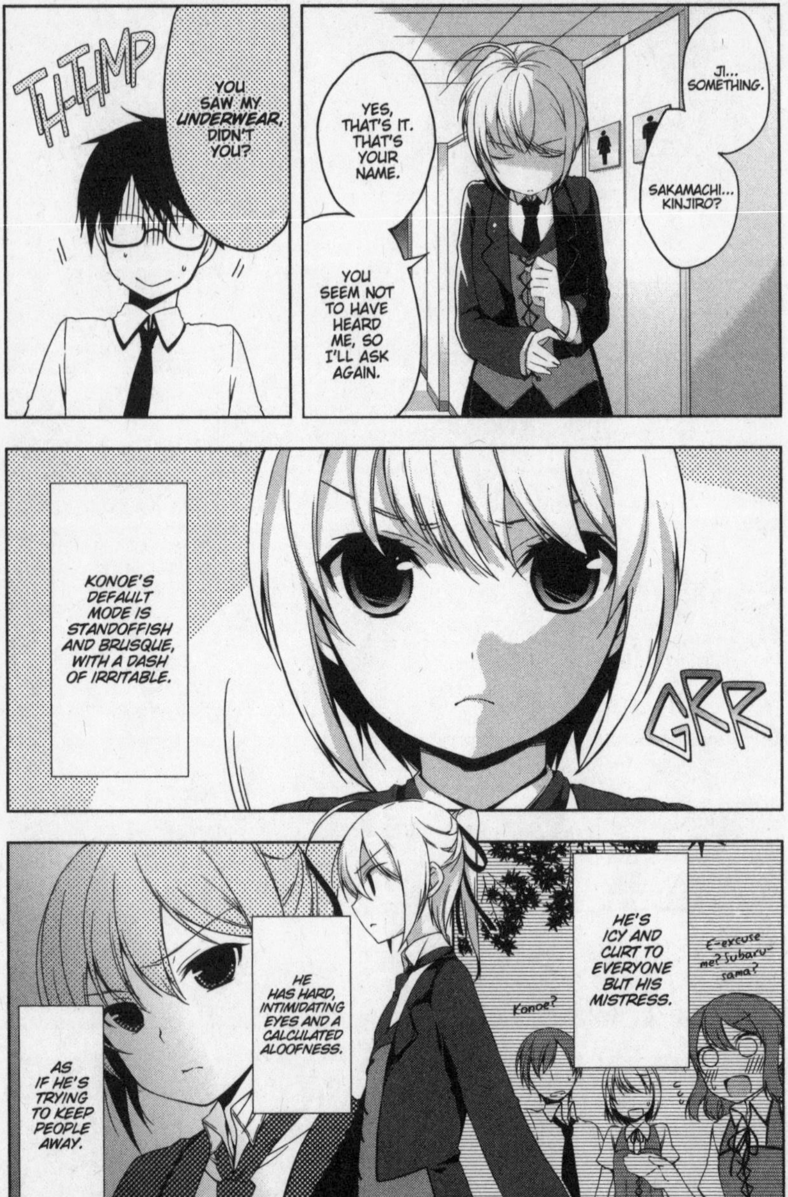
JI... SOMETHING.
SAKAMACHI... KINJIRO?
YES, THAT'S IT. THAT'S YOUR NAME.
YOU SEEM NOT TO HAVE HEARD ME, SO I'LL ASK AGAIN.
YOU SAW MY *UNDERWEAR*, DIDN'T YOU?
TH-THMP
GRR
KONOE'S DEFAULT MODE IS STANDOFFISH AND BRUSQUE, WITH A DASH OF IRRITABLE.
HE'S ICY AND CURT TO EVERYONE BUT HIS MISTRESS.
E-excuse me? Subaru-sama?
Konoe?
HE HAS HARD, INTIMIDATING EYES AND A CALCULATED ALOOFNESS.
AS IF HE'S TRYING TO KEEP PEOPLE AWAY.

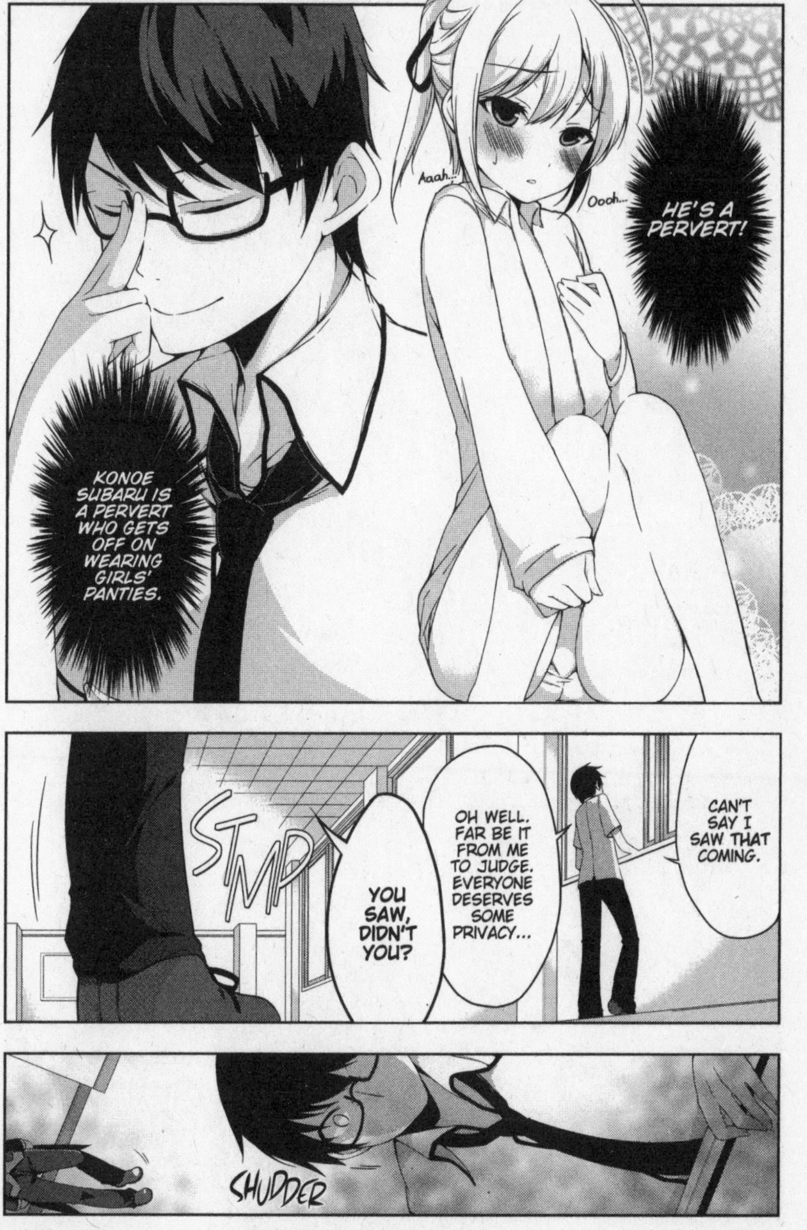
HE'S A PERVERT!
Oooh...
Aaah...
KONOE SUBARU IS A PERVERT WHO GETS OFF ON WEARING GIRLS' PANTIES.
CAN'T SAY I SAW THAT COMING.
OH WELL. FAR BE IT FROM ME TO JUDGE. EVERYONE DESERVES SOME PRIVACY...
YOU SAW, DIDN'T YOU?
STMP
SHUDDER

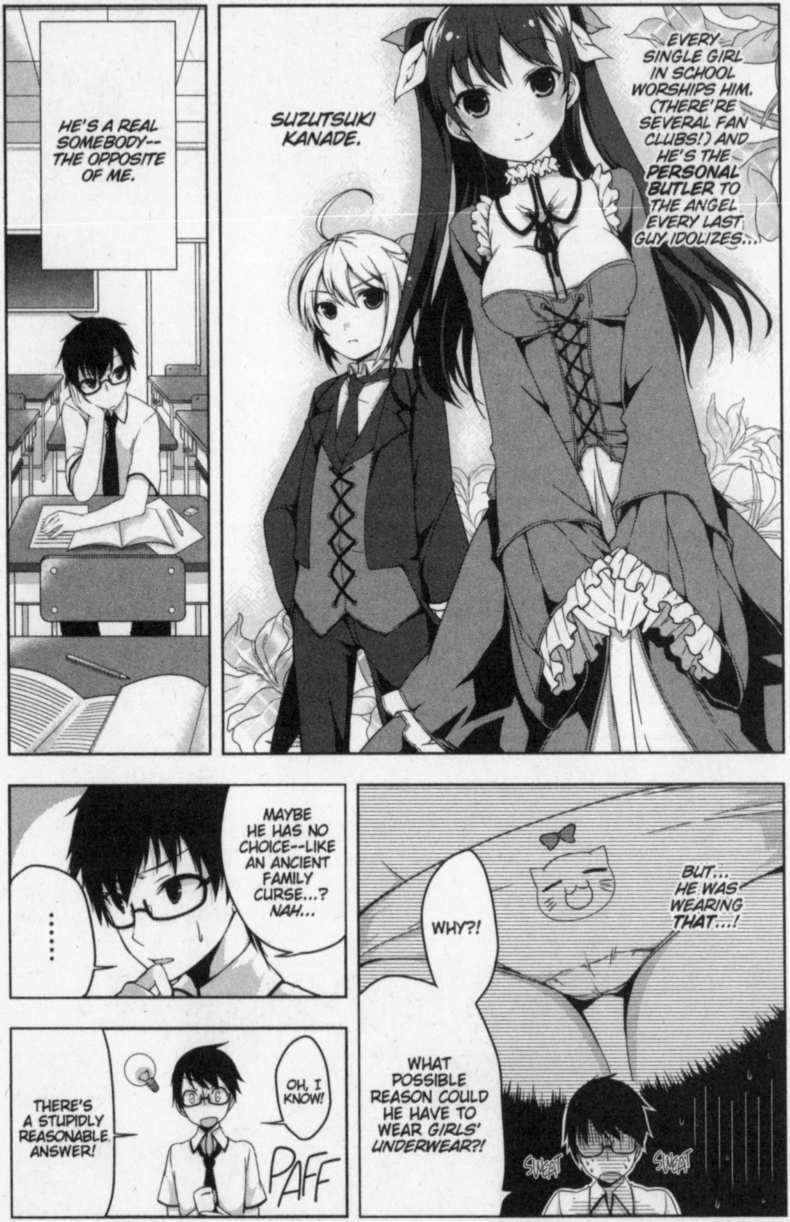
EVERY SINGLE GIRL IN SCHOOL WORSHIPS HIM. (THERE'RE SEVERAL FAN CLUBS!) AND HE'S THE PERSONAL BUTLER TO THE ANGEL EVERY LAST GUY IDOLIZES...
SUZUTSUKI KANADE.
HE'S A REAL SOMEBODY-- THE OPPOSITE OF ME.
BUT... HE WAS WEARING THAT...!
WHY?!
WHAT POSSIBLE REASON COULD HE HAVE TO WEAR GIRLS' UNDERWEAR?!
SWEAT
SWEAT
MAYBE HE HAS NO CHOICE--LIKE AN ANCIENT FAMILY CURSE...? NAH...
......
OH, I KNOW!
THERE'S A STUPIDLY REASONABLE ANSWER!
PAFF

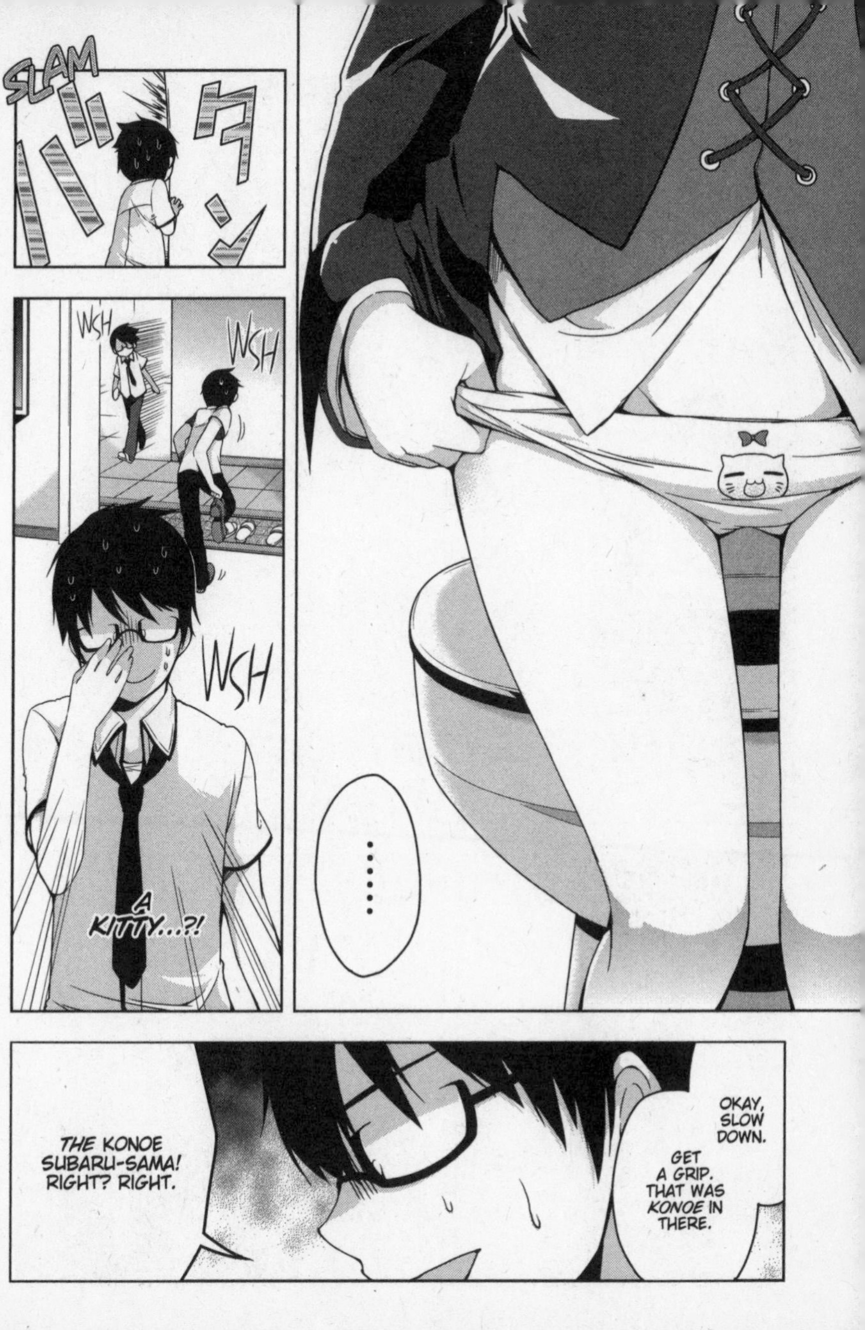
......
SLAM
WSH
WSH
A KITTY...?!
WSH
OKAY, SLOW DOWN.
GET A GRIP. THAT WAS KONOE IN THERE.
THE KONOE SUBARU-SAMA! RIGHT? RIGHT.

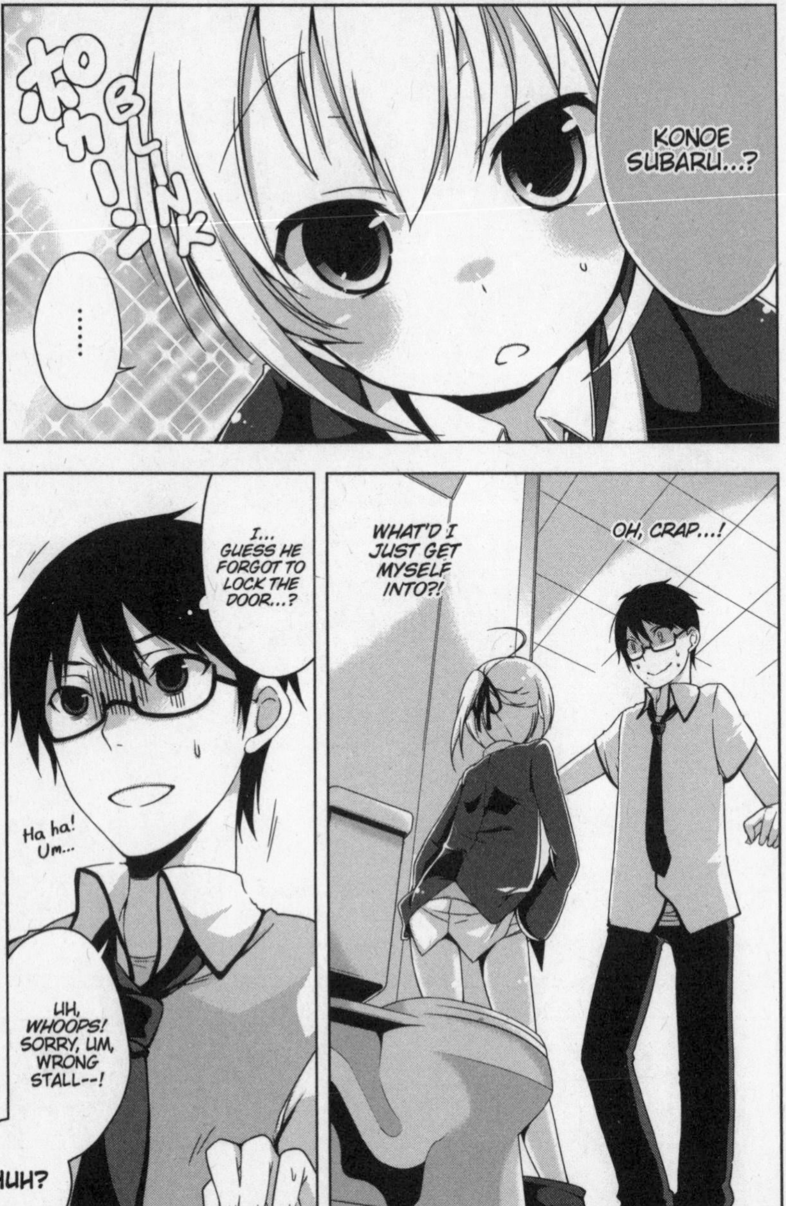

KONOE SUBARU...?
BLINK
......
OH, CRAP...!
WHAT'D I JUST GET MYSELF INTO?!
I... GUESS HE FORGOT TO LOCK THE DOOR...?
Ha ha! Um...
UH, WHOOPS! SORRY, UM, WRONG STALL--!
HUH?

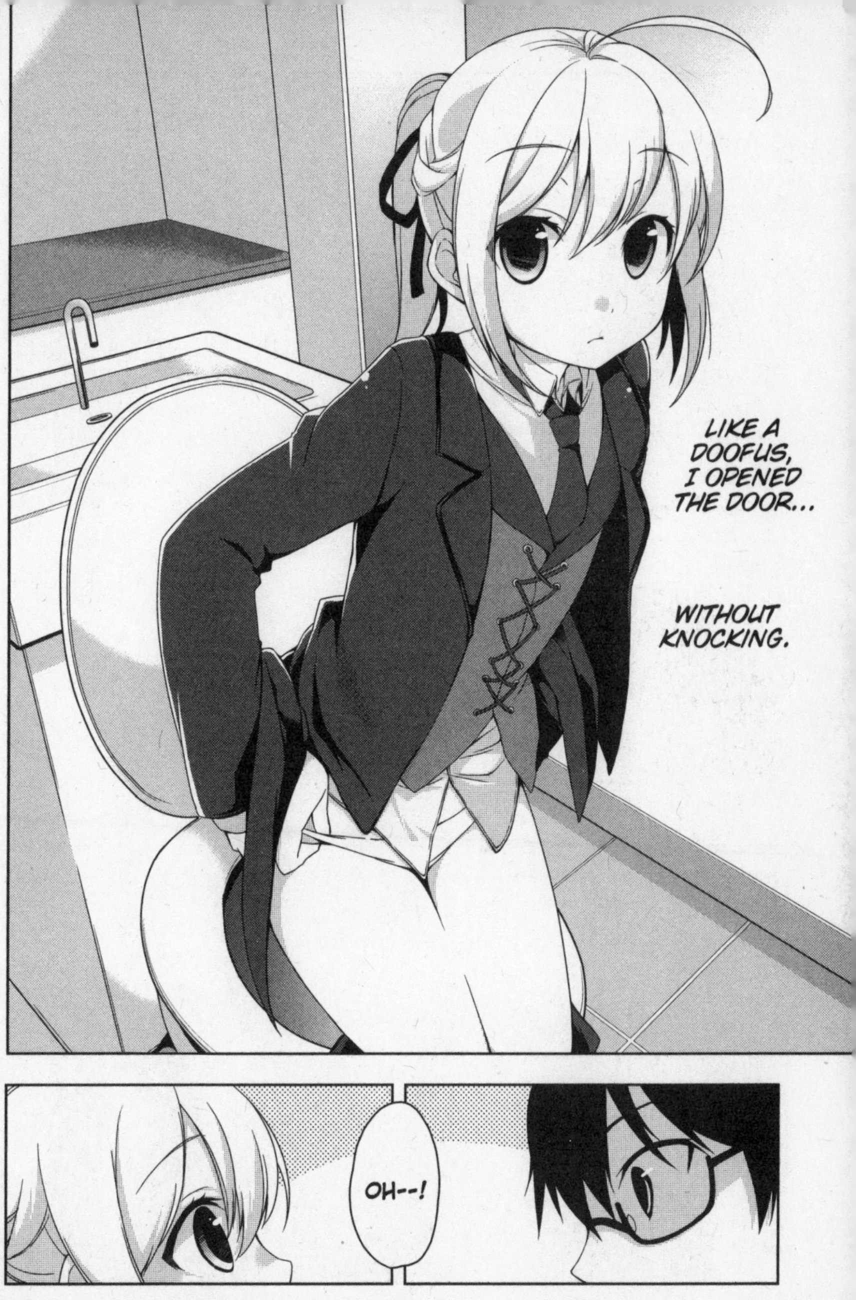
LIKE A DOOFUS, I OPENED THE DOOR...
WITHOUT KNOCKING.
OH--!

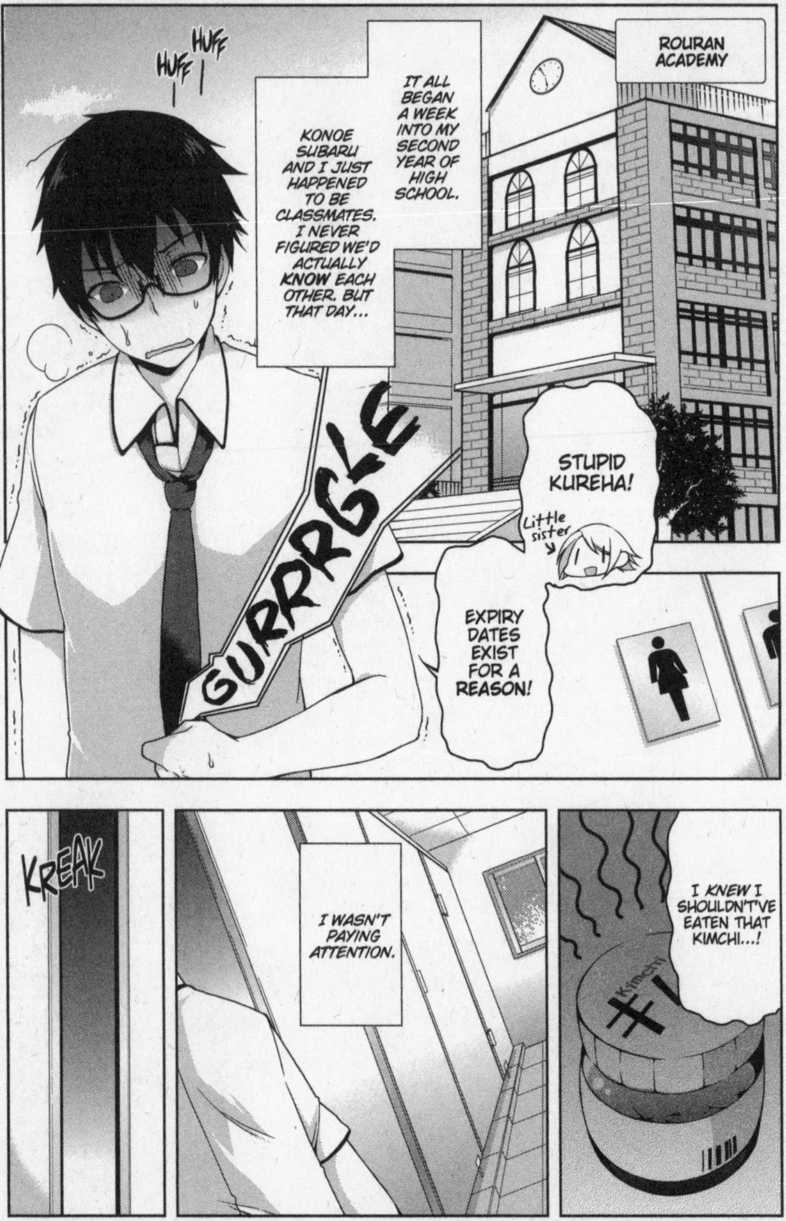
ROURAN ACADEMY
IT ALL BEGAN A WEEK INTO MY SECOND YEAR OF HIGH SCHOOL.
KONOE SUBARU AND I JUST HAPPENED TO BE CLASSMATES. I NEVER FIGURED WE'D ACTUALLY KNOW EACH OTHER. BUT THAT DAY...
HUFF HUFF
GURRRGLE
STUPID KUREHA!
Little sister
EXPIRY DATES EXIST FOR A REASON!
I KNEW I SHOULDN'T'VE EATEN THAT KIMCHI...!
Kimchi
I WASN'T PAYING ATTENTION.
KREAK

MAYO CHIKI!

SPECIAL PREVIEW

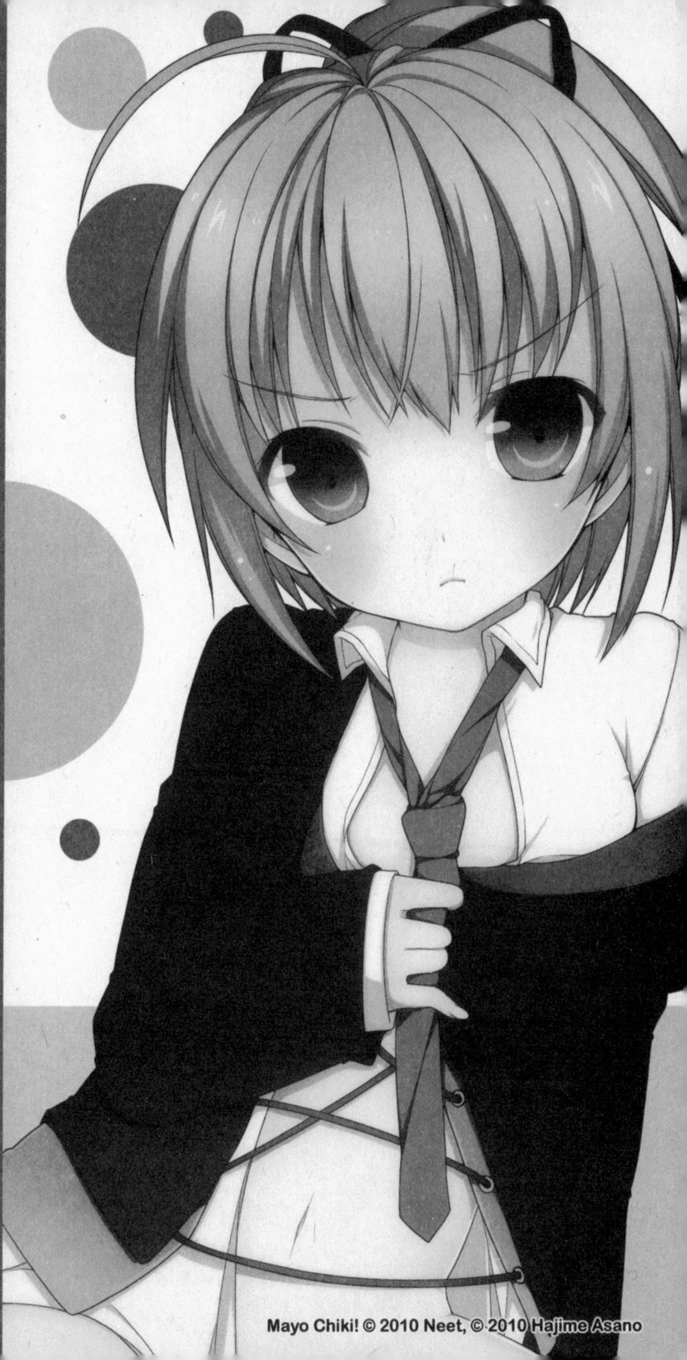

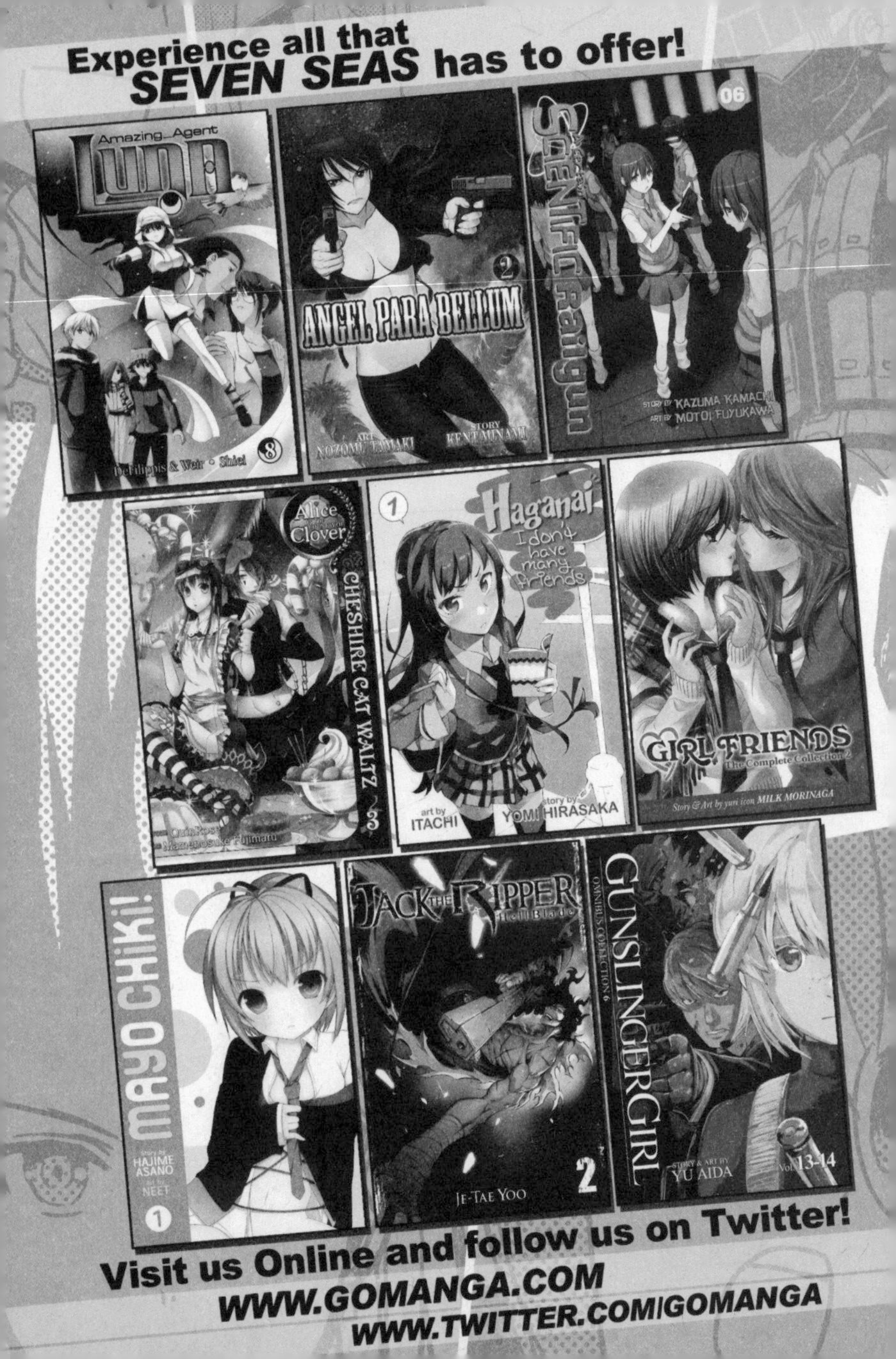
Experience all that
SEVEN SEAS has to offer!
Amazing Agent Luna
DeFilippis & Weir • Shiei
8
ANGEL PARA BELLUM
2
ART NOZOMU TAMAKI
STORY KENT MINAMI
06
Scientific Railgun
STORY BY KAZUMA KAMACHI
ART BY MOTOI FUYUKAWA
Alice in the Country of Clover
CHESHIRE CAT WALTZ
3
Haganai
I don't have many friends
1
art by ITACHI
story by YOMI HIRASAKA
GIRL FRIENDS
The Complete Collection 2
Story & Art by yuri icon MILK MORINAGA
MAYO CHIKI!
Story by HAJIME ASANO
Art by NEET
1
JACK THE RIPPER
Hell Blade
2
JE-TAE YOO
GUNSLINGER GIRL
OMNIBUS COLLECTION 6
STORY & ART BY YU AIDA
VOL. 13-14
Visit us Online and follow us on Twitter!
WWW.GOMANGA.COM
WWW.TWITTER.COM/GOMANGA

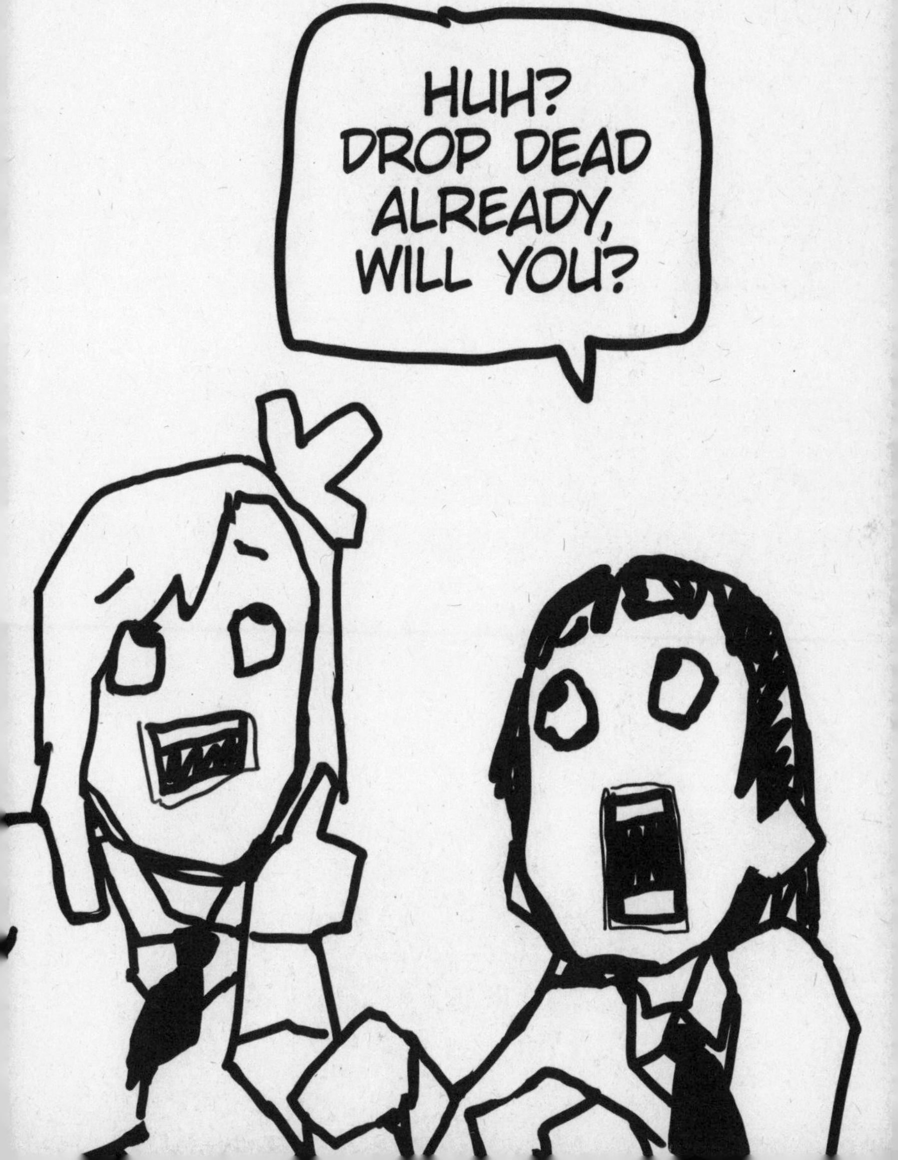
HUH? DROP DEAD ALREADY, WILL YOU?

Haganai

I don't have many friends

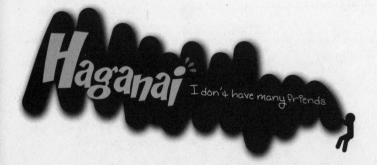

Hello there! I'm Yomi Hirasaka, the original creator of *Boku wa Tomodachi ga Sukunai*. I started just calling it "Haganai" myself, but somehow that seems to have become the official title! Anyway, I'm a regular reader of the manga version of *Haganai* that Itachi-san draws, and I always look forward to the next issue. Kodaka, Yozora, Sena, and Yukimura are all so cute. They all do exactly as they please in the novel as well, but since this is manga, their faces are full of life. I enjoy myself thoroughly just flipping through the pages. Yozora and Sena, in particular, have the most wonderfully unfortunate expressions! Heroines shouldn't make those faces.

Itachi-san is a terrifyingly talented girl! Well, the original creator's not gonna lose! The manga has its strong points and the novels have theirs... But I shouldn't be this submissive. I'll do my best to make sure the original doesn't lose to the manga!

So there you have it. Please check out the original novels too! I think you'll find they have a different feel from the manga.

Yomi Hirasaka

Staff

Pochi-san
Urabi-san
Hayashiyama-san

Thank you so much.
Itachi

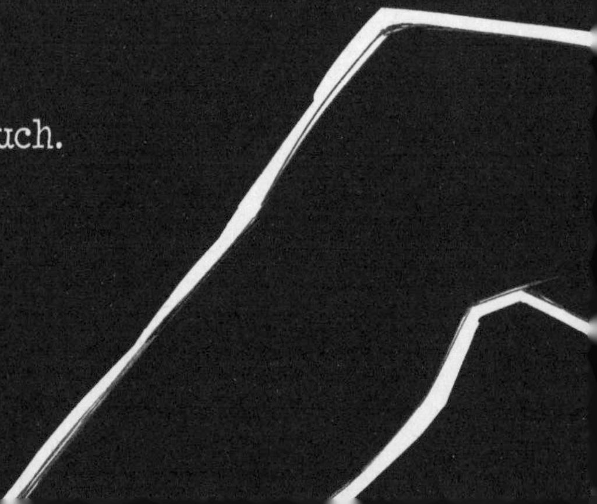

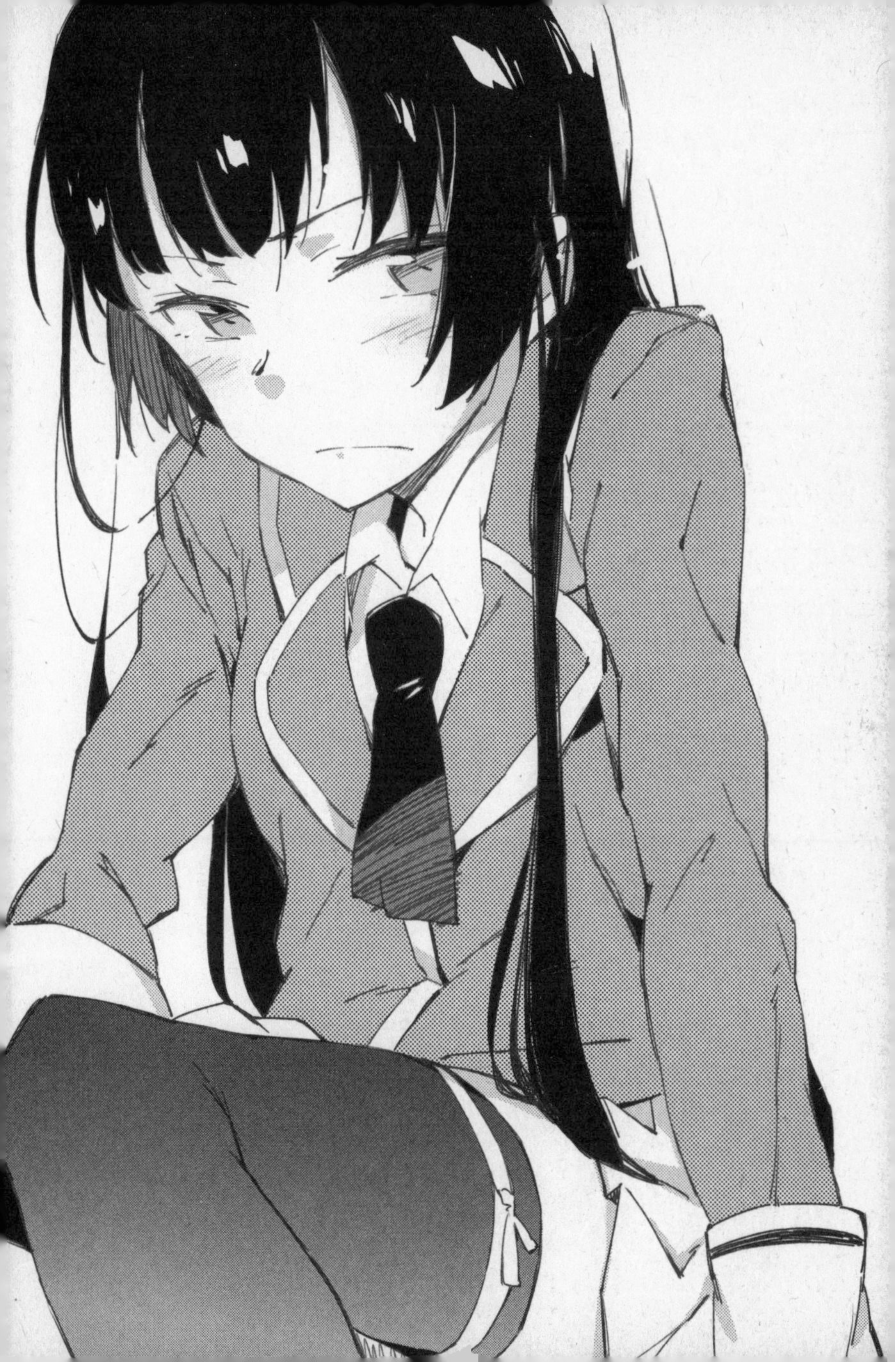

Haganai
I don't have many friends

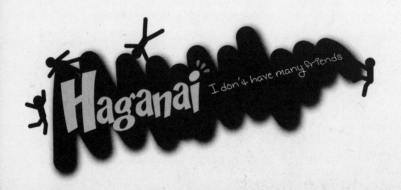

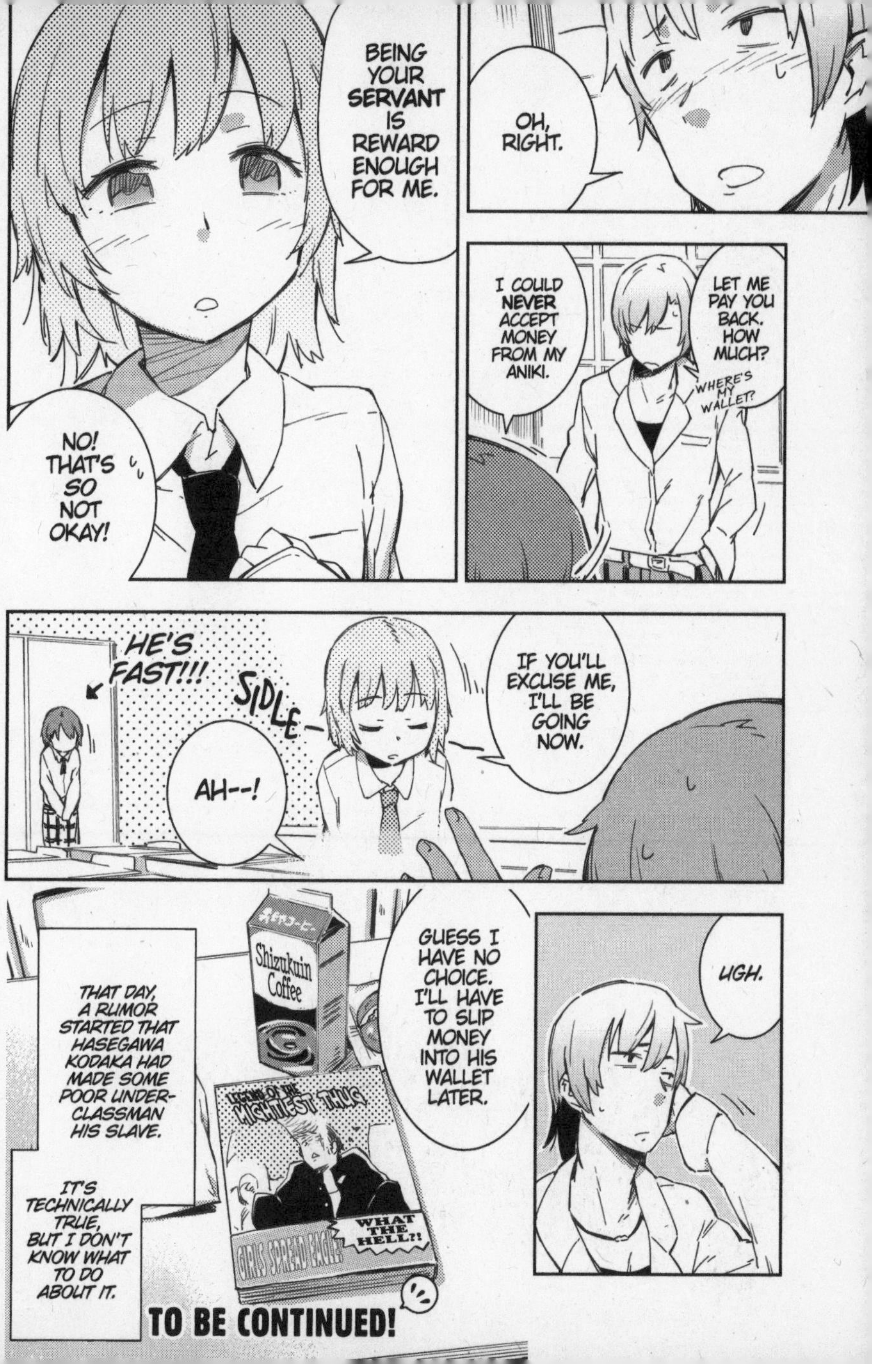
OH, RIGHT.
LET ME PAY YOU BACK. HOW MUCH?
WHERE'S MY WALLET?
I COULD NEVER ACCEPT MONEY FROM MY ANIKI.
BEING YOUR SERVANT IS REWARD ENOUGH FOR ME.
NO! THAT'S SO NOT OKAY!
IF YOU'LL EXCUSE ME, I'LL BE GOING NOW.
SIDLE
AH--!
HE'S FAST!!!
UGH.
GUESS I HAVE NO CHOICE. I'LL HAVE TO SLIP MONEY INTO HIS WALLET LATER.
Shizukuin Coffee
LEGEND OF THE MIGHTIEST THUG
WHAT THE HELL?!
GIRLS SPREAD EAGLE!
THAT DAY, A RUMOR STARTED THAT HASEGAWA KODAKA HAD MADE SOME POOR UNDER-CLASSMAN HIS SLAVE.
IT'S TECHNICALLY TRUE, BUT I DON'T KNOW WHAT TO DO ABOUT IT.
TO BE CONTINUED!

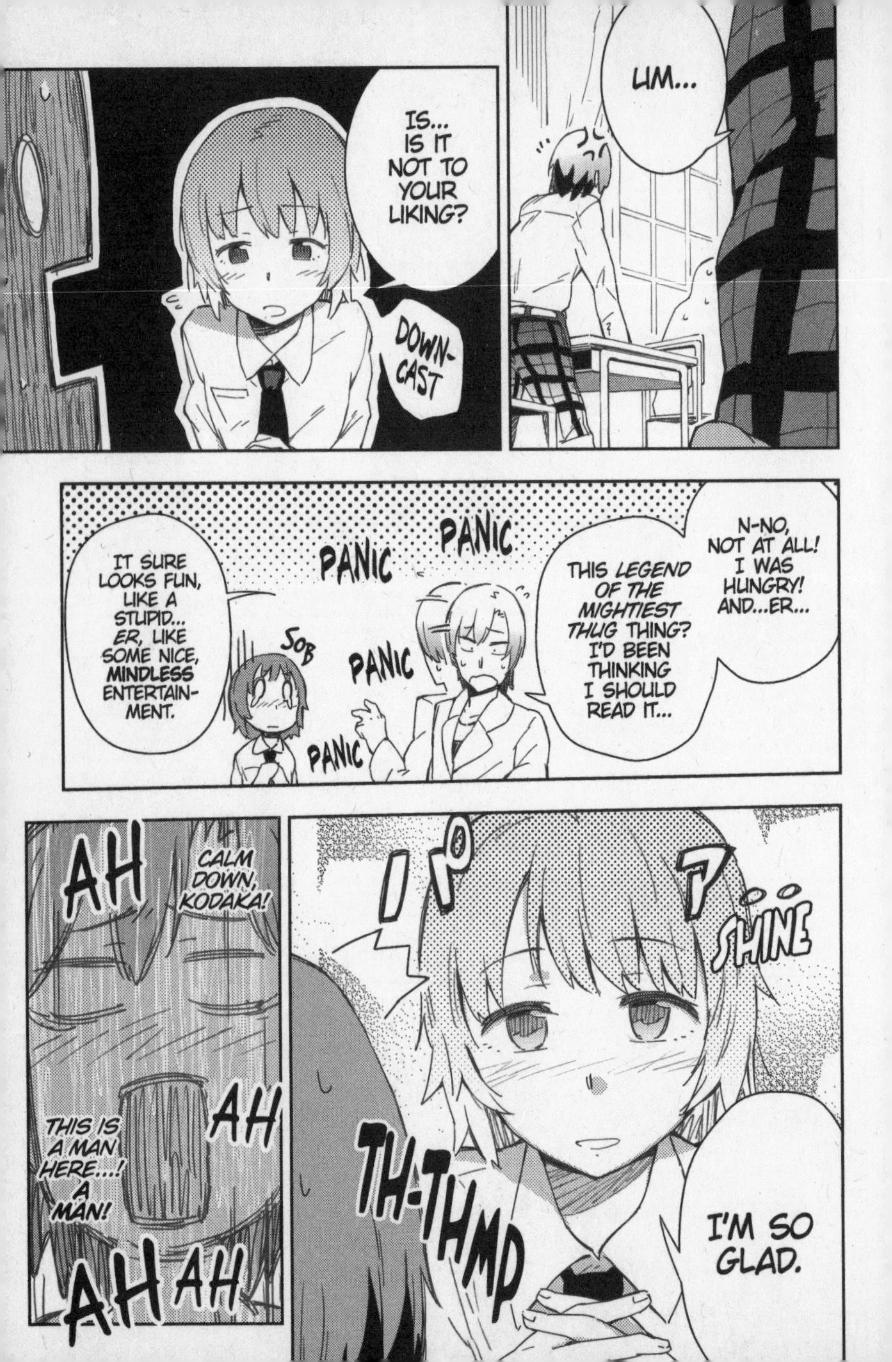
UM...
IS... IS IT NOT TO YOUR LIKING?
DOWN-CAST
N-NO, NOT AT ALL! I WAS HUNGRY! AND...ER...
THIS *LEGEND OF THE MIGHTIEST THUG* THING? I'D BEEN THINKING I SHOULD READ IT...
PANIC
PANIC
PANIC
PANIC
IT SURE LOOKS FUN, LIKE A STUPID... *ER,* LIKE SOME NICE, MINDLESS ENTERTAIN-MENT.
SOB
SHINE
I'M SO GLAD.
TH-THMP
AH
CALM DOWN, KODAKA!
AH
THIS IS A MAN HERE...! A MAN!
AH AH AH

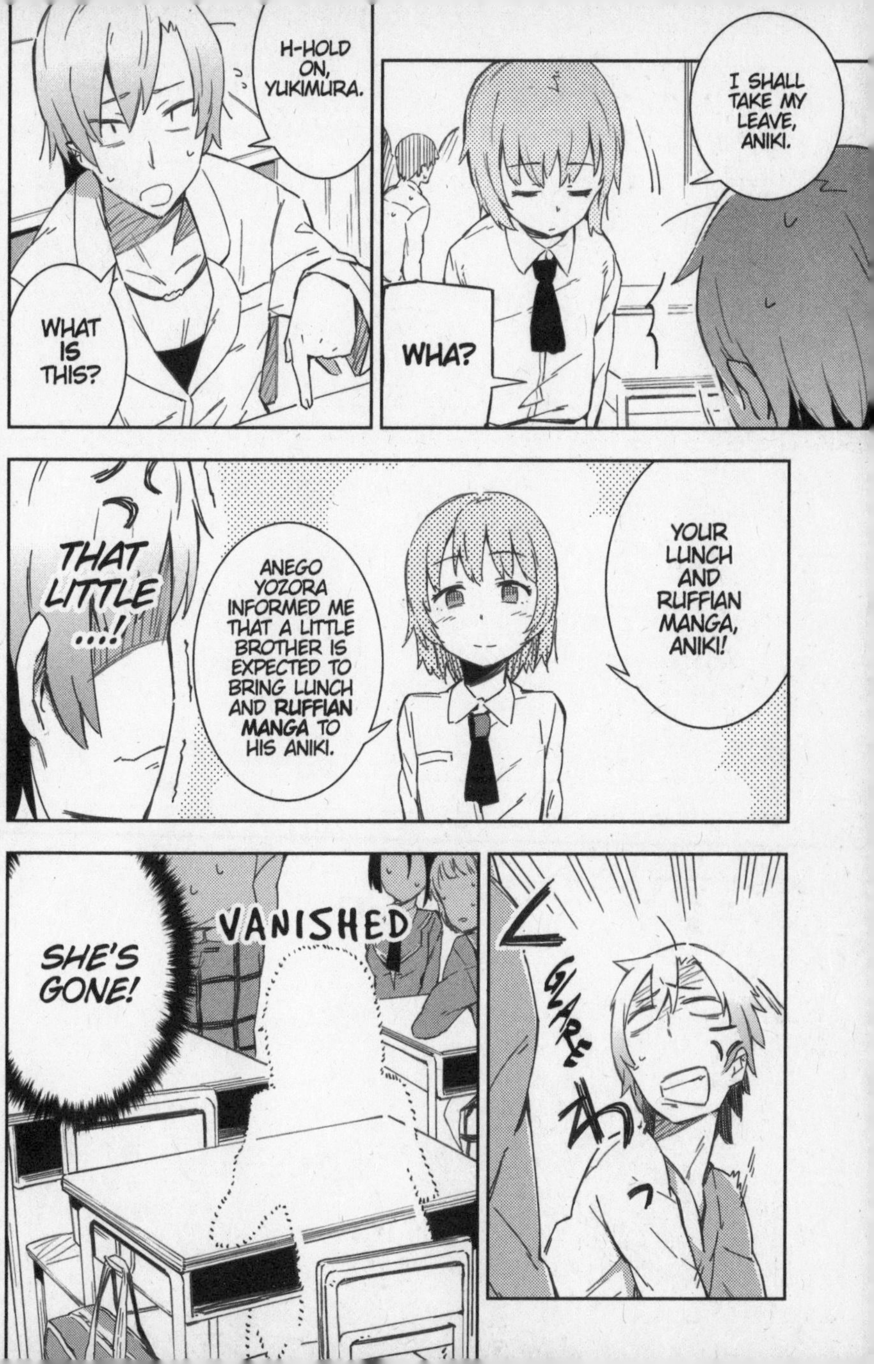
I SHALL TAKE MY LEAVE, ANIKI.
WHA?
H-HOLD ON, YUKIMURA.
WHAT IS THIS?
YOUR LUNCH AND RUFFIAN MANGA, ANIKI!
ANEGO YOZORA INFORMED ME THAT A LITTLE BROTHER IS EXPECTED TO BRING LUNCH AND RUFFIAN MANGA TO HIS ANIKI.
THAT LITTLE ...!
GLARE
VANISHED
SHE'S GONE!

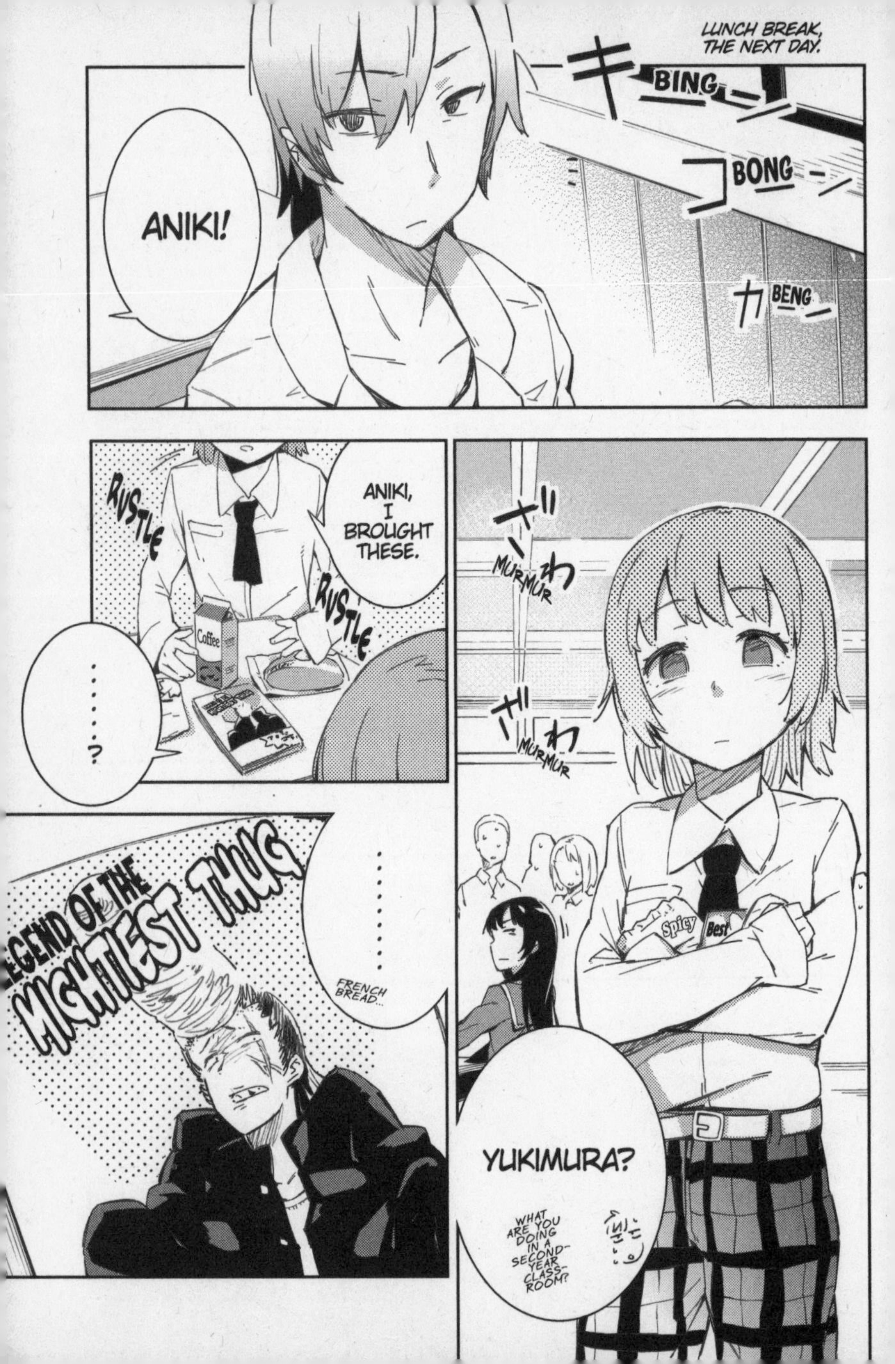
LUNCH BREAK, THE NEXT DAY.
BING
BONG
BENG
ANIKI!
MURMUR
MURMUR
Spicy
Best
YUKIMURA?
WHAT ARE YOU DOING IN A SECOND-YEAR CLASSROOM?
RUSTLE
ANIKI, I BROUGHT THESE.
RUSTLE
Coffee
......?
LEGEND OF THE MIGHTIEST THUG
......
FRENCH BREAD...

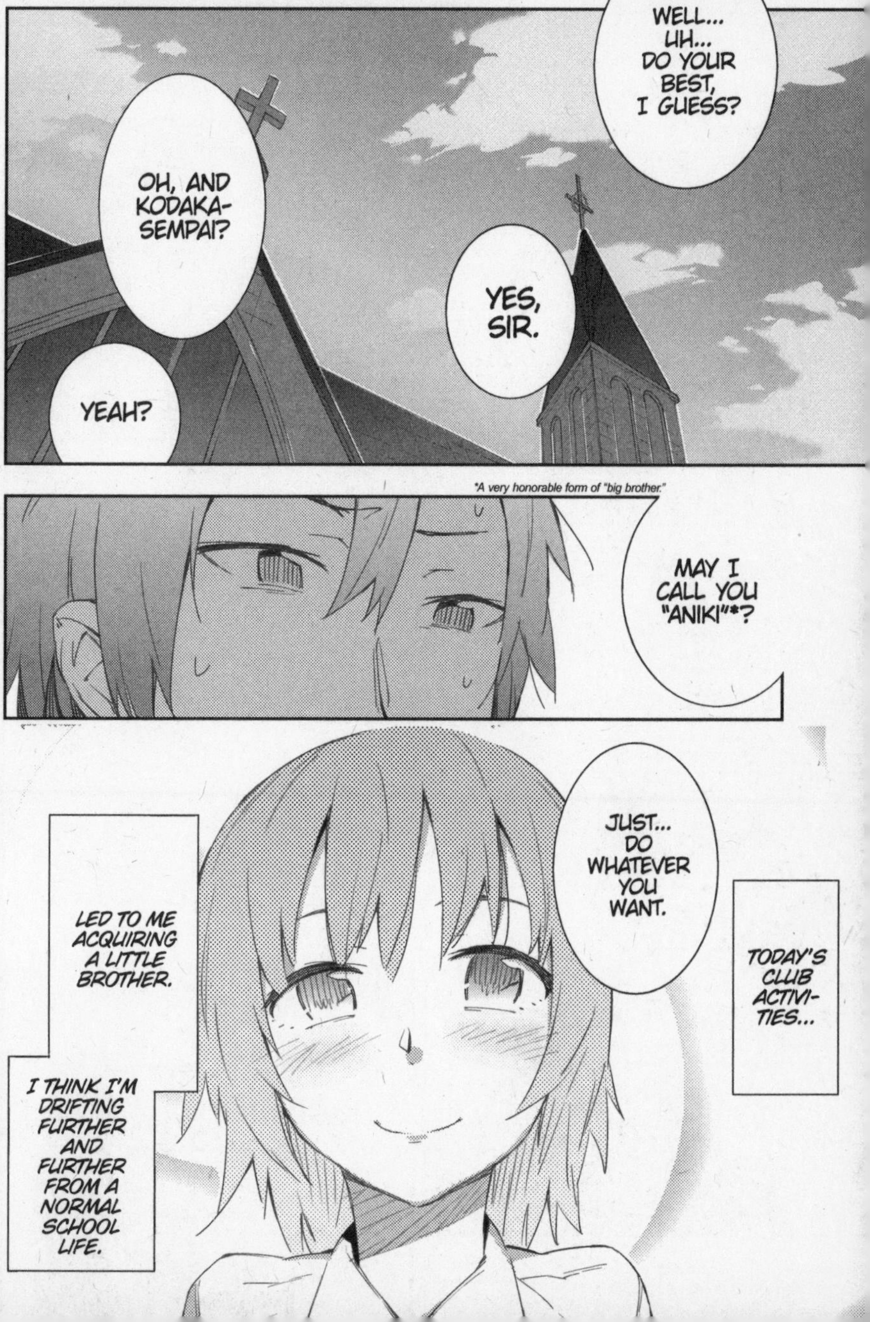
WELL... UH... DO YOUR BEST, I GUESS?
YES, SIR.
OH, AND KODAKA-SEMPAI?
YEAH?
MAY I CALL YOU "ANIKI"*?
*A very honorable form of "big brother."
JUST... DO WHATEVER YOU WANT.
TODAY'S CLUB ACTIVI-TIES...
LED TO ME ACQUIRING A LITTLE BROTHER.
I THINK I'M DRIFTING FURTHER AND FURTHER FROM A NORMAL SCHOOL LIFE.

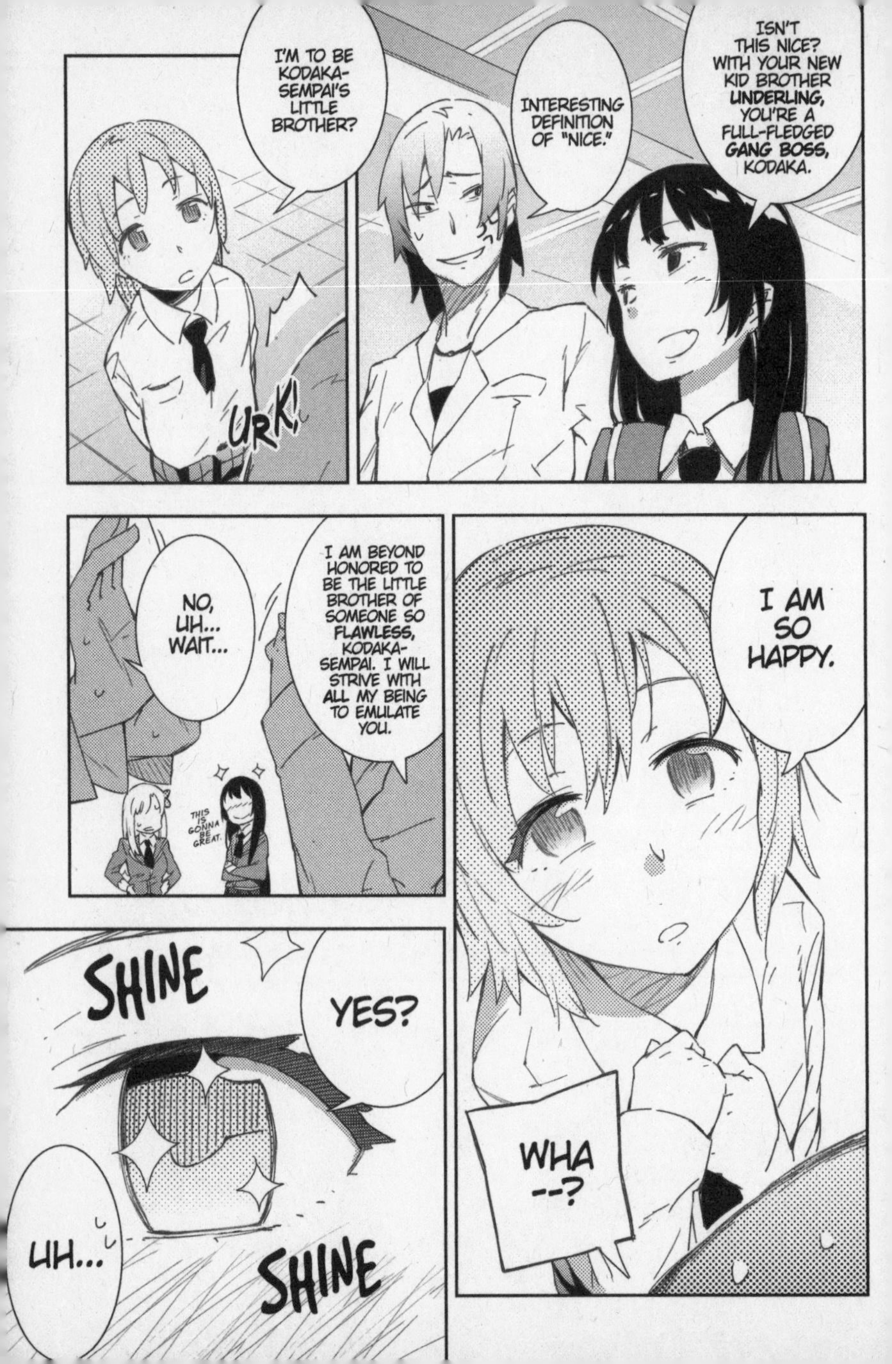
ISN'T THIS NICE? WITH YOUR NEW KID BROTHER **UNDERLING**, YOU'RE A FULL-FLEDGED **GANG BOSS**, KODAKA.
INTERESTING DEFINITION OF "NICE."
I'M TO BE KODAKA-SEMPAI'S LITTLE BROTHER?
URK!
I AM SO HAPPY.
WHA--?
I AM BEYOND HONORED TO BE THE LITTLE BROTHER OF SOMEONE SO **FLAWLESS**, KODAKA-SEMPAI. I WILL STRIVE WITH **ALL MY BEING** TO EMULATE YOU.
NO, UH... WAIT...
THIS IS GONNA BE GREAT.
YES?
SHINE
UH...
SHINE

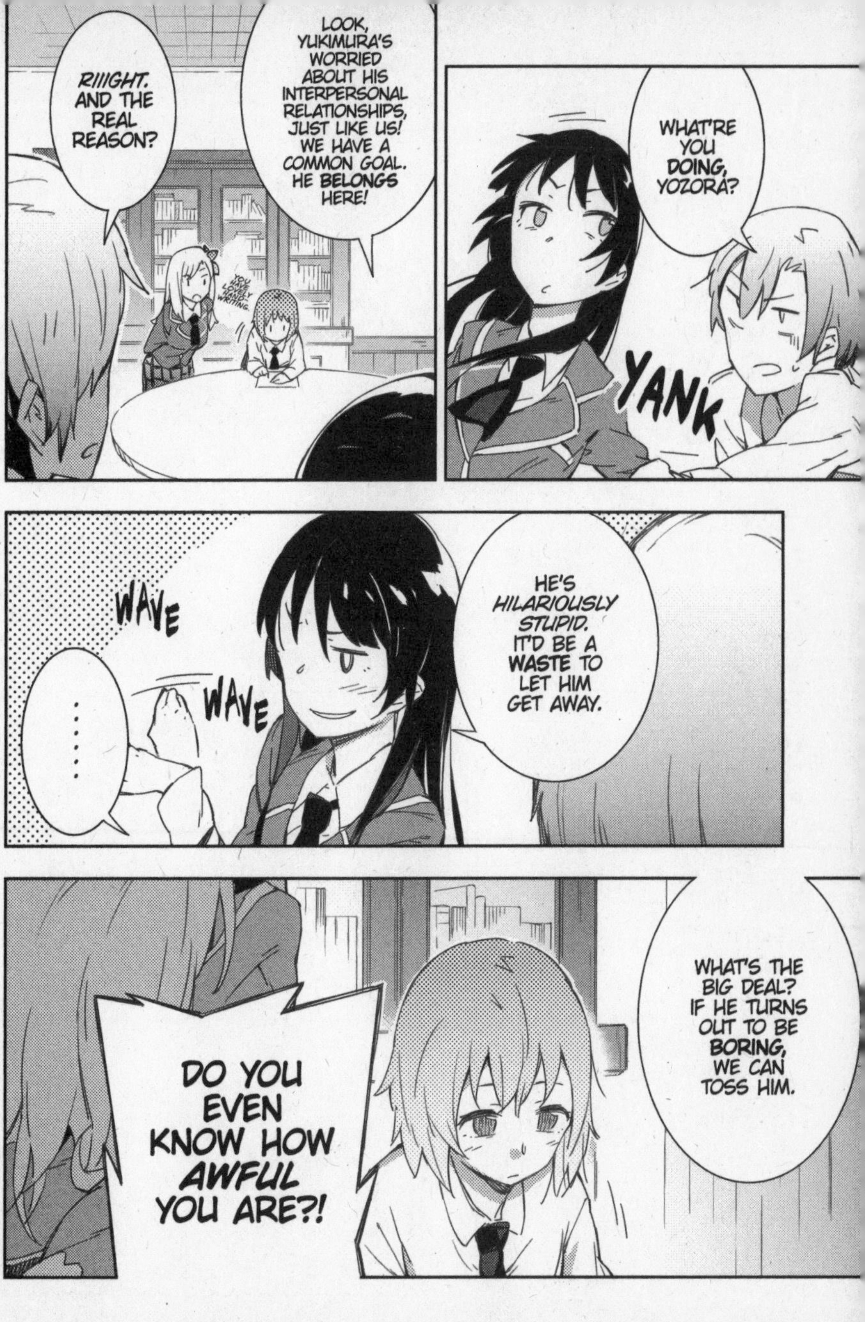
WHAT'RE YOU DOING, YOZORA?
YANK
LOOK, YUKIMURA'S WORRIED ABOUT HIS INTERPERSONAL RELATIONSHIPS, JUST LIKE US! WE HAVE A COMMON GOAL. HE BELONGS HERE!
RIIIGHT. AND THE REAL REASON?
YOU HAVE LOVELY HAND-WRITING.
HE'S HILARIOUSLY STUPID. IT'D BE A WASTE TO LET HIM GET AWAY.
WAVE
WAVE
......
WHAT'S THE BIG DEAL? IF HE TURNS OUT TO BE BORING, WE CAN TOSS HIM.
DO YOU EVEN KNOW HOW AWFUL YOU ARE?!

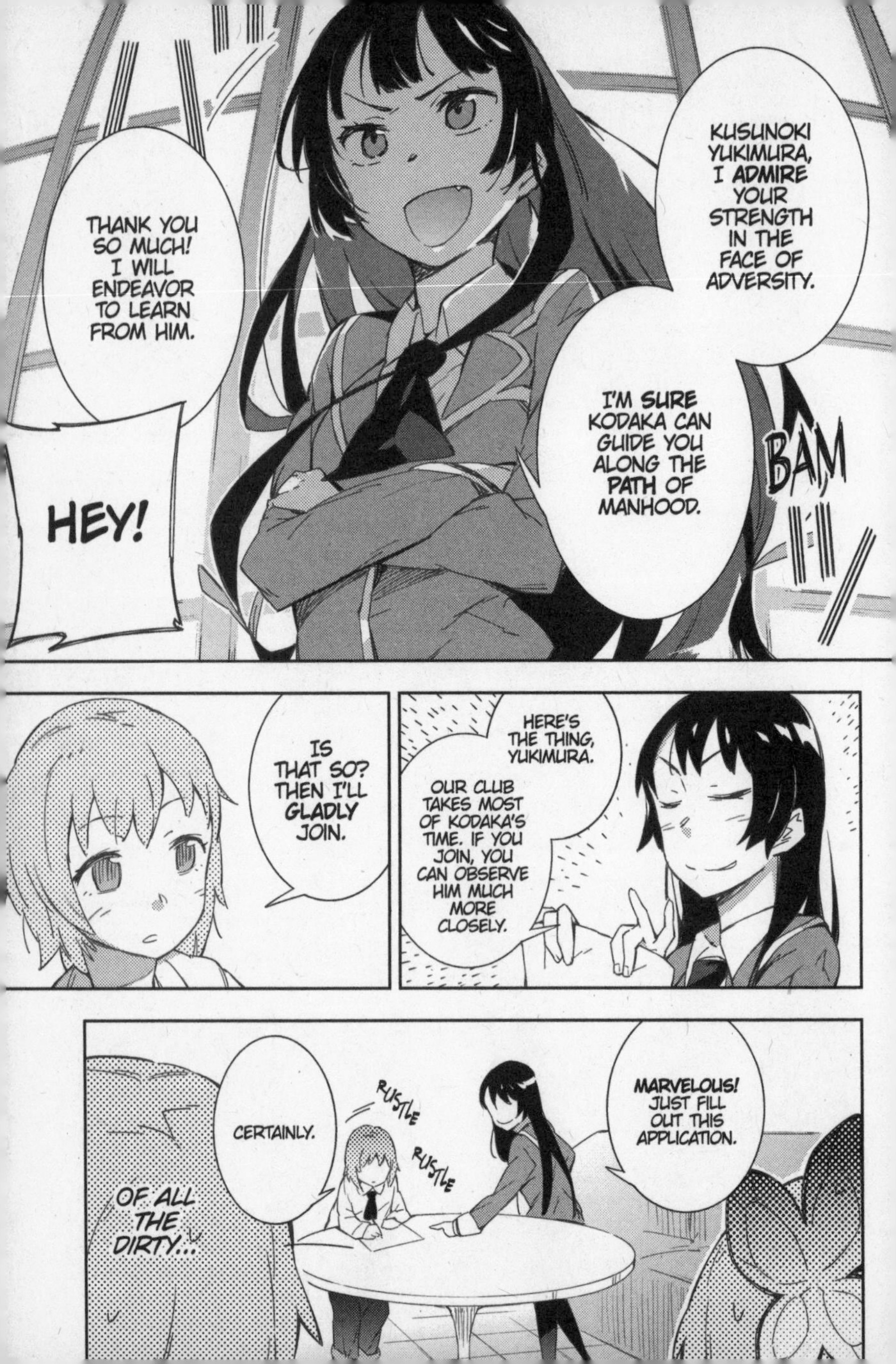
KUSUNOKI YUKIMURA, I ADMIRE YOUR STRENGTH IN THE FACE OF ADVERSITY.
I'M SURE KODAKA CAN GUIDE YOU ALONG THE PATH OF MANHOOD.
BAM
THANK YOU SO MUCH! I WILL ENDEAVOR TO LEARN FROM HIM.
HEY!
HERE'S THE THING, YUKIMURA.
OUR CLUB TAKES MOST OF KODAKA'S TIME. IF YOU JOIN, YOU CAN OBSERVE HIM MUCH MORE CLOSELY.
IS THAT SO? THEN I'LL GLADLY JOIN.
MARVELOUS! JUST FILL OUT THIS APPLICATION.
RUSTLE
RUSTLE
CERTAINLY.
OF ALL THE DIRTY...

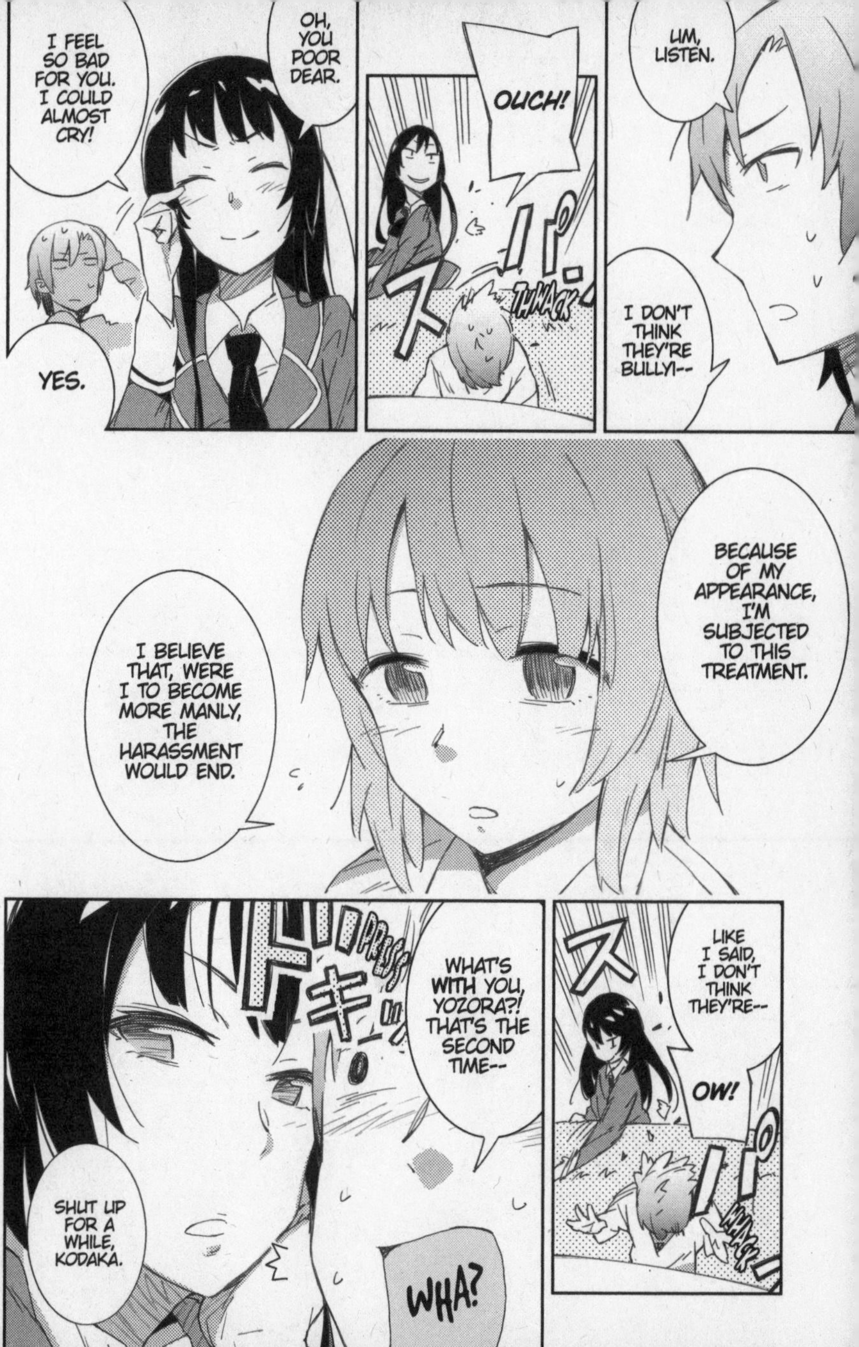
UM, LISTEN.
I DON'T THINK THEY'RE BULLYI--
OUCH!
THWACK
OH, YOU POOR DEAR.
I FEEL SO BAD FOR YOU. I COULD ALMOST CRY!
YES.
BECAUSE OF MY APPEARANCE, I'M SUBJECTED TO THIS TREATMENT.
I BELIEVE THAT, WERE I TO BECOME MORE MANLY, THE HARASSMENT WOULD END.
LIKE I SAID, I DON'T THINK THEY'RE--
OW!
WHACK
WHAT'S WITH YOU, YOZORA?! THAT'S THE SECOND TIME--
SHUT UP FOR A WHILE, KODAKA.
WHA?

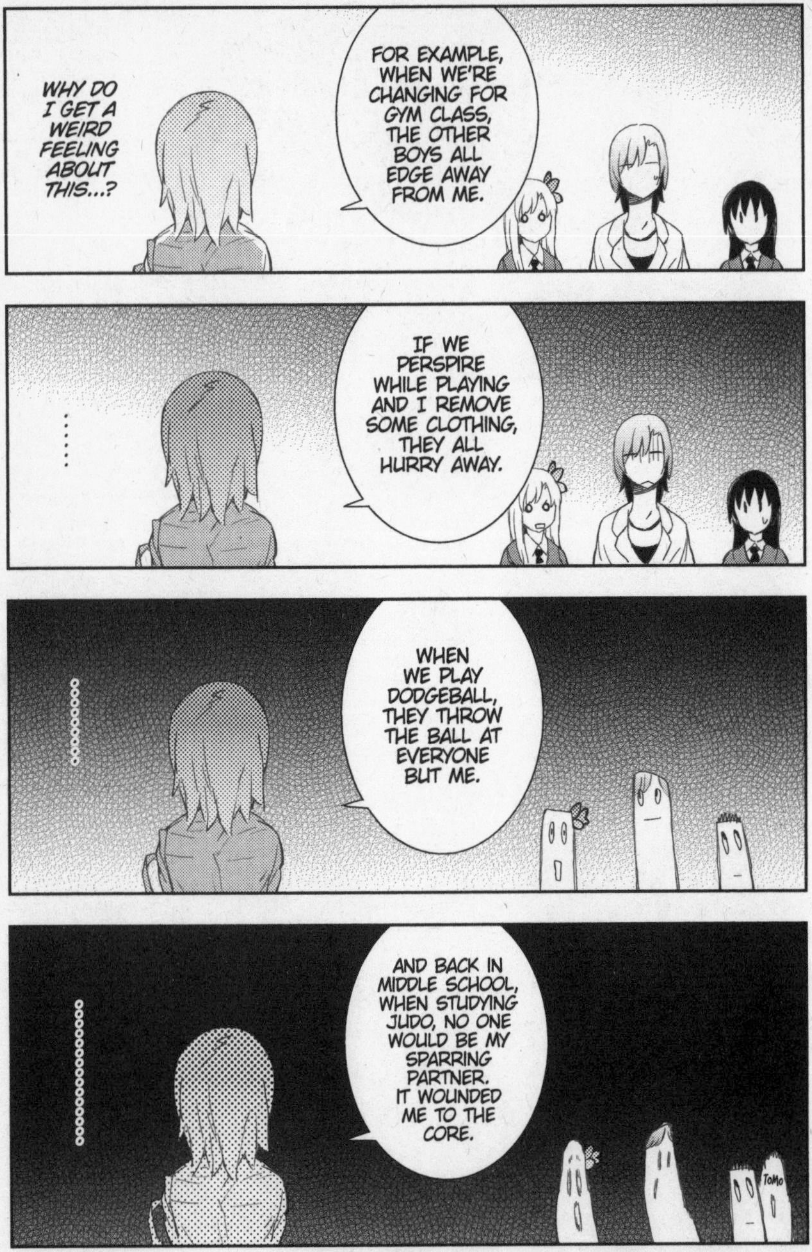
FOR EXAMPLE, WHEN WE'RE CHANGING FOR GYM CLASS, THE OTHER BOYS ALL EDGE AWAY FROM ME.
WHY DO I GET A WEIRD FEELING ABOUT THIS...?
IF WE PERSPIRE WHILE PLAYING AND I REMOVE SOME CLOTHING, THEY ALL HURRY AWAY.
......
WHEN WE PLAY DODGEBALL, THEY THROW THE BALL AT EVERYONE BUT ME.
......
AND BACK IN MIDDLE SCHOOL, WHEN STUDYING JUDO, NO ONE WOULD BE MY SPARRING PARTNER. IT WOUNDED ME TO THE CORE.
......
TOMO

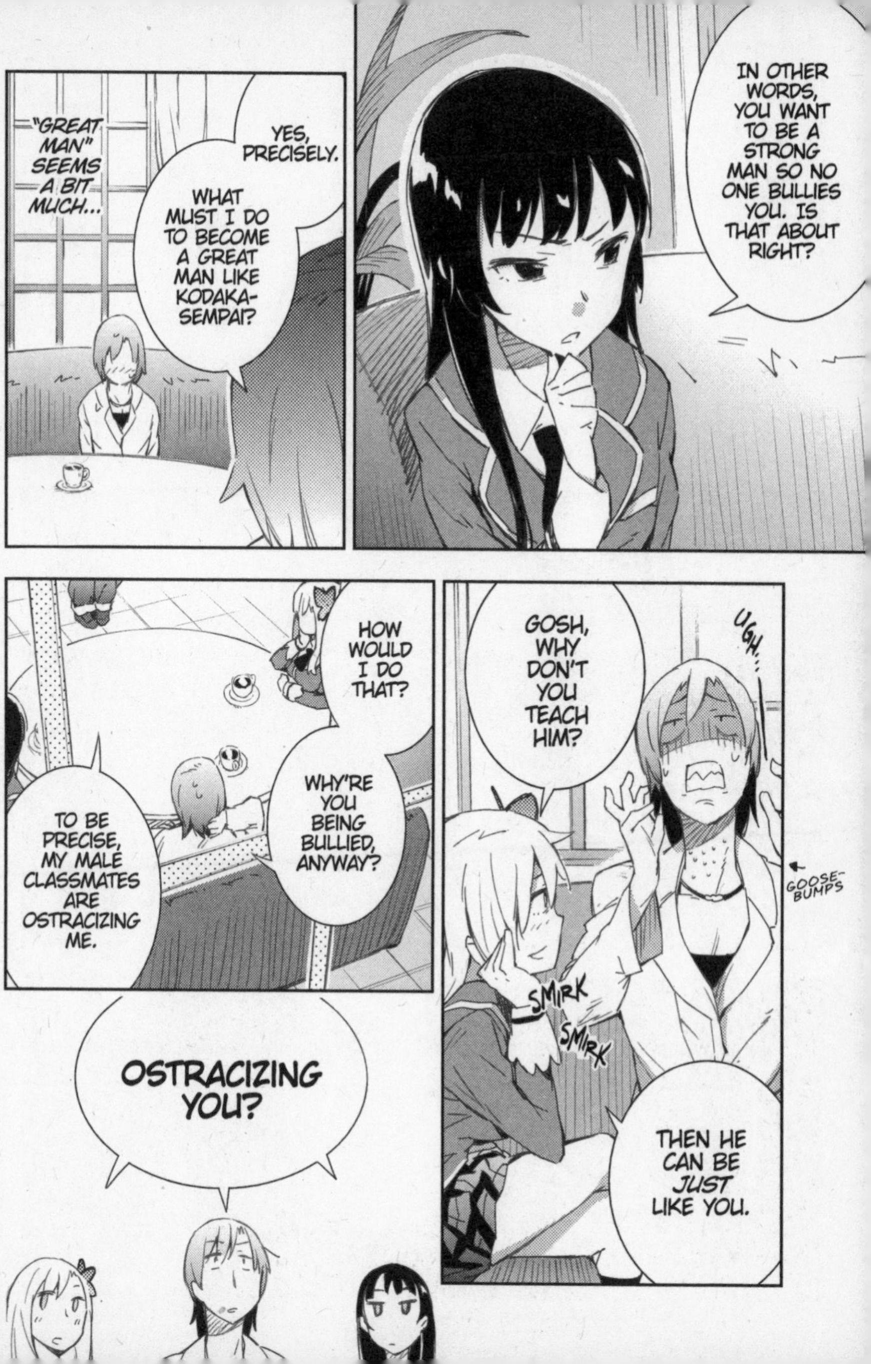
IN OTHER WORDS, YOU WANT TO BE A STRONG MAN SO NO ONE BULLIES YOU. IS THAT ABOUT RIGHT?
YES, PRECISELY.
WHAT MUST I DO TO BECOME A GREAT MAN LIKE KODAKA-SEMPAI?
"GREAT MAN" SEEMS A BIT MUCH...
UGH...
GOSH, WHY DON'T YOU TEACH HIM?
GOOSE-BUMPS
SMIRK
SMIRK
THEN HE CAN BE JUST LIKE YOU.
HOW WOULD I DO THAT?
WHY'RE YOU BEING BULLIED, ANYWAY?
TO BE PRECISE, MY MALE CLASSMATES ARE OSTRACIZING ME.
OSTRACIZING YOU?

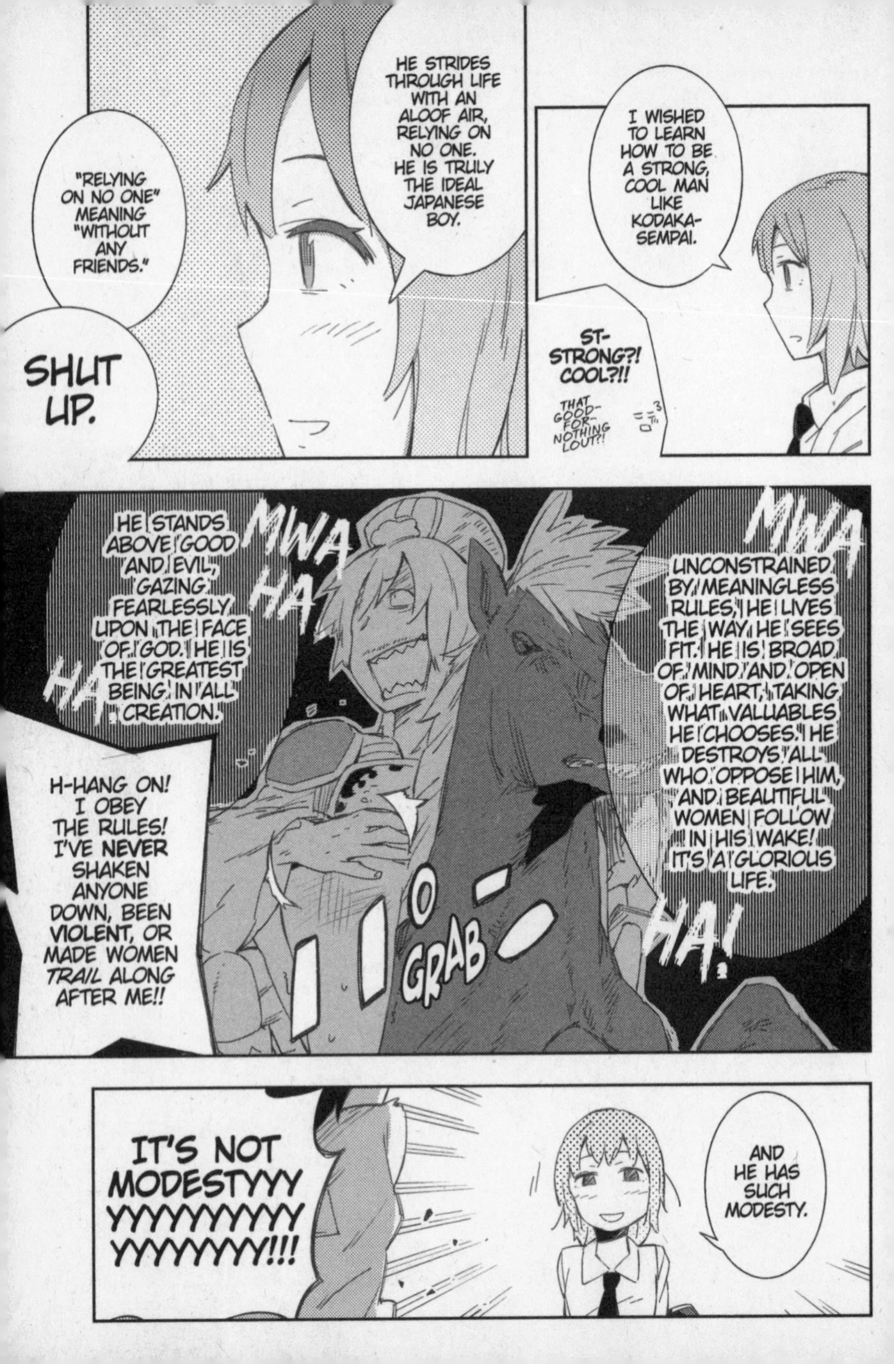
I WISHED TO LEARN HOW TO BE A STRONG, COOL MAN LIKE KODAKA-SEMPAI.
ST-STRONG?! COOL?!!
THAT GOOD-FOR-NOTHING LOUT?!
HE STRIDES THROUGH LIFE WITH AN ALOOF AIR, RELYING ON NO ONE. HE IS TRULY THE IDEAL JAPANESE BOY.
"RELYING ON NO ONE" MEANING "WITHOUT ANY FRIENDS."
SHUT UP.
MWA
UNCONSTRAINED BY MEANINGLESS RULES, HE LIVES THE WAY HE SEES FIT. HE IS BROAD OF MIND AND OPEN OF HEART, TAKING WHAT VALUABLES HE CHOOSES. HE DESTROYS ALL WHO OPPOSE HIM, AND BEAUTIFUL WOMEN FOLLOW IN HIS WAKE! IT'S A GLORIOUS LIFE.
MWA HA HA.
HE STANDS ABOVE GOOD AND EVIL, GAZING FEARLESSLY UPON THE FACE OF GOD. HE IS THE GREATEST BEING IN ALL CREATION.
H-HANG ON! I OBEY THE RULES! I'VE NEVER SHAKEN ANYONE DOWN, BEEN VIOLENT, OR MADE WOMEN TRAIL ALONG AFTER ME!!
GRAB
HA!
AND HE HAS SUCH MODESTY.
IT'S NOT MODESTYYYY YYYYYYYYYY YYYYYYYYY!!!

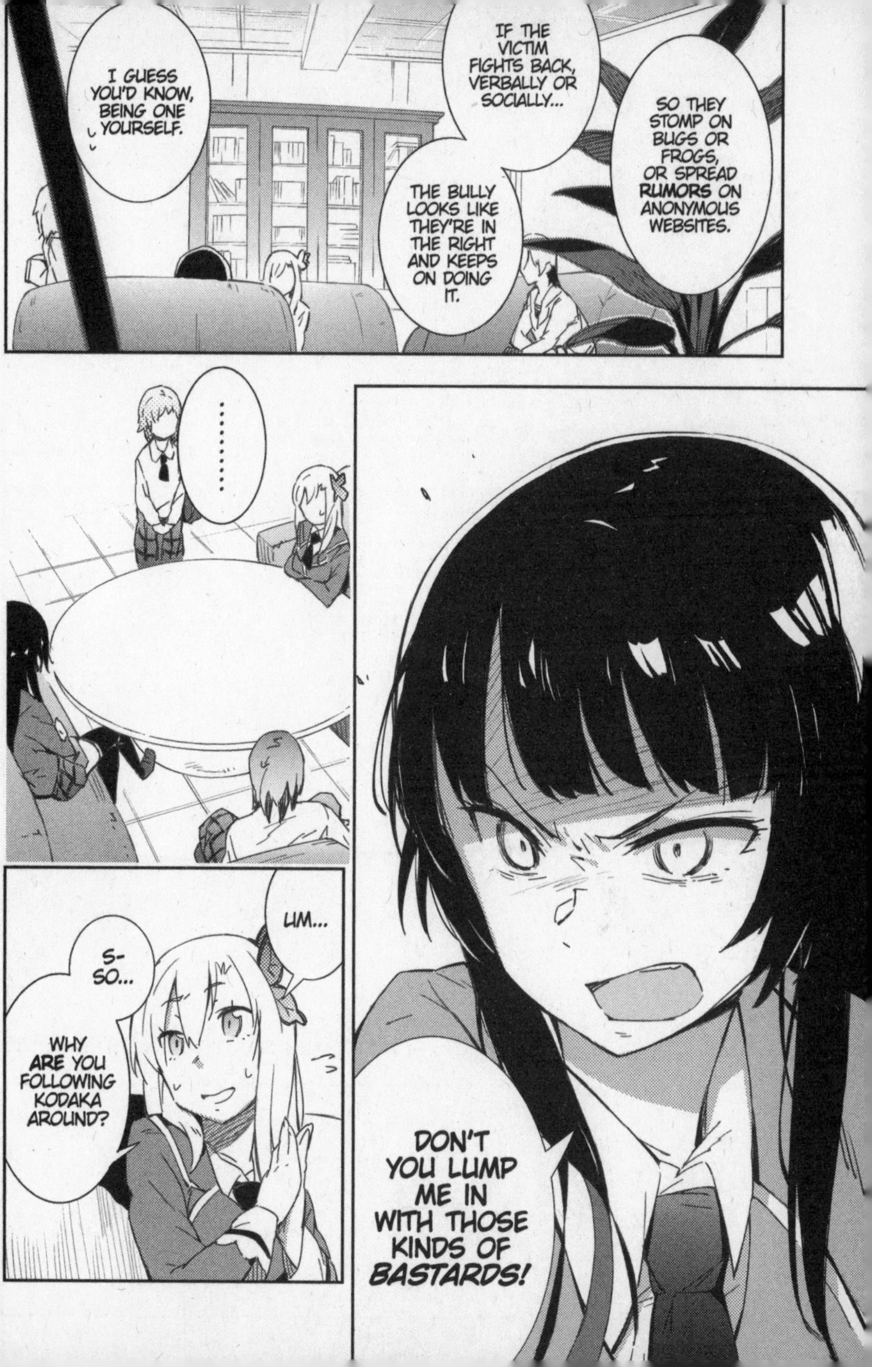
SO THEY STOMP ON BUGS OR FROGS, OR SPREAD RUMORS ON ANONYMOUS WEBSITES.
IF THE VICTIM FIGHTS BACK, VERBALLY OR SOCIALLY...
THE BULLY LOOKS LIKE THEY'RE IN THE RIGHT AND KEEPS ON DOING IT.
I GUESS YOU'D KNOW, BEING ONE YOURSELF.
DON'T YOU LUMP ME IN WITH THOSE KINDS OF BASTARDS!
......
UM...
S-SO...
WHY ARE YOU FOLLOWING KODAKA AROUND?

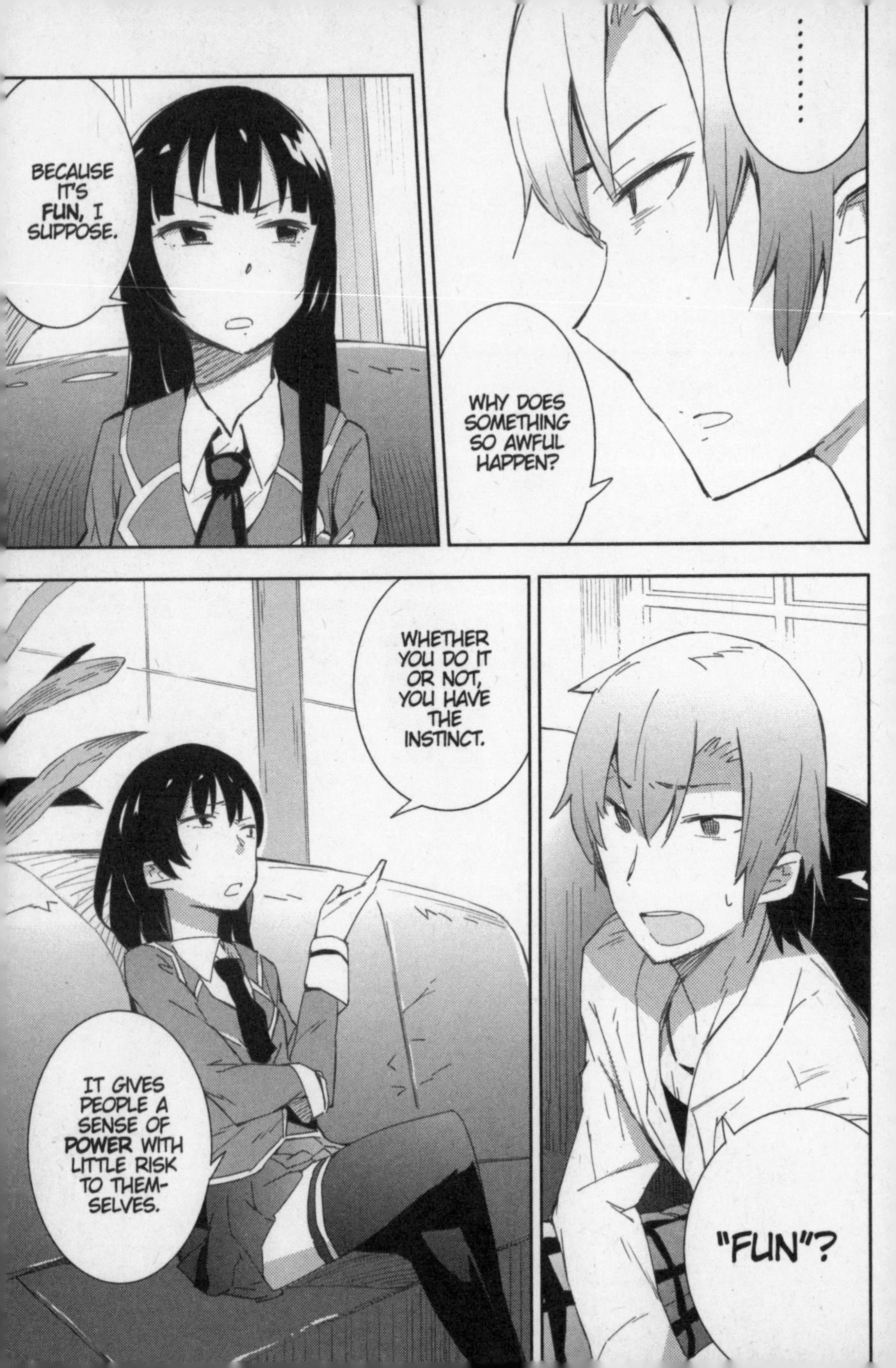

......
WHY DOES SOMETHING SO AWFUL HAPPEN?
BECAUSE IT'S FUN, I SUPPOSE.
"FUN"?
WHETHER YOU DO IT OR NOT, YOU HAVE THE INSTINCT.
IT GIVES PEOPLE A SENSE OF POWER WITH LITTLE RISK TO THEM-SELVES.

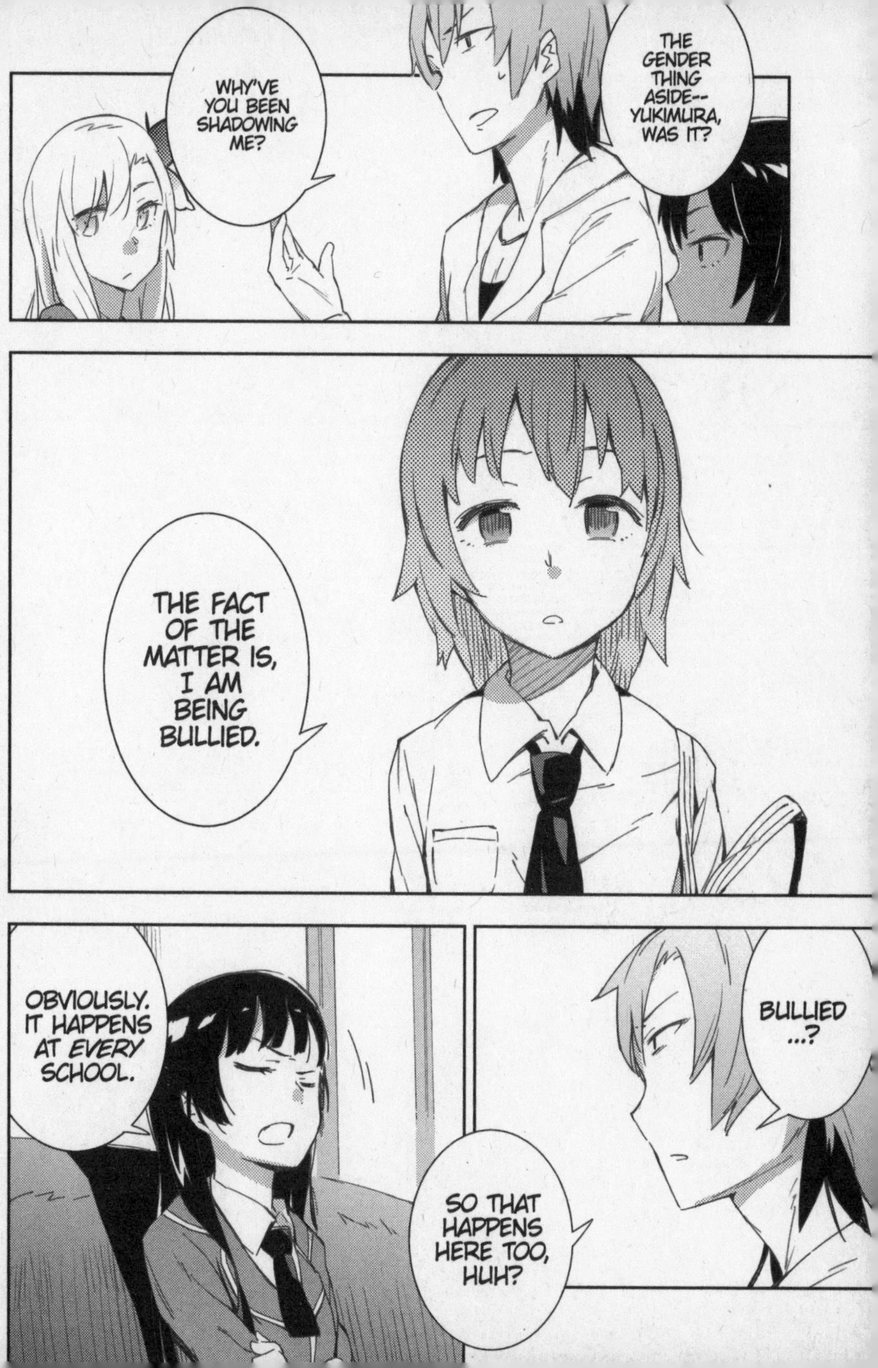
THE GENDER THING ASIDE-- YUKIMURA, WAS IT?
WHY'VE YOU BEEN SHADOWING ME?
THE FACT OF THE MATTER IS, I AM BEING BULLIED.
BULLIED ...?
SO THAT HAPPENS HERE TOO, HUH?
OBVIOUSLY. IT HAPPENS AT *EVERY* SCHOOL.

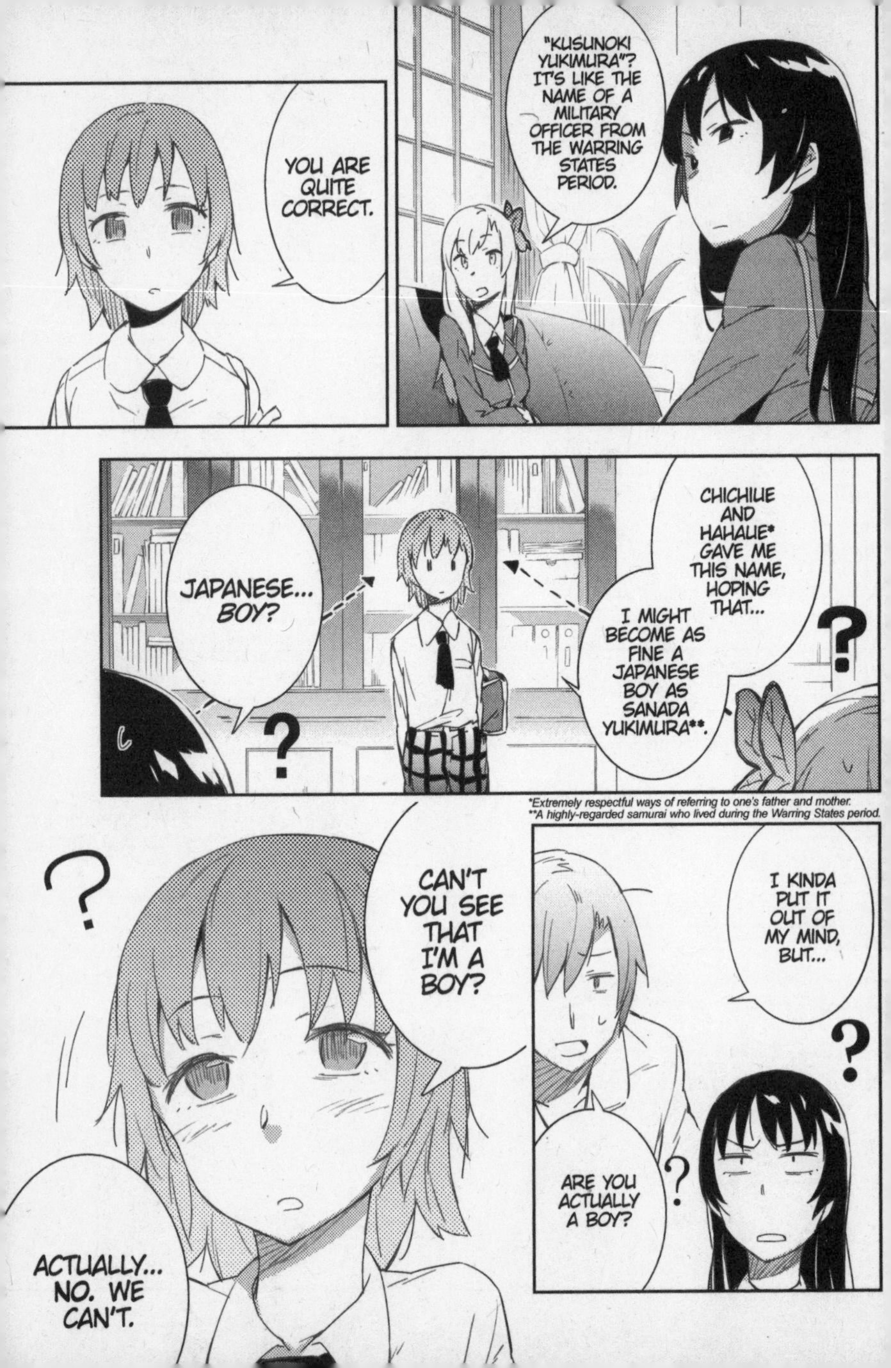
"KUSUNOKI YUKIMURA"? IT'S LIKE THE NAME OF A MILITARY OFFICER FROM THE WARRING STATES PERIOD.
YOU ARE QUITE CORRECT.
CHICHIUE AND HAHAUE* GAVE ME THIS NAME, HOPING THAT...
I MIGHT BECOME AS FINE A JAPANESE BOY AS SANADA YUKIMURA**.
JAPANESE... BOY?
?
?
I KINDA PUT IT OUT OF MY MIND, BUT...
?
ARE YOU ACTUALLY A BOY?
?
?
CAN'T YOU SEE THAT I'M A BOY?
ACTUALLY... NO. WE CAN'T.

*Extremely respectful ways of referring to one's father and mother.
**A highly-regarded samurai who lived during the Warring States period.

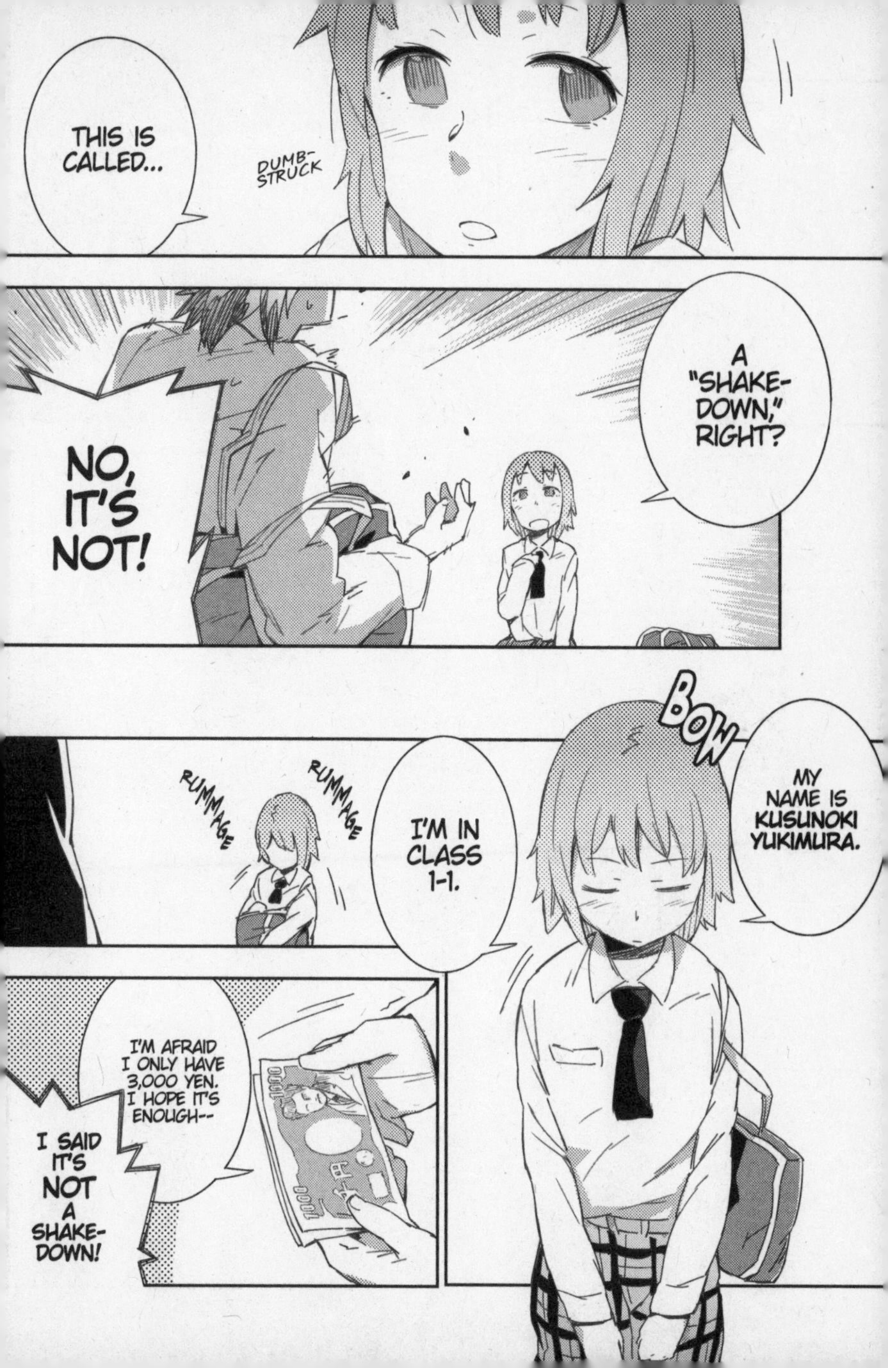
THIS IS CALLED...
DUMB-STRUCK
A "SHAKE-DOWN," RIGHT?
NO, IT'S NOT!
BOW
MY NAME IS KUSUNOKI YUKIMURA.
I'M IN CLASS 1-1.
RUMMAGE
RUMMAGE
I'M AFRAID I ONLY HAVE 3,000 YEN. I HOPE IT'S ENOUGH--
I SAID IT'S NOT A SHAKE-DOWN!

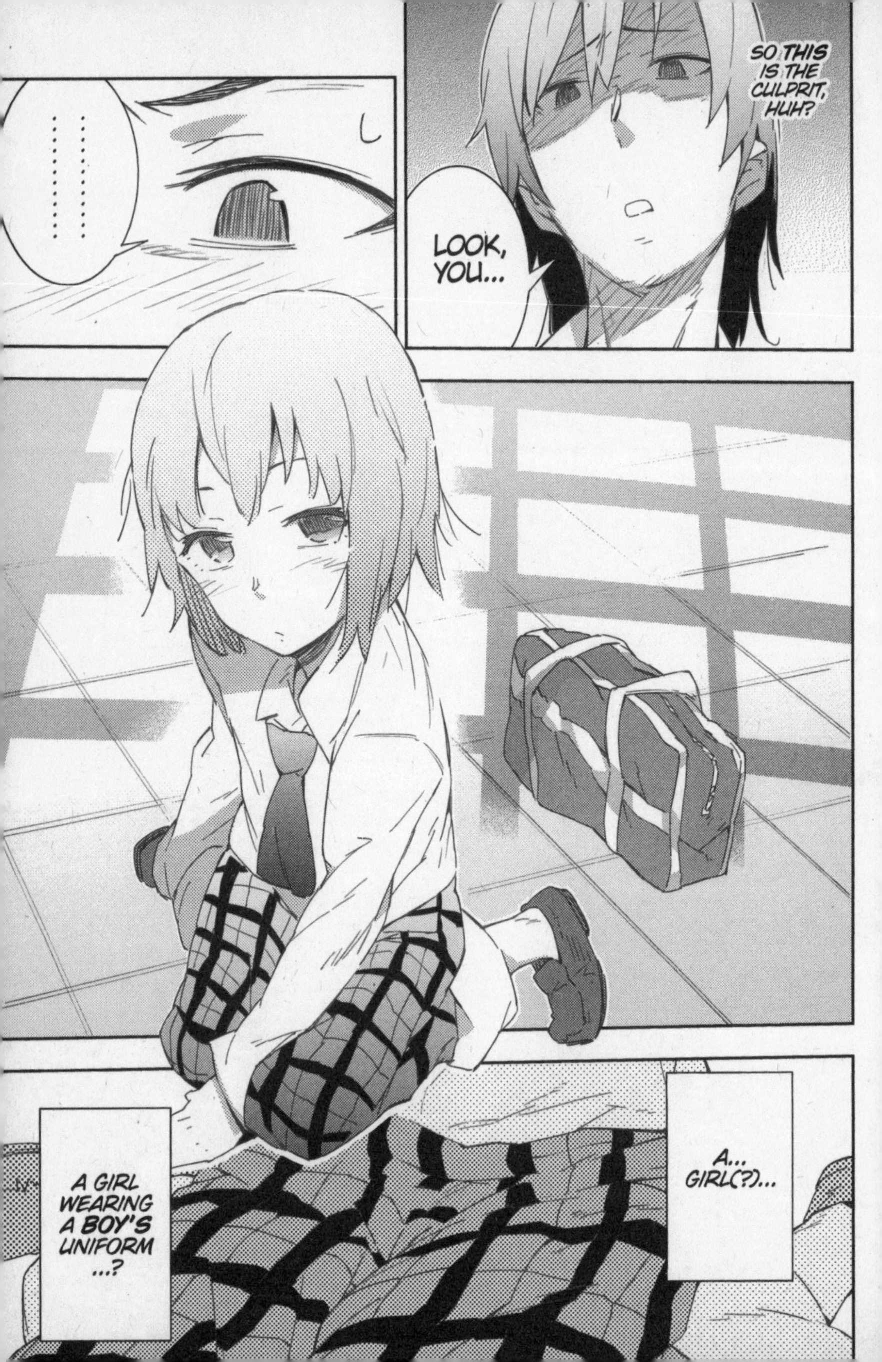
SO THIS IS THE CULPRIT, HUH?
LOOK, YOU...
......
A... GIRL(?)...
A GIRL WEARING A BOY'S UNIFORM ...?

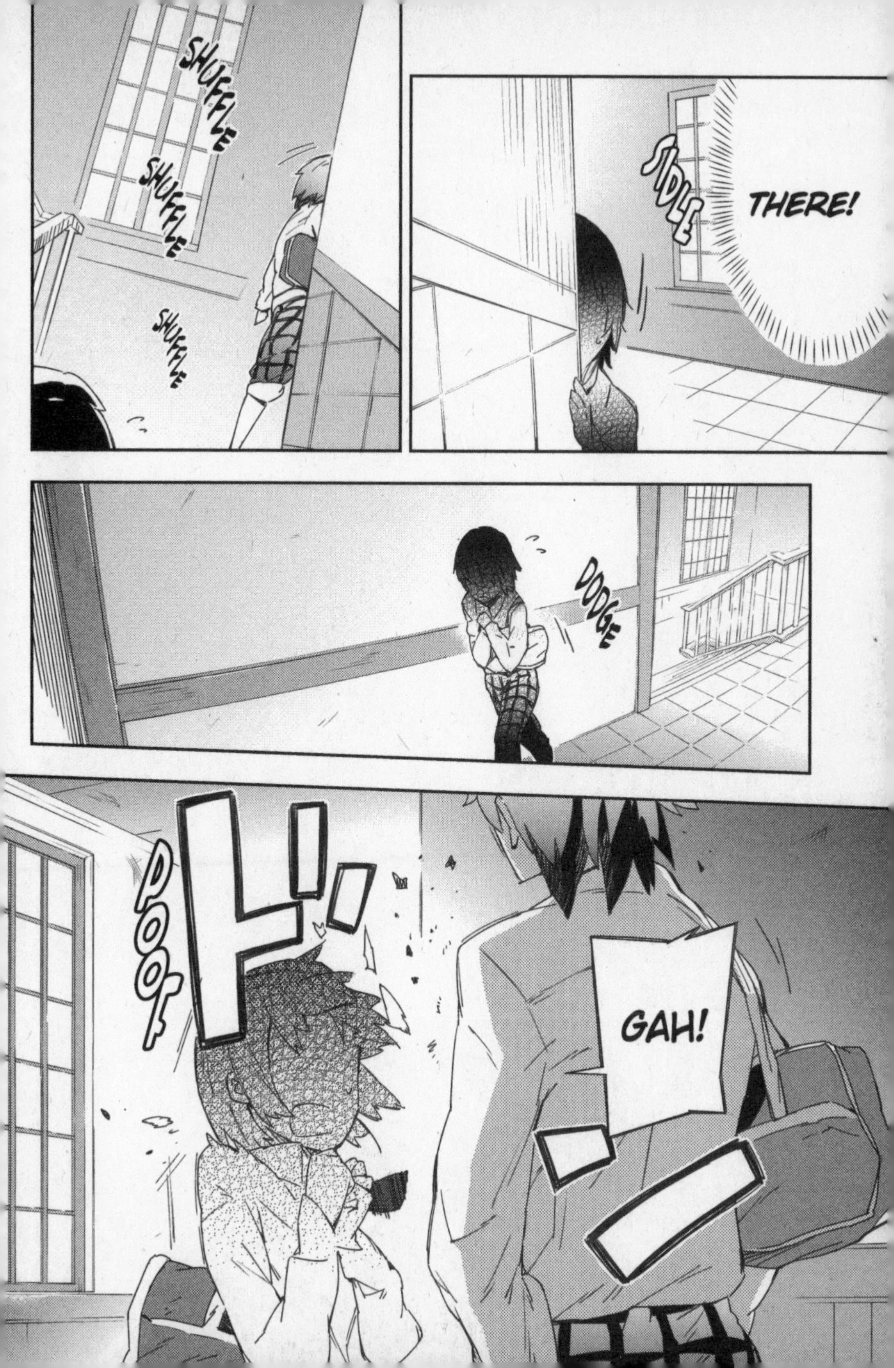
SIDLE
THERE!
SHUFFLE
SHUFFLE
SHUFFLE
DODGE
GAH!
POOF

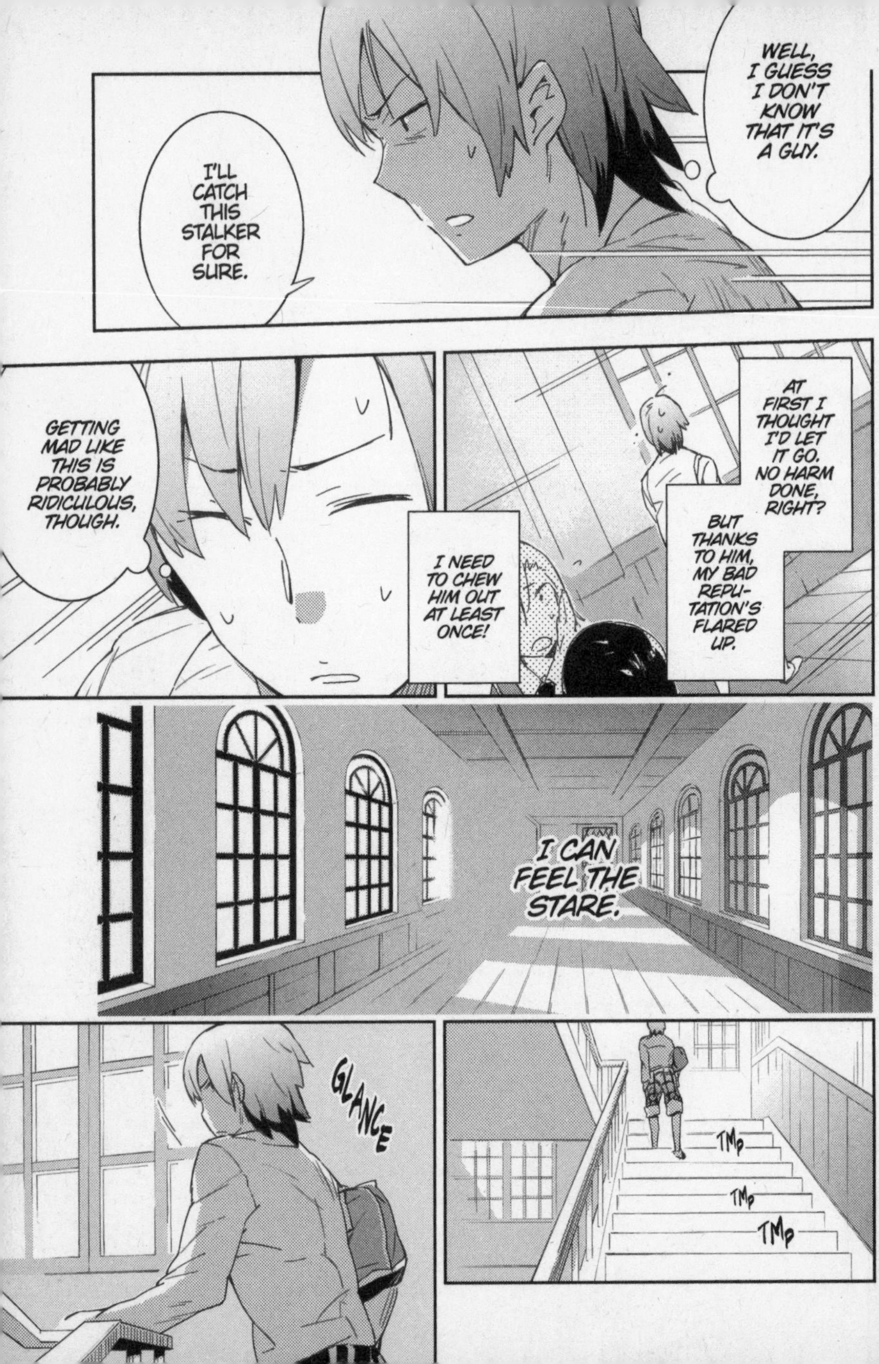
WELL, I GUESS I DON'T KNOW THAT IT'S A GUY.
I'LL CATCH THIS STALKER FOR SURE.
AT FIRST I THOUGHT I'D LET IT GO. NO HARM DONE, RIGHT?
BUT THANKS TO HIM, MY BAD REPU-TATION'S FLARED UP.
I NEED TO CHEW HIM OUT AT LEAST ONCE!
GETTING MAD LIKE THIS IS PROBABLY RIDICULOUS, THOUGH.
I CAN FEEL THE STARE.
TMP
TMP
TMP
GLANCE

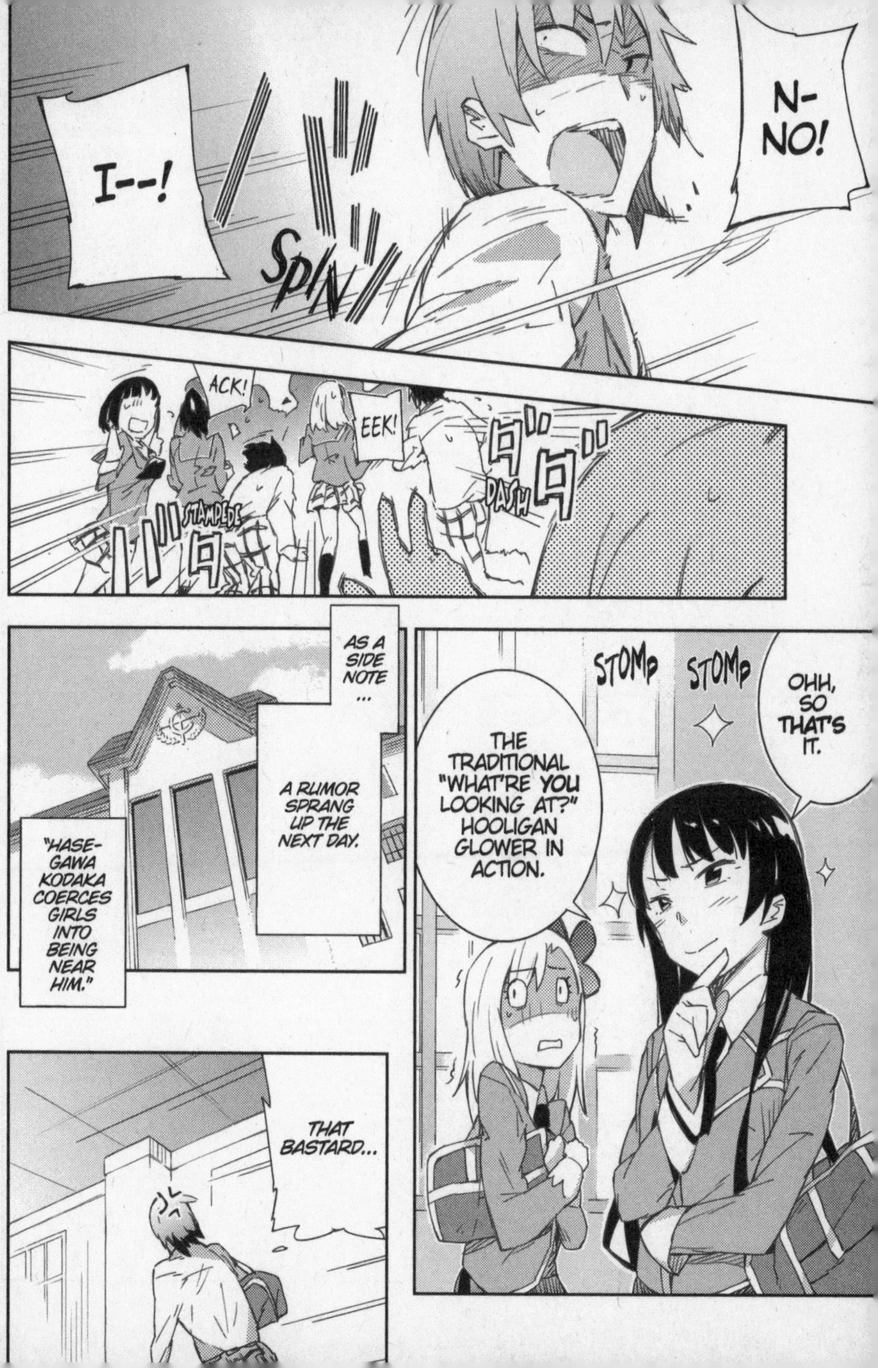
N-NO!
I--!
SPIN
DASH
EEK!
ACK!
STAMPEDE
OHH, SO THAT'S IT.
STOMP
STOMP
THE TRADITIONAL "WHAT'RE YOU LOOKING AT?" HOOLIGAN GLOWER IN ACTION.
AS A SIDE NOTE...
A RUMOR SPRANG UP THE NEXT DAY.
"HASEGAWA KODAKA COERCES GIRLS INTO BEING NEAR HIM."
THAT BASTARD...

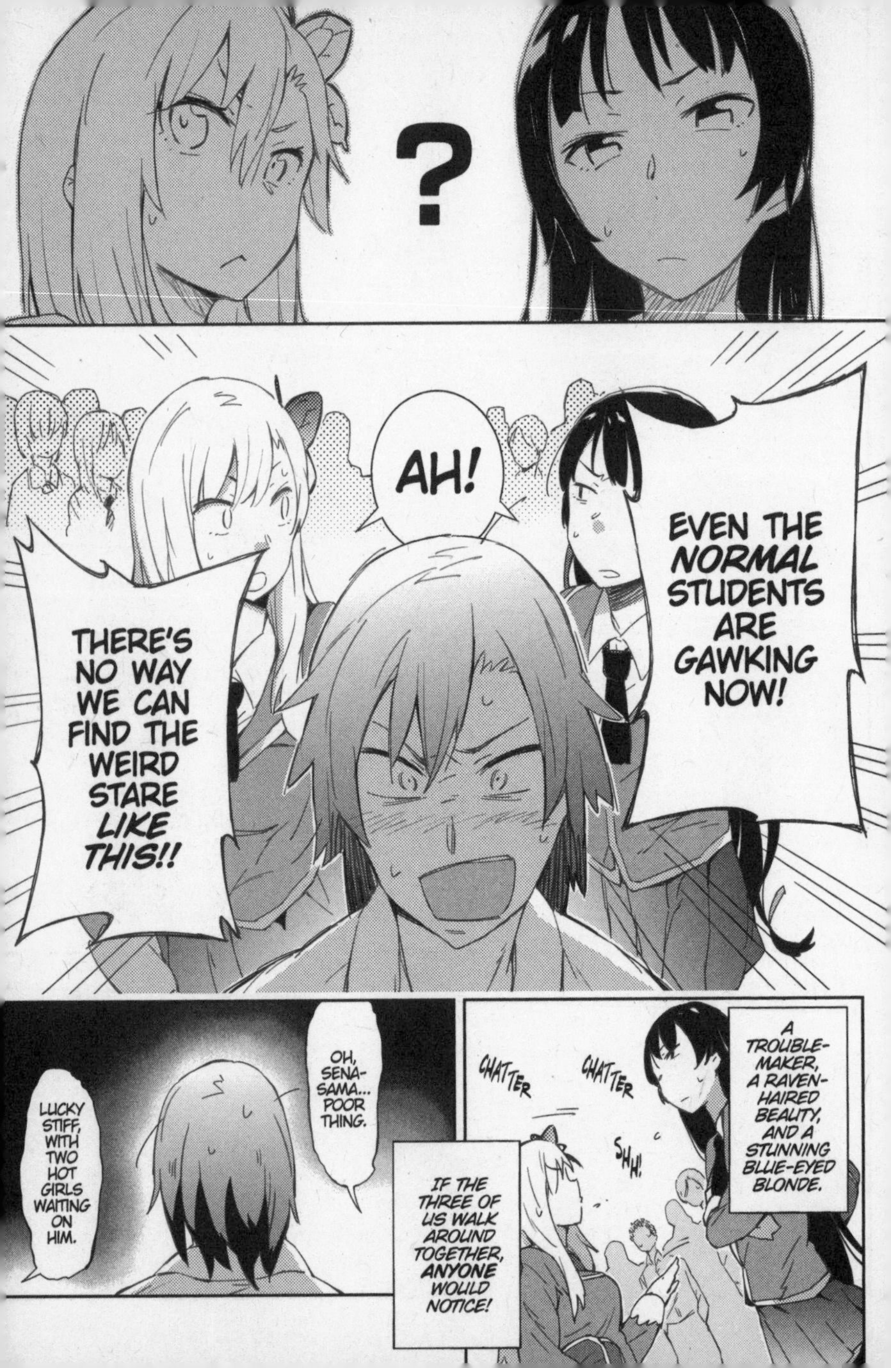
?
AH!
EVEN THE *NORMAL* STUDENTS ARE GAWKING NOW!
THERE'S NO WAY WE CAN FIND THE WEIRD STARE *LIKE THIS!!*
A TROUBLE-MAKER, A RAVEN-HAIRED BEAUTY, AND A STUNNING BLUE-EYED BLONDE.
CHATTER
CHATTER
SHH!
IF THE THREE OF US WALK AROUND TOGETHER, ANYONE WOULD NOTICE!
OH, SENA-SAMA... POOR THING.
LUCKY STIFF, WITH TWO HOT GIRLS WAITING ON HIM.

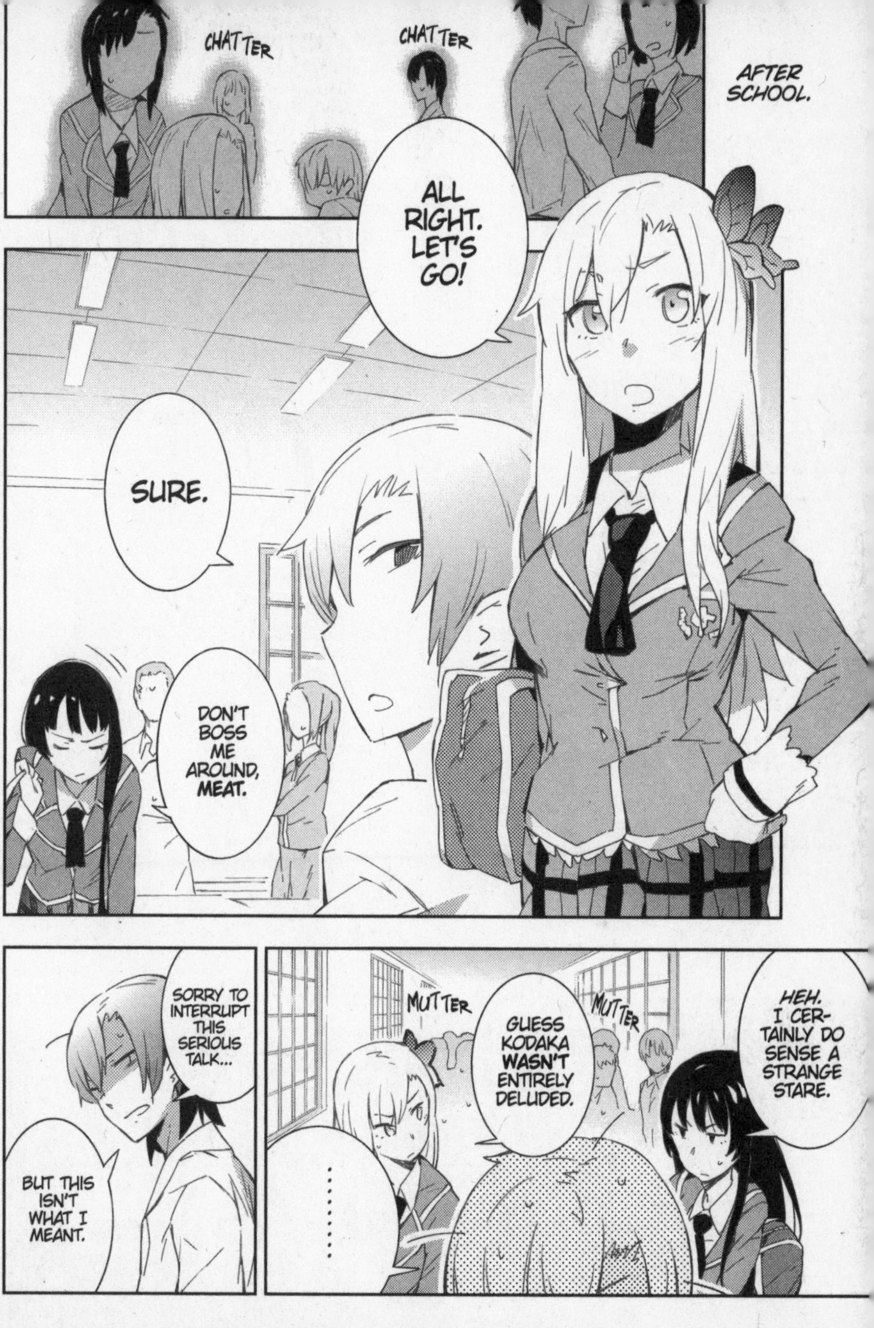
AFTER SCHOOL.
CHATTER
CHATTER
ALL RIGHT. LET'S GO!
SURE.
DON'T BOSS ME AROUND, MEAT.
HEH. I CERTAINLY DO SENSE A STRANGE STARE.
MUTTER
GUESS KODAKA WASN'T ENTIRELY DELUDED.
MUTTER
......
SORRY TO INTERRUPT THIS SERIOUS TALK...
BUT THIS ISN'T WHAT I MEANT.

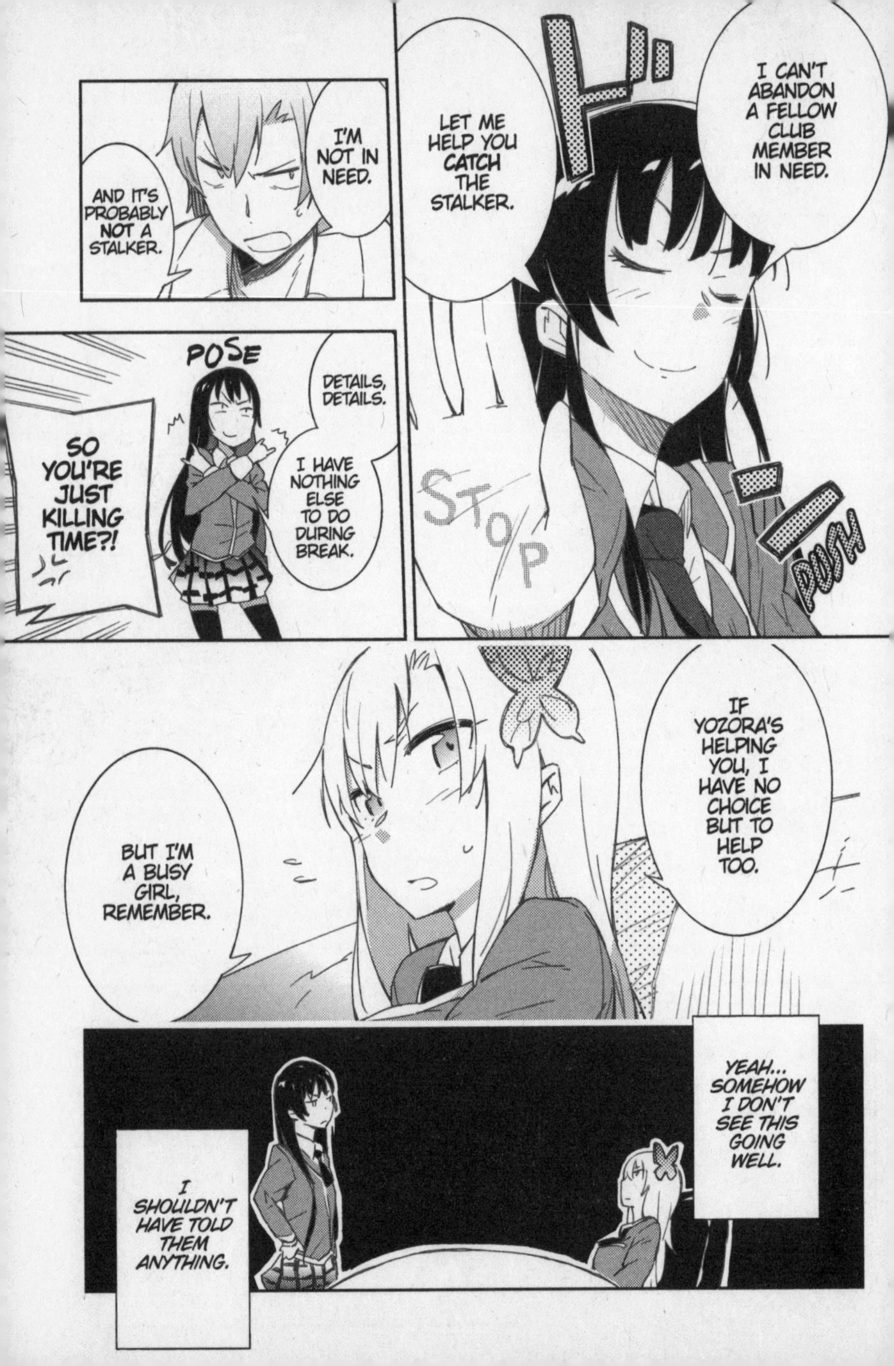
I CAN'T ABANDON A FELLOW CLUB MEMBER IN NEED.
LET ME HELP YOU CATCH THE STALKER.
STOP
PUSH
I'M NOT IN NEED.
AND IT'S PROBABLY NOT A STALKER.
DETAILS, DETAILS.
I HAVE NOTHING ELSE TO DO DURING BREAK.
POSE
SO YOU'RE JUST KILLING TIME?!
IF YOZORA'S HELPING YOU, I HAVE NO CHOICE BUT TO HELP TOO.
BUT I'M A BUSY GIRL, REMEMBER.
YEAH... SOMEHOW I DON'T SEE THIS GOING WELL.
I SHOULDN'T HAVE TOLD THEM ANYTHING.

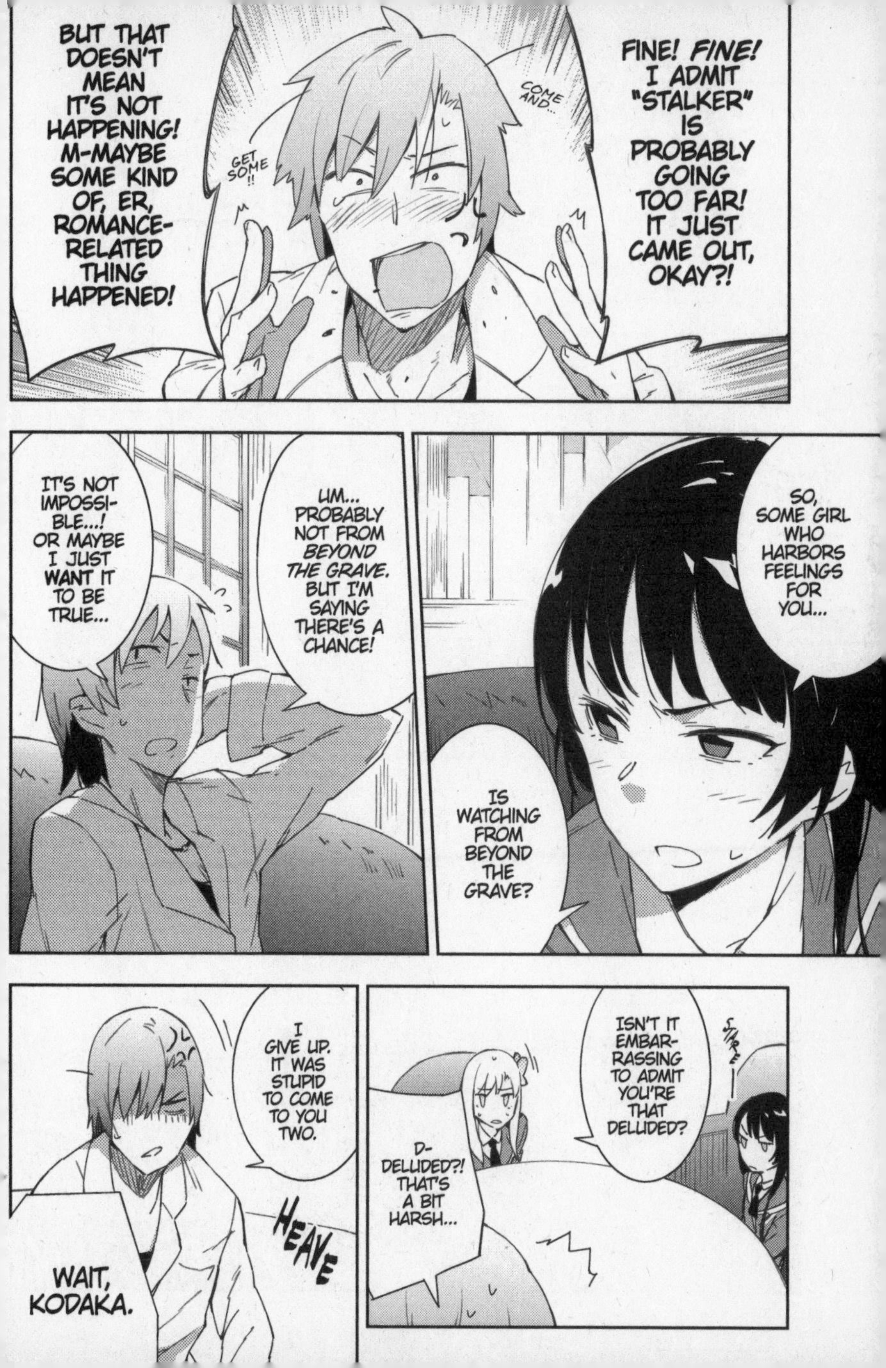
FINE! *FINE!* I ADMIT "STALKER" IS PROBABLY GOING TOO FAR! IT JUST CAME OUT, OKAY?!
COME AND...
GET SOME!!
BUT THAT DOESN'T MEAN IT'S NOT HAPPENING! M-MAYBE SOME KIND OF, ER, ROMANCE-RELATED THING HAPPENED!
SO, SOME GIRL WHO HARBORS FEELINGS FOR YOU...
IS WATCHING FROM BEYOND THE GRAVE?
UM... PROBABLY NOT FROM *BEYOND THE GRAVE.* BUT I'M SAYING THERE'S A CHANCE!
IT'S NOT IMPOSSIBLE...! OR MAYBE I JUST WANT IT TO BE TRUE...
STARE
ISN'T IT EMBARRASSING TO ADMIT YOU'RE THAT DELUDED?
D-DELUDED?! THAT'S A BIT HARSH...
I GIVE UP. IT WAS STUPID TO COME TO YOU TWO.
HEAVE
WAIT, KODAKA.

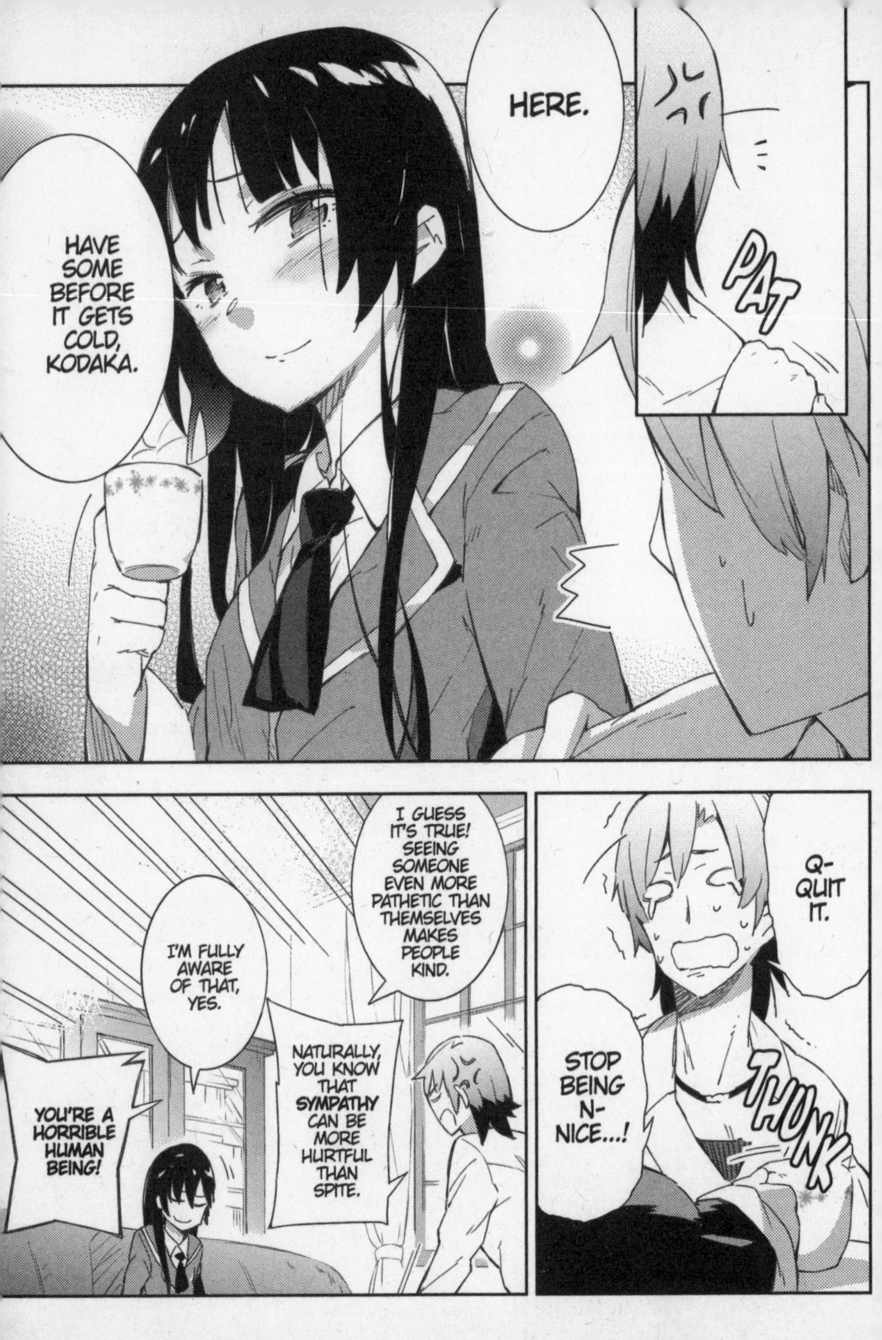
HERE.
PAT
HAVE SOME BEFORE IT GETS COLD, KODAKA.
Q-QUIT IT.
STOP BEING N-NICE...!
THUNK
I GUESS IT'S TRUE! SEEING SOMEONE EVEN MORE PATHETIC THAN THEMSELVES MAKES PEOPLE KIND.
I'M FULLY AWARE OF THAT, YES.
NATURALLY, YOU KNOW THAT SYMPATHY CAN BE MORE HURTFUL THAN SPITE.
YOU'RE A HORRIBLE HUMAN BEING!

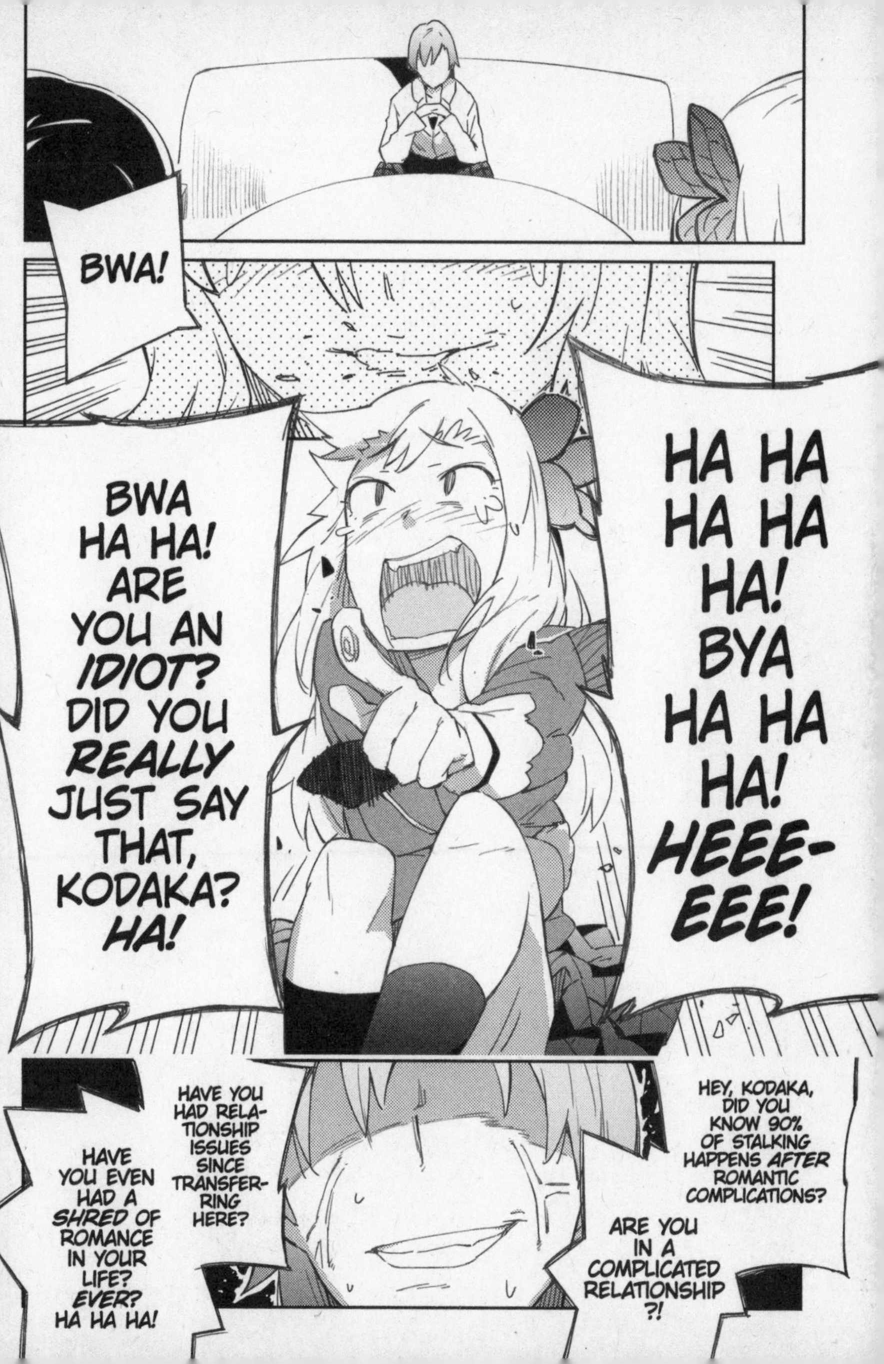
BWA!
HA HA HA HA HA! BYA HA HA HA! HEEE-EEE!
BWA HA HA! ARE YOU AN IDIOT? DID YOU REALLY JUST SAY THAT, KODAKA? HA!
HEY, KODAKA, DID YOU KNOW 90% OF STALKING HAPPENS AFTER ROMANTIC COMPLICATIONS?
ARE YOU IN A COMPLICATED RELATIONSHIP ?!
HAVE YOU HAD RELA-TIONSHIP ISSUES SINCE TRANSFER-RING HERE?
HAVE YOU EVEN HAD A SHRED OF ROMANCE IN YOUR LIFE? EVER? HA HA HA!

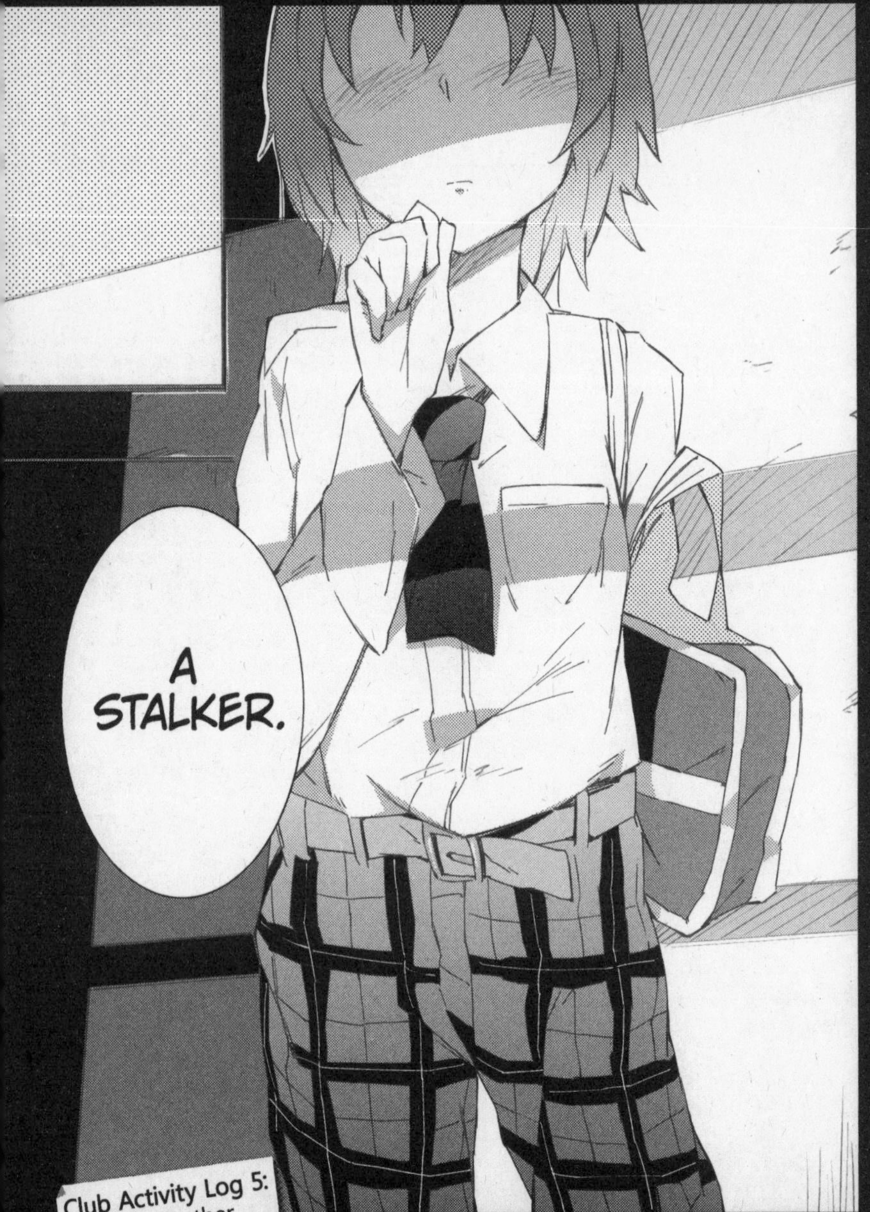
A STALKER.
Club Activity Log 5:
Little Brother

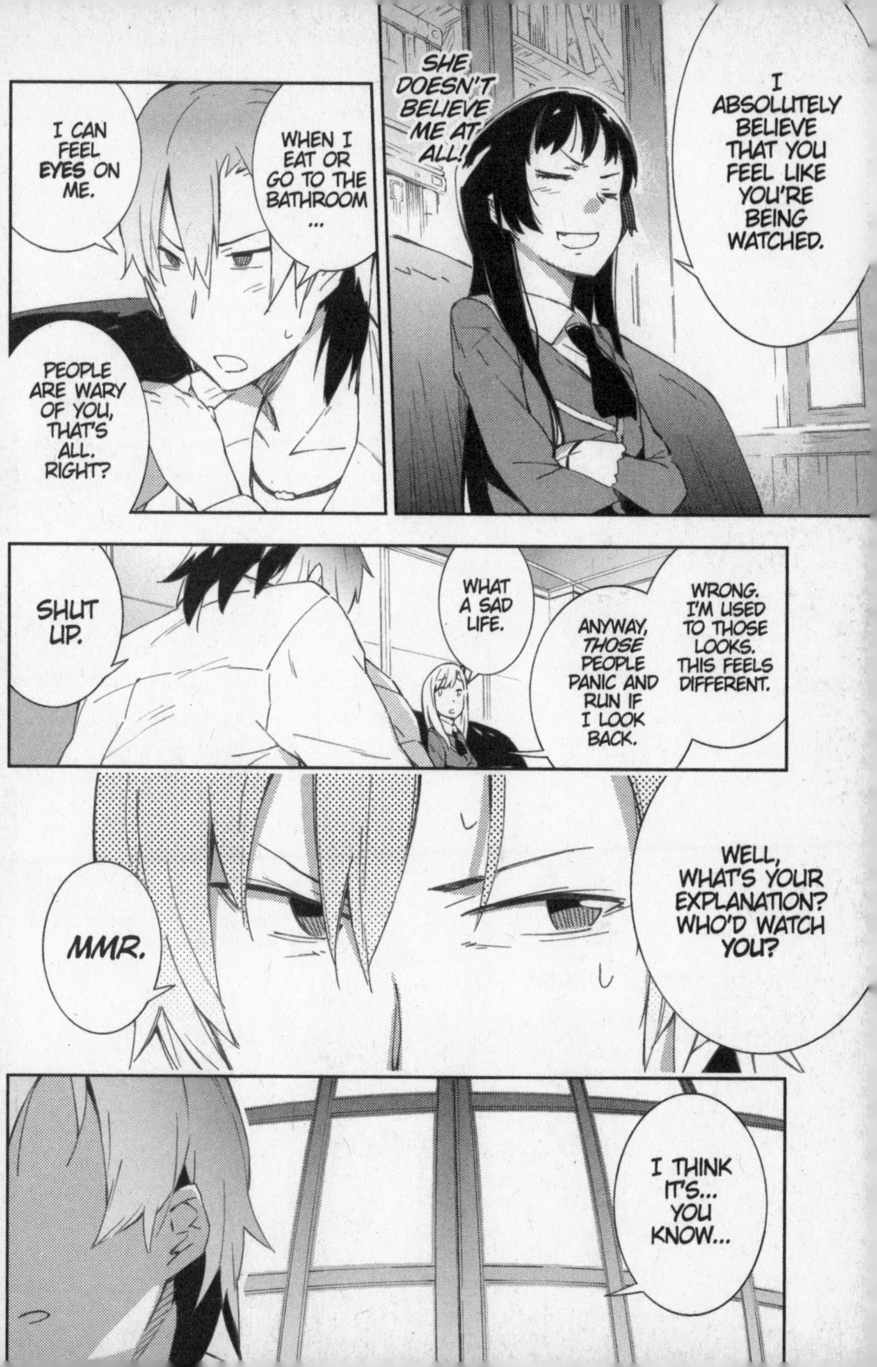
I ABSOLUTELY BELIEVE THAT YOU FEEL LIKE YOU'RE BEING WATCHED.
SHE DOESN'T BELIEVE ME AT ALL!
WHEN I EAT OR GO TO THE BATHROOM ...
I CAN FEEL EYES ON ME.
PEOPLE ARE WARY OF YOU, THAT'S ALL. RIGHT?
WRONG. I'M USED TO THOSE LOOKS. THIS FEELS DIFFERENT.
ANYWAY, *THOSE* PEOPLE PANIC AND RUN IF I LOOK BACK.
WHAT A SAD LIFE.
SHUT UP.
WELL, WHAT'S YOUR EXPLANATION? WHO'D WATCH *YOU*?
MMR.
I THINK IT'S... YOU KNOW...

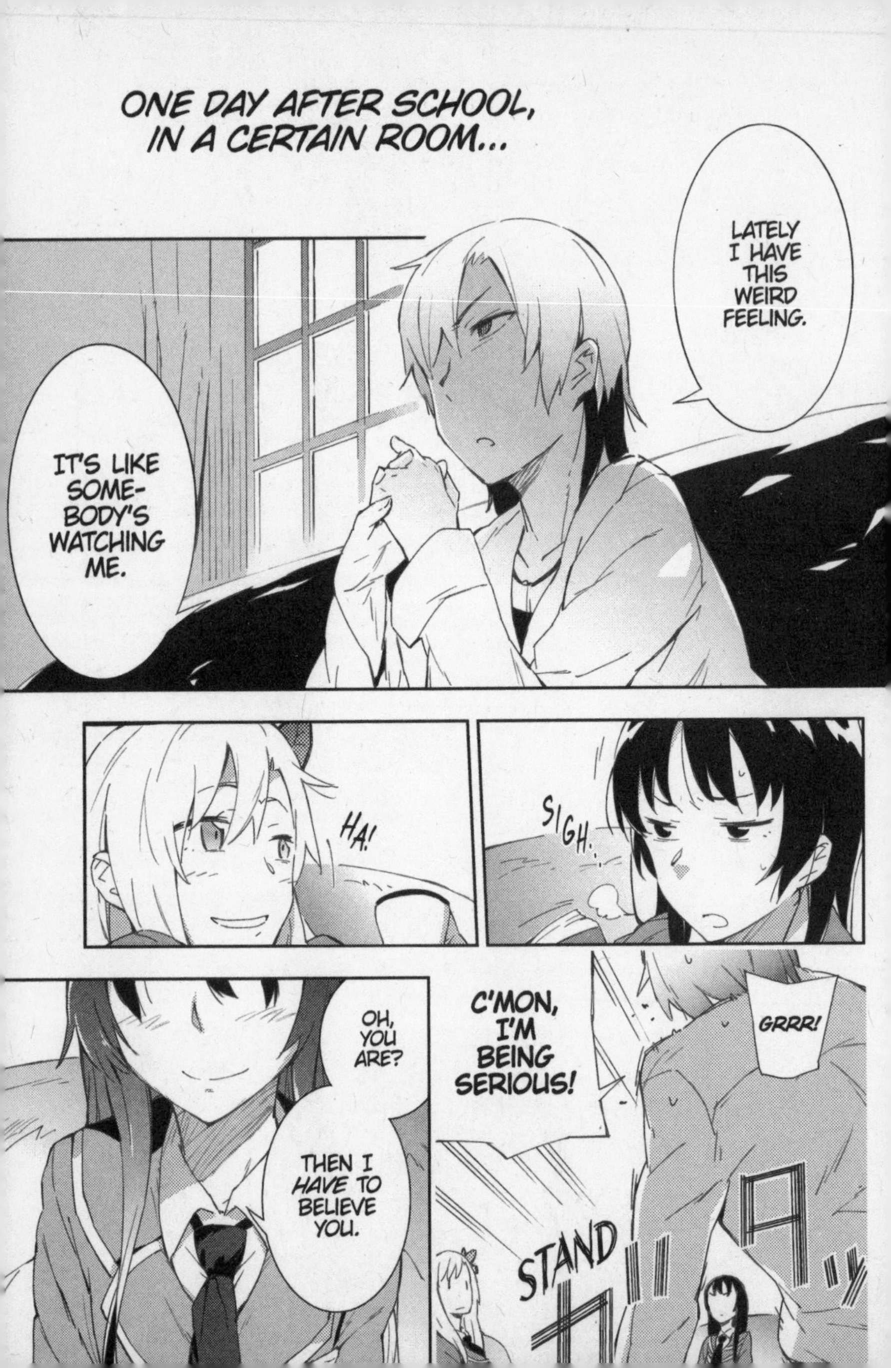
ONE DAY AFTER SCHOOL, IN A CERTAIN ROOM...
LATELY I HAVE THIS WEIRD FEELING.
IT'S LIKE SOME-BODY'S WATCHING ME.
SIGH...
HA!
GRRR!
C'MON, I'M BEING SERIOUS!
STAND
OH, YOU ARE?
THEN I *HAVE* TO BELIEVE YOU.

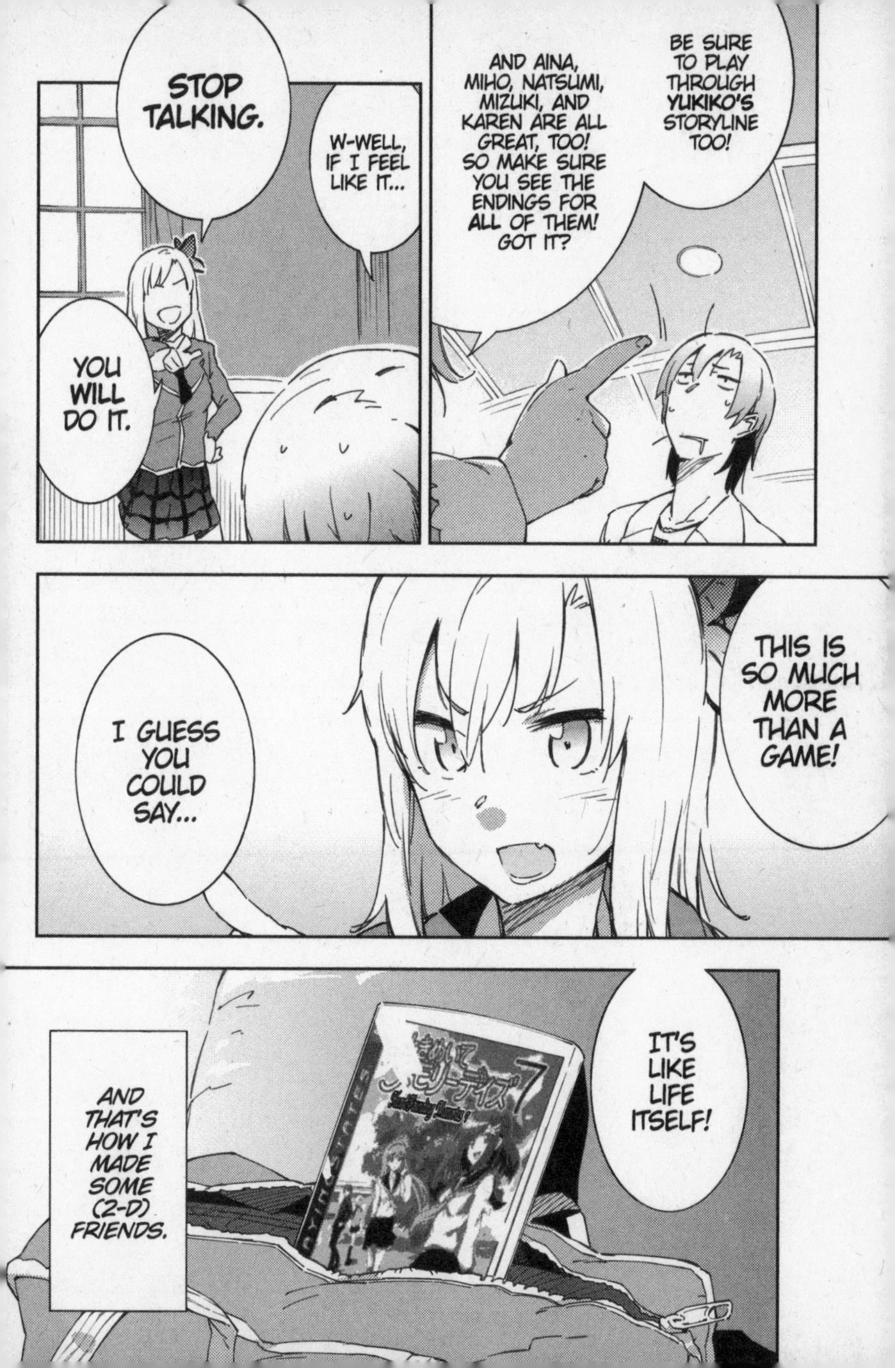
BE SURE TO PLAY THROUGH YUKIKO'S STORYLINE TOO!
AND AINA, MIHO, NATSUMI, MIZUKI, AND KAREN ARE ALL GREAT, TOO! SO MAKE SURE YOU SEE THE ENDINGS FOR ALL OF THEM! GOT IT?
W-WELL, IF I FEEL LIKE IT...
STOP TALKING.
YOU WILL DO IT.
THIS IS SO MUCH MORE THAN A GAME!
I GUESS YOU COULD SAY...
IT'S LIKE LIFE ITSELF!
AND THAT'S HOW I MADE SOME (2-D) FRIENDS.

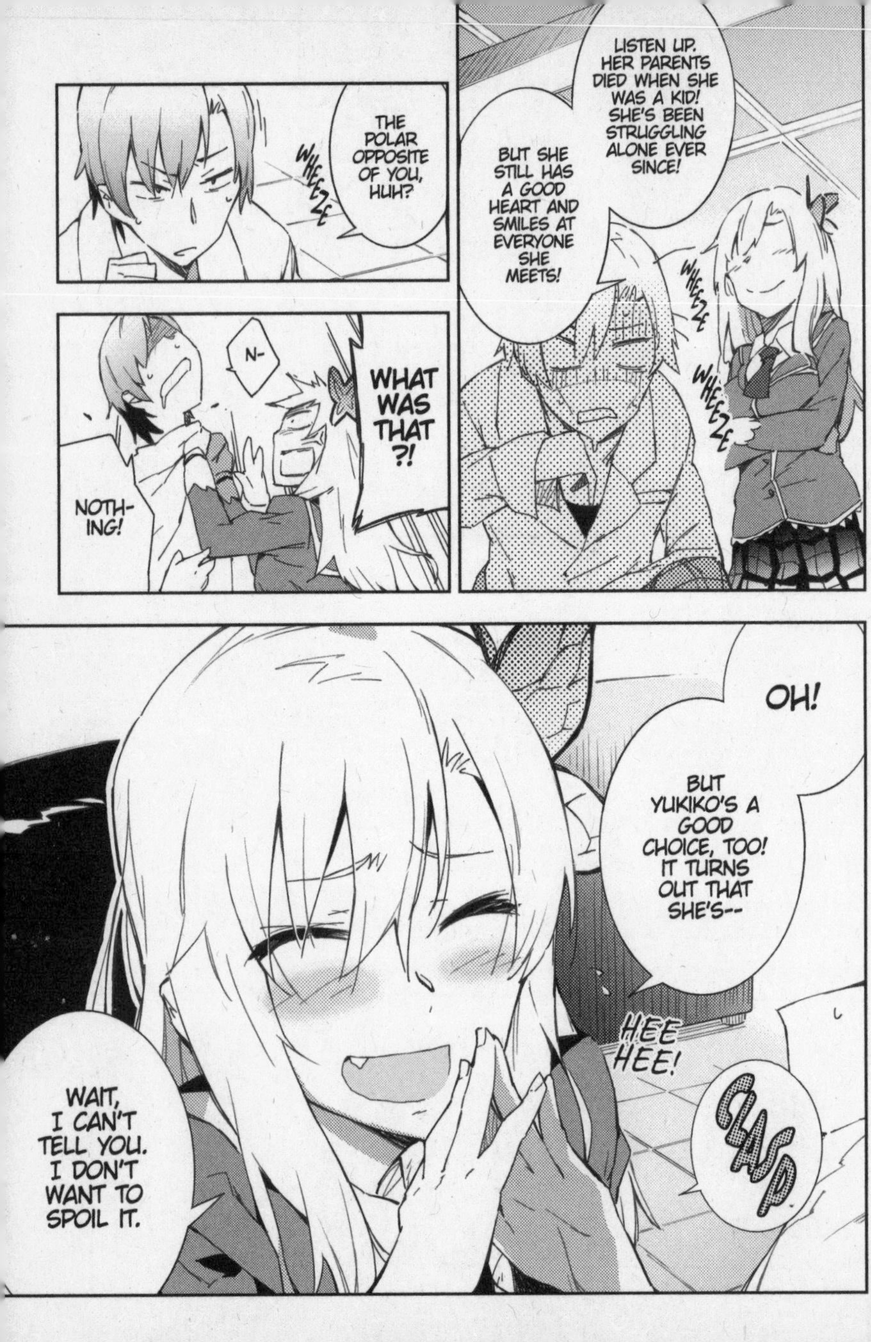
LISTEN UP. HER PARENTS DIED WHEN SHE WAS A KID! SHE'S BEEN STRUGGLING ALONE EVER SINCE!
BUT SHE STILL HAS A GOOD HEART AND SMILES AT EVERYONE SHE MEETS!
WHEEZE
WHEEZE
THE POLAR OPPOSITE OF YOU, HUH?
WHEEZE
WHAT WAS THAT ?!
N-
NOTH-ING!
OH!
BUT YUKIKO'S A GOOD CHOICE, TOO! IT TURNS OUT THAT SHE'S--
HEE HEE!
CLASP
WAIT, I CAN'T TELL YOU. I DON'T WANT TO SPOIL IT.

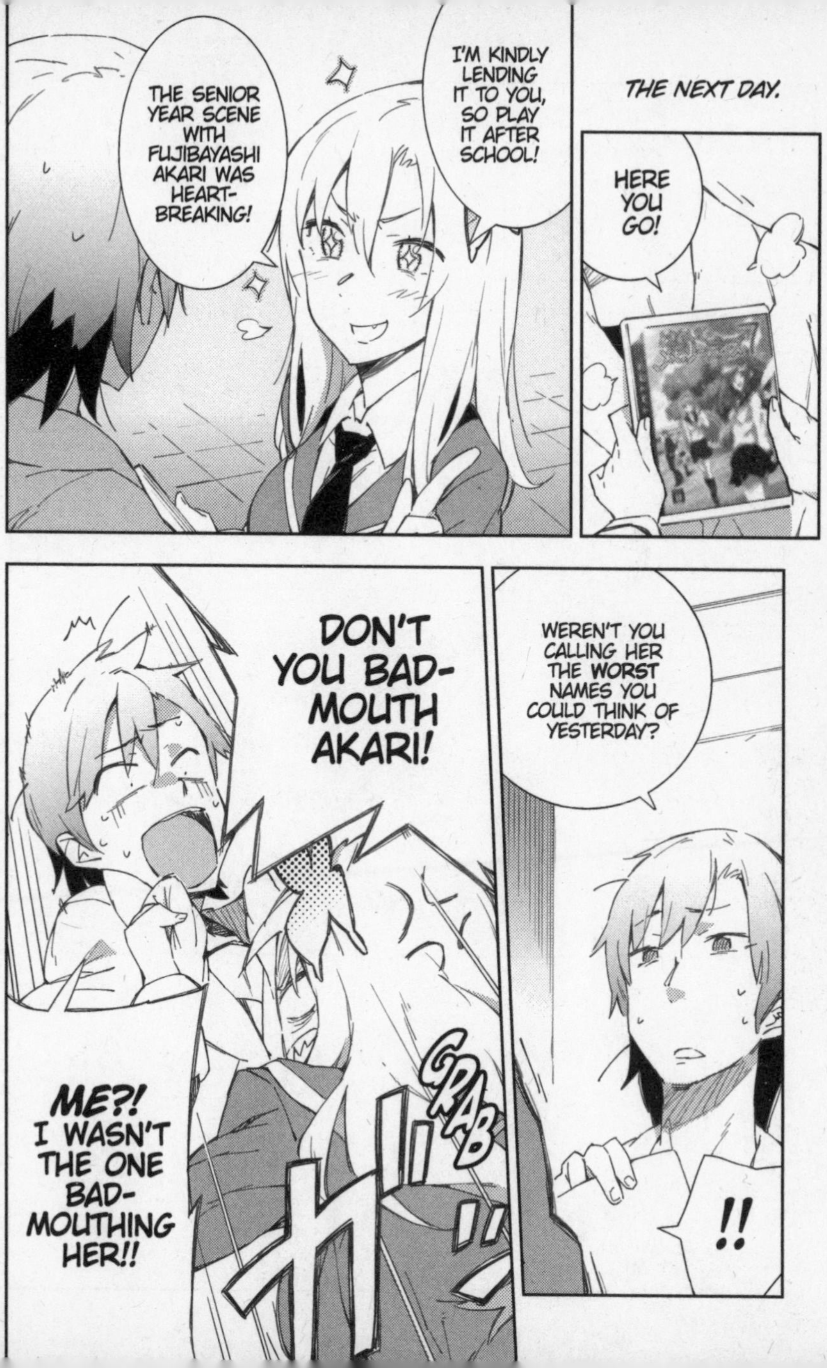
THE NEXT DAY.
HERE YOU GO!
I'M KINDLY LENDING IT TO YOU, SO PLAY IT AFTER SCHOOL!
THE SENIOR YEAR SCENE WITH FUJIBAYASHI AKARI WAS HEART-BREAKING!
WEREN'T YOU CALLING HER THE WORST NAMES YOU COULD THINK OF YESTERDAY?
!!
DON'T YOU BAD-MOUTH AKARI!
GRAB
ME?! I WASN'T THE ONE BAD-MOUTHING HER!!

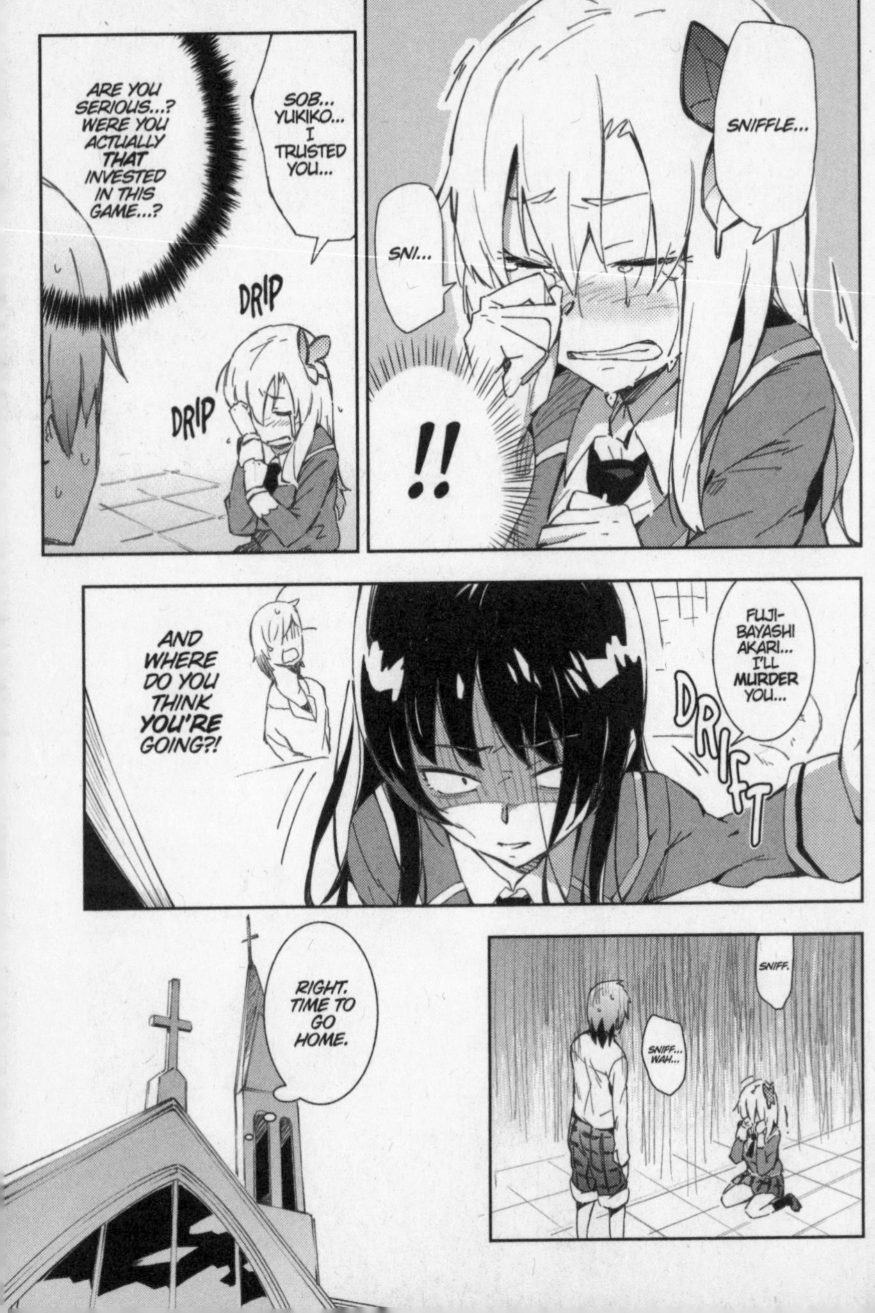
SNIFFLE...
SNI...
!!
SOB... YUKIKO... I TRUSTED YOU...
ARE YOU SERIOUS...? WERE YOU ACTUALLY THAT INVESTED IN THIS GAME...?
DRIP
DRIP
FUJI-BAYASHI AKARI... I'LL MURDER YOU...
DRIFT
AND WHERE DO YOU THINK YOU'RE GOING?!
SNIFF.
SNIFF... WAH...
RIGHT. TIME TO GO HOME.

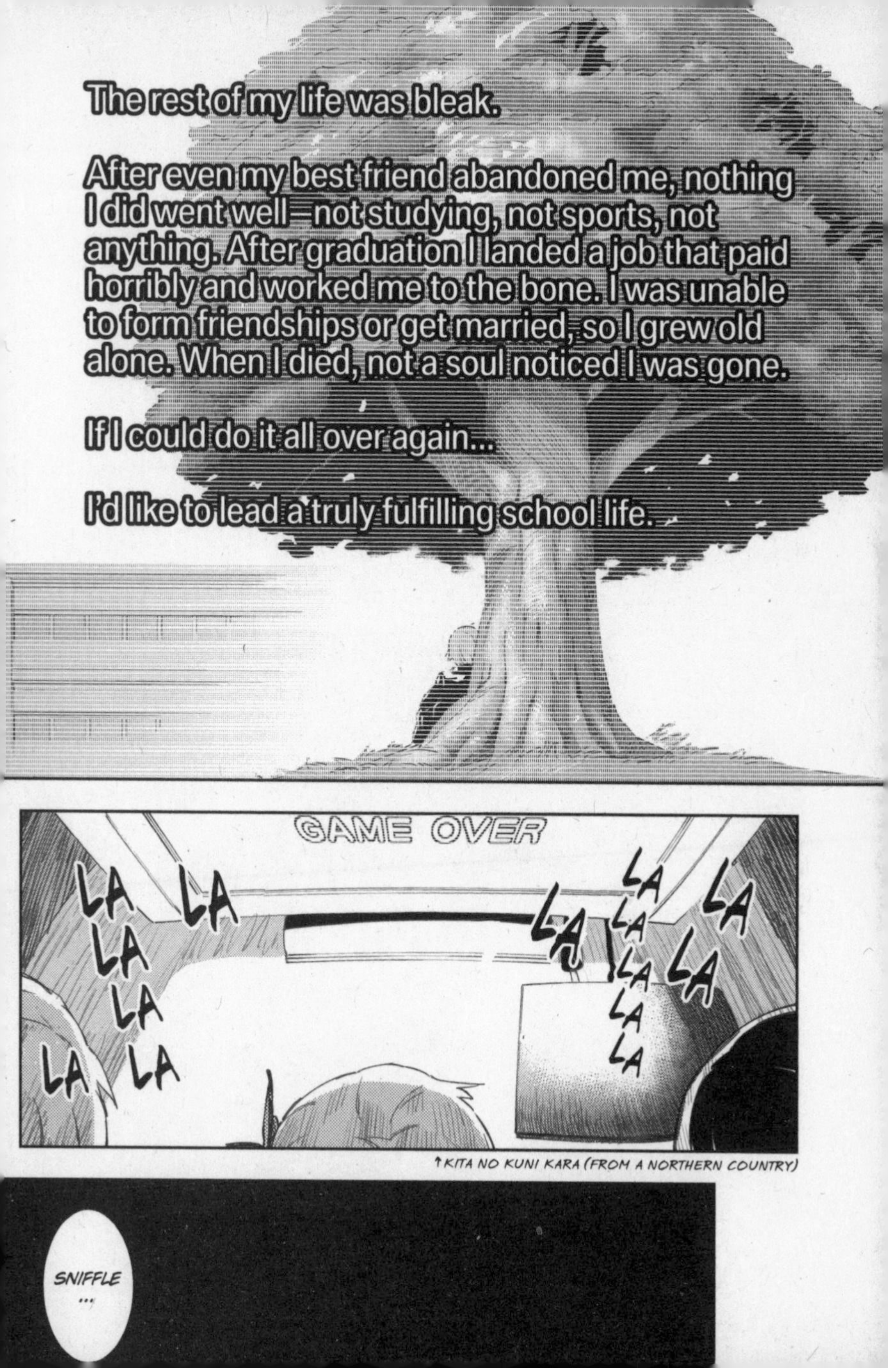
The rest of my life was bleak.
After even my best friend abandoned me, nothing I did went well—not studying, not sports, not anything. After graduation I landed a job that paid horribly and worked me to the bone. I was unable to form friendships or get married, so I grew old alone. When I died, not a soul noticed I was gone.
If I could do it all over again...
I'd like to lead a truly fulfilling school life.
GAME OVER
LA LA LA LA LA LA LA LA LA
LA LA LA LA LA LA LA
↑KITA NO KUNI KARA (FROM A NORTHERN COUNTRY)
SNIFFLE...

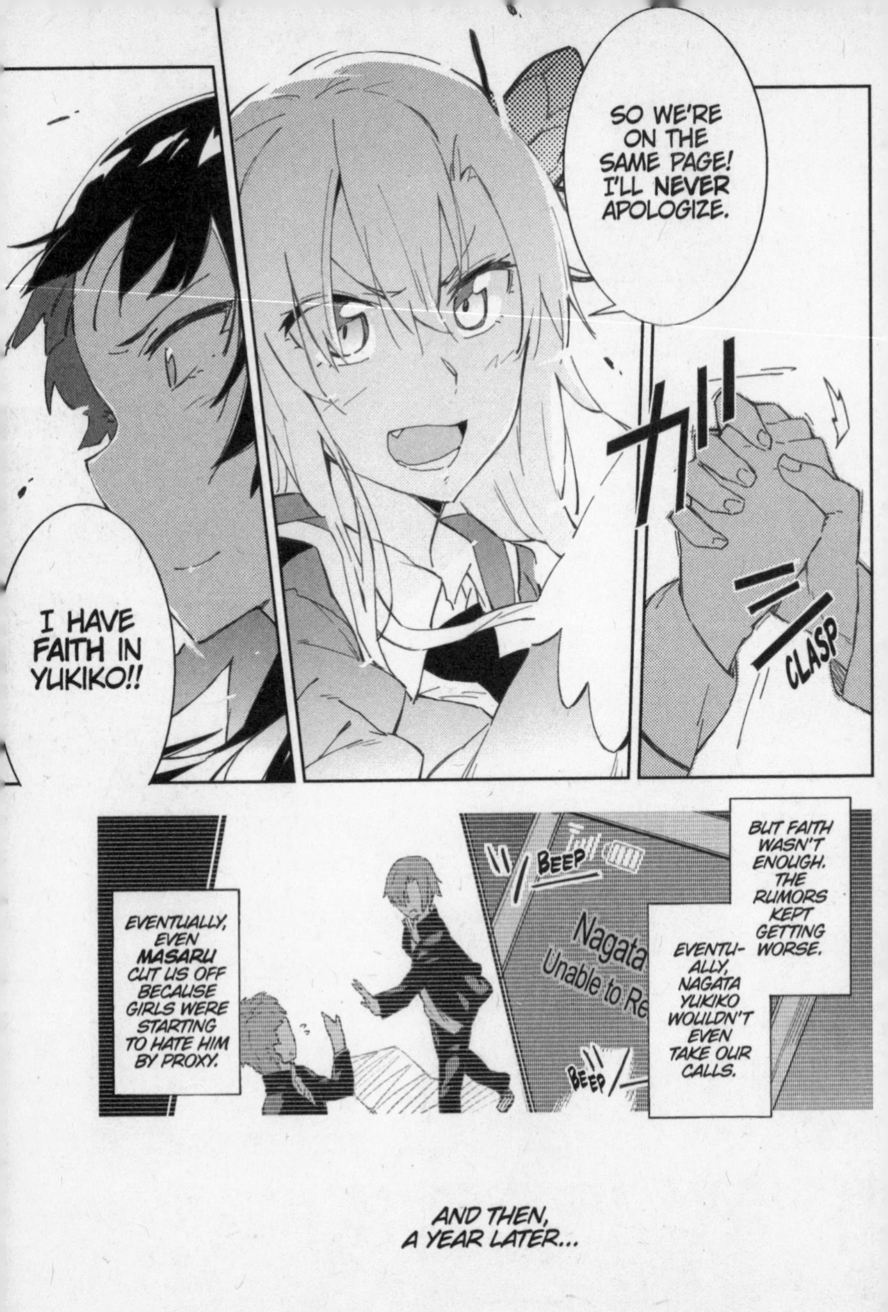
SO WE'RE ON THE SAME PAGE! I'LL NEVER APOLOGIZE.
CLASP
I HAVE FAITH IN YUKIKO!!
BUT FAITH WASN'T ENOUGH. THE RUMORS KEPT GETTING WORSE.
EVENTU-ALLY, NAGATA YUKIKO WOULDN'T EVEN TAKE OUR CALLS.
BEEP
Nagata
Unable to Re
BEEP
EVENTUALLY, EVEN MASARU CUT US OFF BECAUSE GIRLS WERE STARTING TO HATE HIM BY PROXY.
AND THEN, A YEAR LATER...

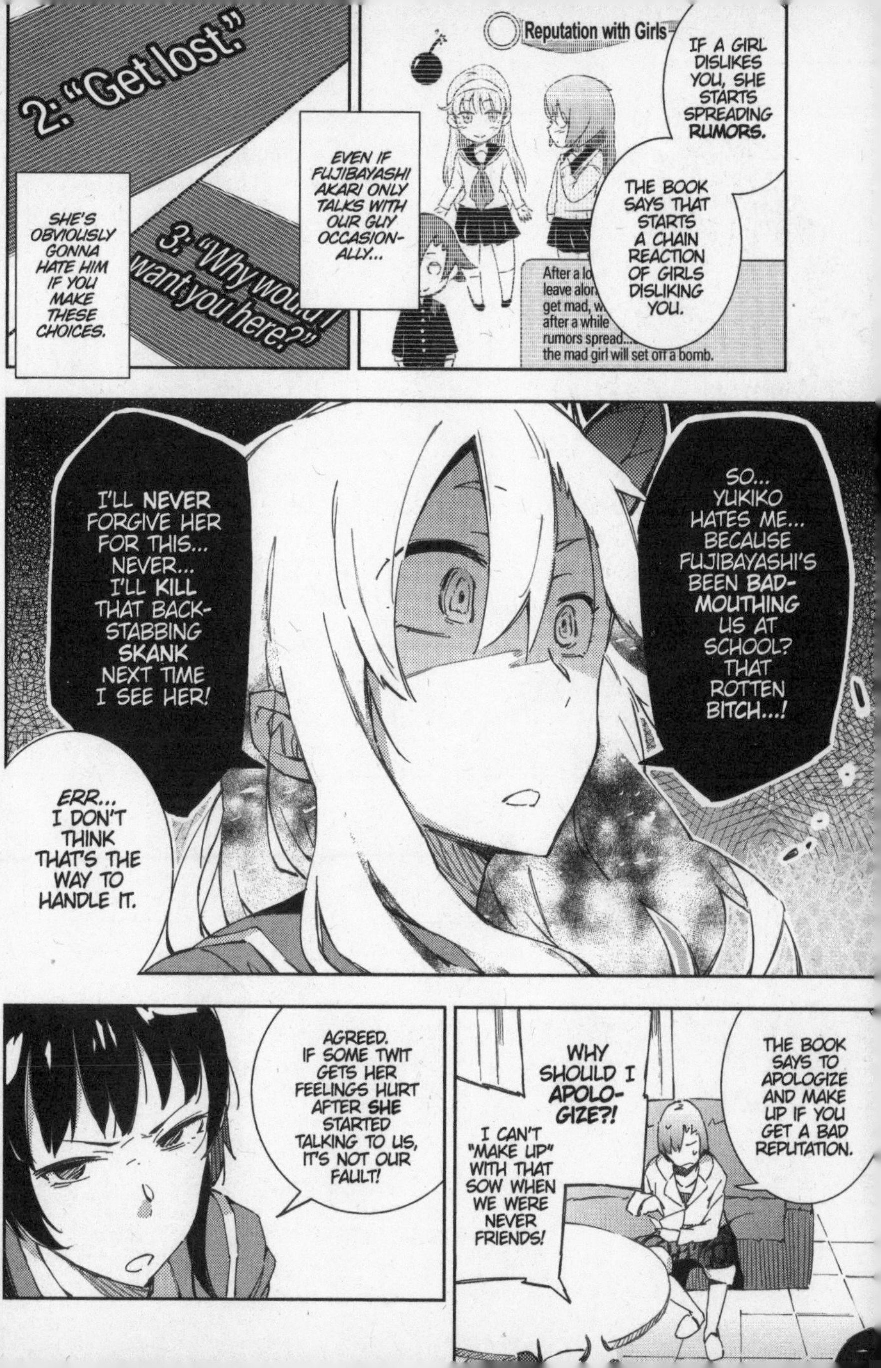

Reputation with Girls
IF A GIRL DISLIKES YOU, SHE STARTS SPREADING RUMORS.
THE BOOK SAYS THAT STARTS A CHAIN REACTION OF GIRLS DISLIKING YOU.
after a while rumors spread... the mad girl will set off a bomb.
EVEN IF FUJIBAYASHI AKARI ONLY TALKS WITH OUR GUY OCCASION-ALLY...
2: "Get lost."
3: "Why woul want you here?"
SHE'S OBVIOUSLY GONNA HATE HIM IF YOU MAKE THESE CHOICES.
SO... YUKIKO HATES ME... BECAUSE FUJIBAYASHI'S BEEN BAD-MOUTHING US AT SCHOOL? THAT ROTTEN BITCH...!
I'LL NEVER FORGIVE HER FOR THIS... NEVER... I'LL KILL THAT BACK-STABBING SKANK NEXT TIME I SEE HER!
ERR... I DON'T THINK THAT'S THE WAY TO HANDLE IT.
THE BOOK SAYS TO APOLOGIZE AND MAKE UP IF YOU GET A BAD REPUTATION.
WHY SHOULD I APOLO-GIZE?!
I CAN'T "MAKE UP" WITH THAT SOW WHEN WE WERE NEVER FRIENDS!
AGREED. IF SOME TWIT GETS HER FEELINGS HURT AFTER SHE STARTED TALKING TO US, IT'S NOT OUR FAULT!

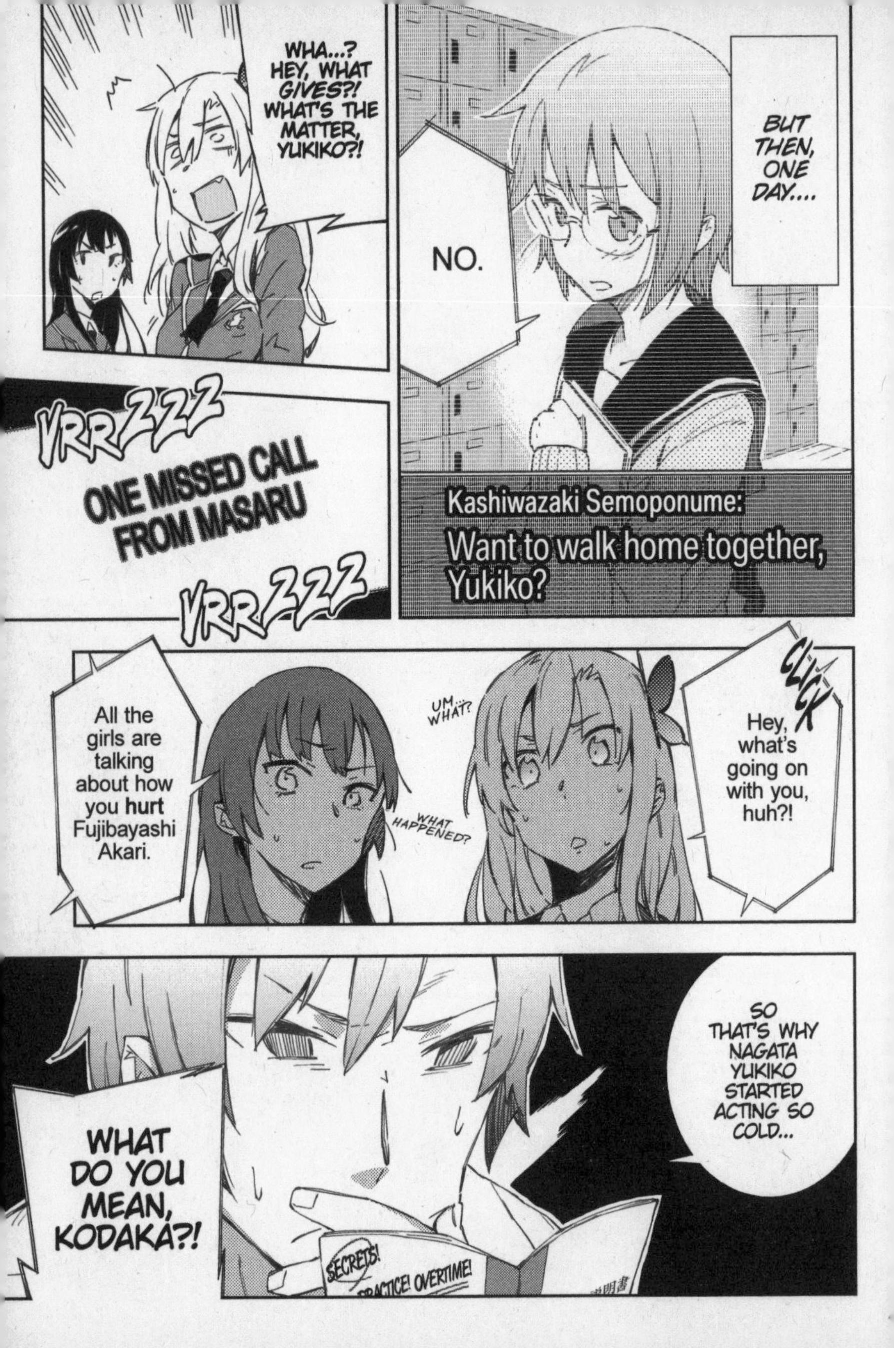

BUT THEN, ONE DAY....
NO.
Kashiwazaki Semoponume:
Want to walk home together, Yukiko?
WHA...? HEY, WHAT GIVES?! WHAT'S THE MATTER, YUKIKO?!
VRRZZZ
ONE MISSED CALL FROM MASARU
VRRZZZ
CLICK
Hey, what's going on with you, huh?!
UM... WHAT?
WHAT HAPPENED?
All the girls are talking about how you **hurt** Fujibayashi Akari.
SO THAT'S WHY NAGATA YUKIKO STARTED ACTING SO COLD...
WHAT DO YOU MEAN, KODAKA?!
SECRETS!
PRACTICE! OVERTIME!

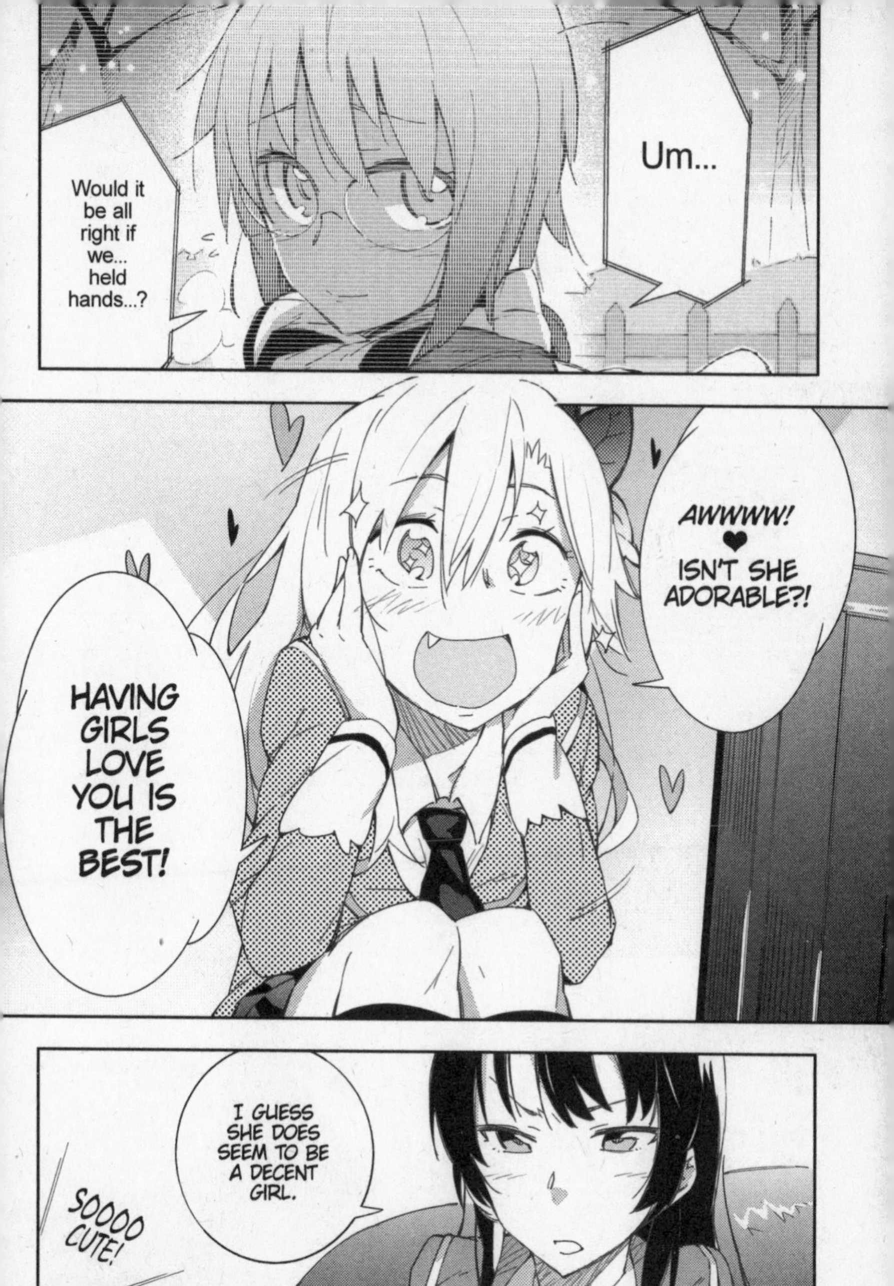
Um...
Would it be all right if we... held hands...?
AWWWW! ❤ ISN'T SHE ADORABLE?!
HAVING GIRLS LOVE YOU IS THE BEST!
I GUESS SHE DOES SEEM TO BE A DECENT GIRL.
SOOOO CUTE!

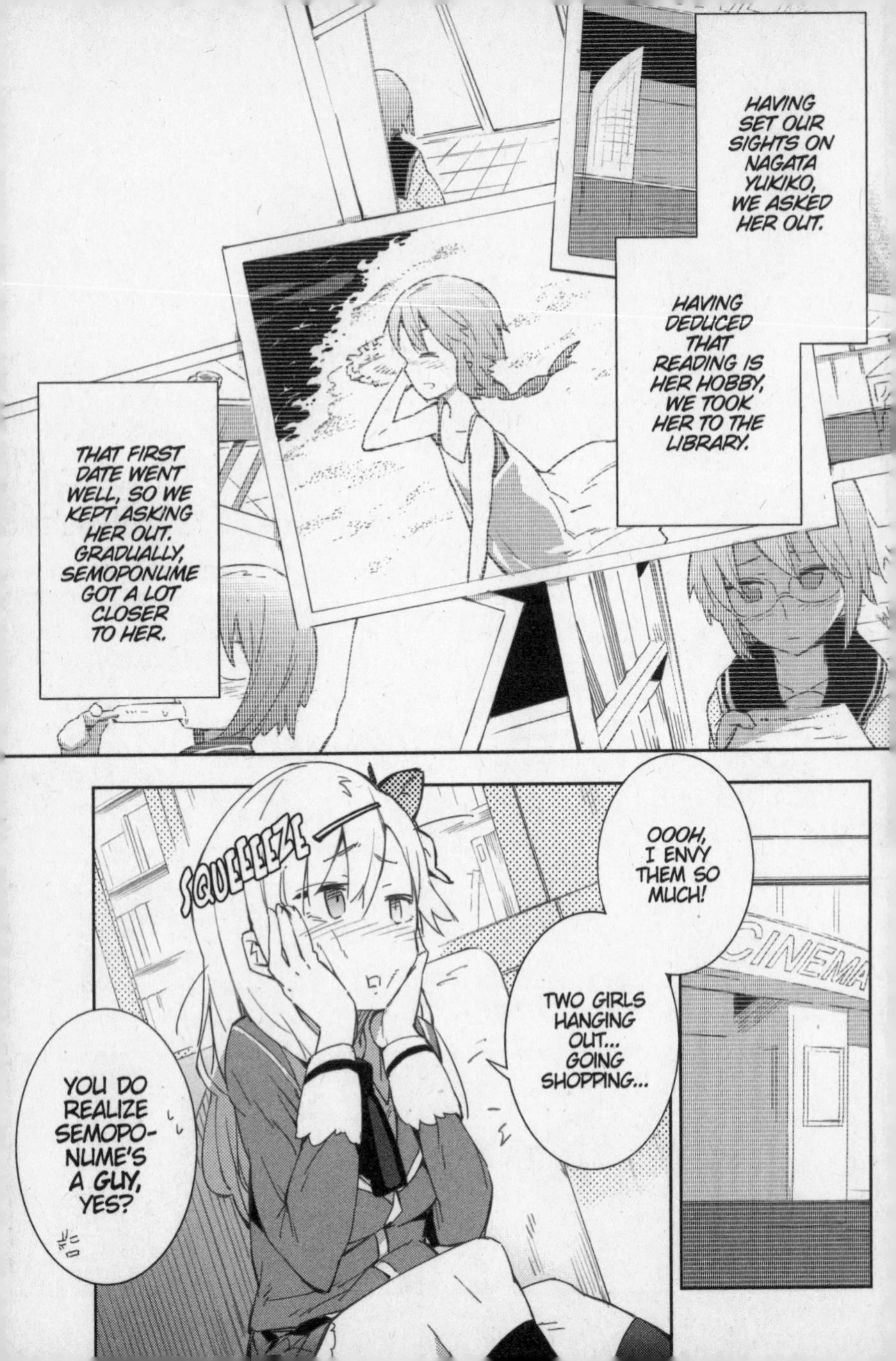
HAVING SET OUR SIGHTS ON NAGATA YUKIKO, WE ASKED HER OUT.
HAVING DEDUCED THAT READING IS HER HOBBY, WE TOOK HER TO THE LIBRARY.
THAT FIRST DATE WENT WELL, SO WE KEPT ASKING HER OUT. GRADUALLY, SEMOPONUME GOT A LOT CLOSER TO HER.
OOOH, I ENVY THEM SO MUCH!
SQUEEEEZE
CINEMA
TWO GIRLS HANGING OUT... GOING SHOPPING...
YOU DO REALIZE SEMOPONUME'S A GUY, YES?

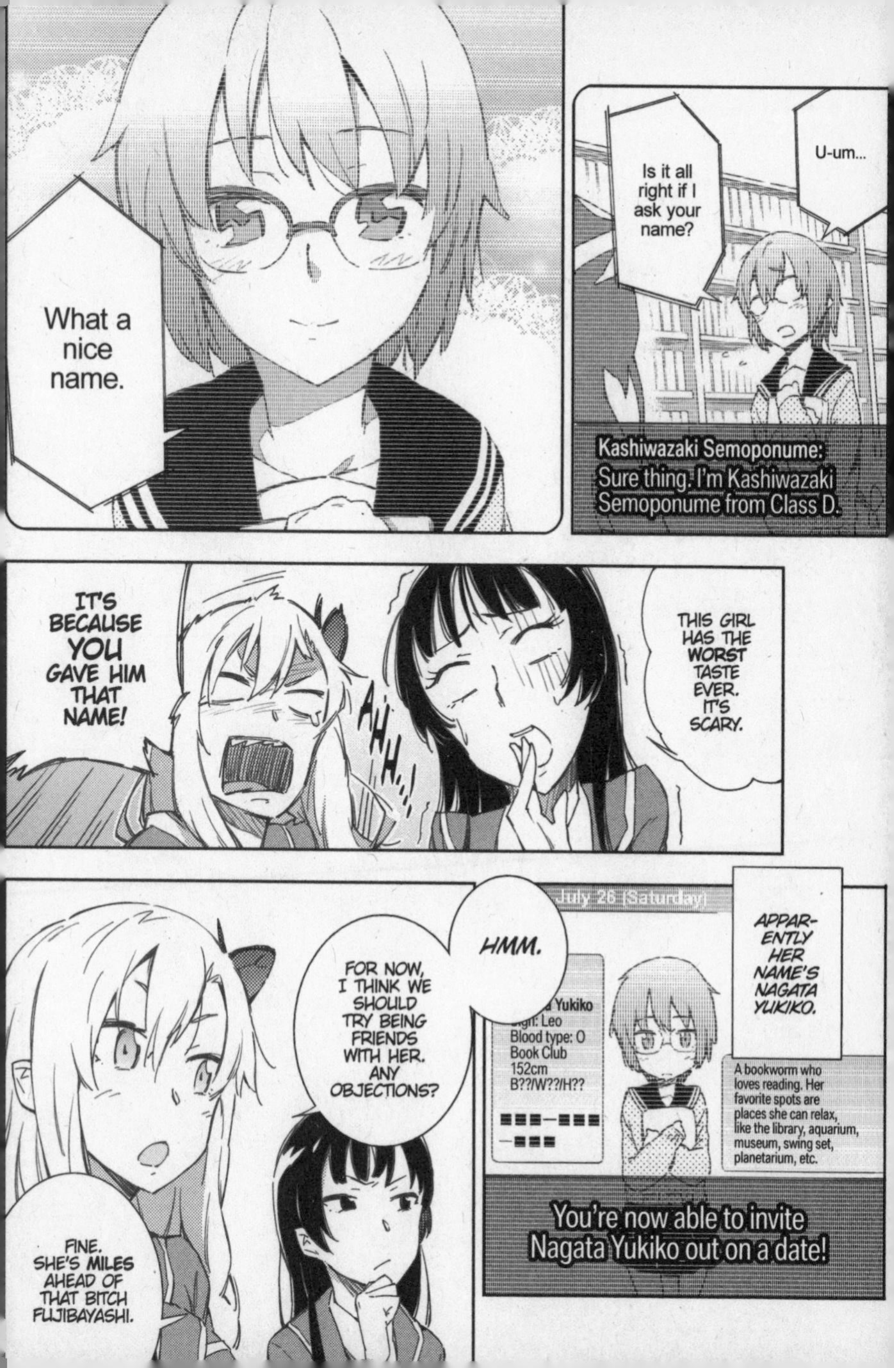
U-um...
Is it all right if I ask your name?
Kashiwazaki Semoponume: Sure thing. I'm Kashiwazaki Semoponume from Class D.
What a nice name.
THIS GIRL HAS THE WORST TASTE EVER. IT'S SCARY.
IT'S BECAUSE YOU GAVE HIM THAT NAME!
AHH...
APPARENTLY HER NAME'S NAGATA YUKIKO.
July 26 (Saturday)
Blood type: O
Book Club
152cm
B??/W??/H??
[redacted]
A bookworm who loves reading. Her favorite spots are places she can relax, like the library, aquarium, museum, swing set, planetarium, etc.
You're now able to invite Nagata Yukiko out on a date!
HMM.
FOR NOW, I THINK WE SHOULD TRY BEING FRIENDS WITH HER. ANY OBJECTIONS?
FINE. SHE'S MILES AHEAD OF THAT BITCH FUJIBAYASHI.

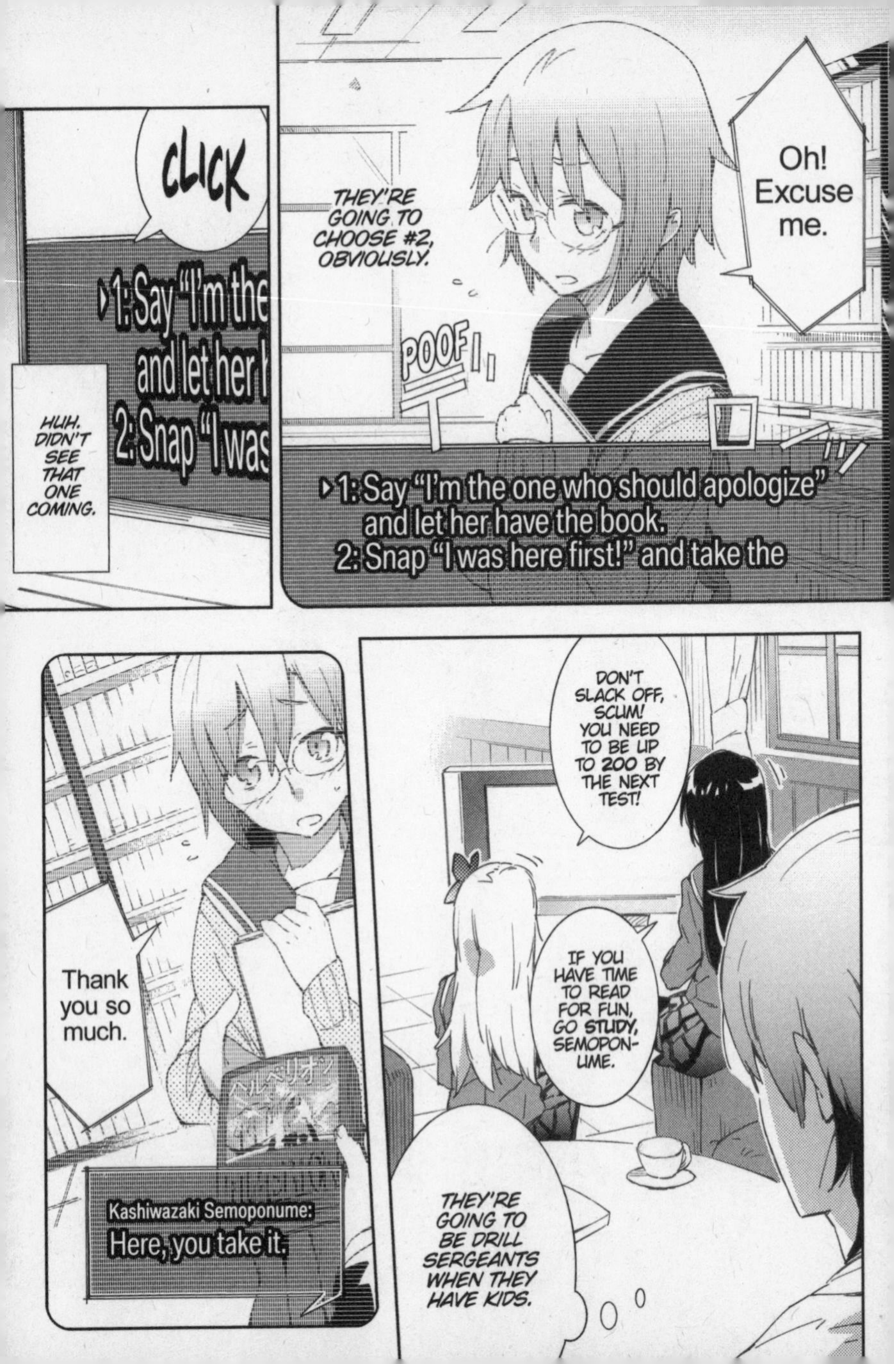

Oh! Excuse me.
THEY'RE GOING TO CHOOSE #2, OBVIOUSLY.
POOF
1: Say "I'm the one who should apologize" and let her have the book.
2: Snap "I was here first!" and take the
CLICK
1: Say "I'm the
and let her h
2: Snap "I was
HUH. DIDN'T SEE THAT ONE COMING.
DON'T SLACK OFF, SCUM! YOU NEED TO BE UP TO 200 BY THE NEXT TEST!
IF YOU HAVE TIME TO READ FOR FUN, GO STUDY, SEMOPON-UME.
THEY'RE GOING TO BE DRILL SERGEANTS WHEN THEY HAVE KIDS.
Thank you so much.
Kashiwazaki Semoponume:
Here, you take it.

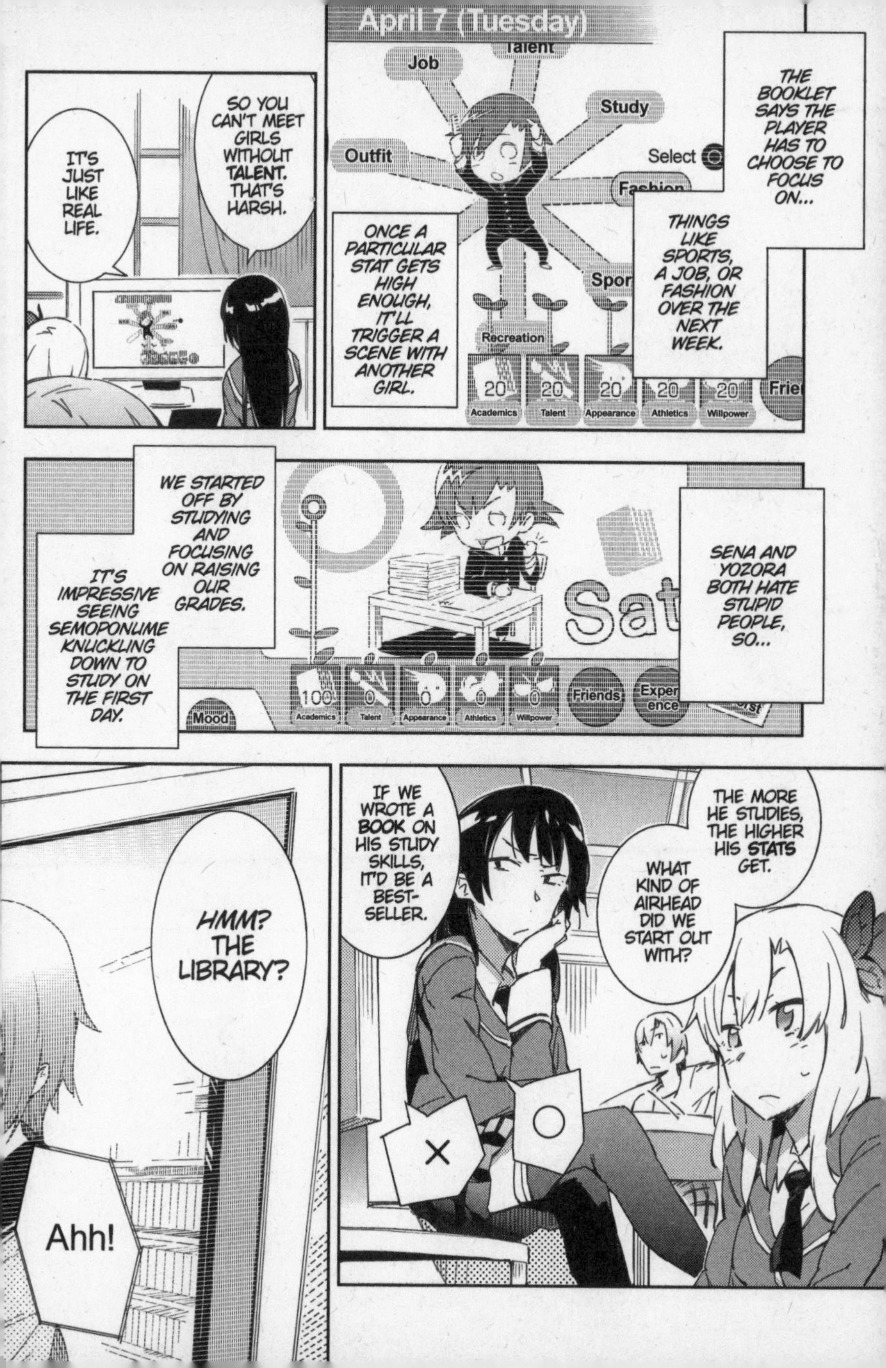

April 7 (Tuesday)
Job
Study
Outfit
Select
THE BOOKLET SAYS THE PLAYER HAS TO CHOOSE TO FOCUS ON...
THINGS LIKE SPORTS, A JOB, OR FASHION OVER THE NEXT WEEK.
ONCE A PARTICULAR STAT GETS HIGH ENOUGH, IT'LL TRIGGER A SCENE WITH ANOTHER GIRL.
Recreation
20 Academics
20 Talent
20 Appearance
20 Athletics
20 Willpower
SO YOU CAN'T MEET GIRLS WITHOUT TALENT. THAT'S HARSH.
IT'S JUST LIKE REAL LIFE.
SENA AND YOZORA BOTH HATE STUPID PEOPLE, SO...
WE STARTED OFF BY STUDYING AND FOCUSING ON RAISING OUR GRADES.
IT'S IMPRESSIVE SEEING SEMOPONUME KNUCKLING DOWN TO STUDY ON THE FIRST DAY.
100 Academics
0 Talent
0 Appearance
0 Athletics
0 Willpower
Friends
Mood
THE MORE HE STUDIES, THE HIGHER HIS STATS GET.
IF WE WROTE A BOOK ON HIS STUDY SKILLS, IT'D BE A BEST-SELLER.
WHAT KIND OF AIRHEAD DID WE START OUT WITH?
○
×
HMM? THE LIBRARY?
Ahh!

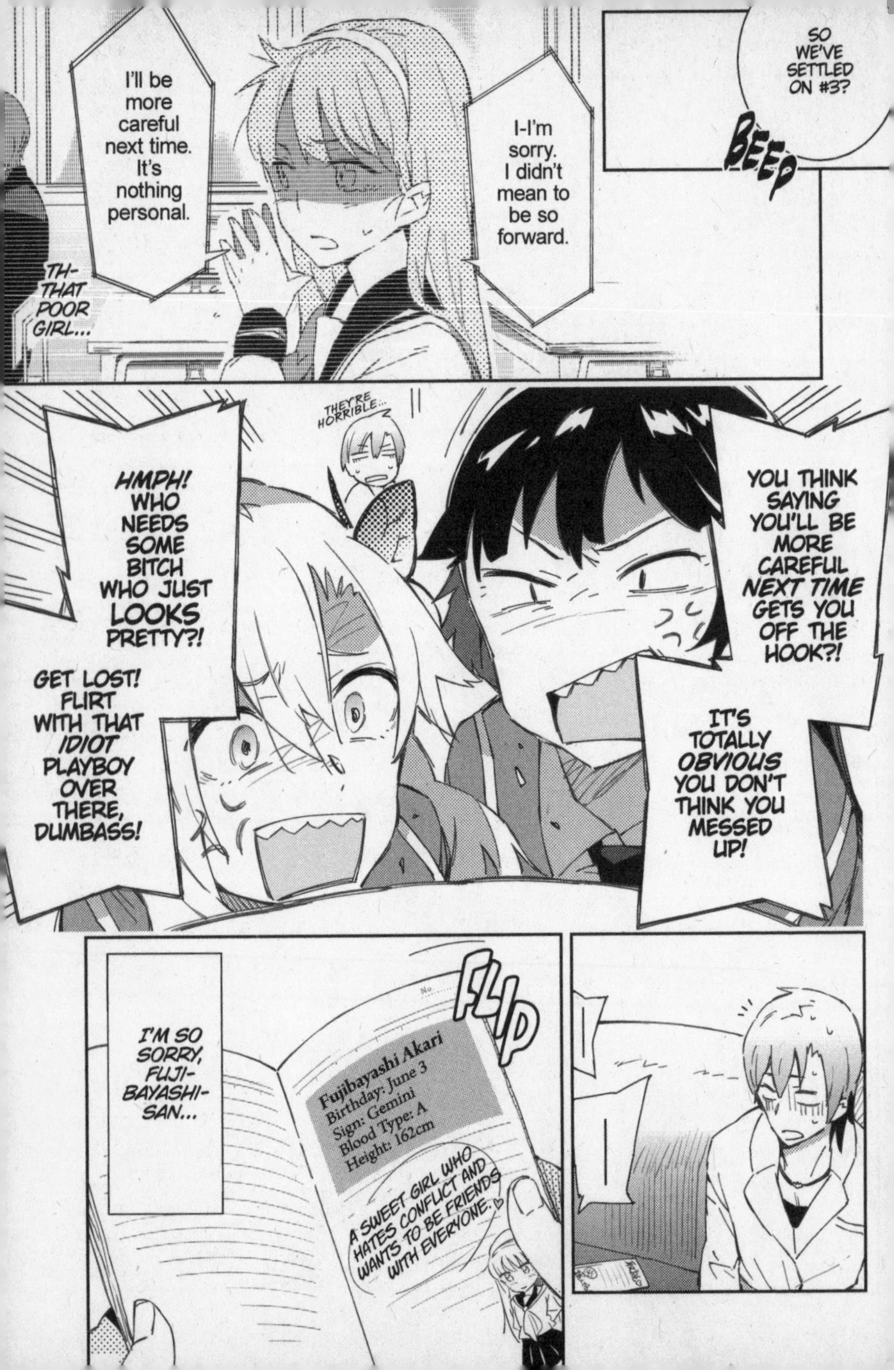
SO WE'VE SETTLED ON #3?
BEEP
I-I'm sorry. I didn't mean to be so forward.
I'll be more careful next time. It's nothing personal.
TH-THAT POOR GIRL...
YOU THINK SAYING YOU'LL BE MORE CAREFUL NEXT TIME GETS YOU OFF THE HOOK?!
IT'S TOTALLY OBVIOUS YOU DON'T THINK YOU MESSED UP!
THEY'RE HORRIBLE...
HMPH! WHO NEEDS SOME BITCH WHO JUST LOOKS PRETTY?!
GET LOST! FLIRT WITH THAT IDIOT PLAYBOY OVER THERE, DUMBASS!
FLIP
Fujibayashi Akari
Birthday: June 3
Sign: Gemini
Blood Type: A
Height: 162cm
A SWEET GIRL WHO HATES CONFLICT AND WANTS TO BE FRIENDS WITH EVERYONE.♡
I'M SO SORRY, FUJIBAYASHI-SAN...

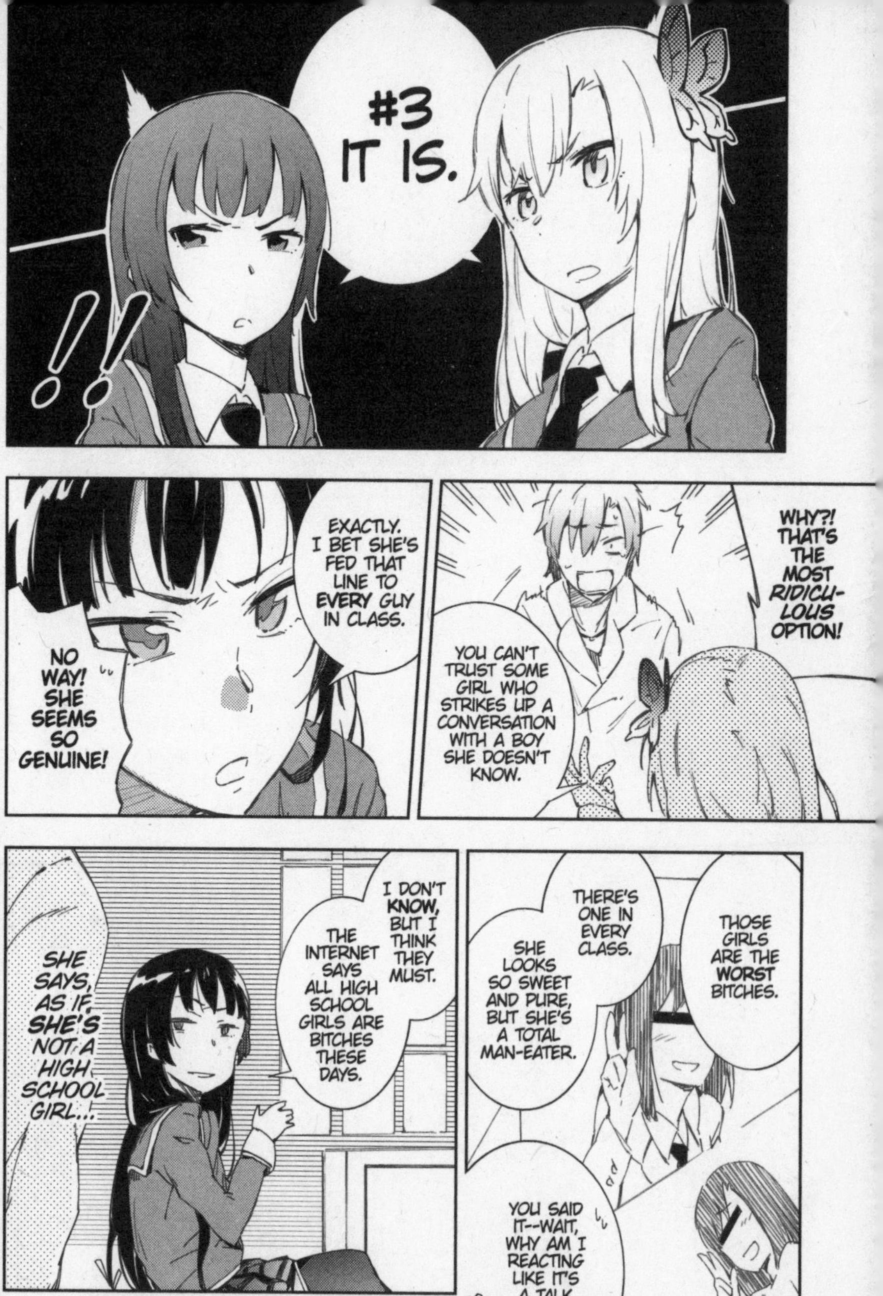
#3 IT IS.
!!
WHY?! THAT'S THE MOST RIDICULOUS OPTION!
YOU CAN'T TRUST SOME GIRL WHO STRIKES UP A CONVERSATION WITH A BOY SHE DOESN'T KNOW.
EXACTLY. I BET SHE'S FED THAT LINE TO EVERY GUY IN CLASS.
NO WAY! SHE SEEMS SO GENUINE!
THOSE GIRLS ARE THE WORST BITCHES.
THERE'S ONE IN EVERY CLASS.
SHE LOOKS SO SWEET AND PURE, BUT SHE'S A TOTAL MAN-EATER.
YOU SAID IT--WAIT, WHY AM I REACTING LIKE IT'S A TALK SHOW...?
DO THESE GIRLS REALLY EXIST?
I DON'T KNOW, BUT I THINK THEY MUST.
THE INTERNET SAYS ALL HIGH SCHOOL GIRLS ARE BITCHES THESE DAYS.
SHE SAYS, AS IF SHE'S NOT A HIGH SCHOOL GIRL...!

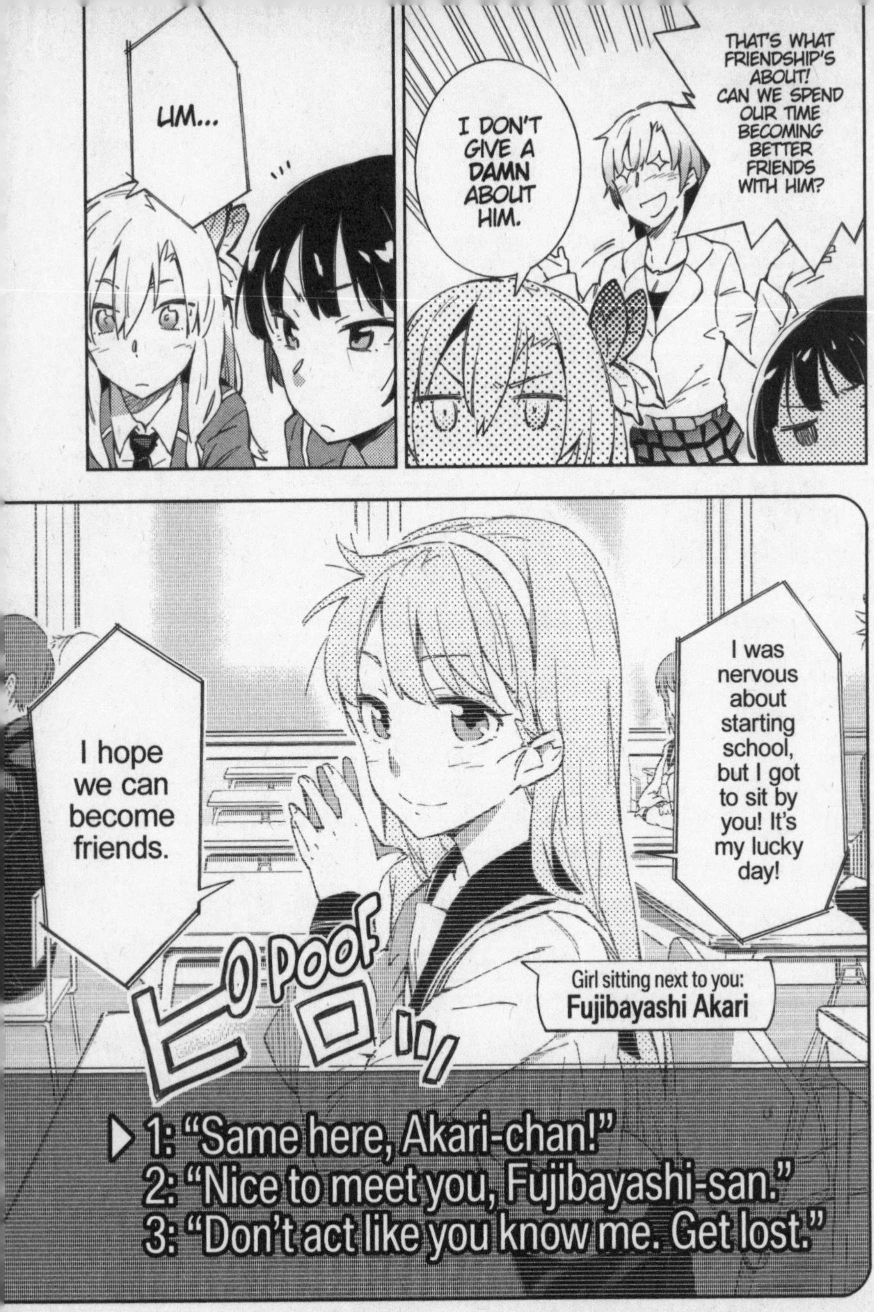
THAT'S WHAT FRIENDSHIP'S ABOUT! CAN WE SPEND OUR TIME BECOMING BETTER FRIENDS WITH HIM?
I DON'T GIVE A DAMN ABOUT HIM.
UM...
I was nervous about starting school, but I got to sit by you! It's my lucky day!
I hope we can become friends.
POOF
Girl sitting next to you: Fujibayashi Akari
1: "Same here, Akari-chan!"
2: "Nice to meet you, Fujibayashi-san."
3: "Don't act like you know me. Get lost."

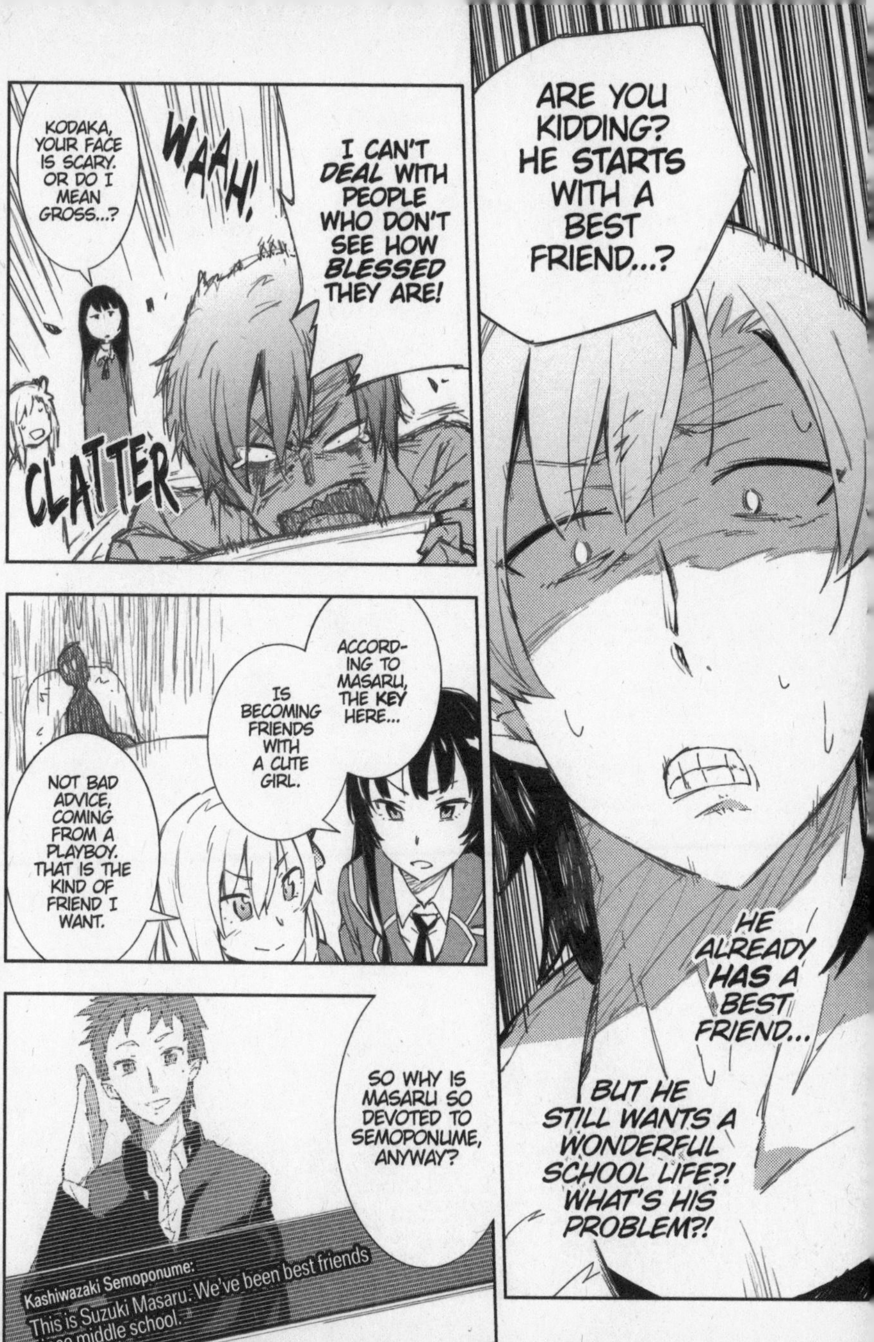
ARE YOU KIDDING? HE STARTS WITH A BEST FRIEND...?
HE ALREADY HAS A BEST FRIEND...
BUT HE STILL WANTS A WONDERFUL SCHOOL LIFE?! WHAT'S HIS PROBLEM?!
I CAN'T DEAL WITH PEOPLE WHO DON'T SEE HOW BLESSED THEY ARE!
WAAH!
KODAKA, YOUR FACE IS SCARY. OR DO I MEAN GROSS...?
CLATTER
ACCORDING TO MASARU, THE KEY HERE...
IS BECOMING FRIENDS WITH A CUTE GIRL.
NOT BAD ADVICE, COMING FROM A PLAYBOY. THAT IS THE KIND OF FRIEND I WANT.
SO WHY IS MASARU SO DEVOTED TO SEMOPONUME, ANYWAY?
Kashiwazaki Semoponume:
This is Suzuki Masaru. We've been best friends since middle school.

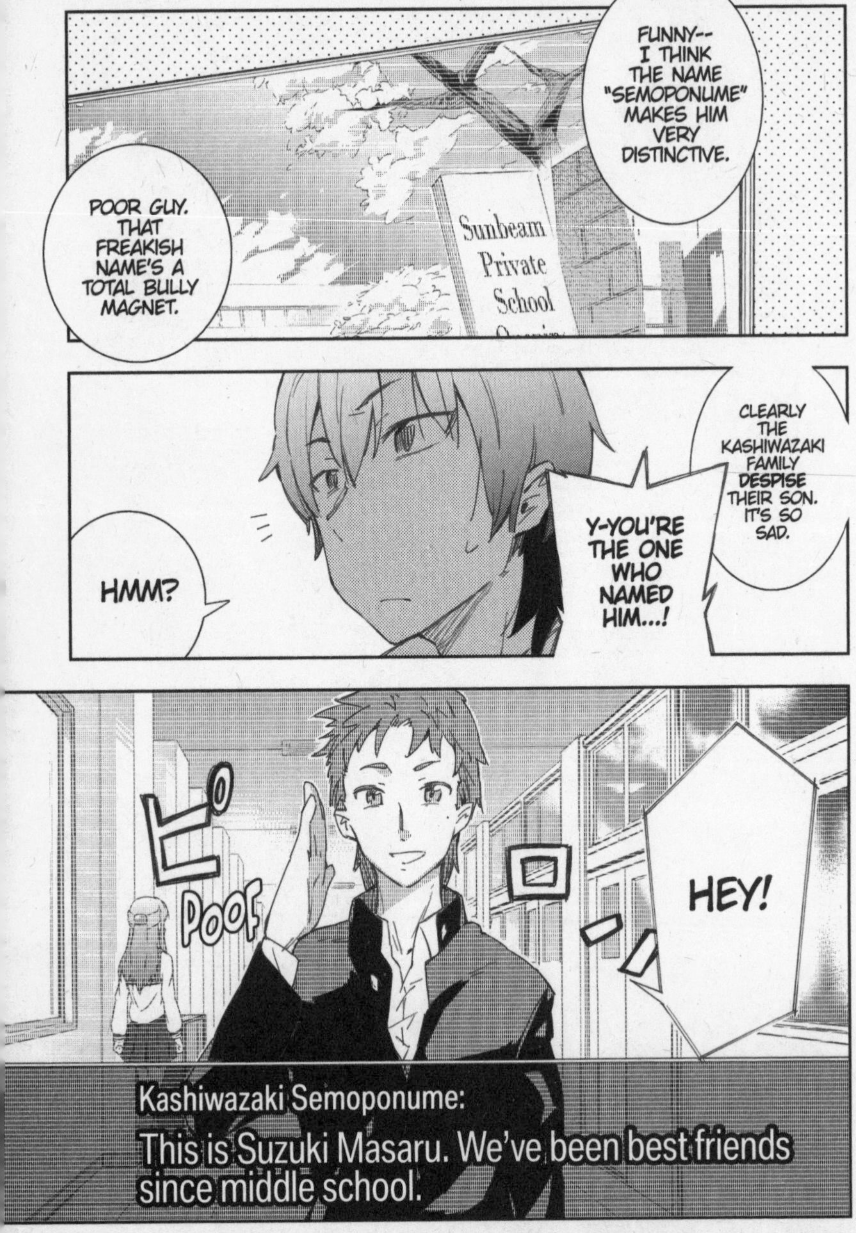
FUNNY-- I THINK THE NAME "SEMOPONUME" MAKES HIM VERY DISTINCTIVE.
POOR GUY. THAT FREAKISH NAME'S A TOTAL BULLY MAGNET.
Sunbeam Private School
CLEARLY THE KASHIWAZAKI FAMILY DESPISE THEIR SON. IT'S SO SAD.
Y-YOU'RE THE ONE WHO NAMED HIM...!
HMM?
HEY!
POOF
Kashiwazaki Semoponume:
This is Suzuki Masaru. We've been best friends since middle school.

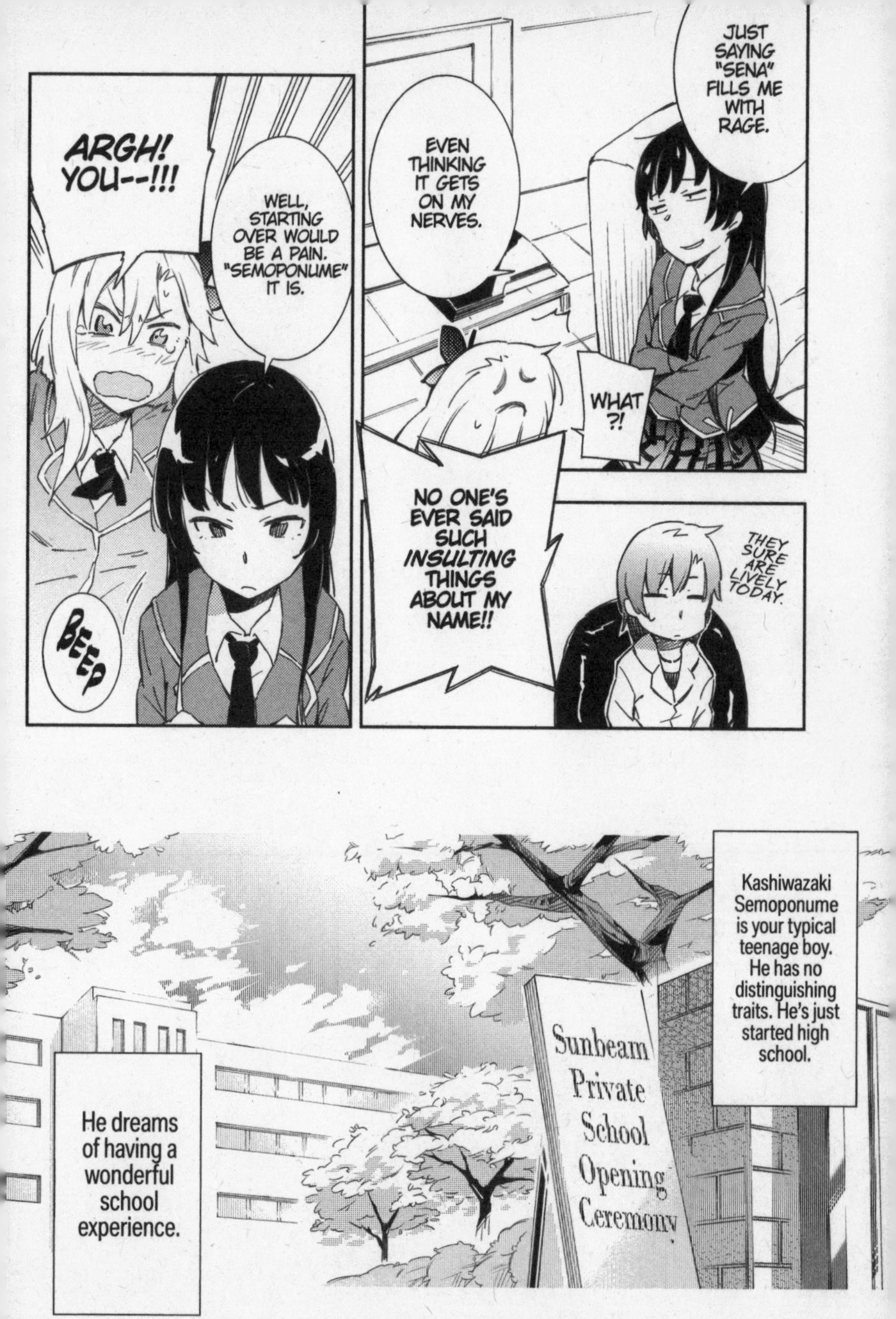
JUST SAYING "SENA" FILLS ME WITH RAGE.
EVEN THINKING IT GETS ON MY NERVES.
WHAT?!
NO ONE'S EVER SAID SUCH *INSULTING* THINGS ABOUT MY NAME!!
THEY SURE ARE LIVELY TODAY.
WELL, STARTING OVER WOULD BE A PAIN. "SEMOPONUME" IT IS.
ARGH! YOU--!!!
BEEP
Kashiwazaki Semoponume is your typical teenage boy. He has no distinguishing traits. He's just started high school.
Sunbeam Private School Opening Ceremony
He dreams of having a wonderful school experience.

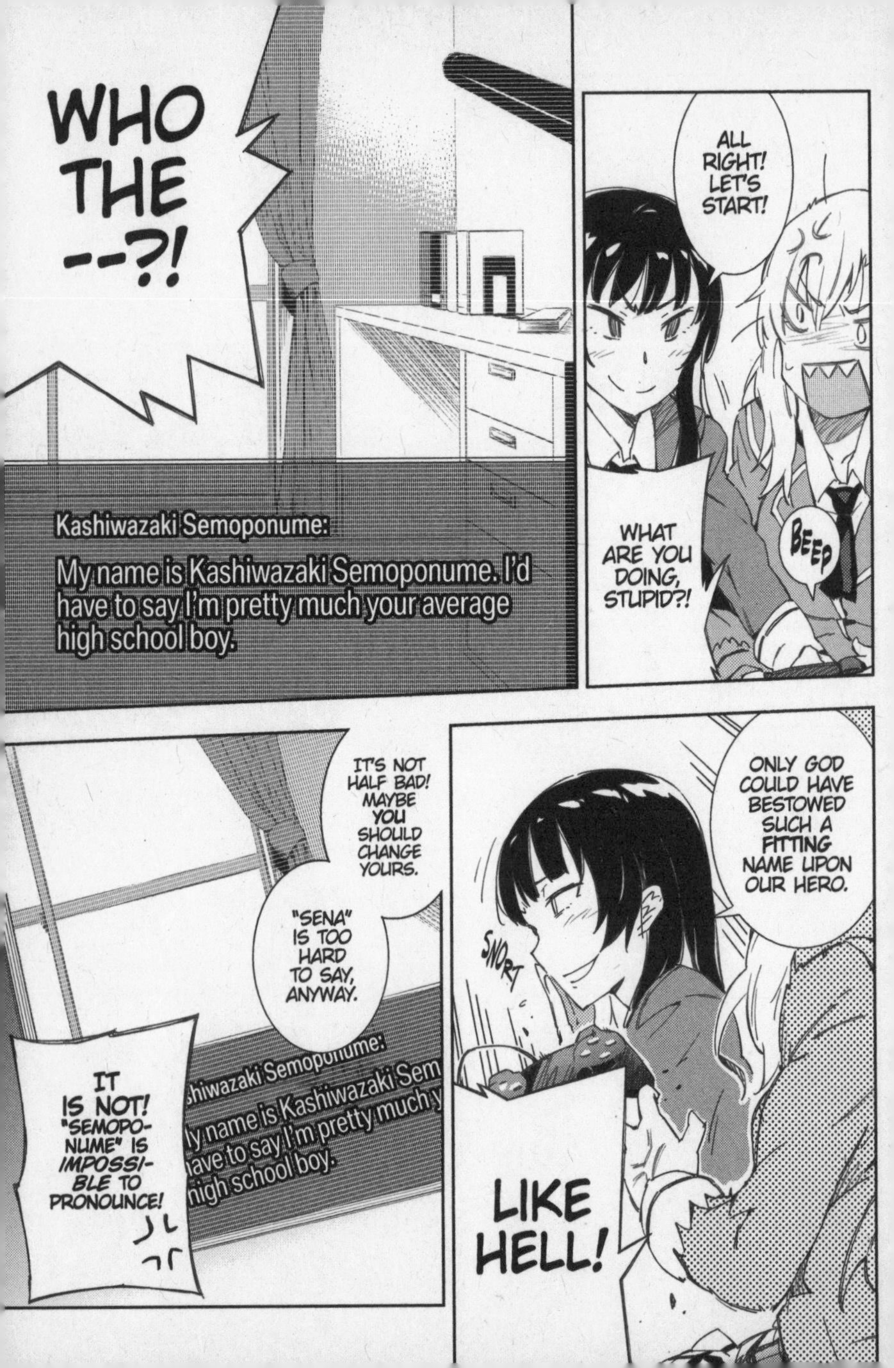
ALL RIGHT! LET'S START!
WHAT ARE YOU DOING, STUPID?!
BEEP
WHO THE --?!
Kashiwazaki Semoponume:
My name is Kashiwazaki Semoponume. I'd have to say I'm pretty much your average high school boy.
ONLY GOD COULD HAVE BESTOWED SUCH A FITTING NAME UPON OUR HERO.
SNORT
LIKE HELL!
IT'S NOT HALF BAD! MAYBE YOU SHOULD CHANGE YOURS.
"SENA" IS TOO HARD TO SAY, ANYWAY.
IT IS NOT! "SEMOPO-NUME" IS IMPOSSI-BLE TO PRONOUNCE!

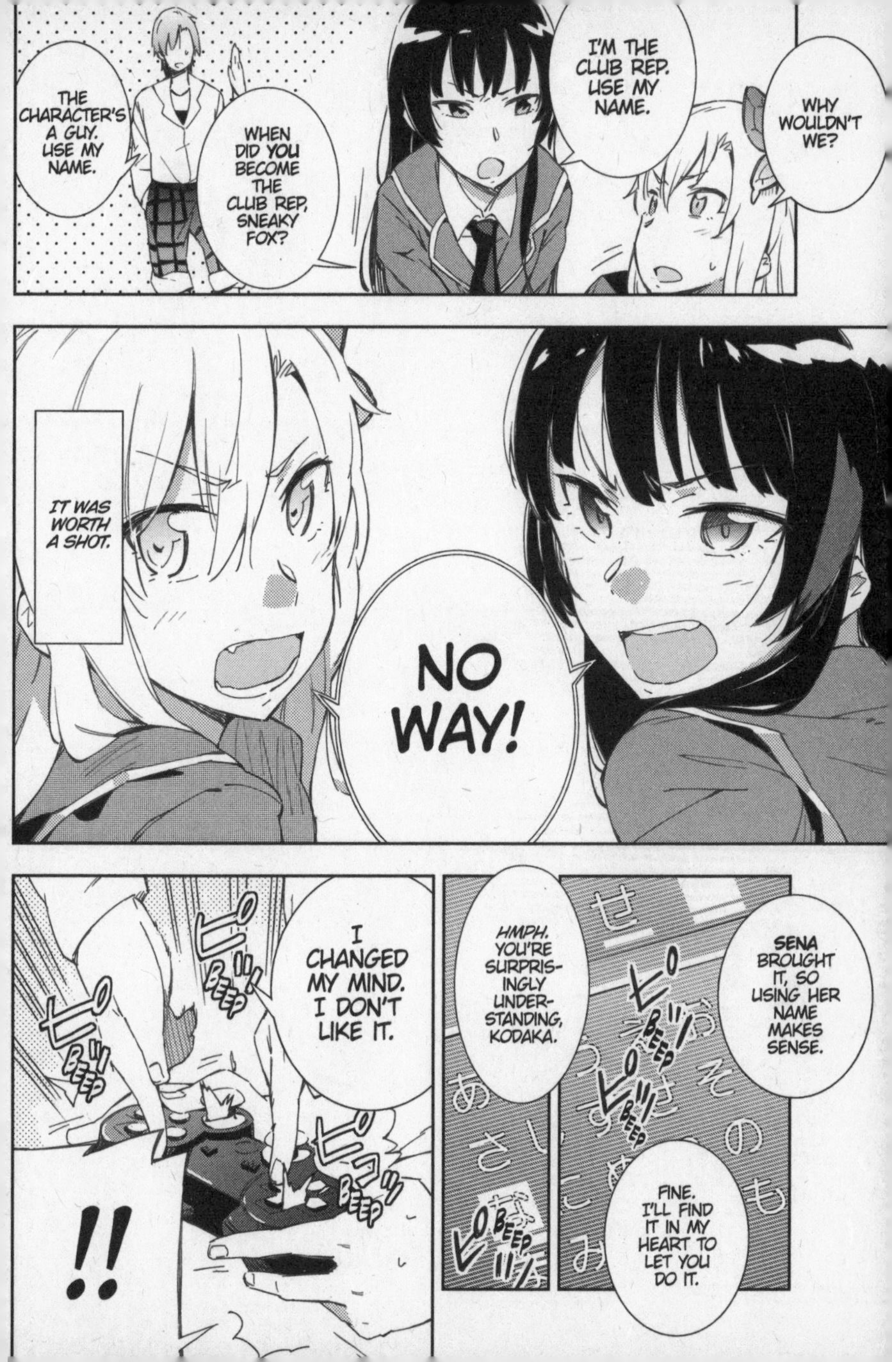
WHY WOULDN'T WE?
I'M THE CLUB REP. USE MY NAME.
WHEN DID YOU BECOME THE CLUB REP, SNEAKY FOX?
THE CHARACTER'S A GUY. USE MY NAME.
NO WAY!
IT WAS WORTH A SHOT.
SENA BROUGHT IT, SO USING HER NAME MAKES SENSE.
HMPH. YOU'RE SURPRISINGLY UNDERSTANDING, KODAKA.
BEEP
BEEP
BEEP
FINE. I'LL FIND IT IN MY HEART TO LET YOU DO IT.
I CHANGED MY MIND. I DON'T LIKE IT.
BEEP
BEEP
BEEP
!!

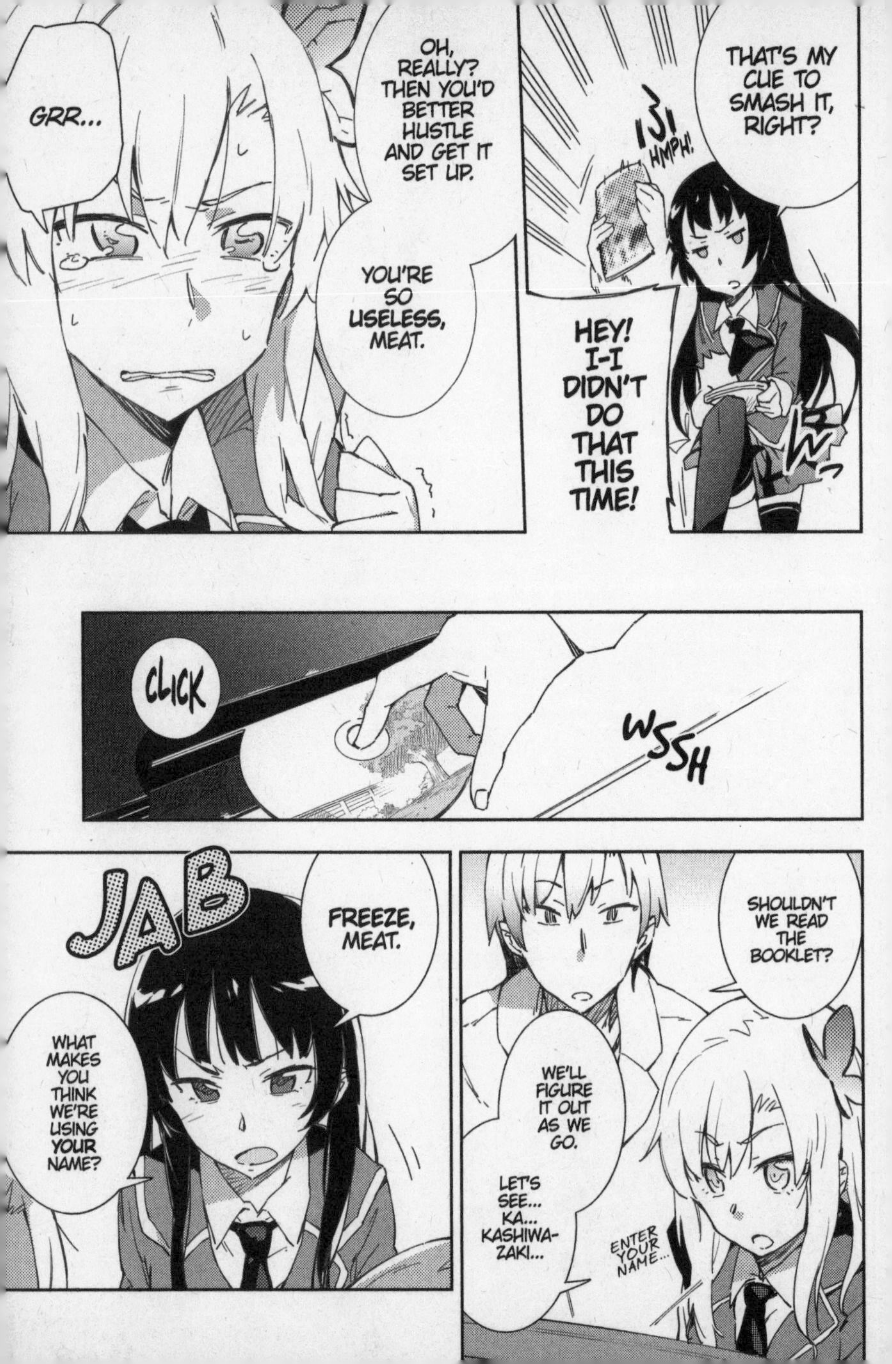
THAT'S MY CUE TO SMASH IT, RIGHT?
HMPH!
HEY! I-I DIDN'T DO THAT THIS TIME!
OH, REALLY? THEN YOU'D BETTER HUSTLE AND GET IT SET UP.
YOU'RE SO USELESS, MEAT.
GRR...
CLICK
WSSH
SHOULDN'T WE READ THE BOOKLET?
WE'LL FIGURE IT OUT AS WE GO.
ENTER YOUR NAME...
LET'S SEE... KA... KASHIWA-ZAKI...
JAB
FREEZE, MEAT.
WHAT MAKES YOU THINK WE'RE USING YOUR NAME?

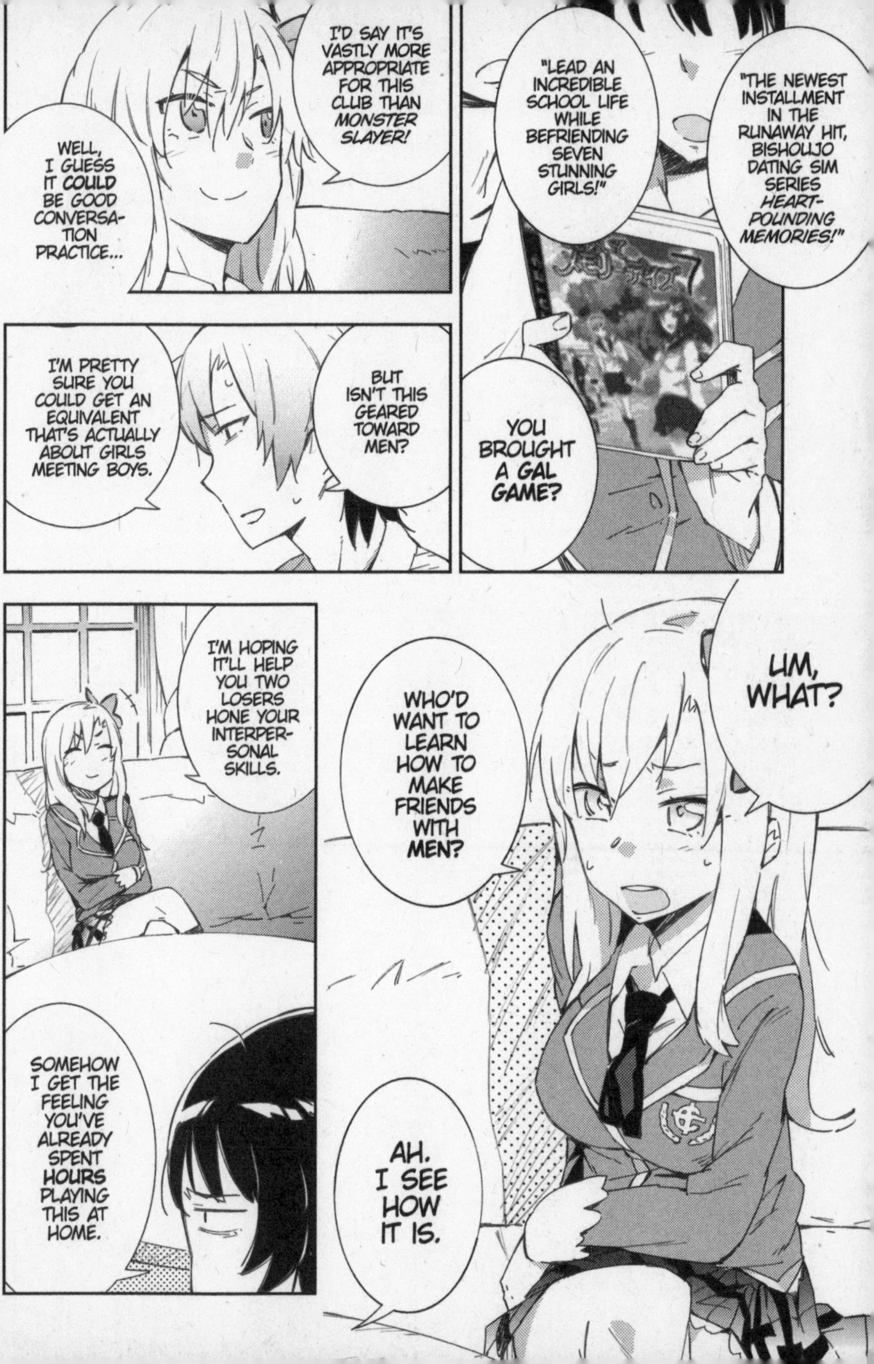
"THE NEWEST INSTALLMENT IN THE RUNAWAY HIT, BISHOUJO DATING SIM SERIES *HEART-POUNDING MEMORIES!*"
"LEAD AN INCREDIBLE SCHOOL LIFE WHILE BEFRIENDING SEVEN STUNNING GIRLS!"
YOU BROUGHT A GAL GAME?
I'D SAY IT'S VASTLY MORE APPROPRIATE FOR THIS CLUB THAN *MONSTER SLAYER!*
WELL, I GUESS IT COULD BE GOOD CONVERSATION PRACTICE...
BUT ISN'T THIS GEARED TOWARD MEN?
I'M PRETTY SURE YOU COULD GET AN EQUIVALENT THAT'S ACTUALLY ABOUT GIRLS MEETING BOYS.
UM, WHAT?
WHO'D WANT TO LEARN HOW TO MAKE FRIENDS WITH MEN?
AH. I SEE HOW IT IS.
I'M HOPING IT'LL HELP YOU TWO LOSERS HONE YOUR INTERPERSONAL SKILLS.
SOMEHOW I GET THE FEELING YOU'VE ALREADY SPENT HOURS PLAYING THIS AT HOME.

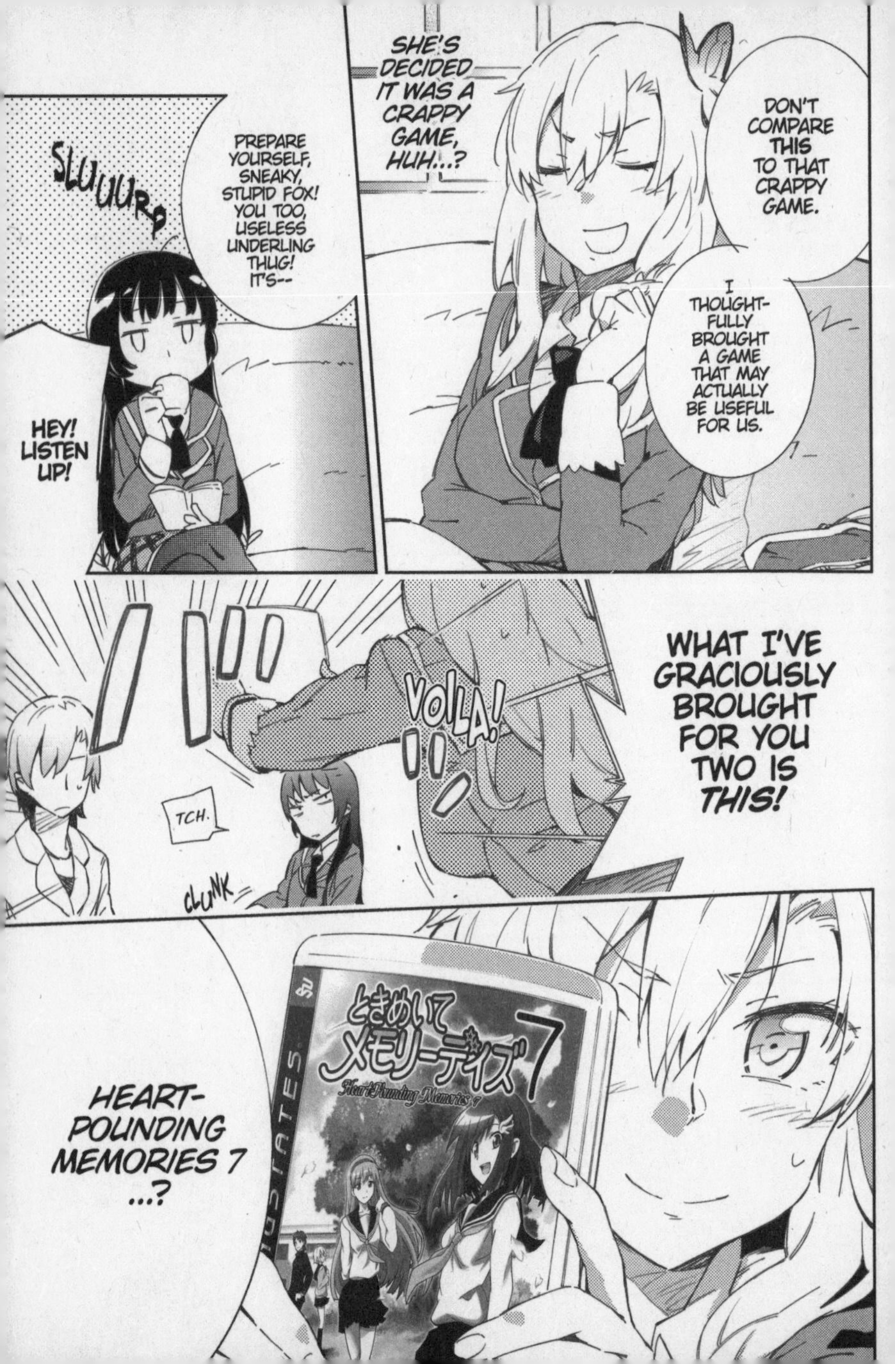

SHE'S DECIDED IT WAS A CRAPPY GAME, HUH...?
DON'T COMPARE THIS TO THAT CRAPPY GAME.
I THOUGHTFULLY BROUGHT A GAME THAT MAY ACTUALLY BE USEFUL FOR US.
PREPARE YOURSELF, SNEAKY, STUPID FOX! YOU TOO, USELESS UNDERLING THUG! IT'S--
SLUUURP
HEY! LISTEN UP!
WHAT I'VE GRACIOUSLY BROUGHT FOR YOU TWO IS THIS!
VOILA!
TCH.
CLUNK
ときめいて
メモリー☆デイズ 7
Heart Pounding Memories 7
HEART-POUNDING MEMORIES 7 ...?

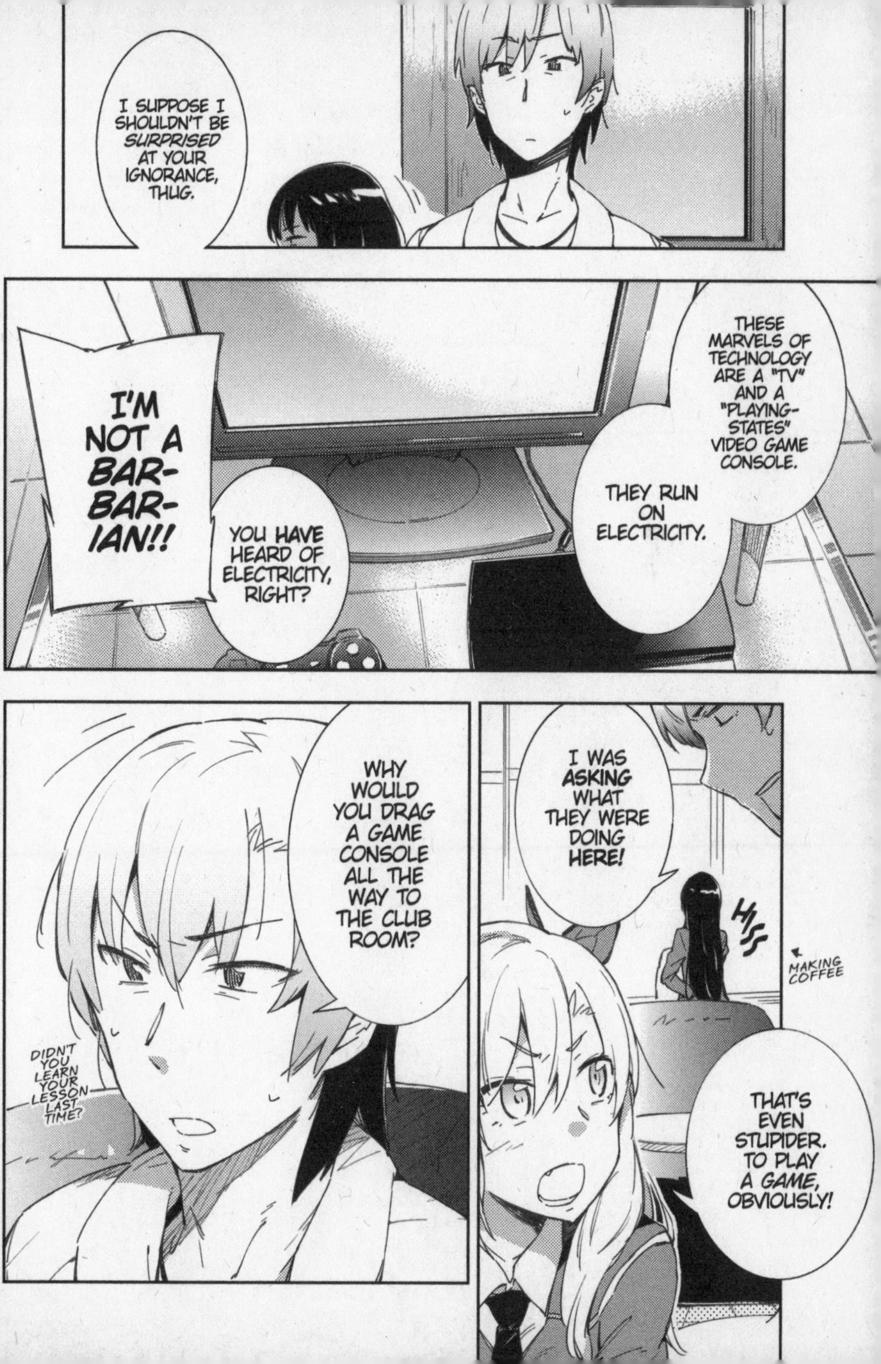
I SUPPOSE I SHOULDN'T BE SURPRISED AT YOUR IGNORANCE, THUG.
THESE MARVELS OF TECHNOLOGY ARE A "TV" AND A "PLAYING-STATES" VIDEO GAME CONSOLE.
THEY RUN ON ELECTRICITY.
YOU HAVE HEARD OF ELECTRICITY, RIGHT?
I'M NOT A BAR-BAR-IAN!!
I WAS ASKING WHAT THEY WERE DOING HERE!
HISS
MAKING COFFEE
THAT'S EVEN STUPIDER. TO PLAY A GAME, OBVIOUSLY!
WHY WOULD YOU DRAG A GAME CONSOLE ALL THE WAY TO THE CLUB ROOM?
DIDN'T YOU LEARN YOUR LESSON LAST TIME?

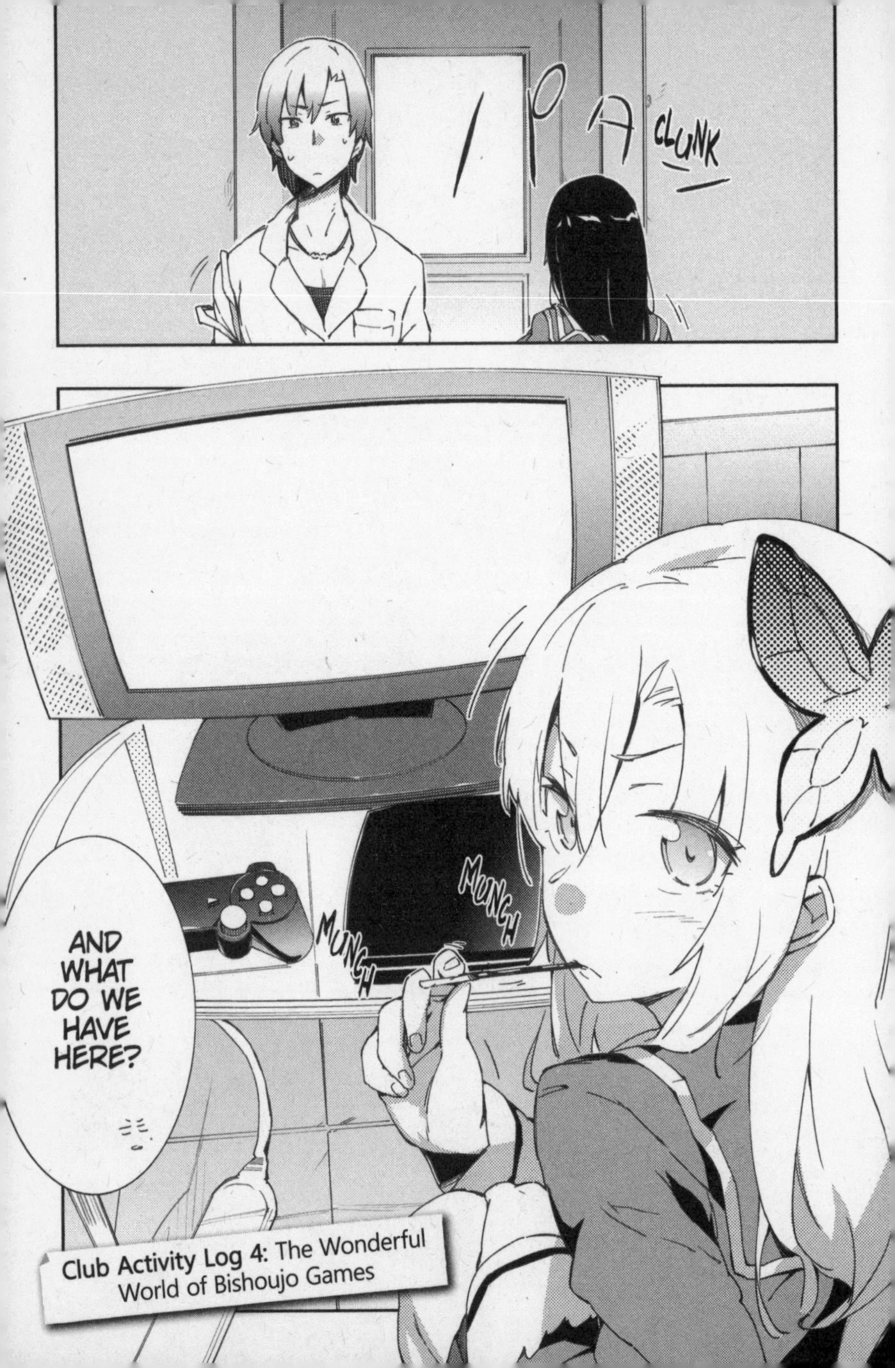
CLUNK
MUNCH
MUNCH
AND WHAT DO WE HAVE HERE?
Club Activity Log 4: The Wonderful World of Bishoujo Games

Haganai
I don't have many friends

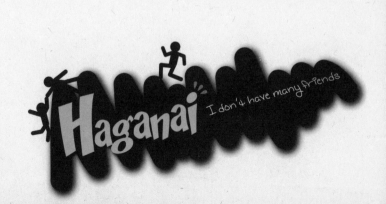

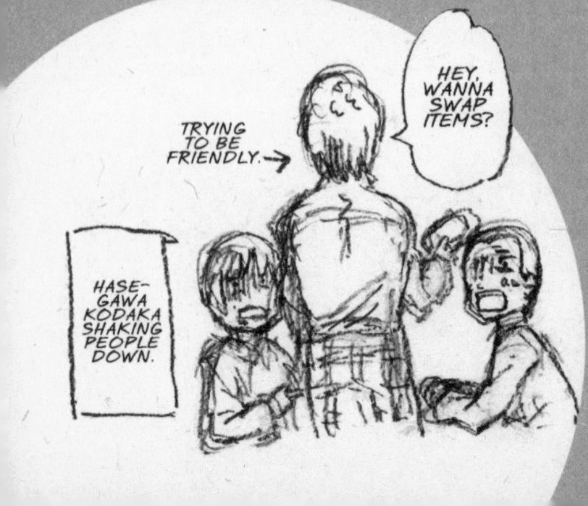
HEY, WANNA SWAP ITEMS?
TRYING TO BE FRIENDLY.
HASE-GAWA KODAKA SHAKING PEOPLE DOWN.

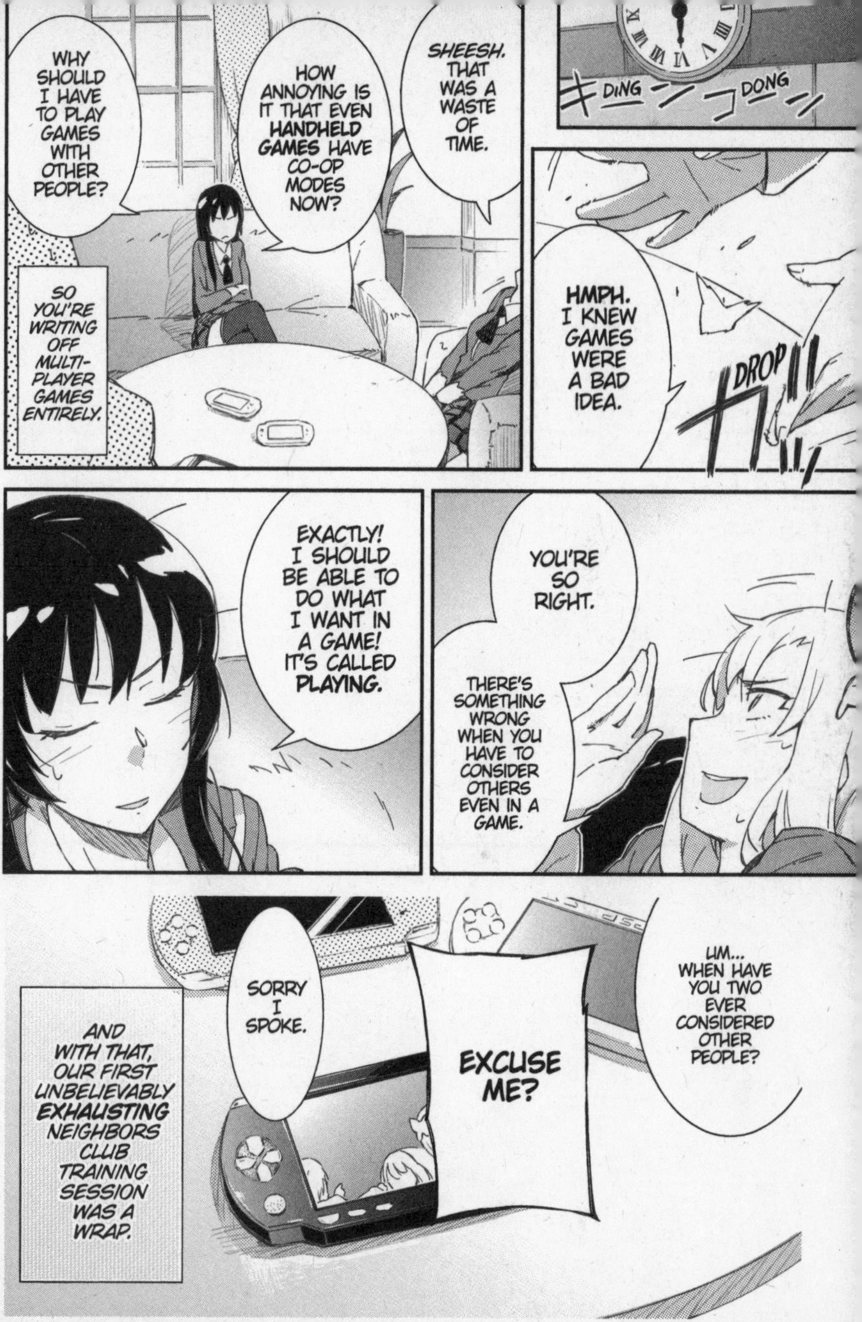
DING DONG
HMPH. I KNEW GAMES WERE A BAD IDEA.
DROP
SHEESH. THAT WAS A WASTE OF TIME.
HOW ANNOYING IS IT THAT EVEN HANDHELD GAMES HAVE CO-OP MODES NOW?
WHY SHOULD I HAVE TO PLAY GAMES WITH OTHER PEOPLE?
SO YOU'RE WRITING OFF MULTI-PLAYER GAMES ENTIRELY.
YOU'RE SO RIGHT.
THERE'S SOMETHING WRONG WHEN YOU HAVE TO CONSIDER OTHERS EVEN IN A GAME.
EXACTLY! I SHOULD BE ABLE TO DO WHAT I WANT IN A GAME! IT'S CALLED PLAYING.
UM... WHEN HAVE YOU TWO EVER CONSIDERED OTHER PEOPLE?
EXCUSE ME?
SORRY I SPOKE.
AND WITH THAT, OUR FIRST UNBELIEVABLY EXHAUSTING NEIGHBORS CLUB TRAINING SESSION WAS A WRAP.

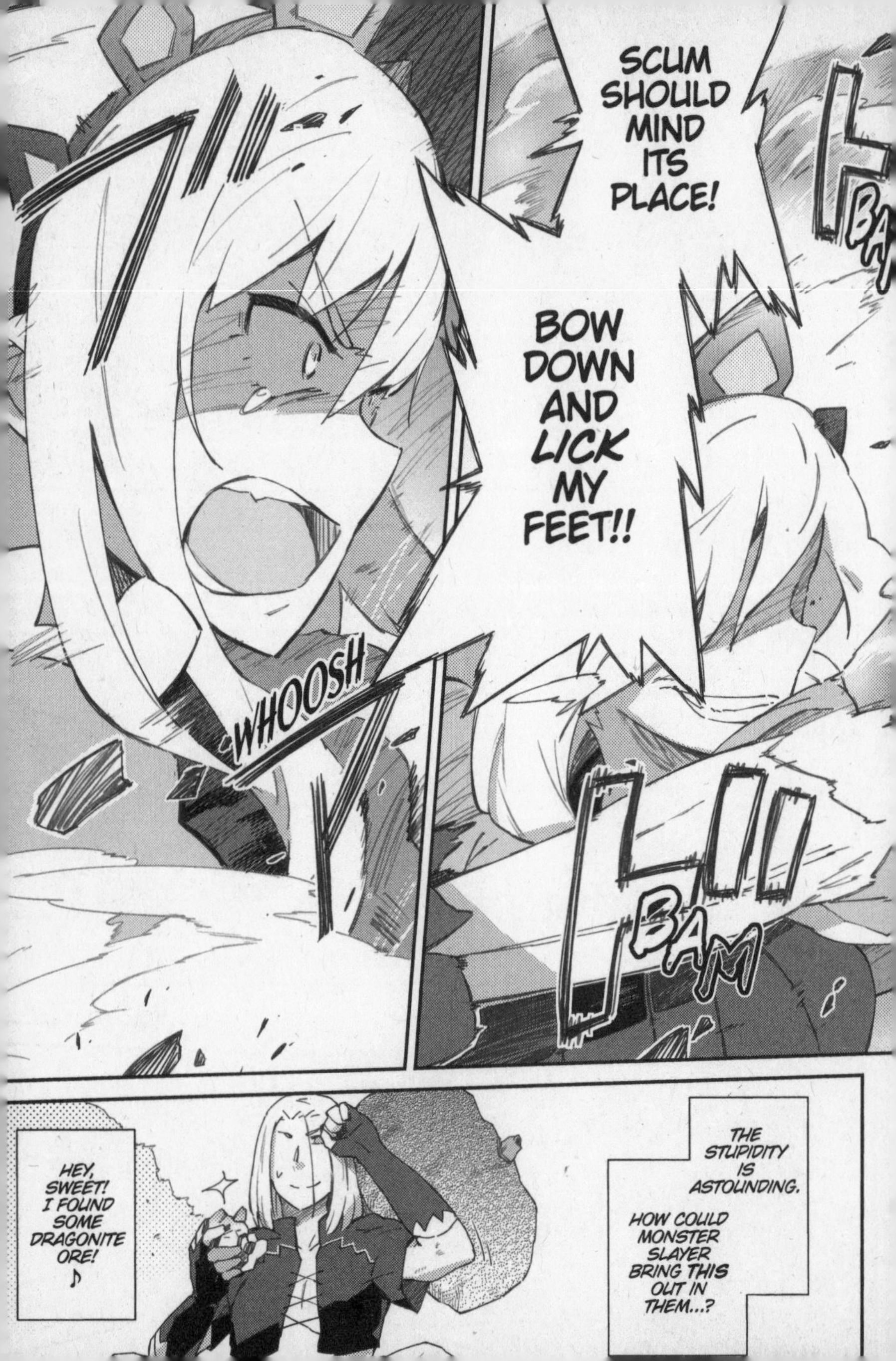
SCUM SHOULD MIND ITS PLACE!
BOW DOWN AND LICK MY FEET!!
BAM
WHOOSH
THE STUPIDITY IS ASTOUNDING.
HOW COULD MONSTER SLAYER BRING THIS OUT IN THEM...?
HEY, SWEET! I FOUND SOME DRAGONITE ORE! ♪

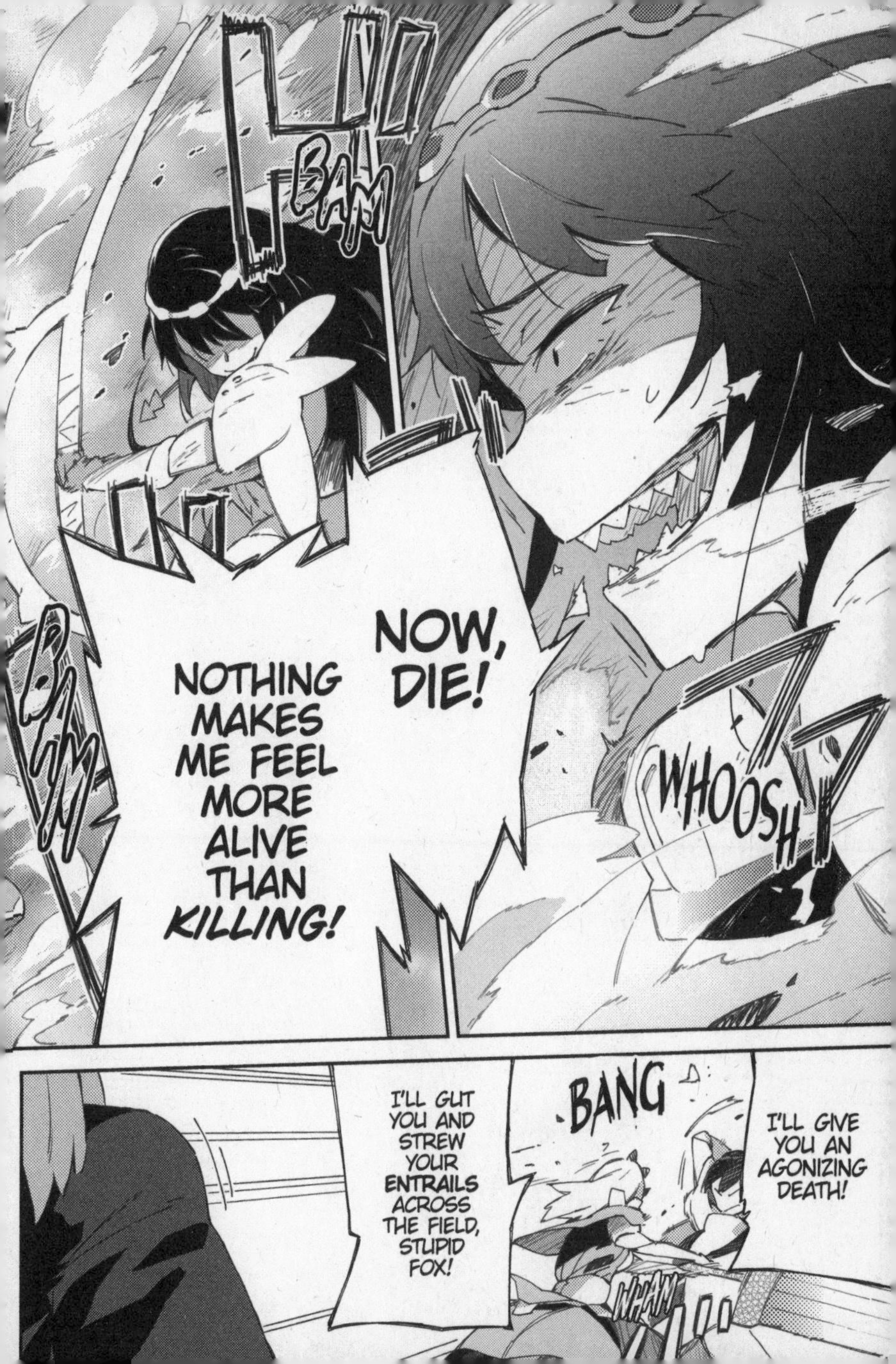
BAM
WHOOSH
NOW, DIE!
NOTHING MAKES ME FEEL MORE ALIVE THAN KILLING!
BAM
I'LL GIVE YOU AN AGONIZING DEATH!
BANG
WHAM
I'LL GUT YOU AND STREW YOUR ENTRAILS ACROSS THE FIELD, STUPID FOX!

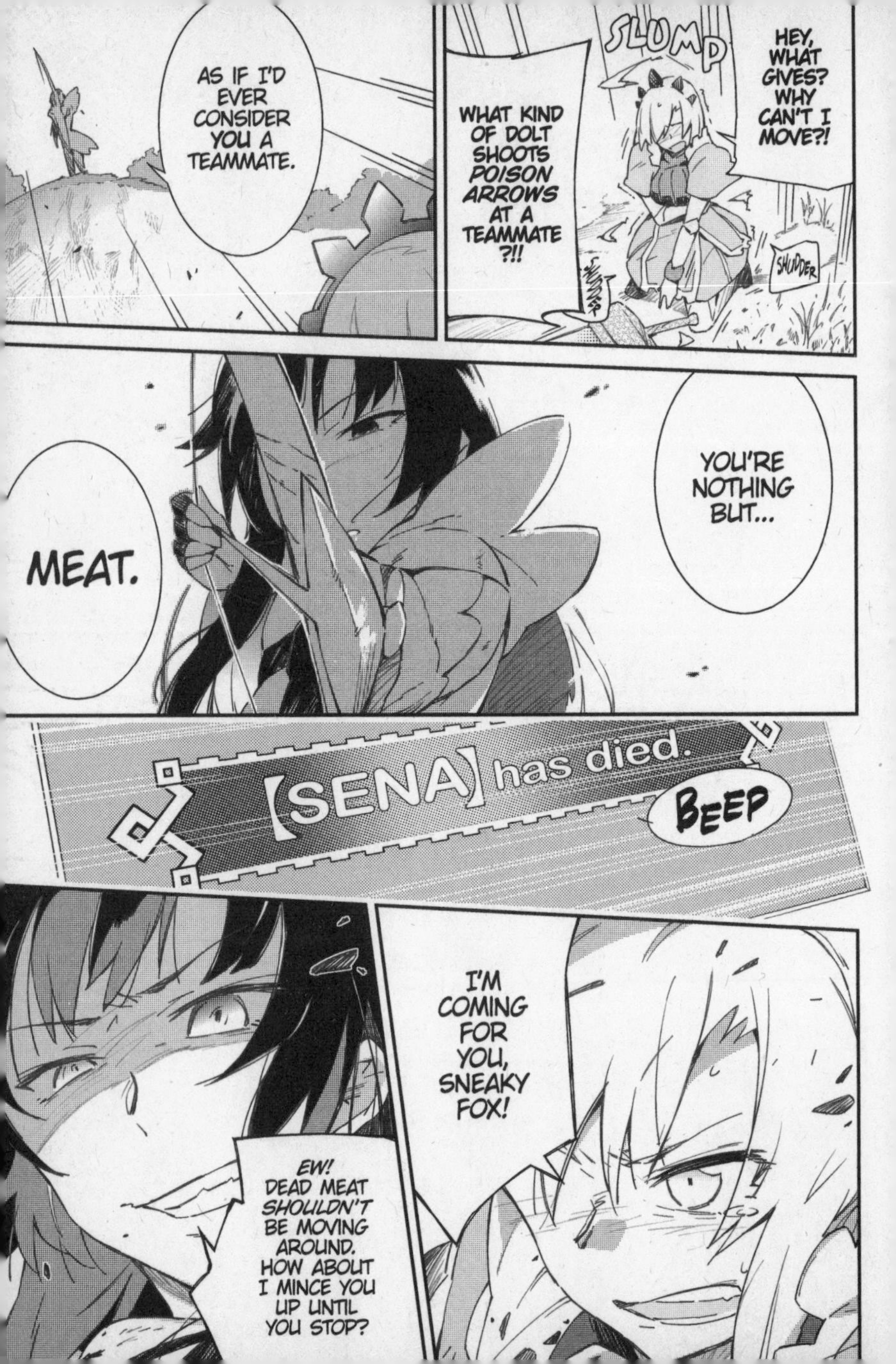
HEY, WHAT GIVES? WHY CAN'T I MOVE?!
SLUMP
WHAT KIND OF DOLT SHOOTS *POISON ARROWS* AT A TEAMMATE ?!!
SHUDDER
AS IF I'D EVER CONSIDER YOU A TEAMMATE.
YOU'RE NOTHING BUT...
MEAT.
【SENA】has died.
BEEP
I'M COMING FOR YOU, SNEAKY FOX!
EW! DEAD MEAT *SHOULDN'T* BE MOVING AROUND. HOW ABOUT I MINCE YOU UP UNTIL YOU STOP?

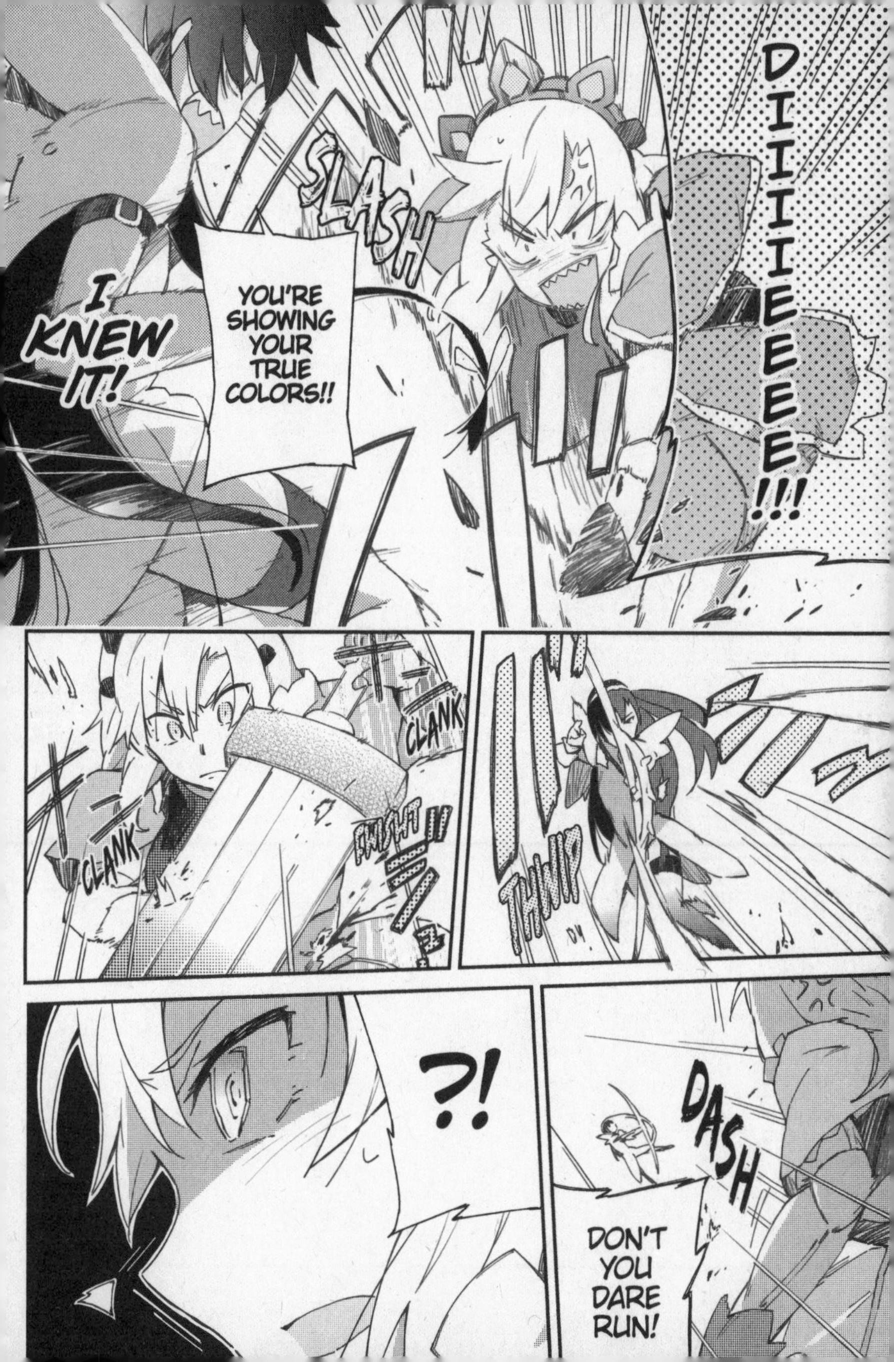
DIIIIEEEE!!!
SLASH
YOU'RE SHOWING YOUR TRUE COLORS!!
I KNEW IT!
THWIP
CLANK
FWISHT
CLANK
DASH
DON'T YOU DARE RUN!
?!

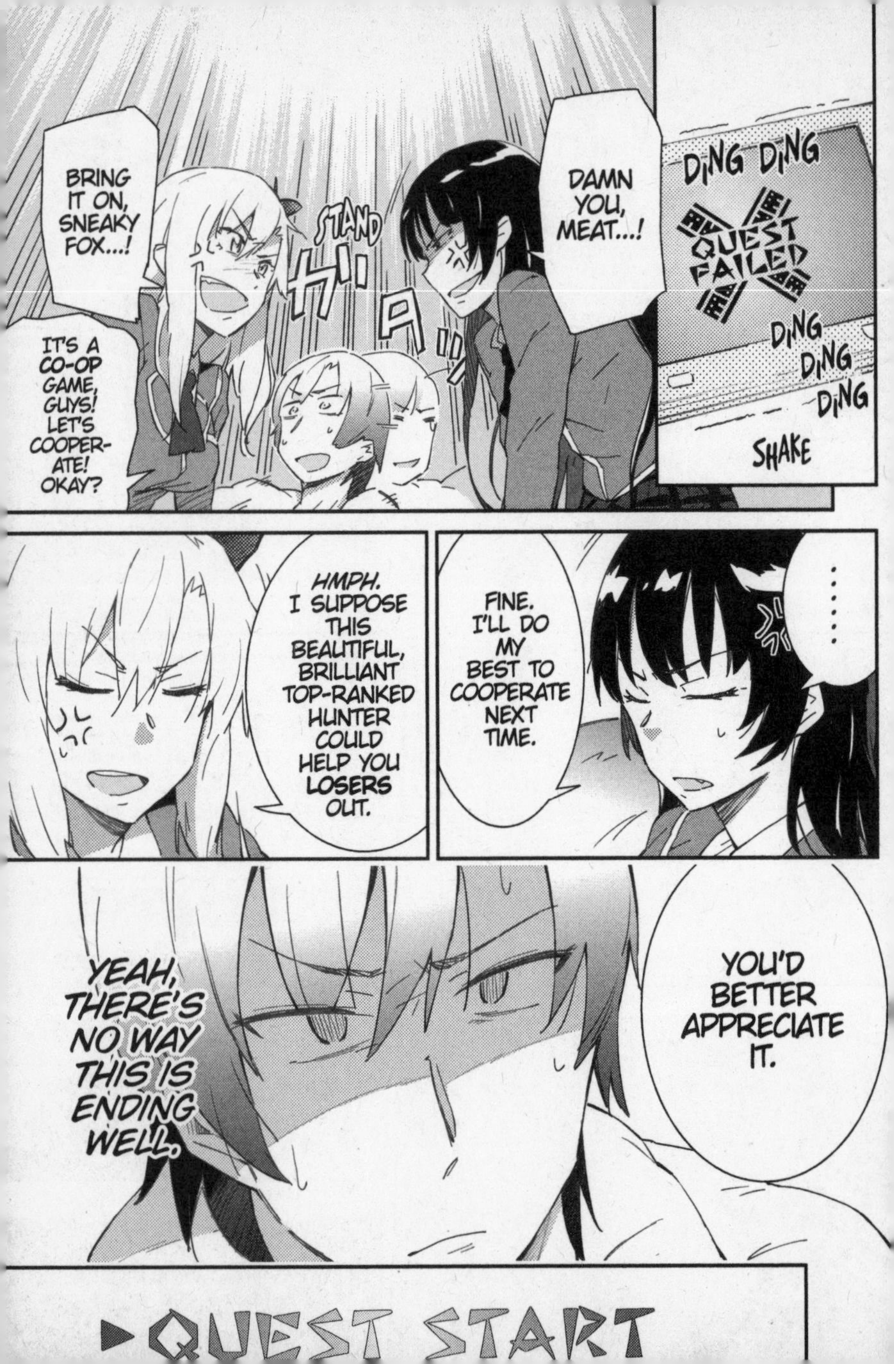
DING DING
QUEST FAILED
DING DING DING
SHAKE
DAMN YOU, MEAT...!
STAND
BRING IT ON, SNEAKY FOX...!
IT'S A CO-OP GAME, GUYS! LET'S COOPERATE! OKAY?
......
FINE. I'LL DO MY BEST TO COOPERATE NEXT TIME.
HMPH. I SUPPOSE THIS BEAUTIFUL, BRILLIANT TOP-RANKED HUNTER COULD HELP YOU LOSERS OUT.
YOU'D BETTER APPRECIATE IT.
YEAH, THERE'S NO WAY THIS IS ENDING WELL.
▶QUEST START

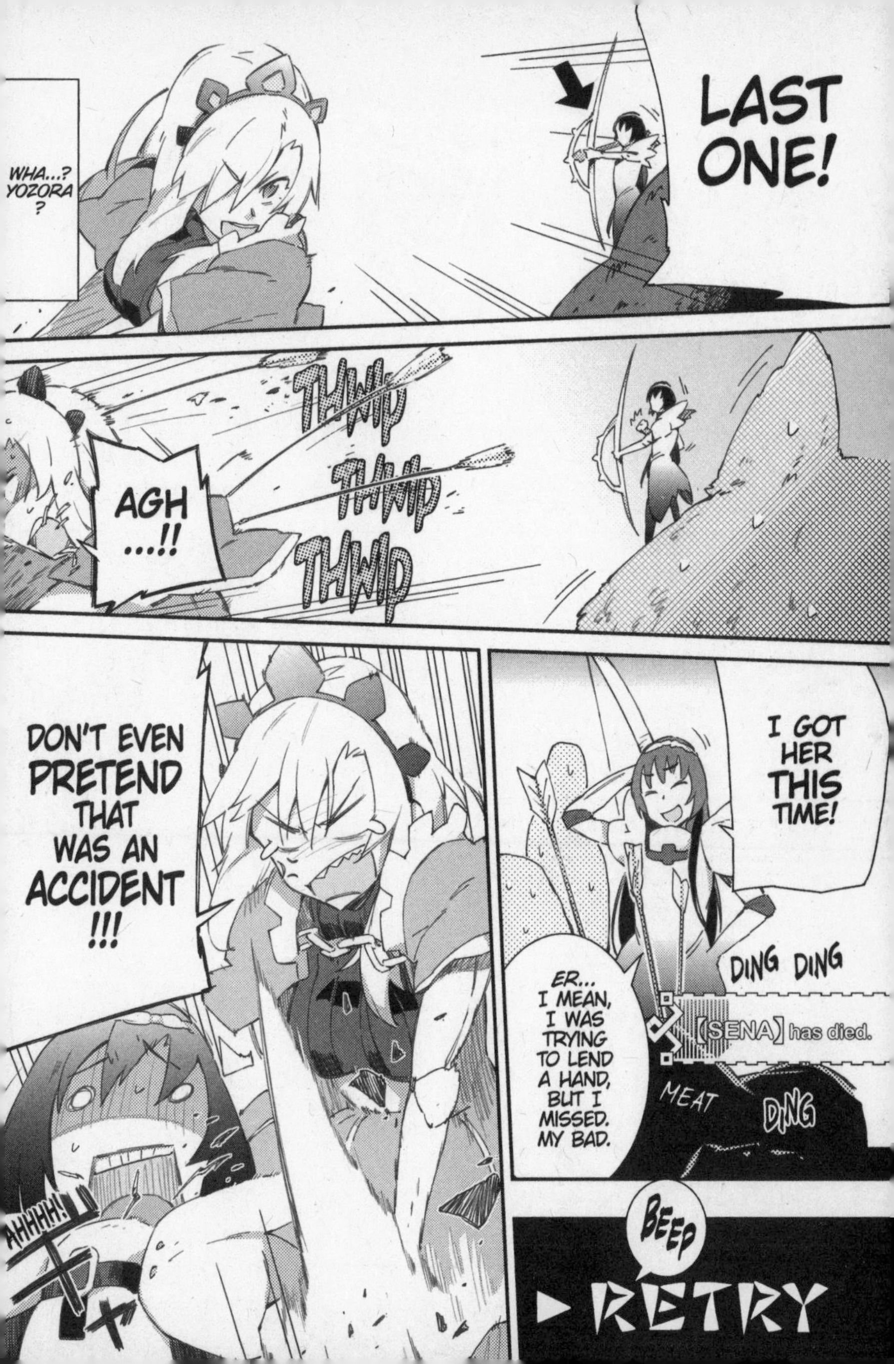
LAST ONE!
WHA...? YOZORA?
THWIP
THWIP
THWIP
AGH ...!!
I GOT HER THIS TIME!
DING DING
【SENA】 has died.
MEAT
DING
ER... I MEAN, I WAS TRYING TO LEND A HAND, BUT I MISSED. MY BAD.
BEEP
▶ RETRY
DON'T EVEN PRETEND THAT WAS AN ACCIDENT !!!
AHHHH!

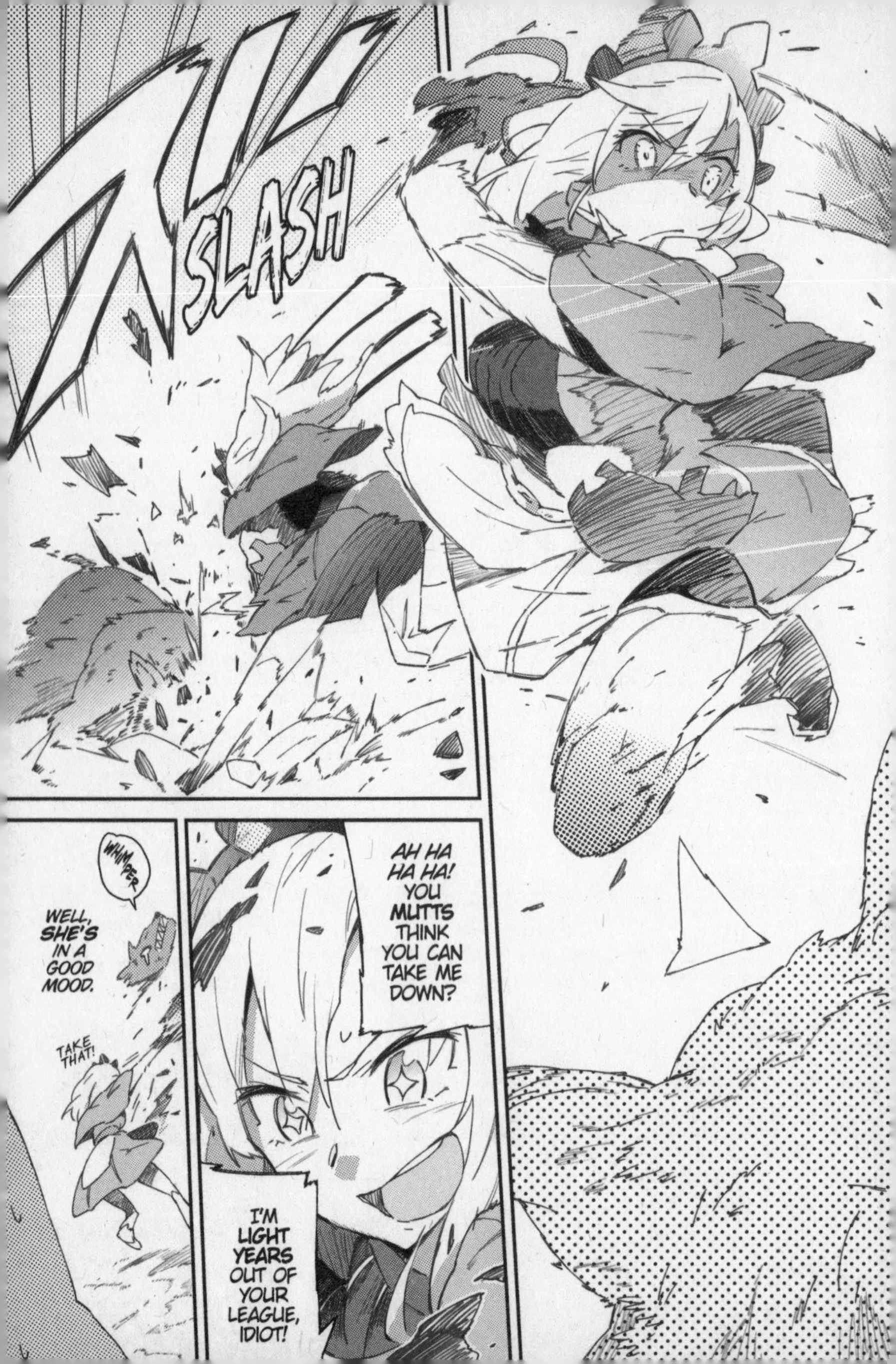
SLASH
AH HA HA HA! YOU MUTTS THINK YOU CAN TAKE ME DOWN?
I'M LIGHT YEARS OUT OF YOUR LEAGUE, IDIOT!
WHIMPER
WELL, SHE'S IN A GOOD MOOD.
TAKE THAT!

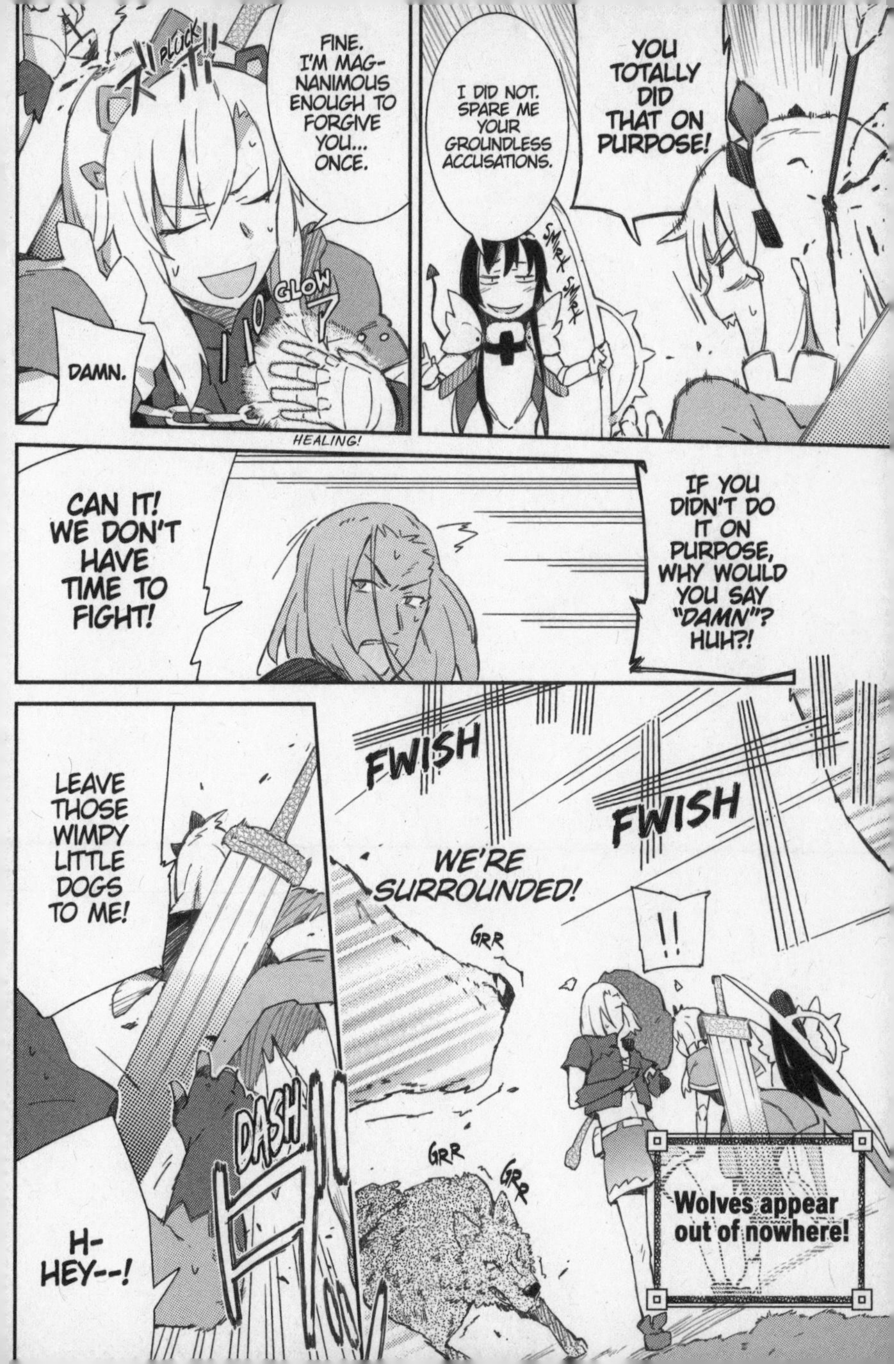
YOU TOTALLY DID THAT ON PURPOSE!
I DID NOT. SPARE ME YOUR GROUNDLESS ACCUSATIONS.
SMIRK SMIRK
FINE. I'M MAG-NANIMOUS ENOUGH TO FORGIVE YOU... ONCE.
PLUCK
GLOW
DAMN.
HEALING!
IF YOU DIDN'T DO IT ON PURPOSE, WHY WOULD YOU SAY "DAMN"? HUH?!
CAN IT! WE DON'T HAVE TIME TO FIGHT!
FWISH
FWISH
WE'RE SURROUNDED!
!!
GRR
GRR
GRR
Wolves appear out of nowhere!
LEAVE THOSE WIMPY LITTLE DOGS TO ME!
DASH
H-HEY--!

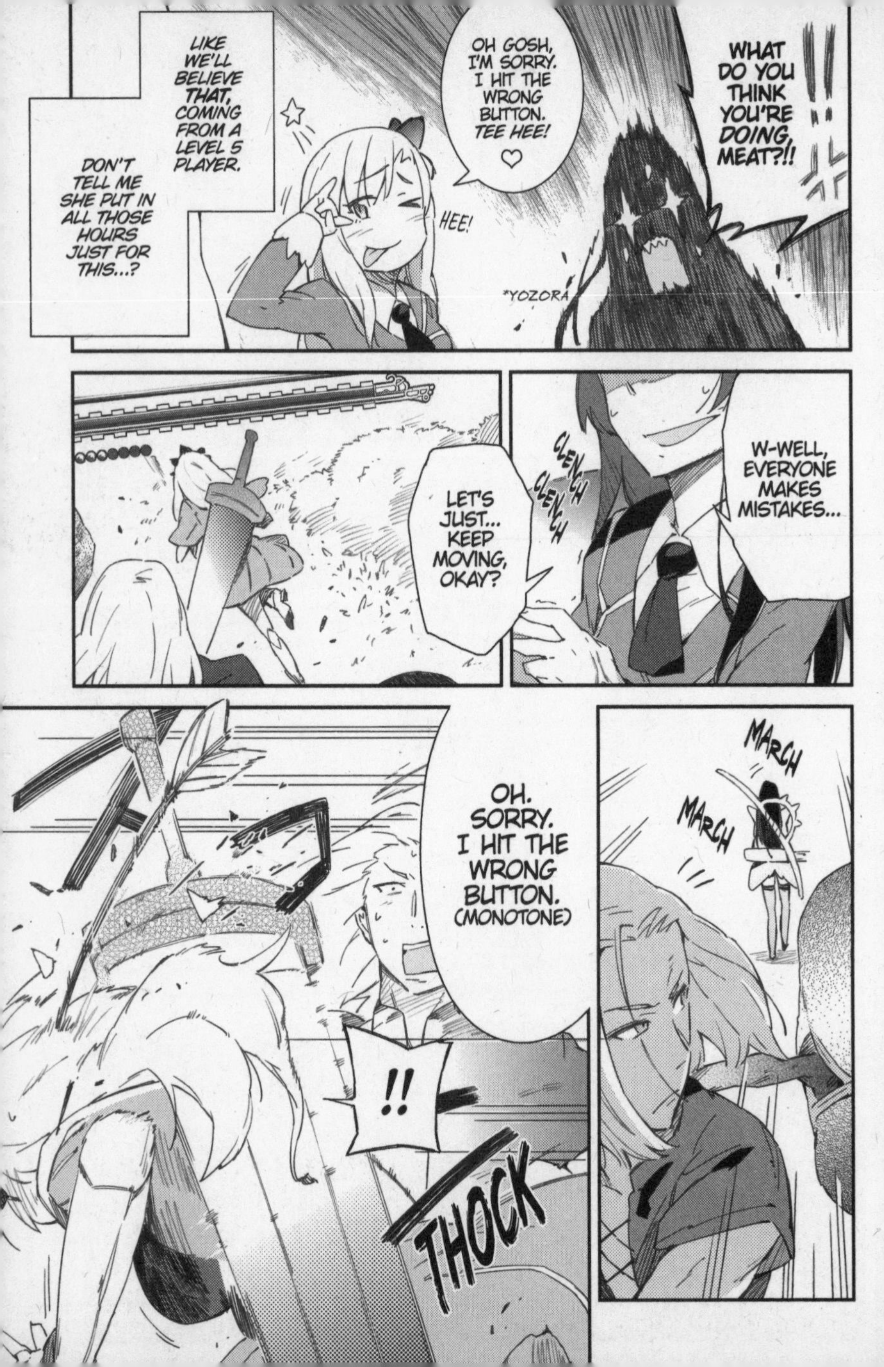
WHAT DO YOU THINK YOU'RE DOING, MEAT?!!
OH GOSH, I'M SORRY. I HIT THE WRONG BUTTON. TEE HEE! ♡
HEE!
*YOZORA
LIKE WE'LL BELIEVE THAT, COMING FROM A LEVEL 5 PLAYER.
DON'T TELL ME SHE PUT IN ALL THOSE HOURS JUST FOR THIS...?
W-WELL, EVERYONE MAKES MISTAKES...
CLENCH CLENCH
LET'S JUST... KEEP MOVING, OKAY?
MARCH
MARCH
OH. SORRY. I HIT THE WRONG BUTTON. (MONOTONE)
!!
THOCK

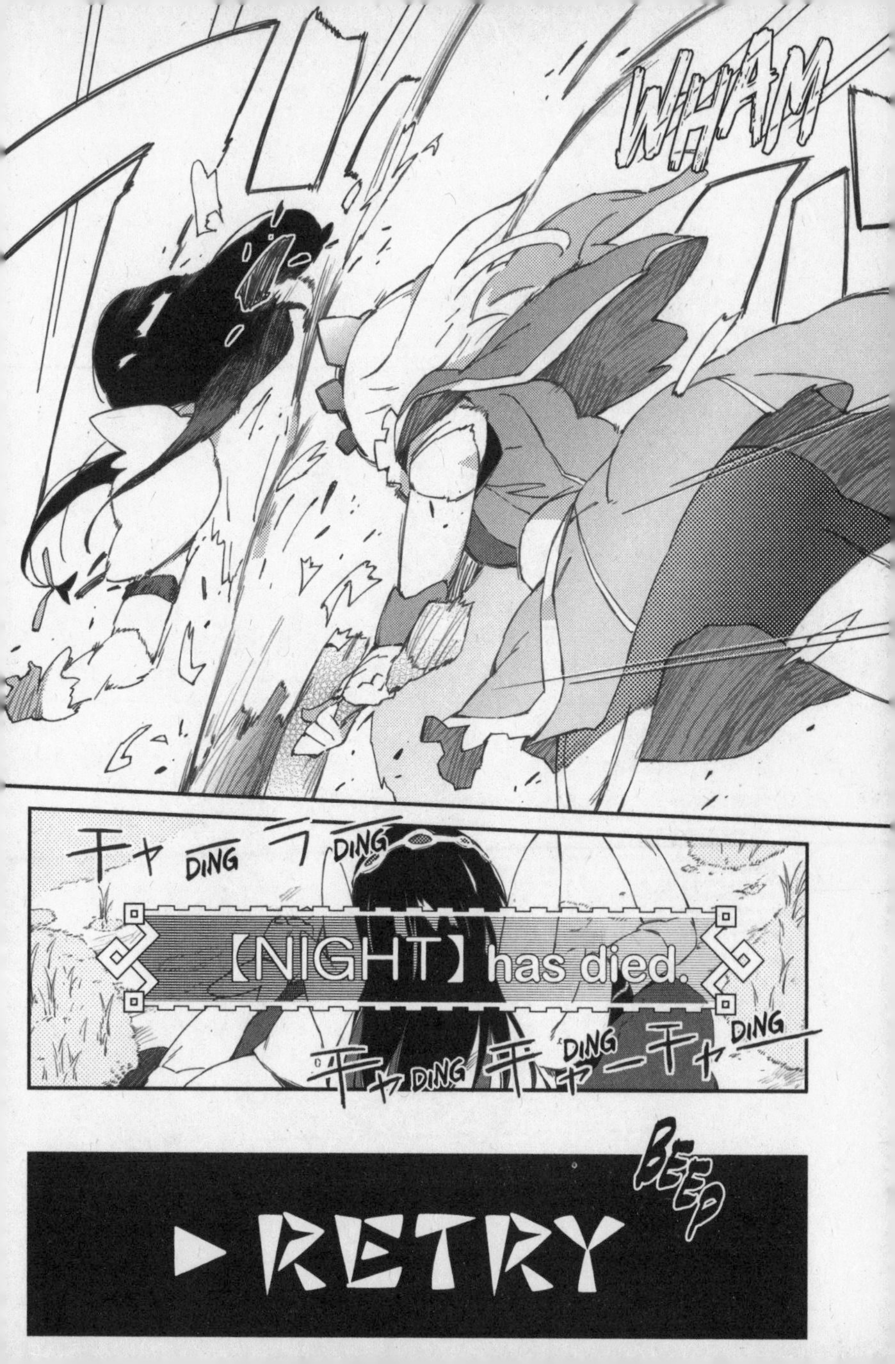
WHAM
チャ DING ラ DING
【NIGHT】 has died.
チャ DING チャ DING ーチャ DING
BEEP
▶RETRY

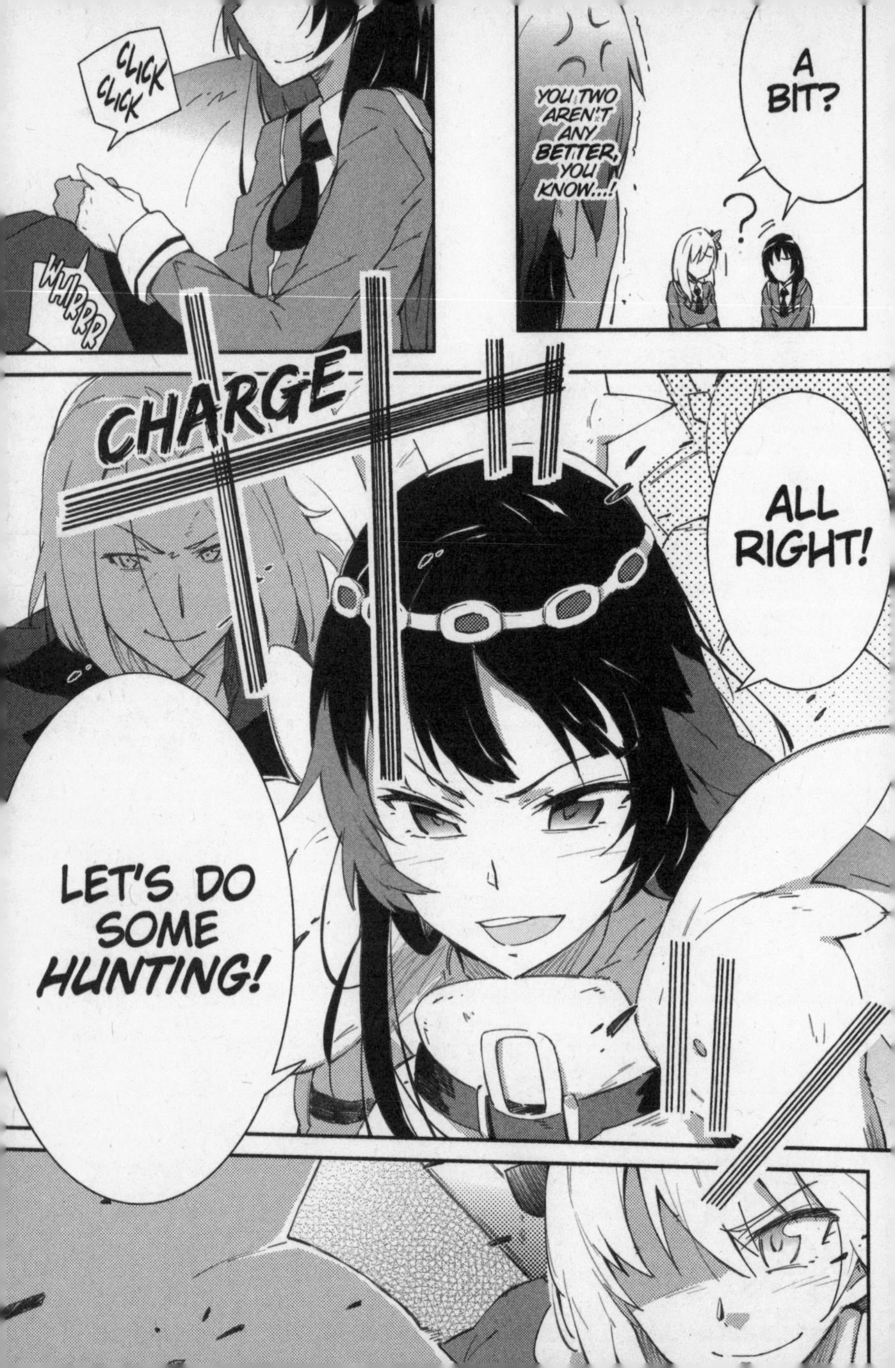
A BIT?
YOU TWO AREN'T ANY BETTER, YOU KNOW...!
CLICK CLICK
WHRRR
ALL RIGHT!
CHARGE
LET'S DO SOME HUNTING!

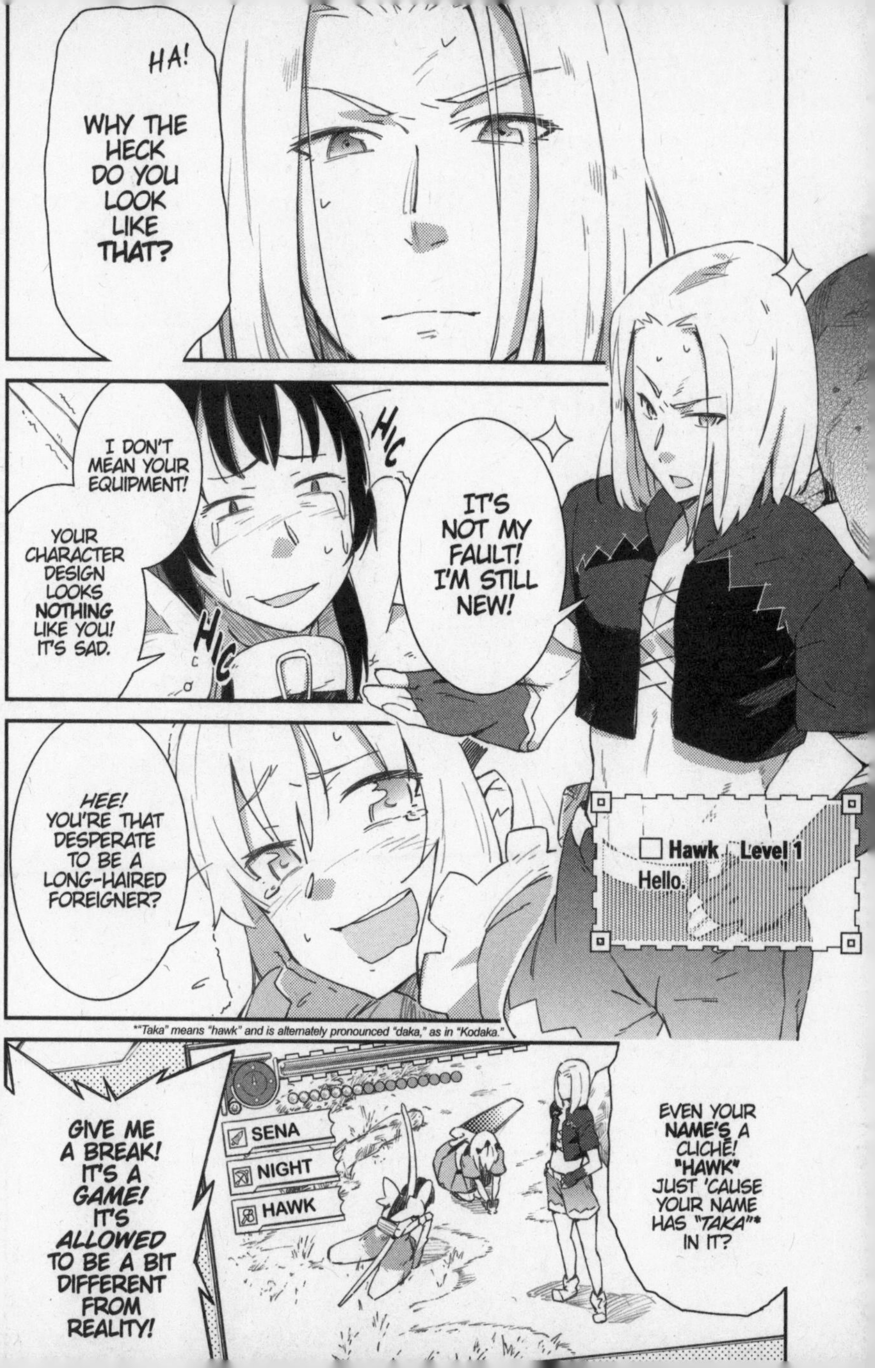
HA!
WHY THE HECK DO YOU LOOK LIKE THAT?
IT'S NOT MY FAULT! I'M STILL NEW!
HIC
I DON'T MEAN YOUR EQUIPMENT!
YOUR CHARACTER DESIGN LOOKS NOTHING LIKE YOU! IT'S SAD.
HIC
Hawk Level 1
Hello.
HEE! YOU'RE THAT DESPERATE TO BE A LONG-HAIRED FOREIGNER?
EVEN YOUR NAME'S A CLICHÉ! "HAWK" JUST 'CAUSE YOUR NAME HAS "TAKA"* IN IT?
SENA
NIGHT
HAWK
GIVE ME A BREAK! IT'S A GAME! IT'S ALLOWED TO BE A BIT DIFFERENT FROM REALITY!

*"Taka" means "hawk" and is alternately pronounced "daka," as in "Kodaka."

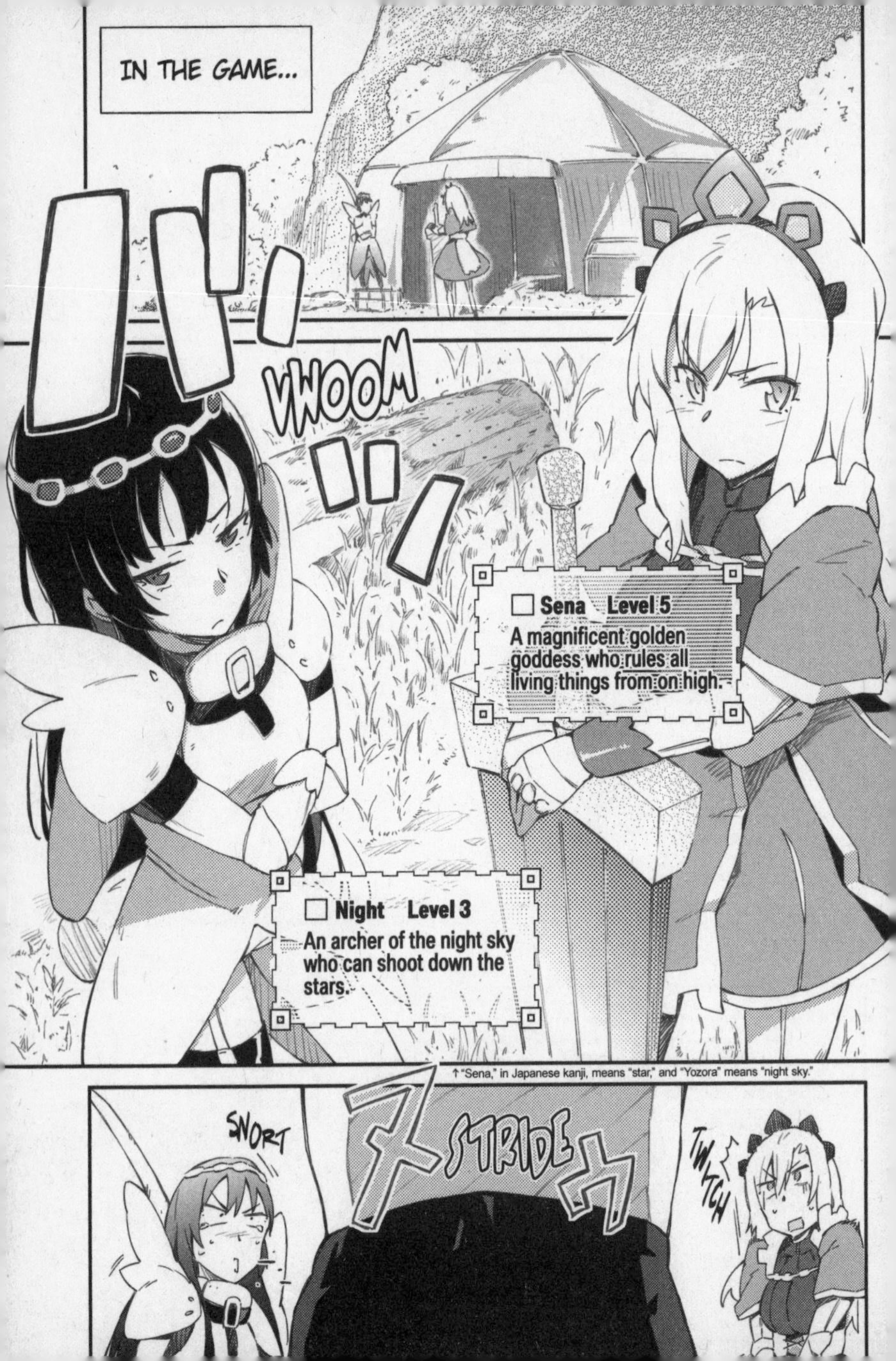
IN THE GAME...
VWOOM
Sena Level 5
A magnificent golden goddess who rules all living things from on high.
Night Level 3
An archer of the night sky who can shoot down the stars.
TWITCH
STRIDE
SNORT
↑"Sena," in Japanese kanji, means "star," and "Yozora" means "night sky."

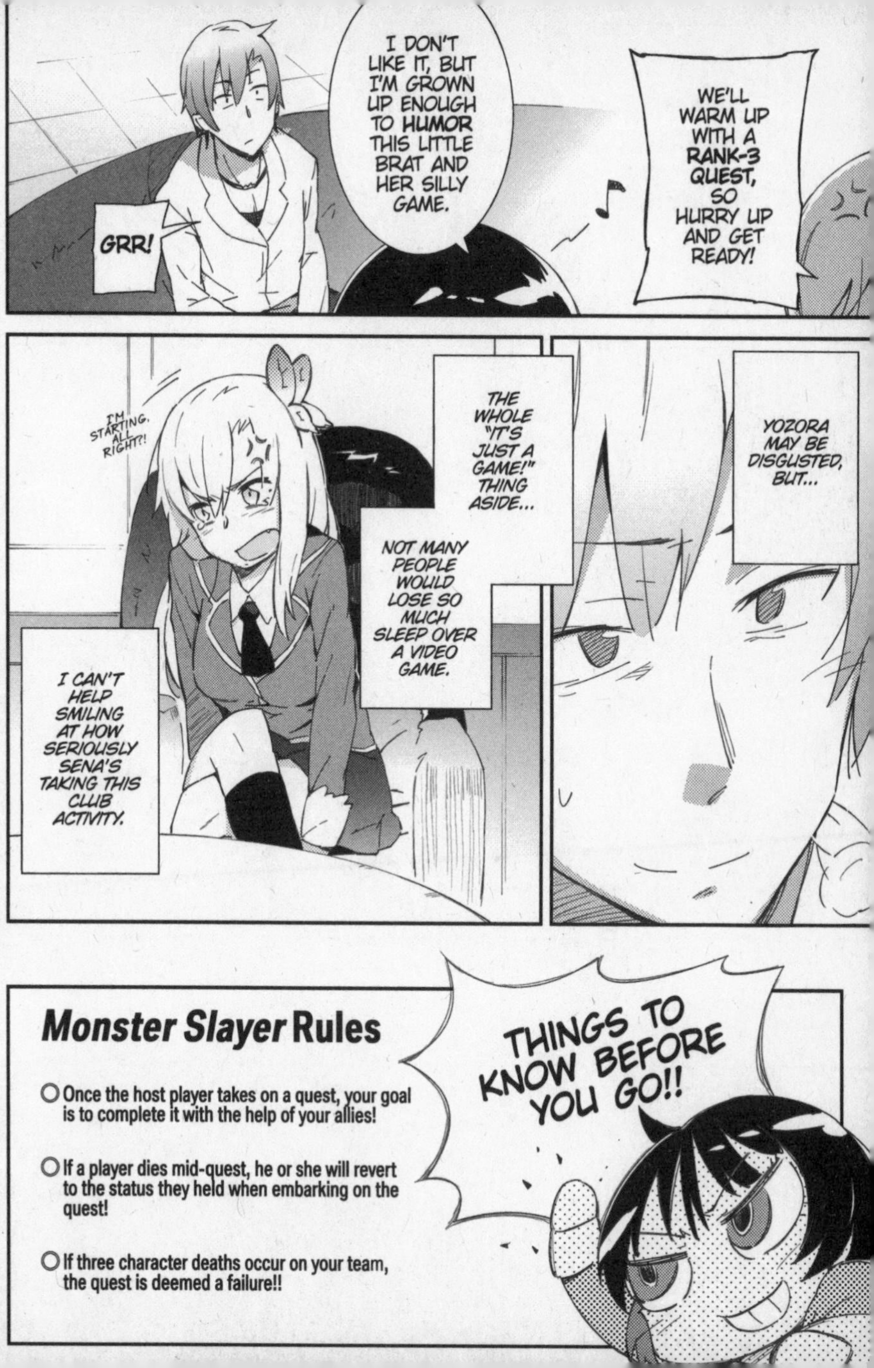
WE'LL WARM UP WITH A RANK-3 QUEST, SO HURRY UP AND GET READY!
I DON'T LIKE IT, BUT I'M GROWN UP ENOUGH TO HUMOR THIS LITTLE BRAT AND HER SILLY GAME.
GRR!
YOZORA MAY BE DISGUSTED, BUT...
THE WHOLE "IT'S JUST A GAME!" THING ASIDE...
NOT MANY PEOPLE WOULD LOSE SO MUCH SLEEP OVER A VIDEO GAME.
I'M STARTING, ALL RIGHT?!
I CAN'T HELP SMILING AT HOW SERIOUSLY SENA'S TAKING THIS CLUB ACTIVITY.
THINGS TO KNOW BEFORE YOU GO!!
Monster Slayer Rules
Once the host player takes on a quest, your goal is to complete it with the help of your allies!
If a player dies mid-quest, he or she will revert to the status they held when embarking on the quest!
If three character deaths occur on your team, the quest is deemed a failure!!

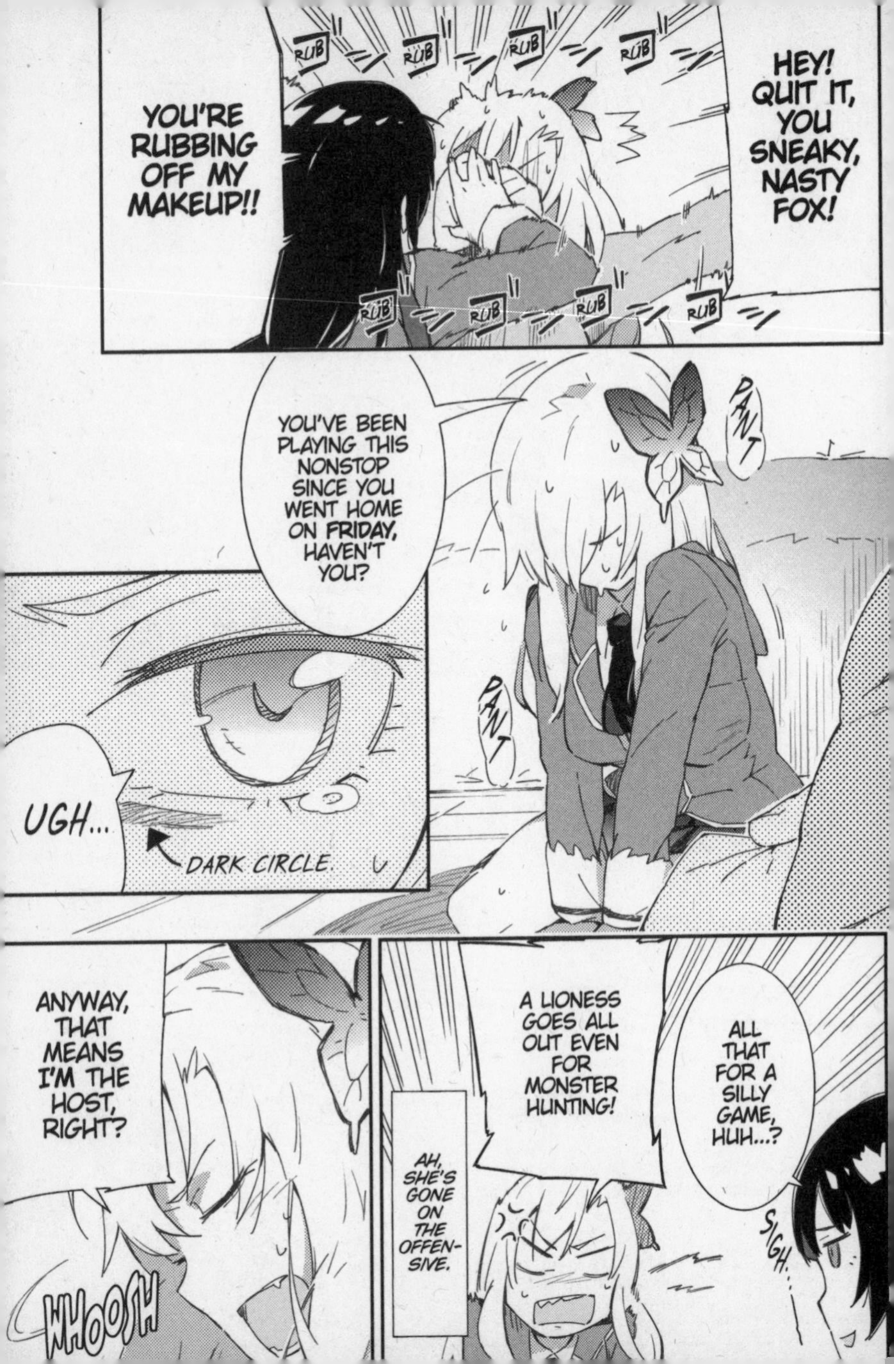
HEY! QUIT IT, YOU SNEAKY, NASTY FOX!
RUB RUB RUB RUB
YOU'RE RUBBING OFF MY MAKEUP!!
RUB RUB RUB RUB
PANT
YOU'VE BEEN PLAYING THIS NONSTOP SINCE YOU WENT HOME ON FRIDAY, HAVEN'T YOU?
PANT
UGH...
DARK CIRCLE
ALL THAT FOR A SILLY GAME, HUH...?
SIGH...
A LIONESS GOES ALL OUT EVEN FOR MONSTER HUNTING!
AH, SHE'S GONE ON THE OFFEN-SIVE.
ANYWAY, THAT MEANS I'M THE HOST, RIGHT?
WHOOSH

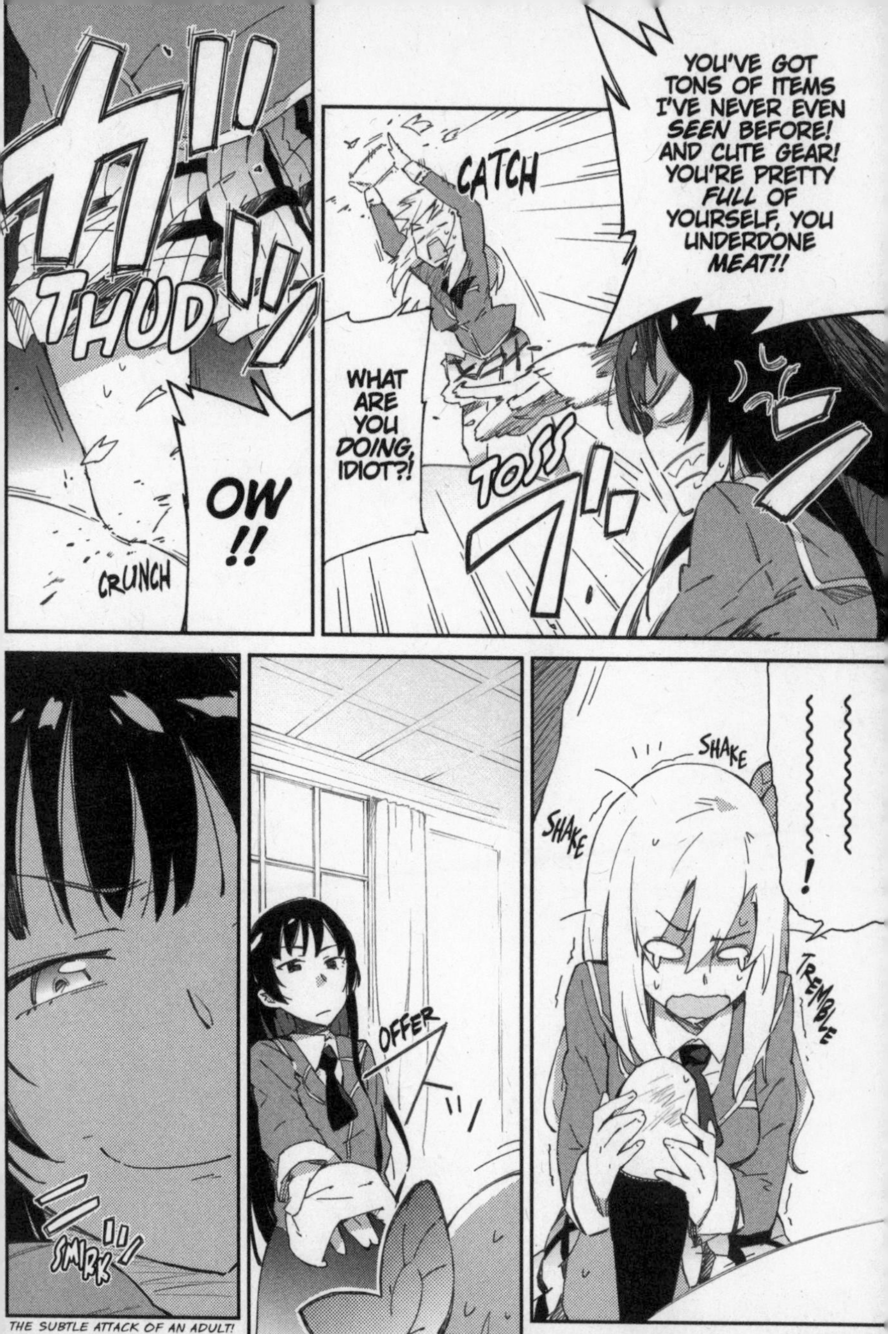
YOU'VE GOT TONS OF ITEMS I'VE NEVER EVEN SEEN BEFORE! AND CUTE GEAR! YOU'RE PRETTY FULL OF YOURSELF, YOU UNDERDONE MEAT!!
CATCH
WHAT ARE YOU DOING, IDIOT?!
TOSS
THUD
OW!!
CRUNCH
SHAKE
SHAKE
TREMBLE
OFFER
SMIRK

THE SUBTLE ATTACK OF AN ADULT!

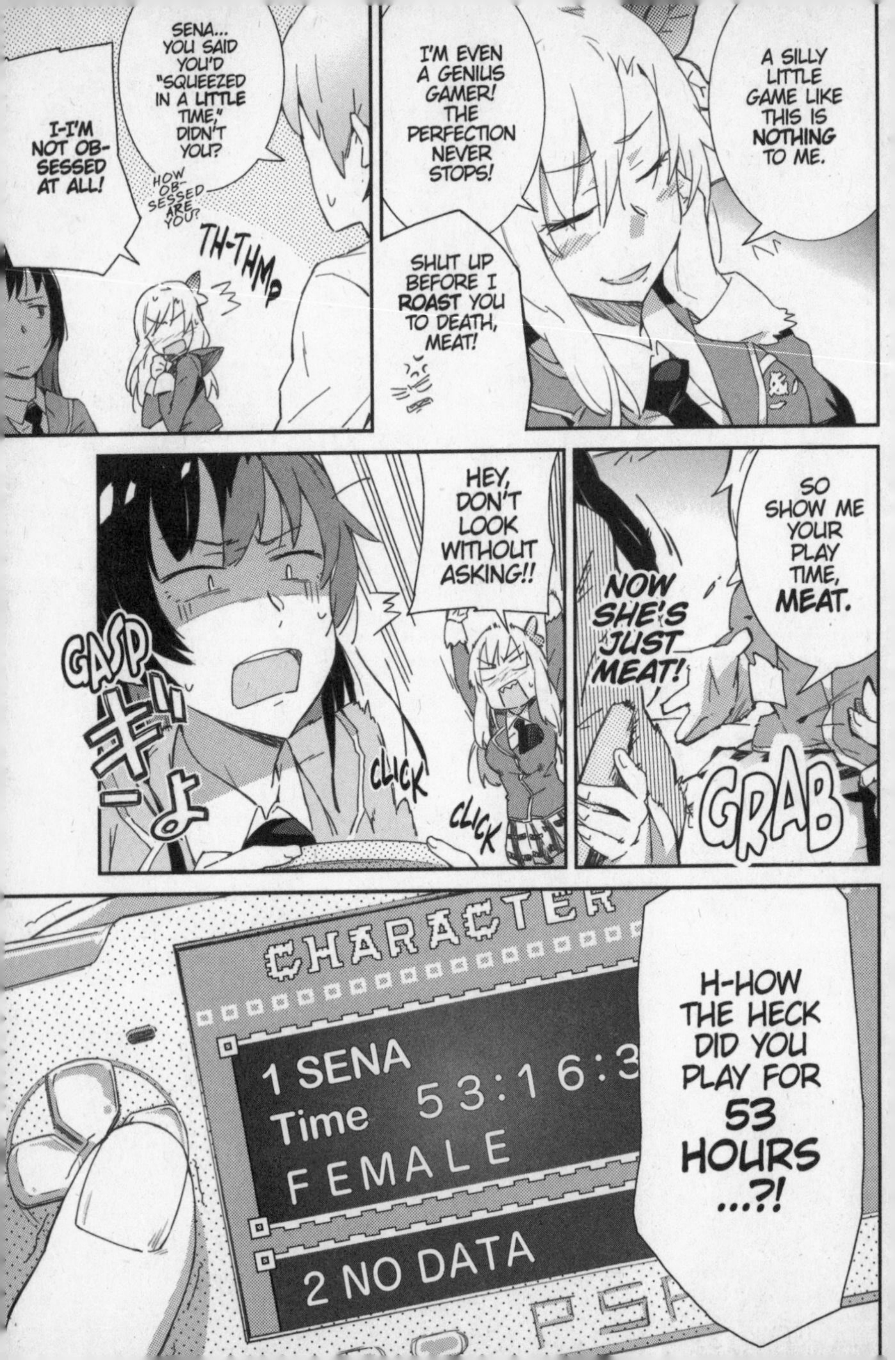
A SILLY LITTLE GAME LIKE THIS IS NOTHING TO ME.
I'M EVEN A GENIUS GAMER! THE PERFECTION NEVER STOPS!
SHUT UP BEFORE I ROAST YOU TO DEATH, MEAT!
SENA... YOU SAID YOU'D "SQUEEZED IN A LITTLE TIME," DIDN'T YOU?
HOW OB-SESSED ARE YOU?
I-I'M NOT OB-SESSED AT ALL!
TH-THMP
SO SHOW ME YOUR PLAY TIME, MEAT.
NOW SHE'S JUST MEAT!
GRAB
HEY, DON'T LOOK WITHOUT ASKING!!
GASP
CLICK
CLICK
CHARACTER
1 SENA
Time 53:16:3
FEMALE
2 NO DATA
H-HOW THE HECK DID YOU PLAY FOR 53 HOURS ...?!

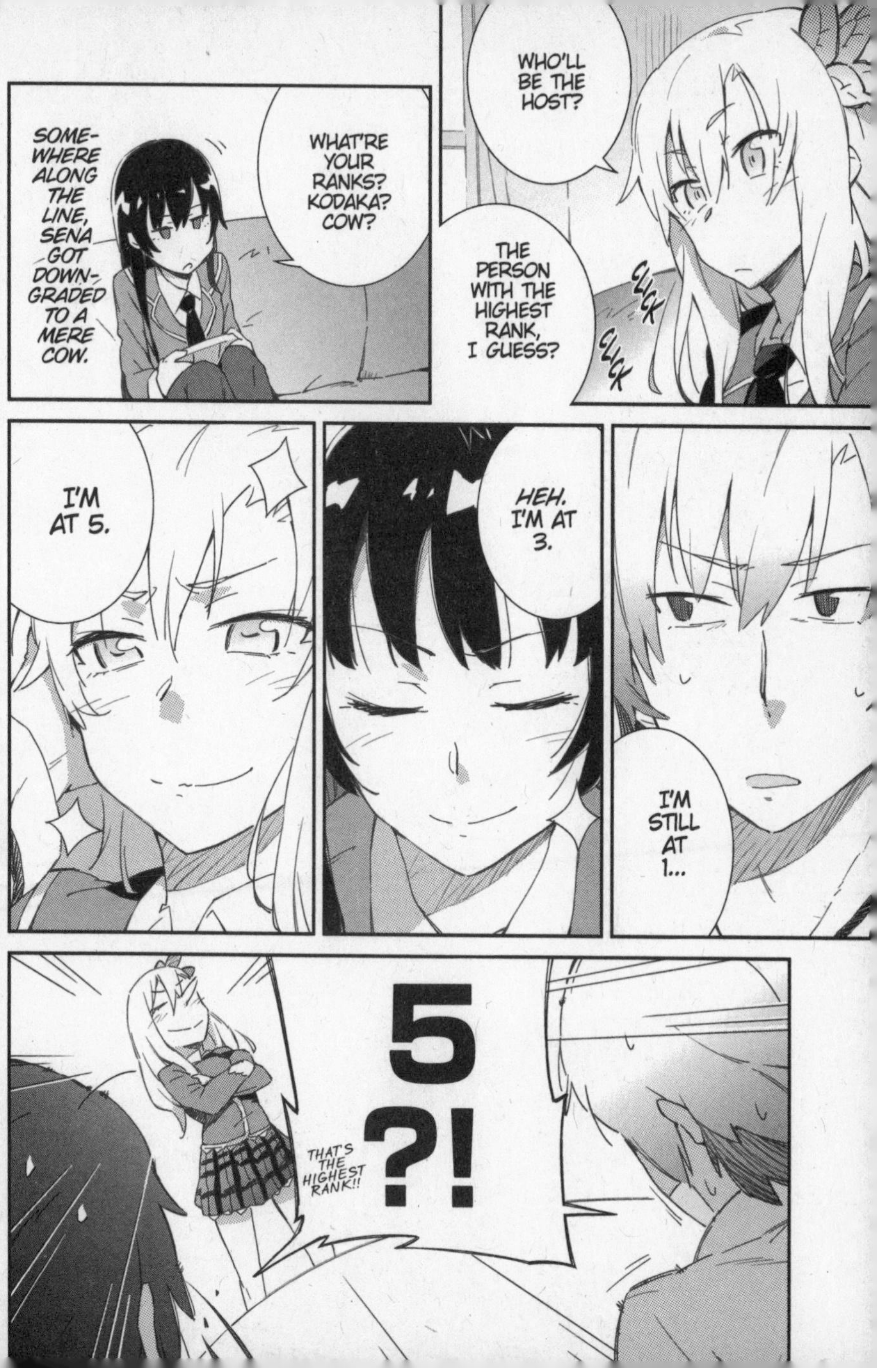
WHO'LL BE THE HOST?
THE PERSON WITH THE HIGHEST RANK, I GUESS?
CLICK CLICK
WHAT'RE YOUR RANKS? KODAKA? COW?
SOME-WHERE ALONG THE LINE, SENA GOT DOWN-GRADED TO A MERE COW.
I'M STILL AT 1...
HEH. I'M AT 3.
I'M AT 5.
5?!
THAT'S THE HIGHEST RANK!!

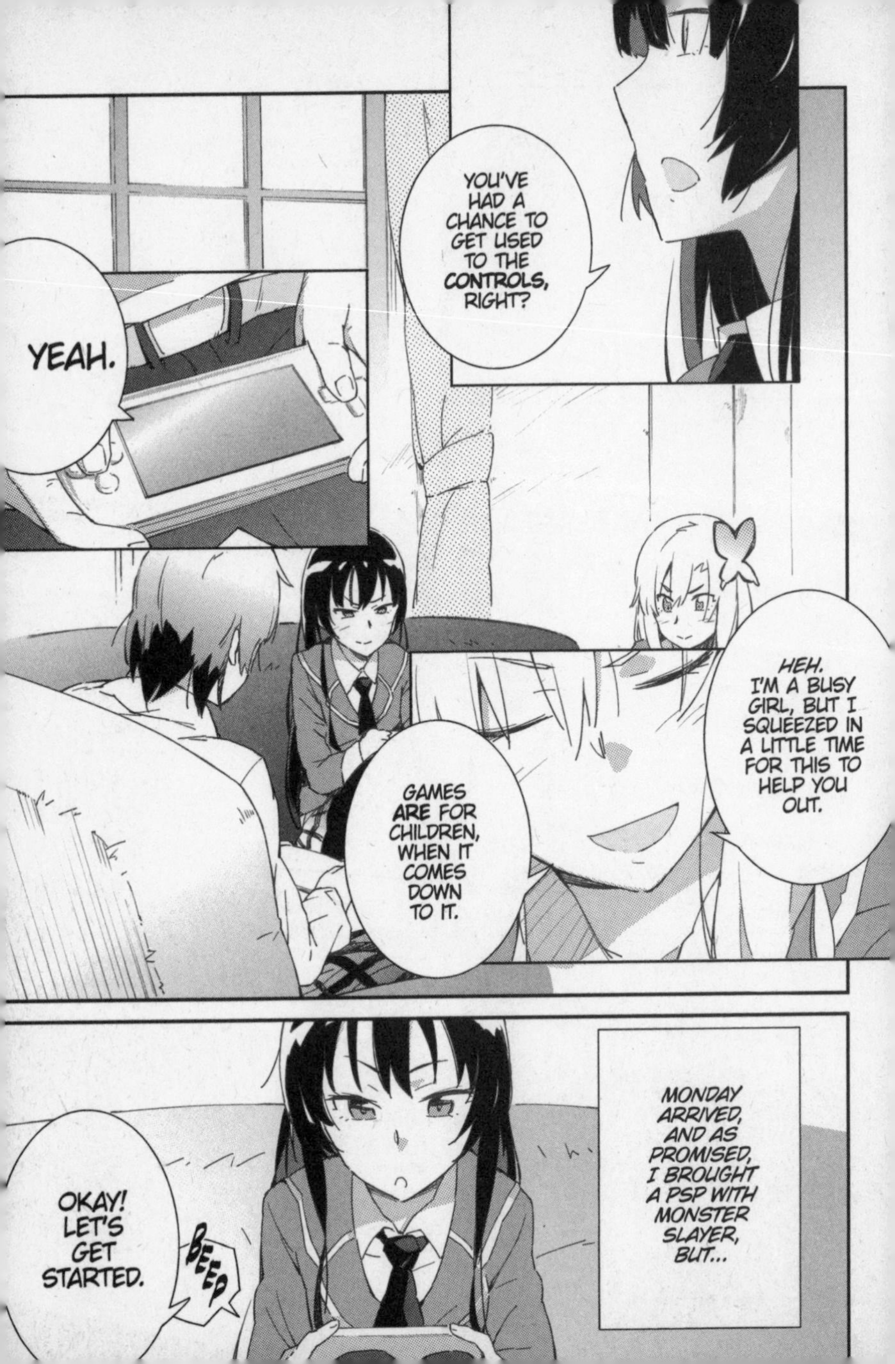
YOU'VE HAD A CHANCE TO GET USED TO THE CONTROLS, RIGHT?
YEAH.
HEH. I'M A BUSY GIRL, BUT I SQUEEZED IN A LITTLE TIME FOR THIS TO HELP YOU OUT.
GAMES ARE FOR CHILDREN, WHEN IT COMES DOWN TO IT.
MONDAY ARRIVED, AND AS PROMISED, I BROUGHT A PSP WITH MONSTER SLAYER, BUT...
OKAY! LET'S GET STARTED.
BEEP

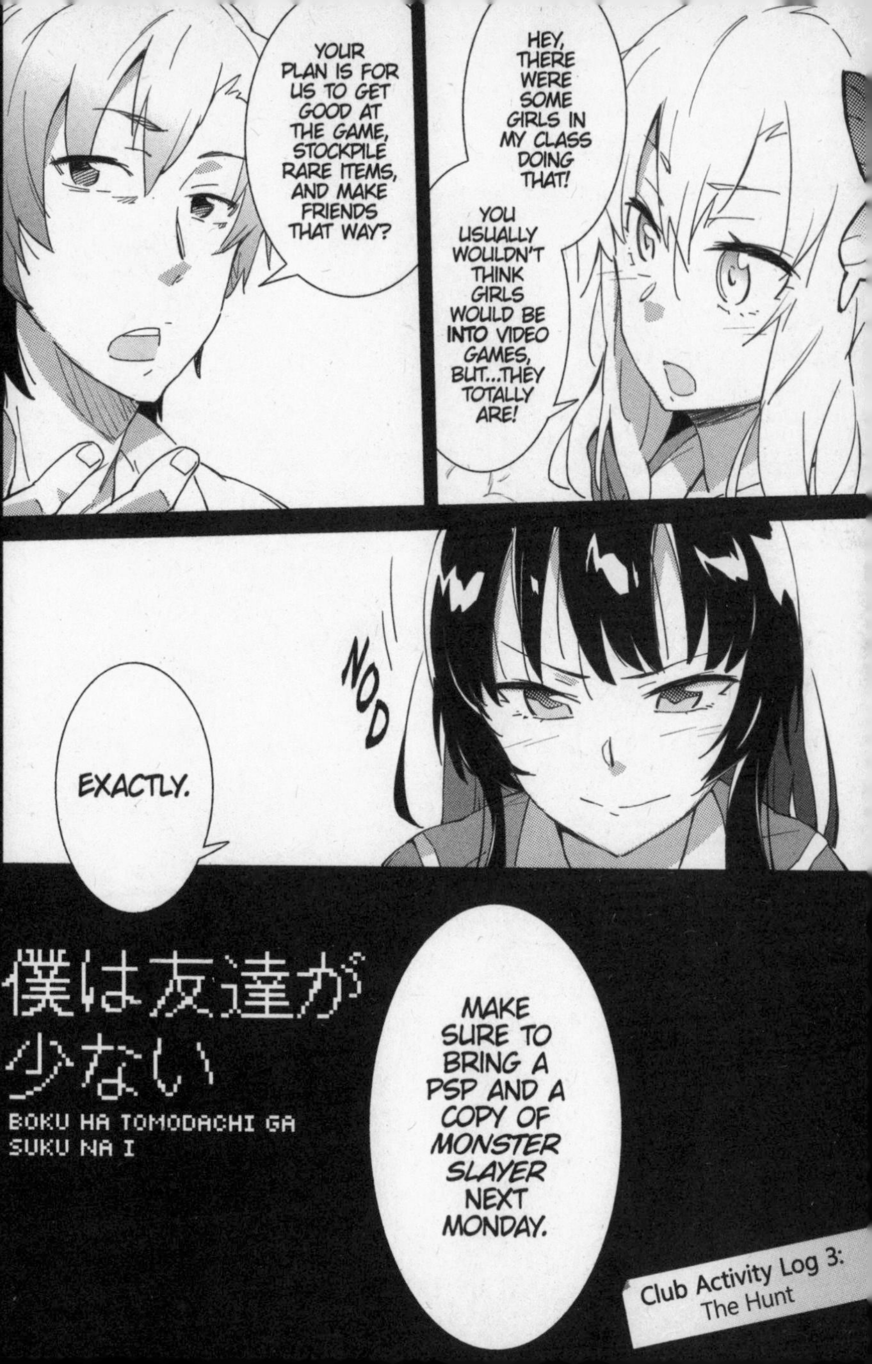
HEY, THERE WERE SOME GIRLS IN MY CLASS DOING THAT!
YOU USUALLY WOULDN'T THINK GIRLS WOULD BE INTO VIDEO GAMES, BUT...THEY TOTALLY ARE!
YOUR PLAN IS FOR US TO GET GOOD AT THE GAME, STOCKPILE RARE ITEMS, AND MAKE FRIENDS THAT WAY?
NOD
EXACTLY.
MAKE SURE TO BRING A PSP AND A COPY OF *MONSTER SLAYER* NEXT MONDAY.
僕は友達が少ない
BOKU HA TOMODACHI GA SUKU NA I
Club Activity Log 3: The Hunt

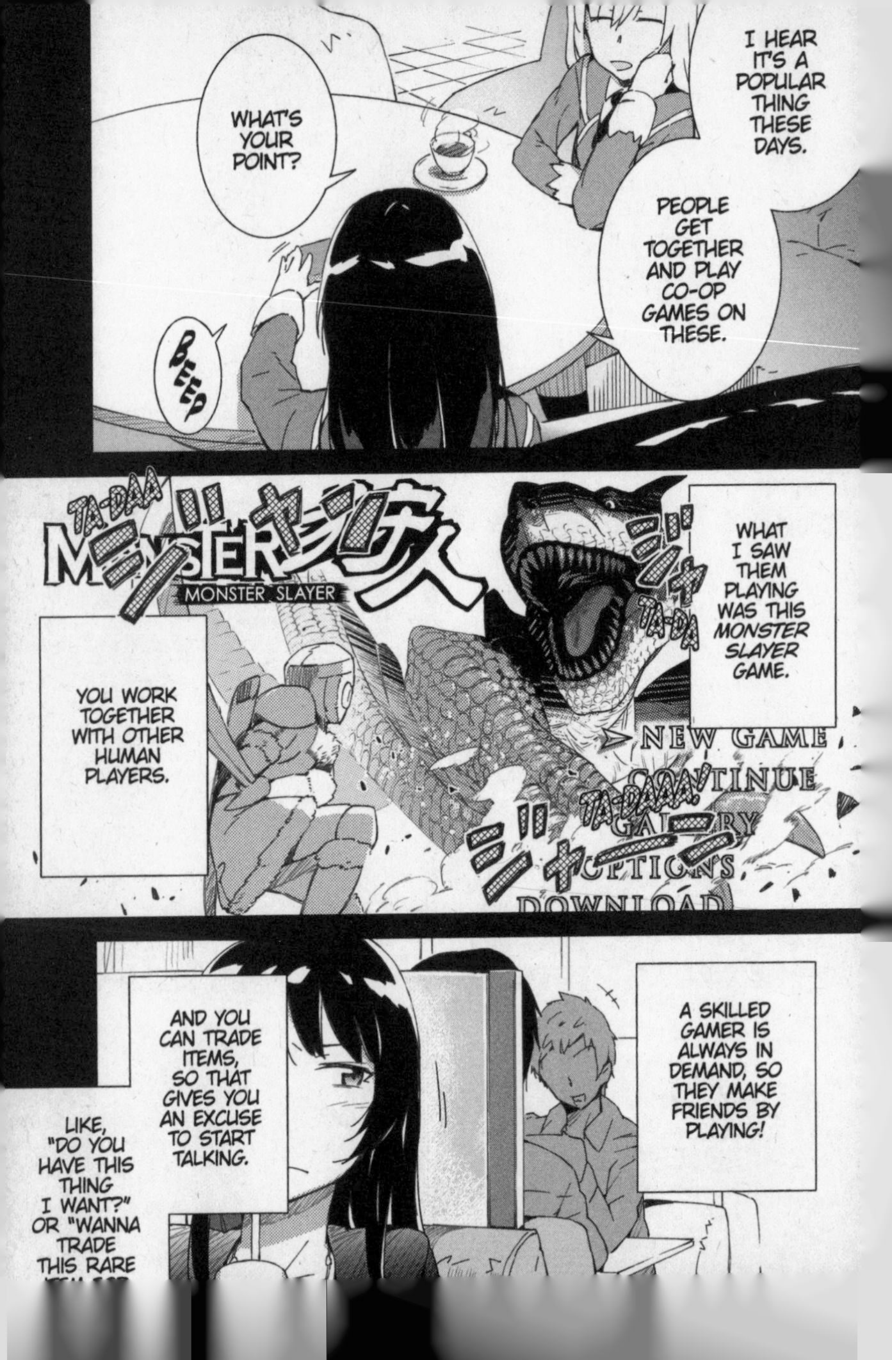
I HEAR IT'S A POPULAR THING THESE DAYS.
PEOPLE GET TOGETHER AND PLAY CO-OP GAMES ON THESE.
WHAT'S YOUR POINT?
BEEP
WHAT I SAW THEM PLAYING WAS THIS MONSTER SLAYER GAME.
TA-DA
NEW GAME
CONTINUE
OPTIONS
TA-DAAA!
TA-DAA
MONSTER
MONSTER SLAYER
YOU WORK TOGETHER WITH OTHER HUMAN PLAYERS.
A SKILLED GAMER IS ALWAYS IN DEMAND, SO THEY MAKE FRIENDS BY PLAYING!
AND YOU CAN TRADE ITEMS, SO THAT GIVES YOU AN EXCUSE TO START TALKING.
LIKE, "DO YOU HAVE THIS THING I WANT?" OR "WANNA TRADE THIS RARE

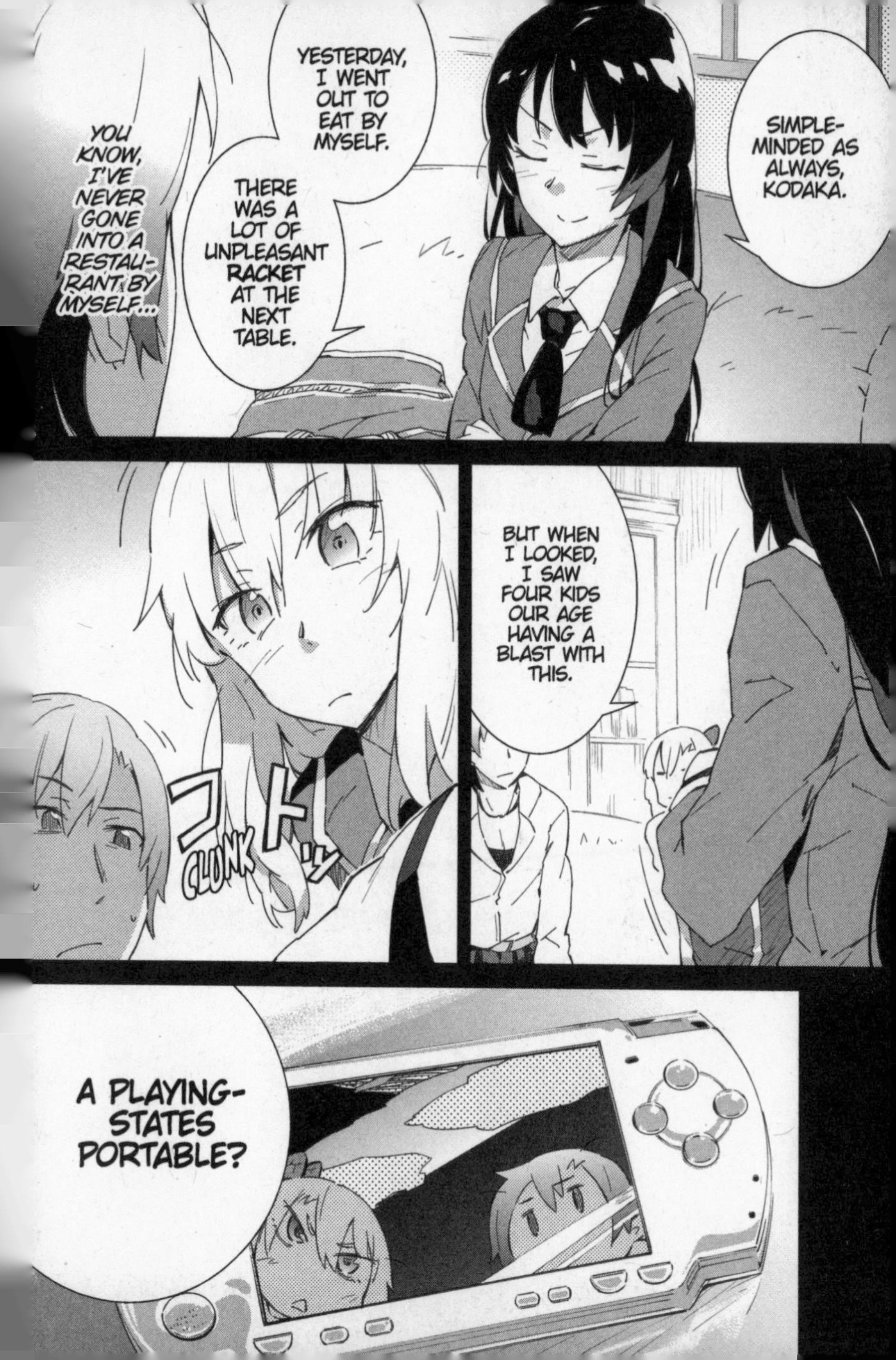
SIMPLE-MINDED AS ALWAYS, KODAKA.
YESTERDAY, I WENT OUT TO EAT BY MYSELF.
THERE WAS A LOT OF UNPLEASANT RACKET AT THE NEXT TABLE.
YOU KNOW, I'VE NEVER GONE INTO A RESTAURANT BY MYSELF...
BUT WHEN I LOOKED, I SAW FOUR KIDS OUR AGE HAVING A BLAST WITH THIS.
コトッ
CLUNK
A PLAYING-STATES PORTABLE?

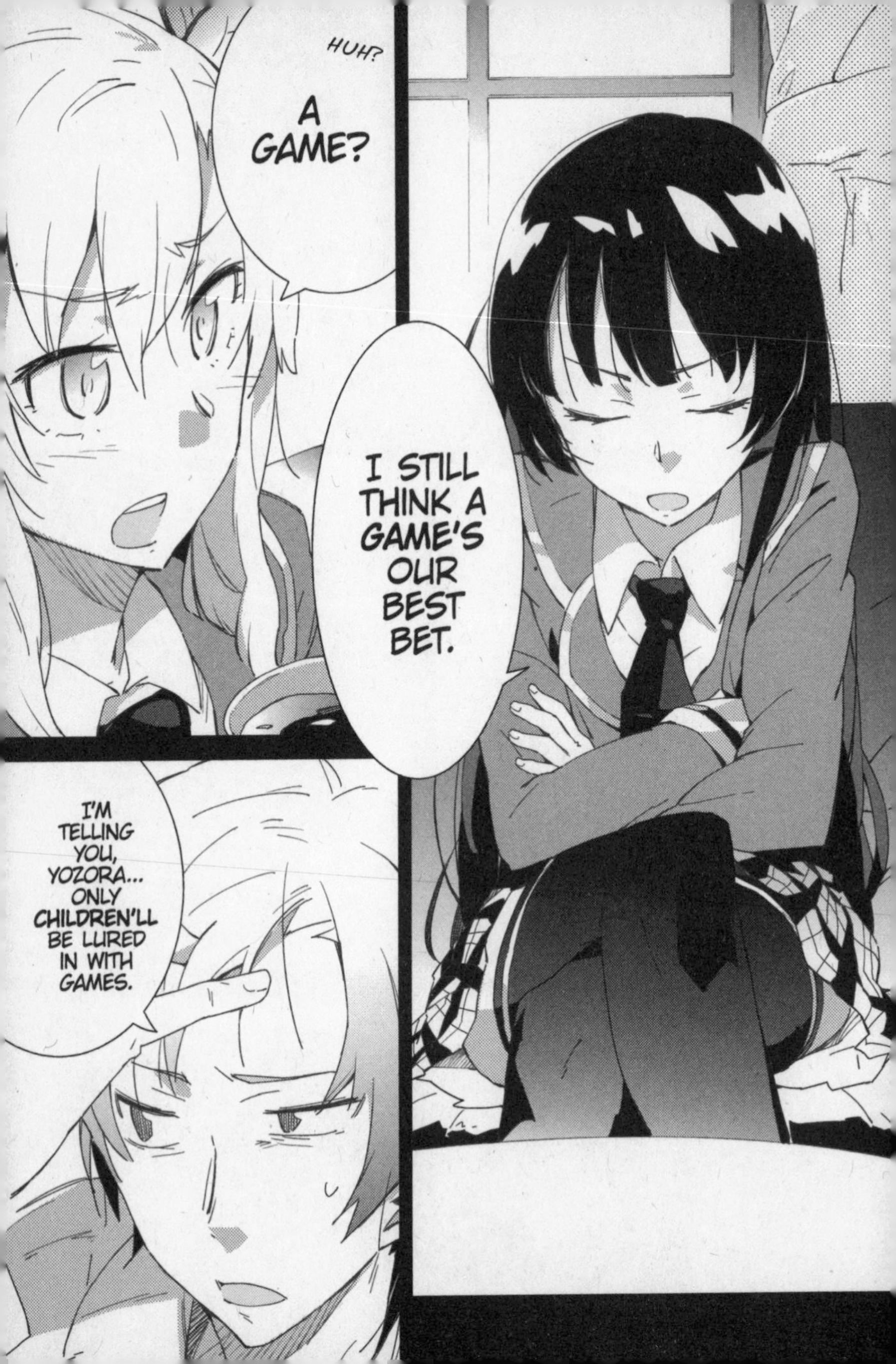
I STILL THINK A GAME'S OUR BEST BET.
HUH?
A GAME?
I'M TELLING YOU, YOZORA... ONLY CHILDREN'LL BE LURED IN WITH GAMES.

Haganai

I don't have many friends

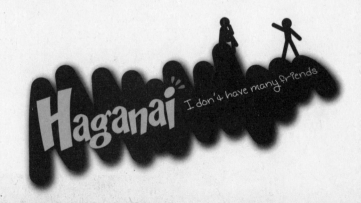

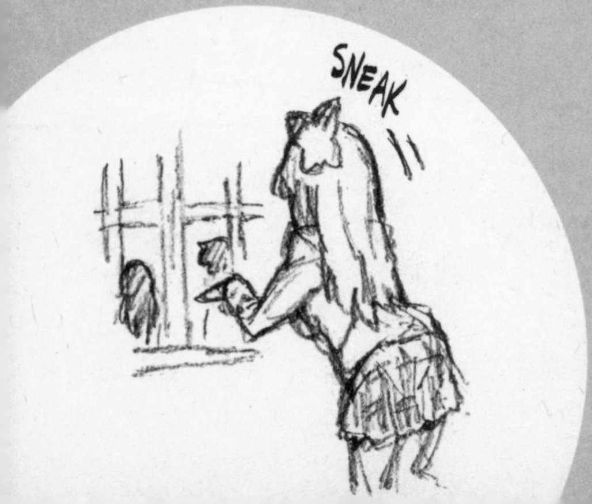
SNEAK

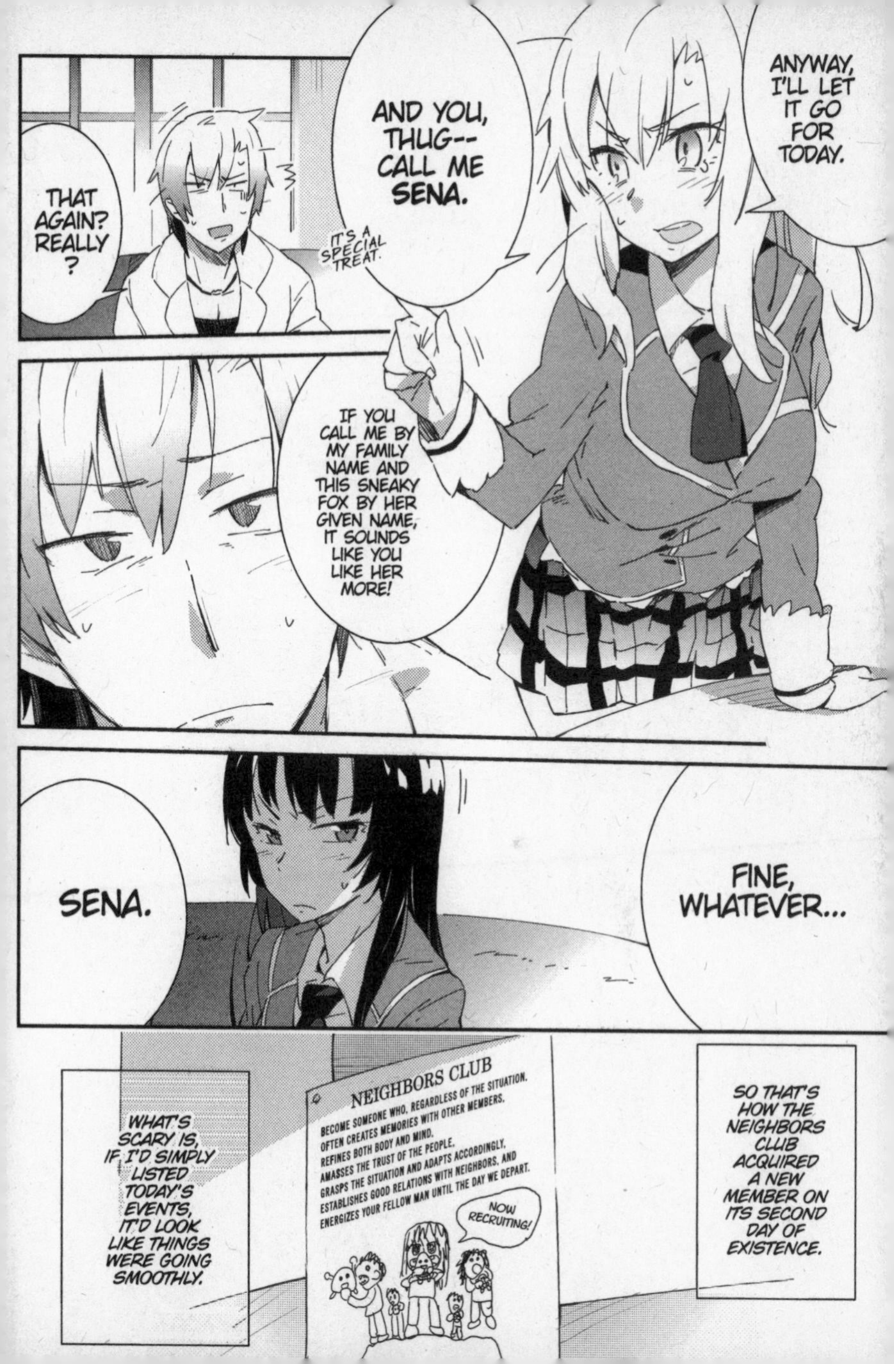
ANYWAY, I'LL LET IT GO FOR TODAY.
AND YOU, THUG-- CALL ME SENA.
IT'S A SPECIAL TREAT.
THAT AGAIN? REALLY?
IF YOU CALL ME BY MY FAMILY NAME AND THIS SNEAKY FOX BY HER GIVEN NAME, IT SOUNDS LIKE YOU LIKE HER MORE!
FINE, WHATEVER...
SENA.
SO THAT'S HOW THE NEIGHBORS CLUB ACQUIRED A NEW MEMBER ON ITS SECOND DAY OF EXISTENCE.
NEIGHBORS CLUB
BECOME SOMEONE WHO, REGARDLESS OF THE SITUATION,
OFTEN CREATES MEMORIES WITH OTHER MEMBERS,
REFINES BOTH BODY AND MIND,
AMASSES THE TRUST OF THE PEOPLE,
GRASPS THE SITUATION AND ADAPTS ACCORDINGLY,
ESTABLISHES GOOD RELATIONS WITH NEIGHBORS, AND
ENERGIZES YOUR FELLOW MAN UNTIL THE DAY WE DEPART.
NOW RECRUITING!
WHAT'S SCARY IS, IF I'D SIMPLY LISTED TODAY'S EVENTS, IT'D LOOK LIKE THINGS WERE GOING SMOOTHLY.

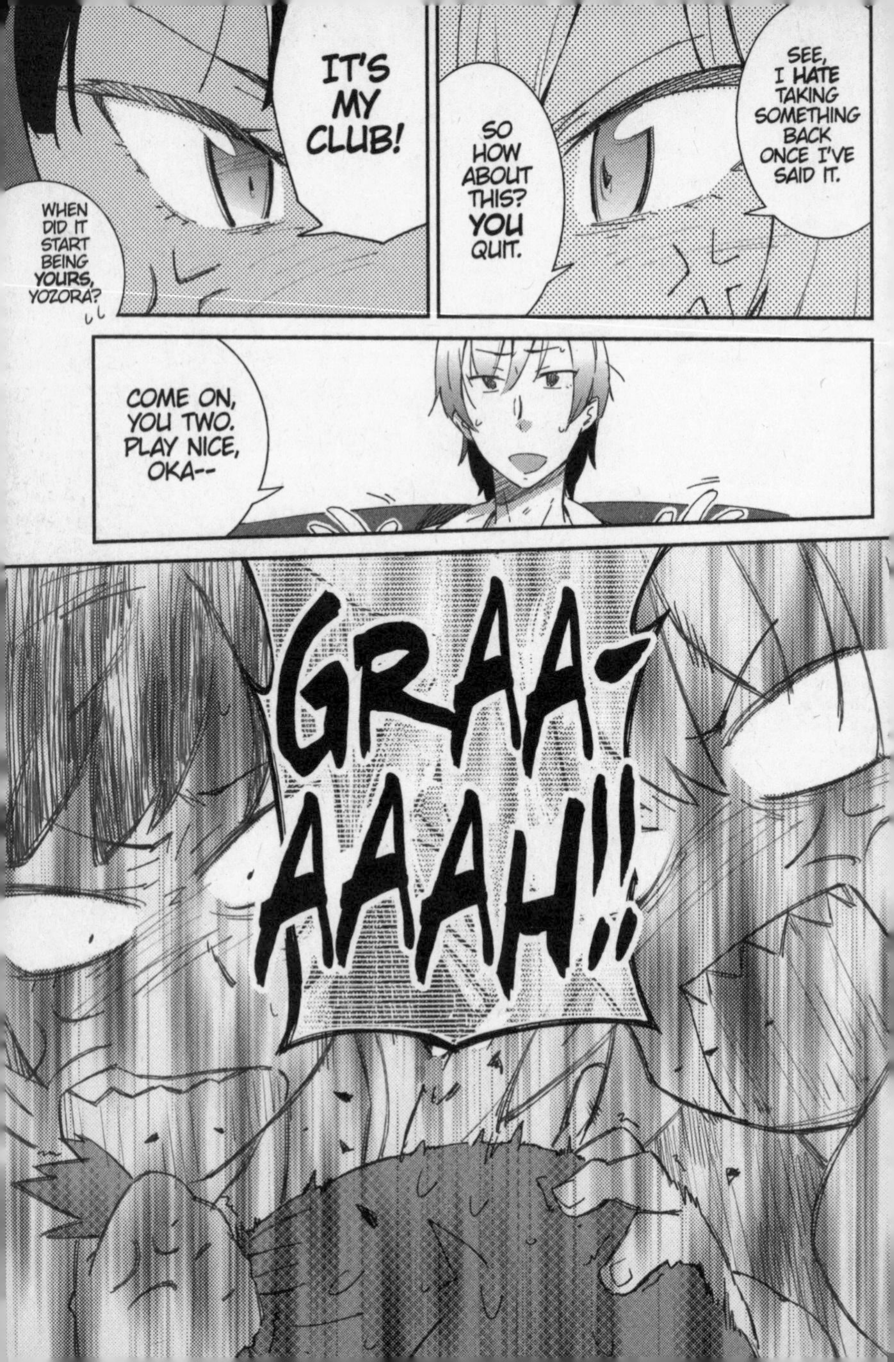
SEE, I HATE TAKING SOMETHING BACK ONCE I'VE SAID IT.
SO HOW ABOUT THIS? YOU QUIT.
IT'S MY CLUB!
WHEN DID IT START BEING YOURS, YOZORA?
COME ON, YOU TWO. PLAY NICE, OKA--
GRAA-AAAH!!

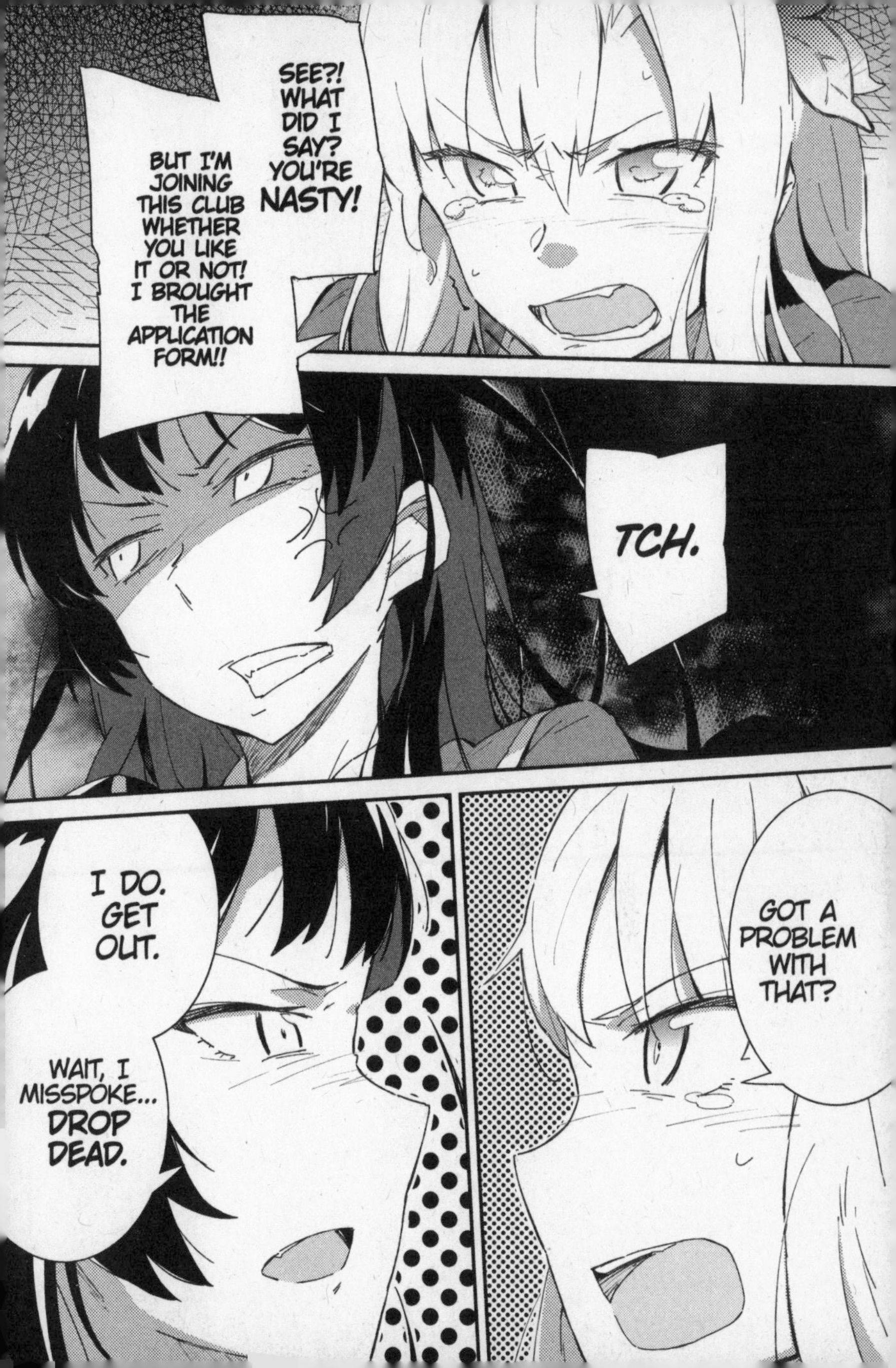
SEE?! WHAT DID I SAY? YOU'RE NASTY!
BUT I'M JOINING THIS CLUB WHETHER YOU LIKE IT OR NOT! I BROUGHT THE APPLICATION FORM!!
TCH.
GOT A PROBLEM WITH THAT?
I DO. GET OUT.
WAIT, I MISSPOKE... DROP DEAD.

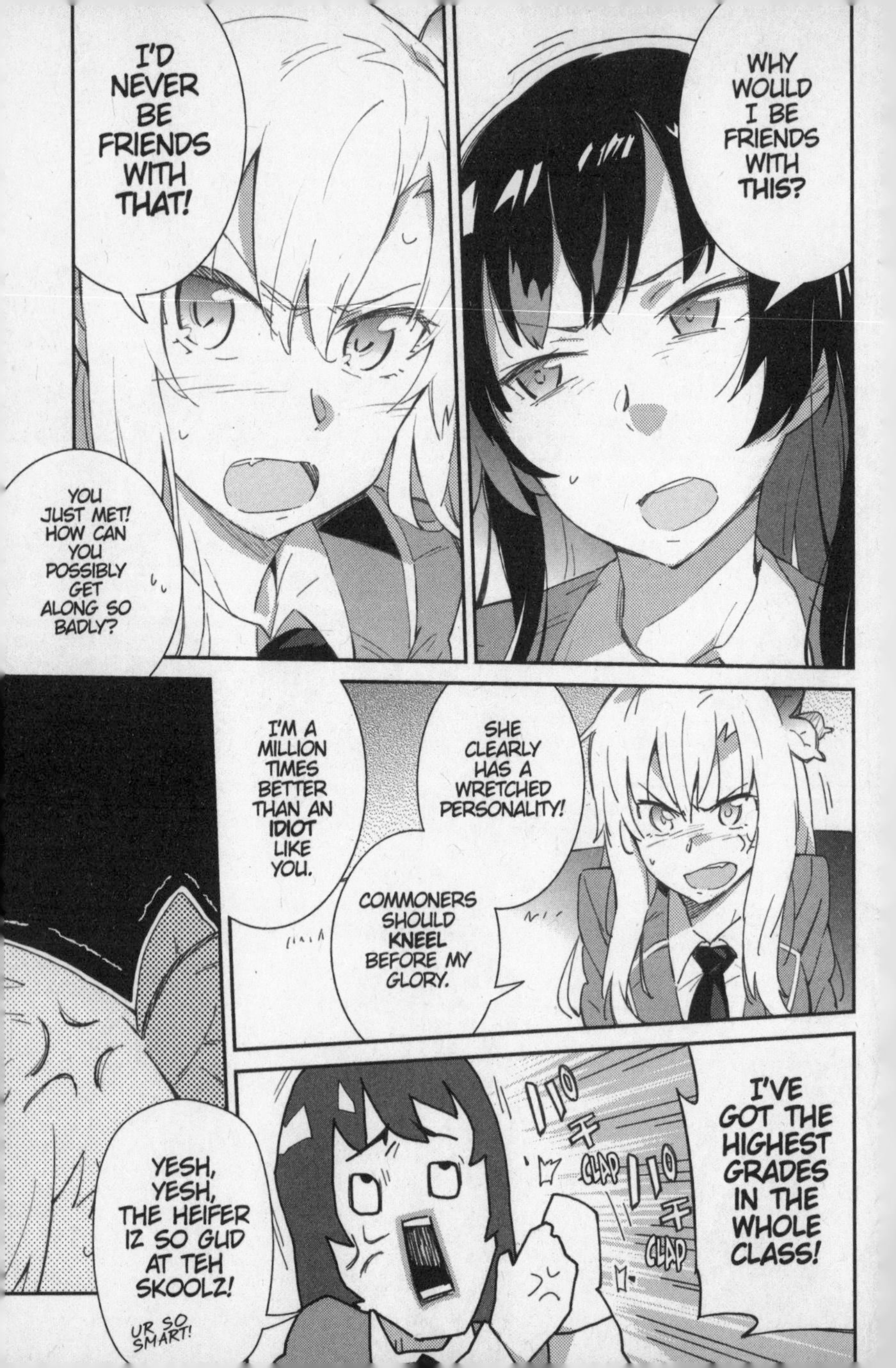
WHY WOULD I BE FRIENDS WITH THIS?
I'D NEVER BE FRIENDS WITH THAT!
YOU JUST MET! HOW CAN YOU POSSIBLY GET ALONG SO BADLY?
SHE CLEARLY HAS A WRETCHED PERSONALITY!
I'M A MILLION TIMES BETTER THAN AN IDIOT LIKE YOU.
COMMONERS SHOULD KNEEL BEFORE MY GLORY.
I'VE GOT THE HIGHEST GRADES IN THE WHOLE CLASS!
CLAP
CLAP
YESH, YESH, THE HEIFER IZ SO GUD AT TEH SKOOLZ!
UR SO SMART!

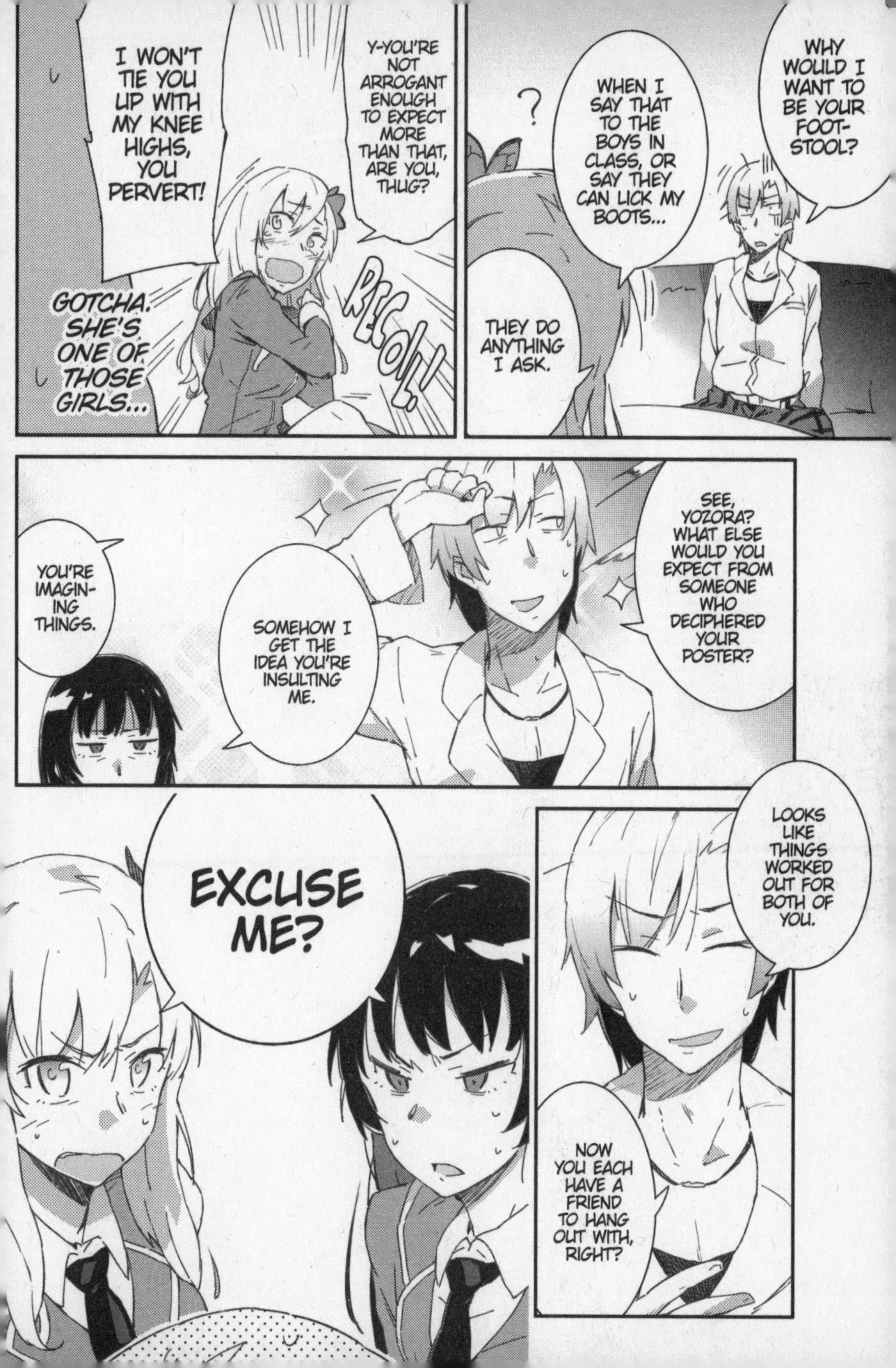
WHY WOULD I WANT TO BE YOUR FOOT-STOOL?
WHEN I SAY THAT TO THE BOYS IN CLASS, OR SAY THEY CAN LICK MY BOOTS...
THEY DO ANYTHING I ASK.
Y-YOU'RE NOT ARROGANT ENOUGH TO EXPECT MORE THAN THAT, ARE YOU, THUG?
I WON'T TIE YOU UP WITH MY KNEE HIGHS, YOU PERVERT!
RECOIL!
GOTCHA. SHE'S ONE OF THOSE GIRLS...
SEE, YOZORA? WHAT ELSE WOULD YOU EXPECT FROM SOMEONE WHO DECIPHERED YOUR POSTER?
SOMEHOW I GET THE IDEA YOU'RE INSULTING ME.
YOU'RE IMAGINING THINGS.
LOOKS LIKE THINGS WORKED OUT FOR BOTH OF YOU.
NOW YOU EACH HAVE A FRIEND TO HANG OUT WITH, RIGHT?
EXCUSE ME?

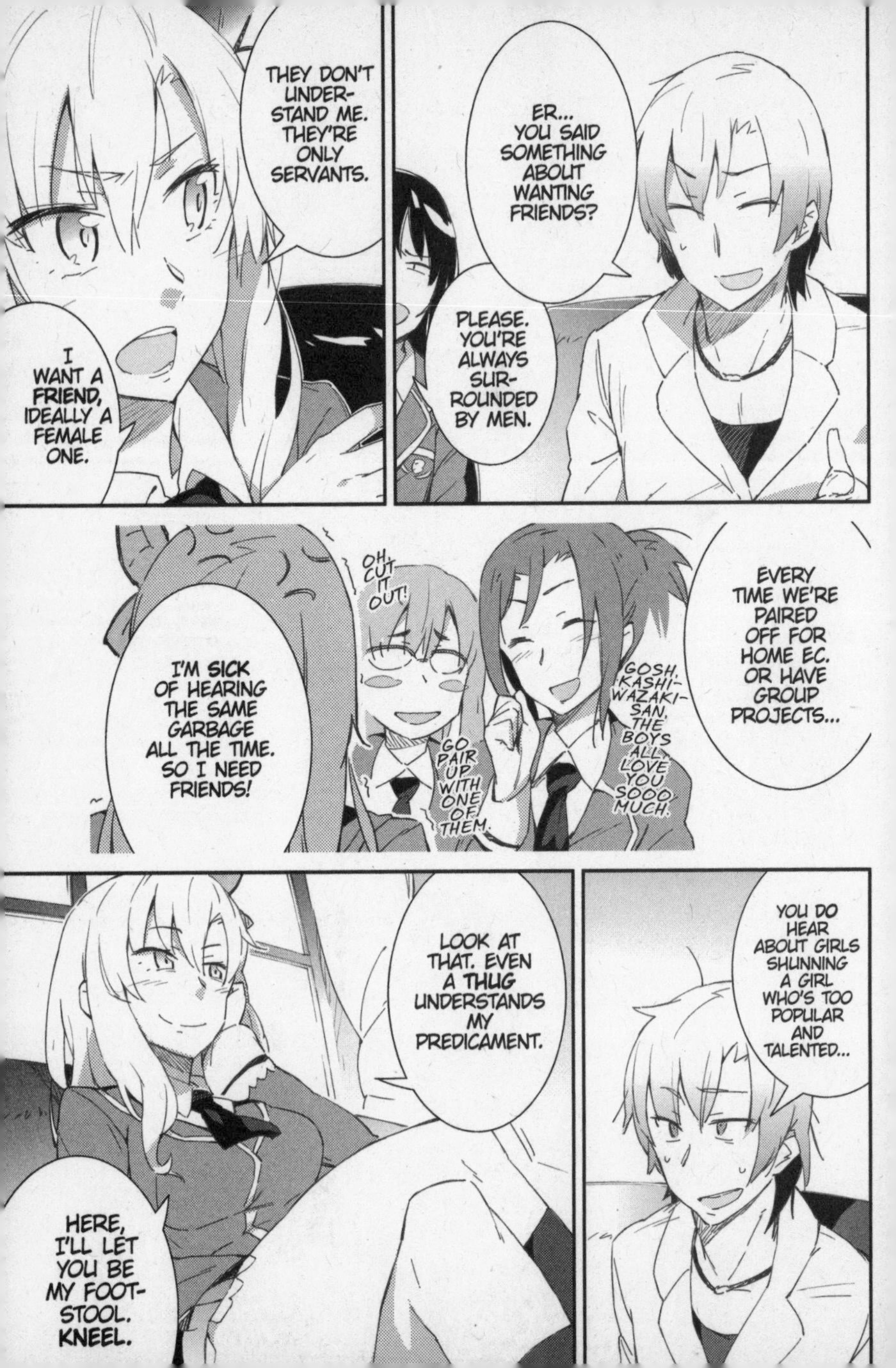
ER... YOU SAID SOMETHING ABOUT WANTING FRIENDS?
PLEASE. YOU'RE ALWAYS SURROUNDED BY MEN.
THEY DON'T UNDERSTAND ME. THEY'RE ONLY SERVANTS.
I WANT A FRIEND, IDEALLY A FEMALE ONE.
EVERY TIME WE'RE PAIRED OFF FOR HOME EC. OR HAVE GROUP PROJECTS...
GOSH. KASHIWAZAKI-SAN. THE BOYS ALL LOVE YOU SOOO MUCH.
OH, CUT IT OUT!
GO PAIR UP WITH ONE OF THEM.
I'M SICK OF HEARING THE SAME GARBAGE ALL THE TIME. SO I NEED FRIENDS!
YOU DO HEAR ABOUT GIRLS SHUNNING A GIRL WHO'S TOO POPULAR AND TALENTED...
LOOK AT THAT. EVEN A THUG UNDERSTANDS MY PREDICAMENT.
HERE, I'LL LET YOU BE MY FOOTSTOOL. KNEEL.

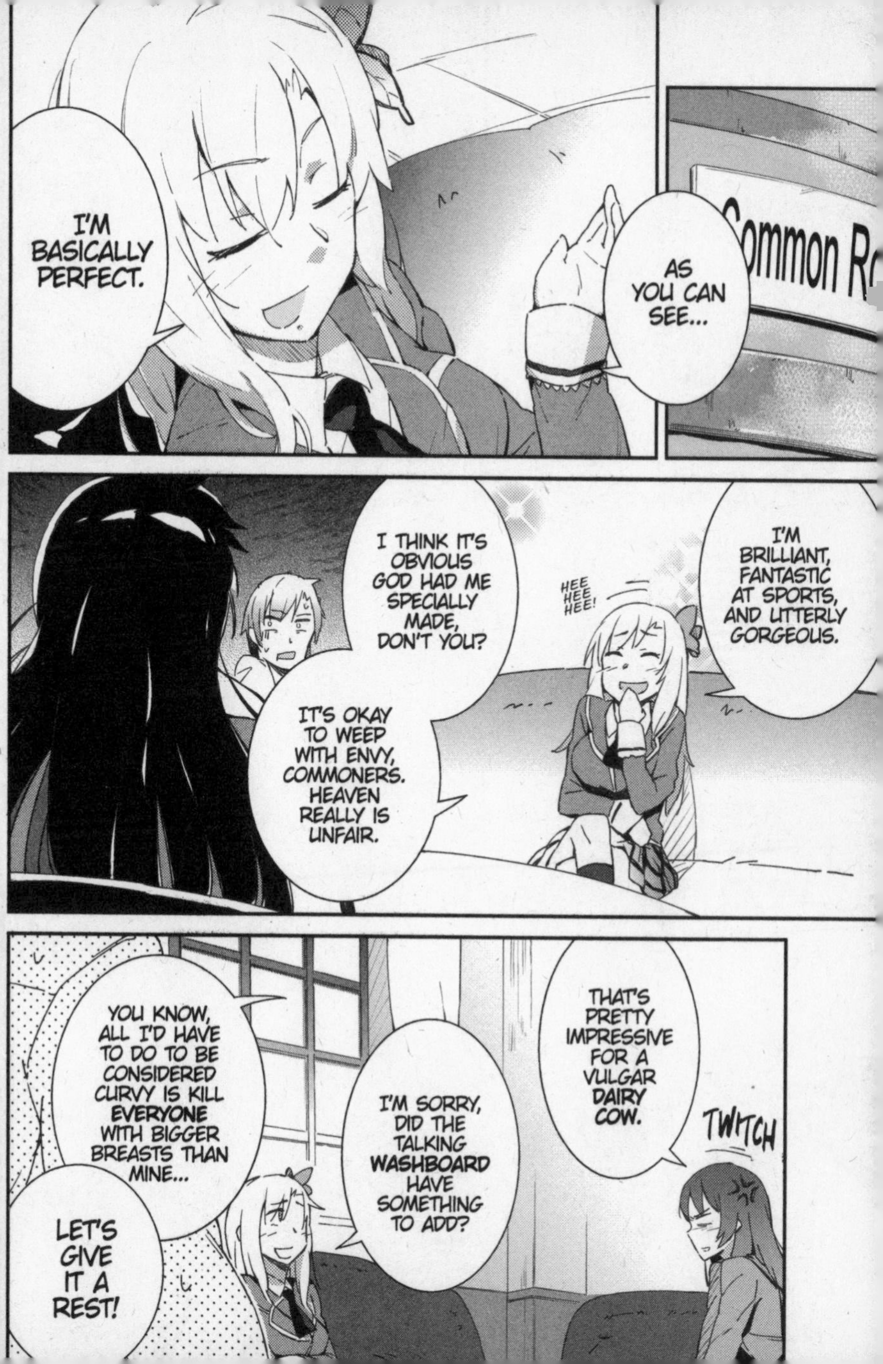
Common R
AS YOU CAN SEE...
I'M BASICALLY PERFECT.
I'M BRILLIANT, FANTASTIC AT SPORTS, AND UTTERLY GORGEOUS.
HEE HEE HEE!
I THINK IT'S OBVIOUS GOD HAD ME SPECIALLY MADE, DON'T YOU?
IT'S OKAY TO WEEP WITH ENVY, COMMONERS. HEAVEN REALLY IS UNFAIR.
THAT'S PRETTY IMPRESSIVE FOR A VULGAR DAIRY COW.
TWITCH
I'M SORRY, DID THE TALKING WASHBOARD HAVE SOMETHING TO ADD?
YOU KNOW, ALL I'D HAVE TO DO TO BE CONSIDERED CURVY IS KILL EVERYONE WITH BIGGER BREASTS THAN MINE...
LET'S GIVE IT A REST!

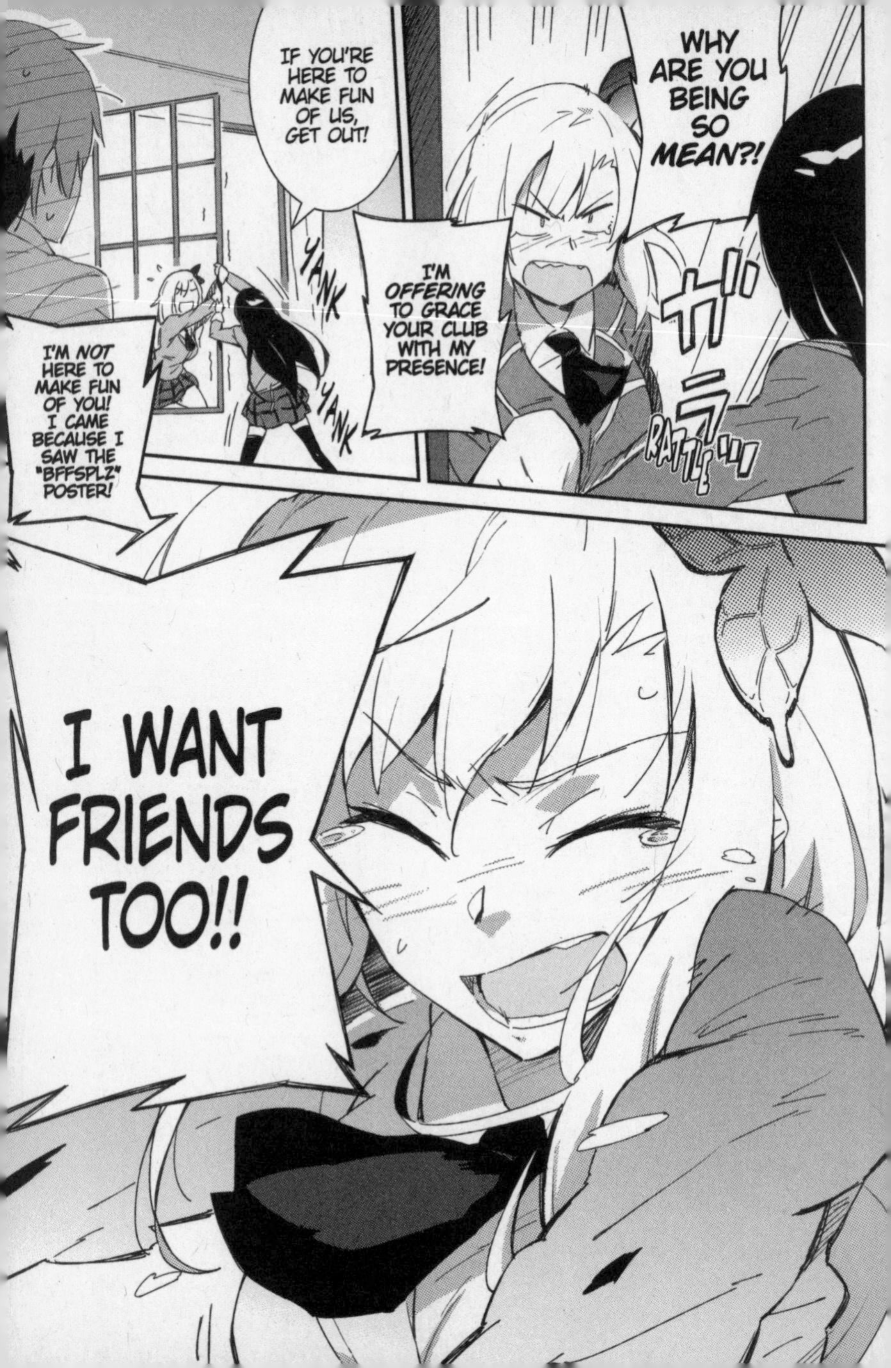
WHY ARE YOU BEING SO MEAN?!
ガラ
RATTLE
I'M OFFERING TO GRACE YOUR CLUB WITH MY PRESENCE!
IF YOU'RE HERE TO MAKE FUN OF US, GET OUT!
YANK
YANK
I'M NOT HERE TO MAKE FUN OF YOU! I CAME BECAUSE I SAW THE "BFFSPLZ" POSTER!
I WANT FRIENDS TOO!!

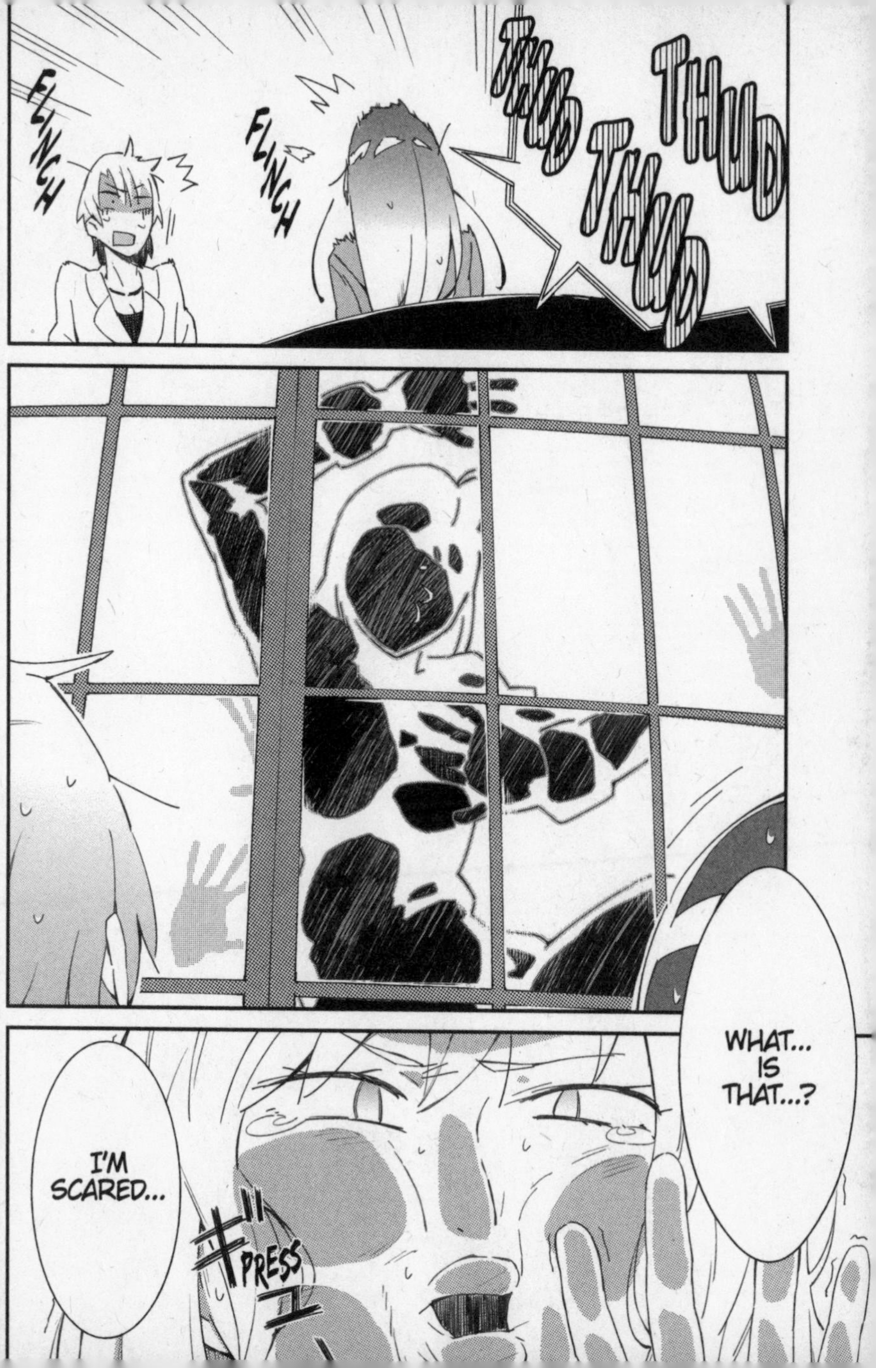
THUD
THUD
THUD
FLINCH
FLINCH
WHAT... IS THAT...?
I'M SCARED...
PRESS

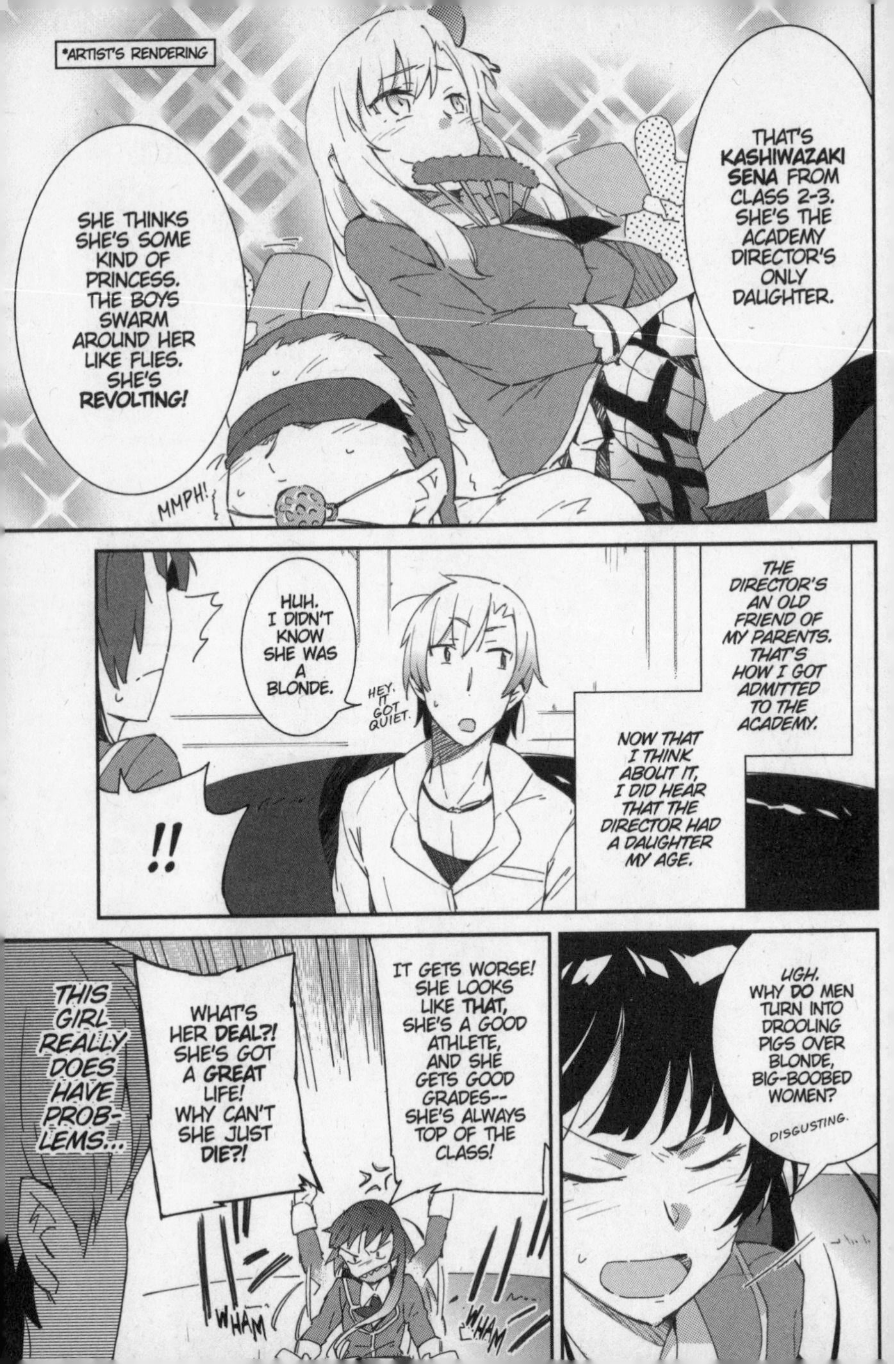
THAT'S KASHIWAZAKI SENA FROM CLASS 2-3. SHE'S THE ACADEMY DIRECTOR'S ONLY DAUGHTER.
*ARTIST'S RENDERING
SHE THINKS SHE'S SOME KIND OF PRINCESS. THE BOYS SWARM AROUND HER LIKE FLIES. SHE'S REVOLTING!
MMPH!
THE DIRECTOR'S AN OLD FRIEND OF MY PARENTS. THAT'S HOW I GOT ADMITTED TO THE ACADEMY.
NOW THAT I THINK ABOUT IT, I DID HEAR THAT THE DIRECTOR HAD A DAUGHTER MY AGE.
HUH. I DIDN'T KNOW SHE WAS A BLONDE.
HEY. IT GOT QUIET.
!!
UGH. WHY DO MEN TURN INTO DROOLING PIGS OVER BLONDE, BIG-BOOBED WOMEN?
DISGUSTING.
IT GETS WORSE! SHE LOOKS LIKE THAT, SHE'S A GOOD ATHLETE, AND SHE GETS GOOD GRADES-- SHE'S ALWAYS TOP OF THE CLASS!
WHAT'S HER DEAL?! SHE'S GOT A GREAT LIFE! WHY CAN'T SHE JUST DIE?!
THIS GIRL REALLY DOES HAVE PROB-LEMS...
WHAM
WHAM

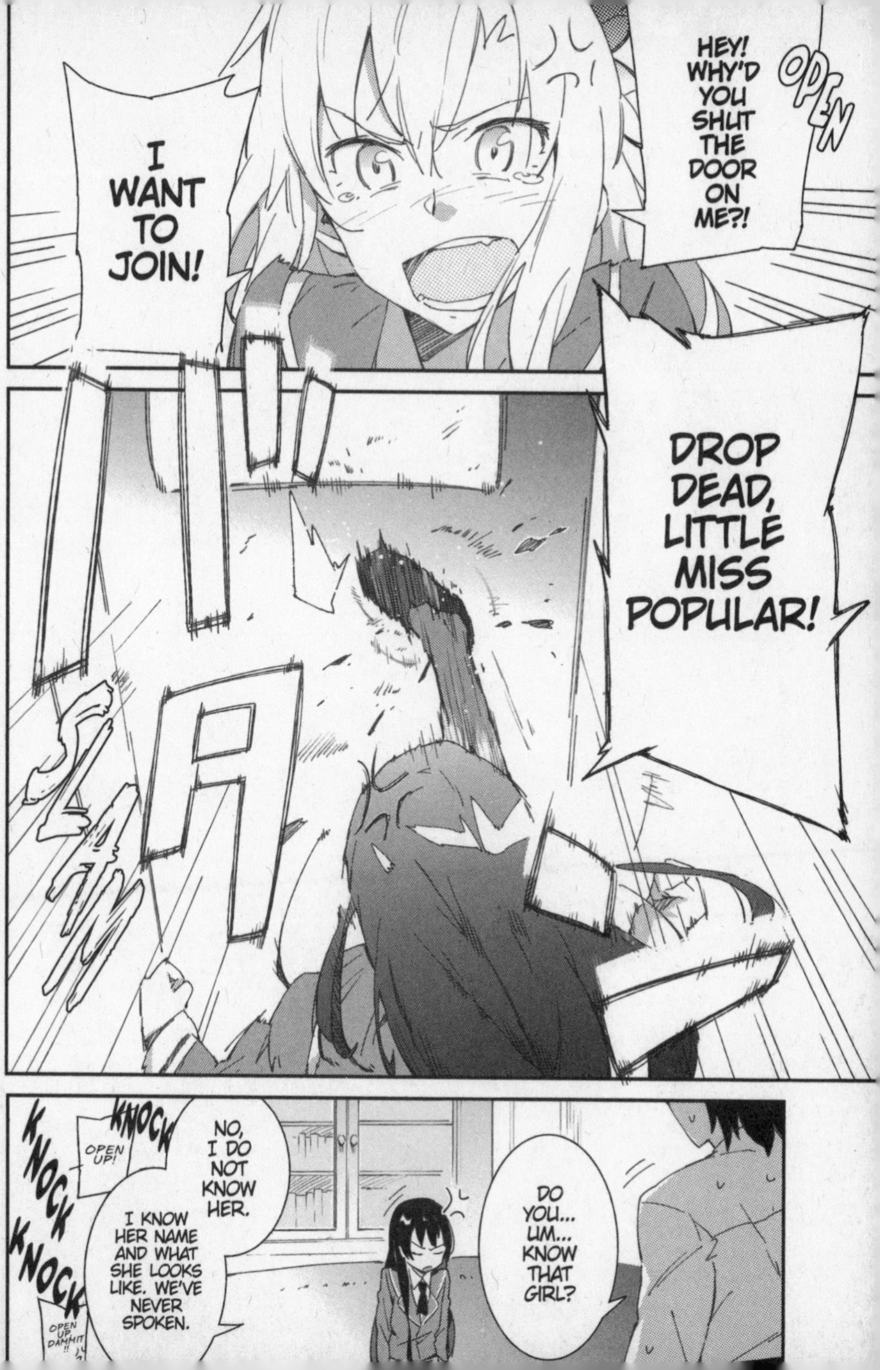
OPEN
HEY! WHY'D YOU SHUT THE DOOR ON ME?!
I WANT TO JOIN!
DROP DEAD, LITTLE MISS POPULAR!
DO YOU... UM... KNOW THAT GIRL?
NO, I DO NOT KNOW HER.
I KNOW HER NAME AND WHAT SHE LOOKS LIKE. WE'VE NEVER SPOKEN.
KNOCK
OPEN UP!
KNOCK KNOCK
OPEN UP DAMMIT!!

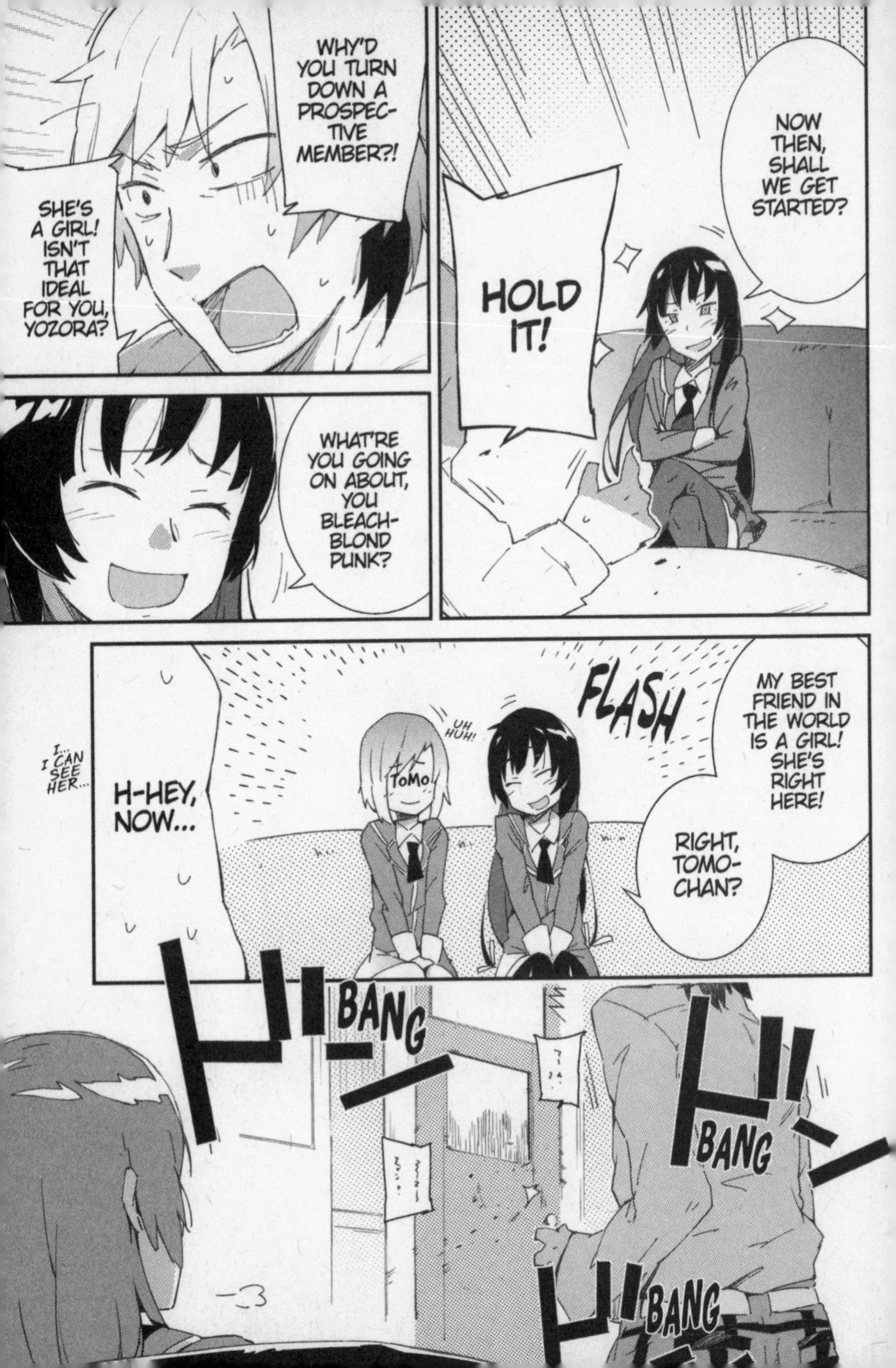
NOW THEN, SHALL WE GET STARTED?
HOLD IT!
WHY'D YOU TURN DOWN A PROSPECTIVE MEMBER?!
SHE'S A GIRL! ISN'T THAT IDEAL FOR YOU, YOZORA?
WHAT'RE YOU GOING ON ABOUT, YOU BLEACH-BLOND PUNK?
FLASH
MY BEST FRIEND IN THE WORLD IS A GIRL! SHE'S RIGHT HERE!
RIGHT, TOMO-CHAN?
UH HUH!
TOMO
H-HEY, NOW...
I... I CAN SEE HER...
BANG
BANG
BANG

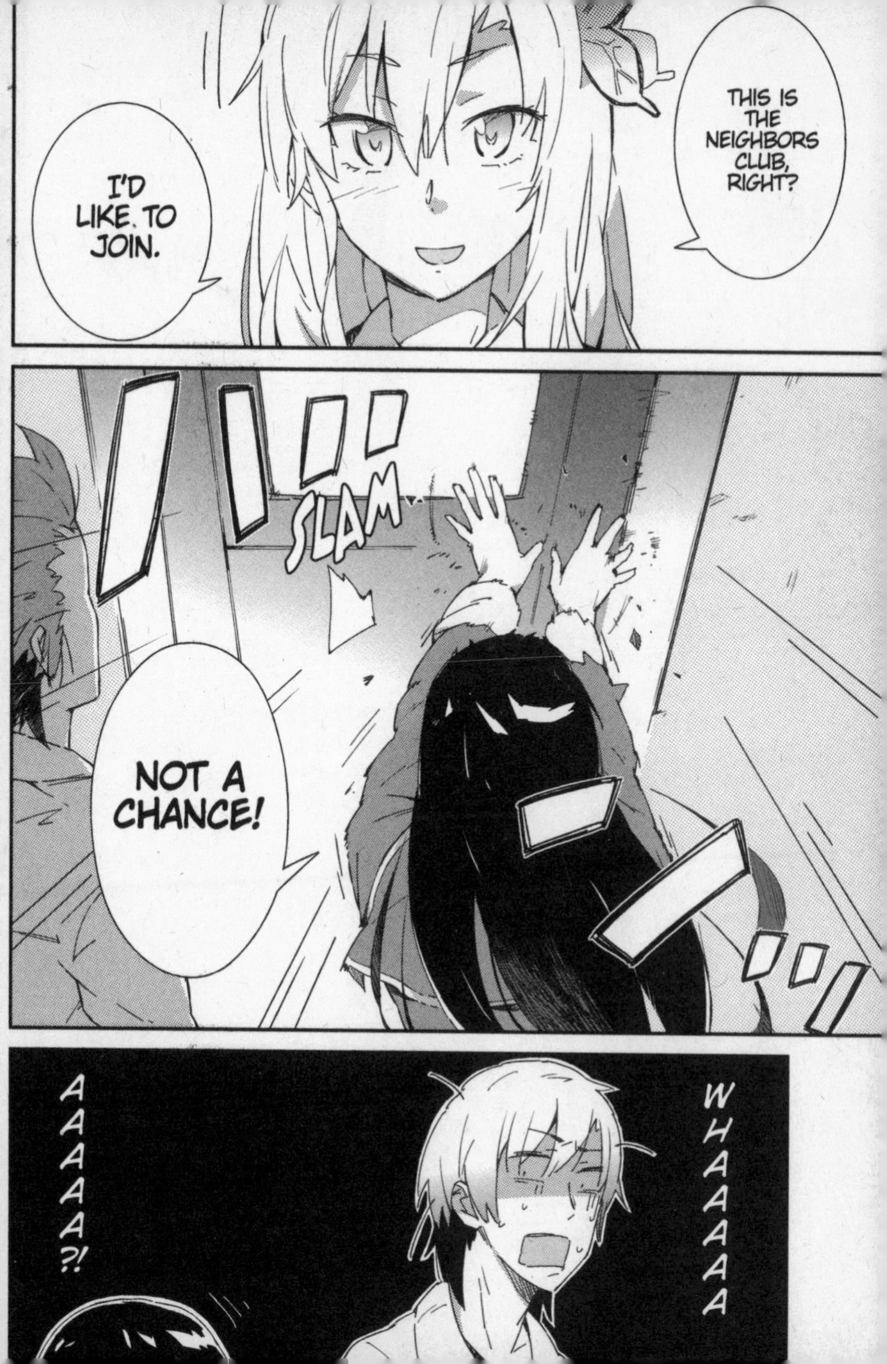
THIS IS THE NEIGHBORS CLUB, RIGHT?
I'D LIKE TO JOIN.
SLAM
NOT A CHANCE!
WHAAAAAA
AAAAAA?!

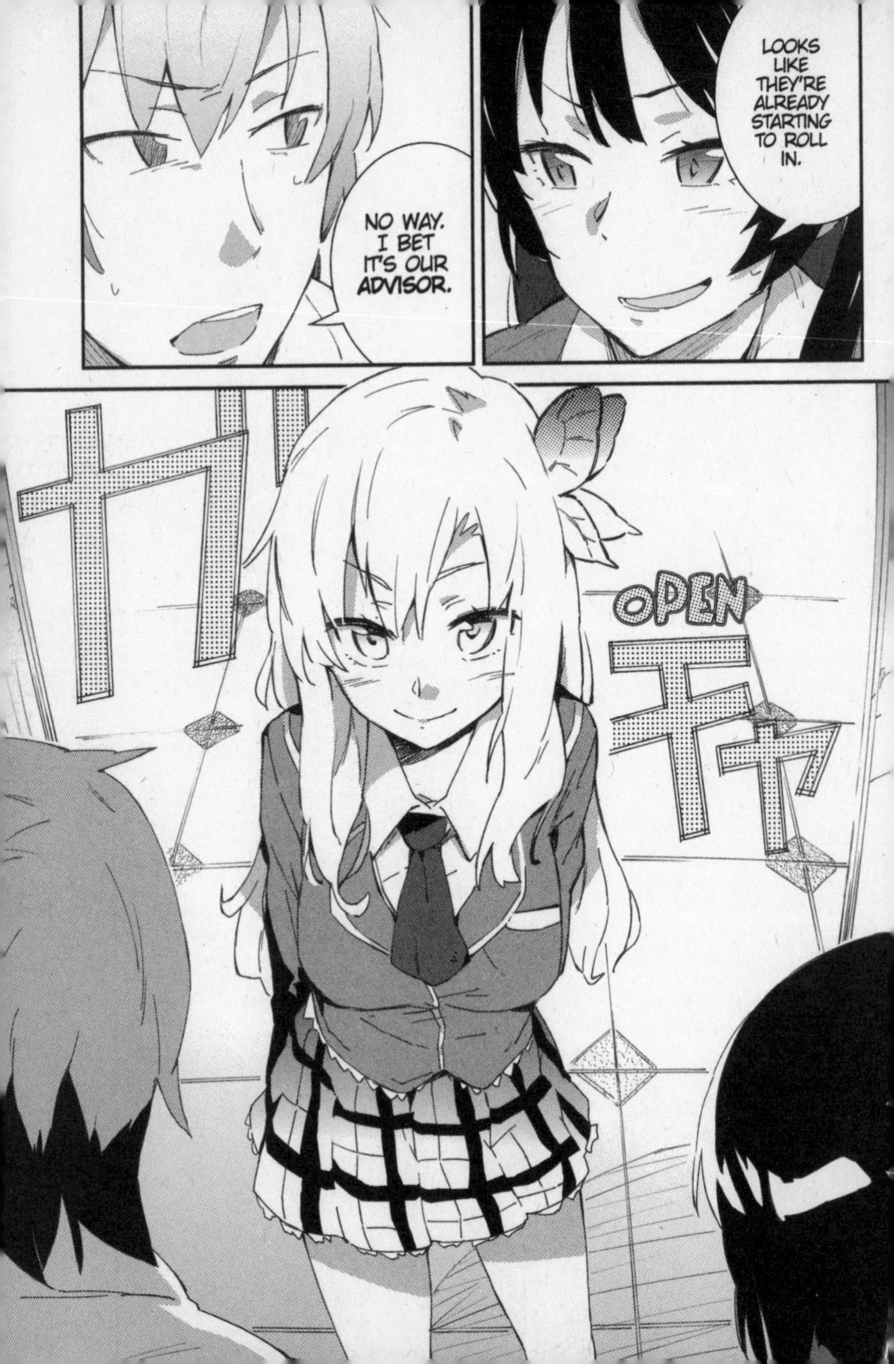
LOOKS LIKE THEY'RE ALREADY STARTING TO ROLL IN.
NO WAY. I BET IT'S OUR ADVISOR.
OPEN

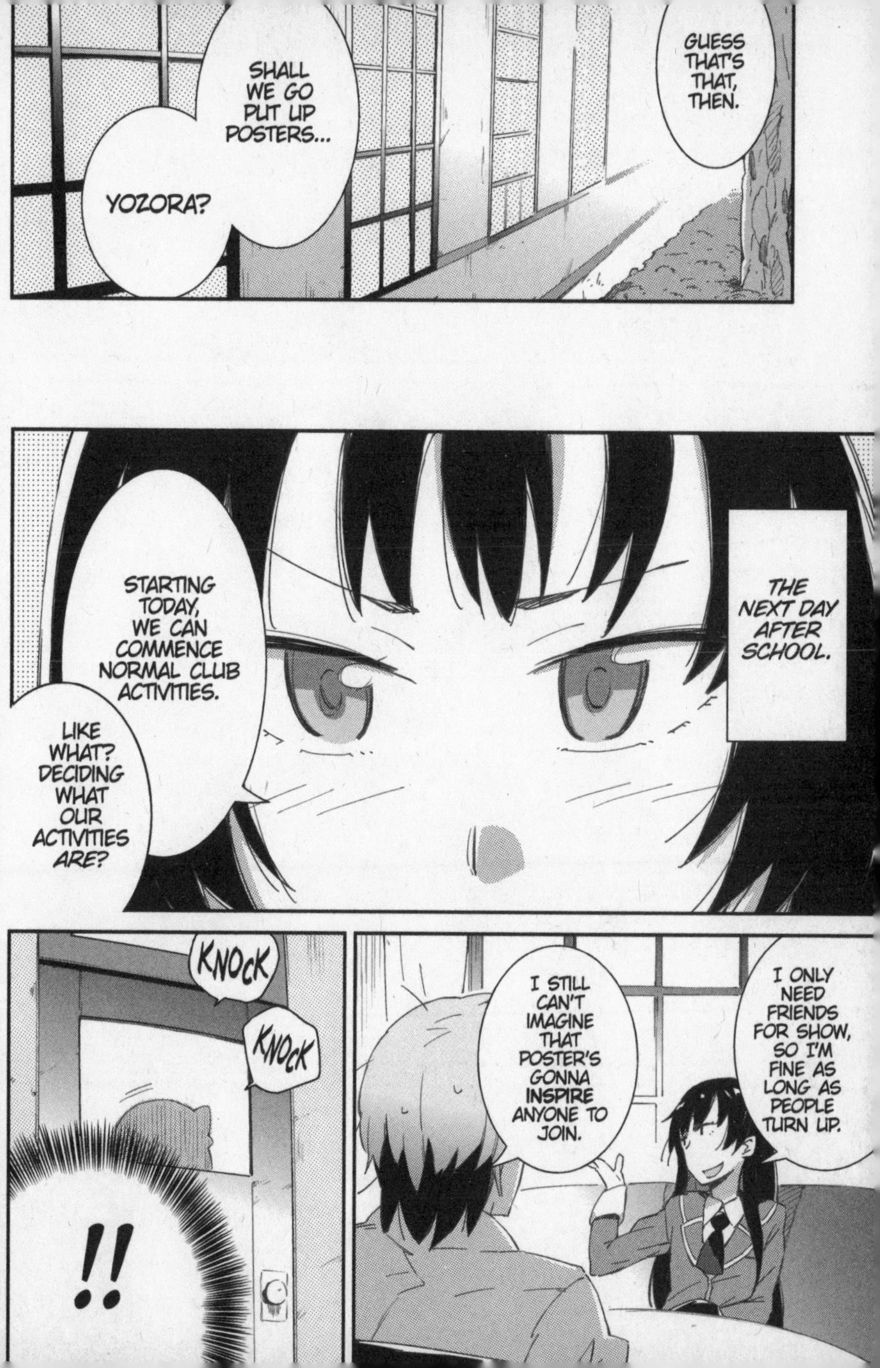
GUESS THAT'S THAT, THEN.
SHALL WE GO PUT UP POSTERS...
YOZORA?
THE NEXT DAY AFTER SCHOOL.
STARTING TODAY, WE CAN COMMENCE NORMAL CLUB ACTIVITIES.
LIKE WHAT? DECIDING WHAT OUR ACTIVITIES ARE?
I ONLY NEED FRIENDS FOR SHOW, SO I'M FINE AS LONG AS PEOPLE TURN UP.
I STILL CAN'T IMAGINE THAT POSTER'S GONNA **INSPIRE** ANYONE TO JOIN.
KNOCK
KNOCK
!!

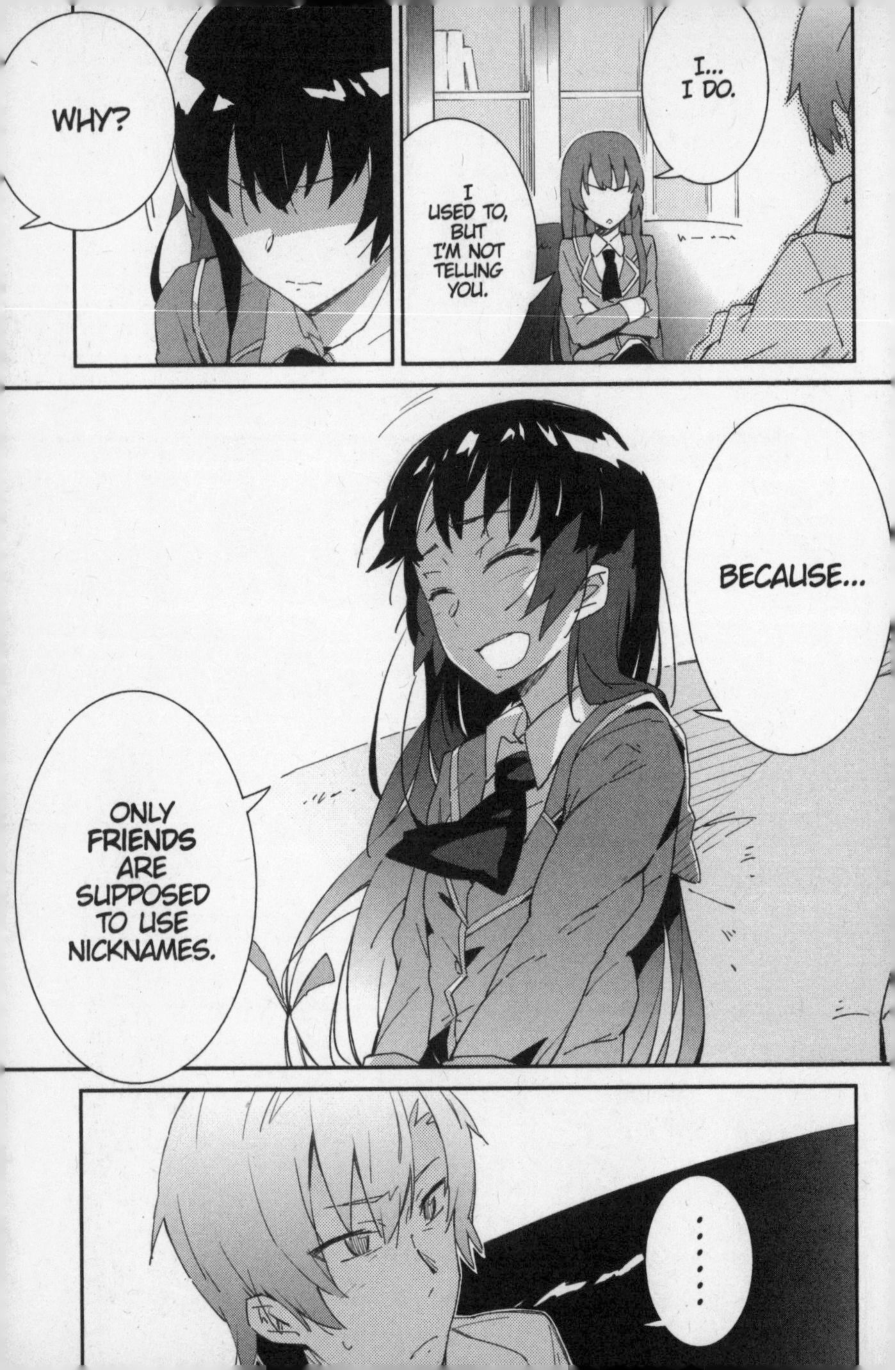
I... I DO.
I USED TO, BUT I'M NOT TELLING YOU.
WHY?
BECAUSE...
ONLY FRIENDS ARE SUPPOSED TO USE NICKNAMES.
......

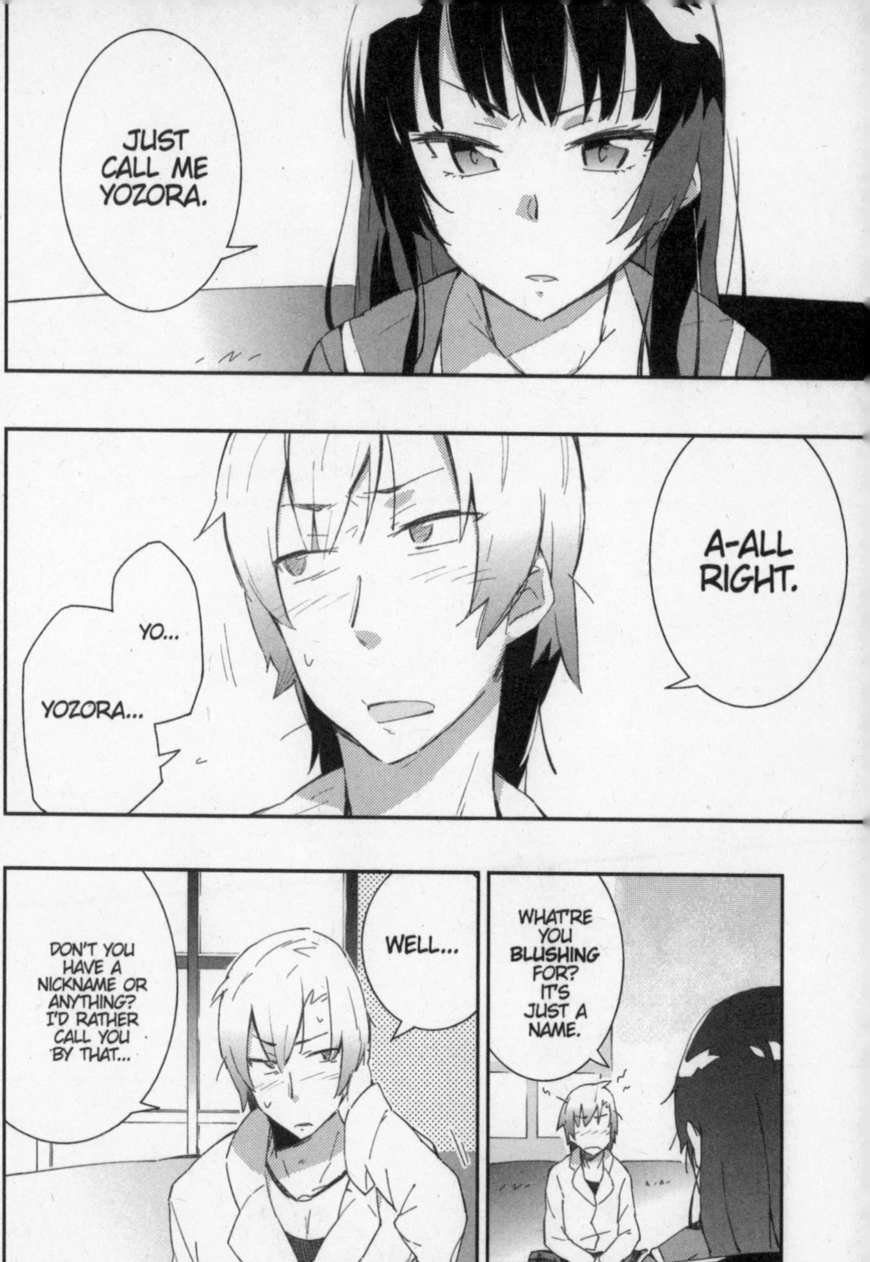
JUST CALL ME YOZORA.
A-ALL RIGHT.
YO...
YOZORA...
WHAT'RE YOU BLUSHING FOR? IT'S JUST A NAME.
WELL...
DON'T YOU HAVE A NICKNAME OR ANYTHING? I'D RATHER CALL YOU BY THAT...

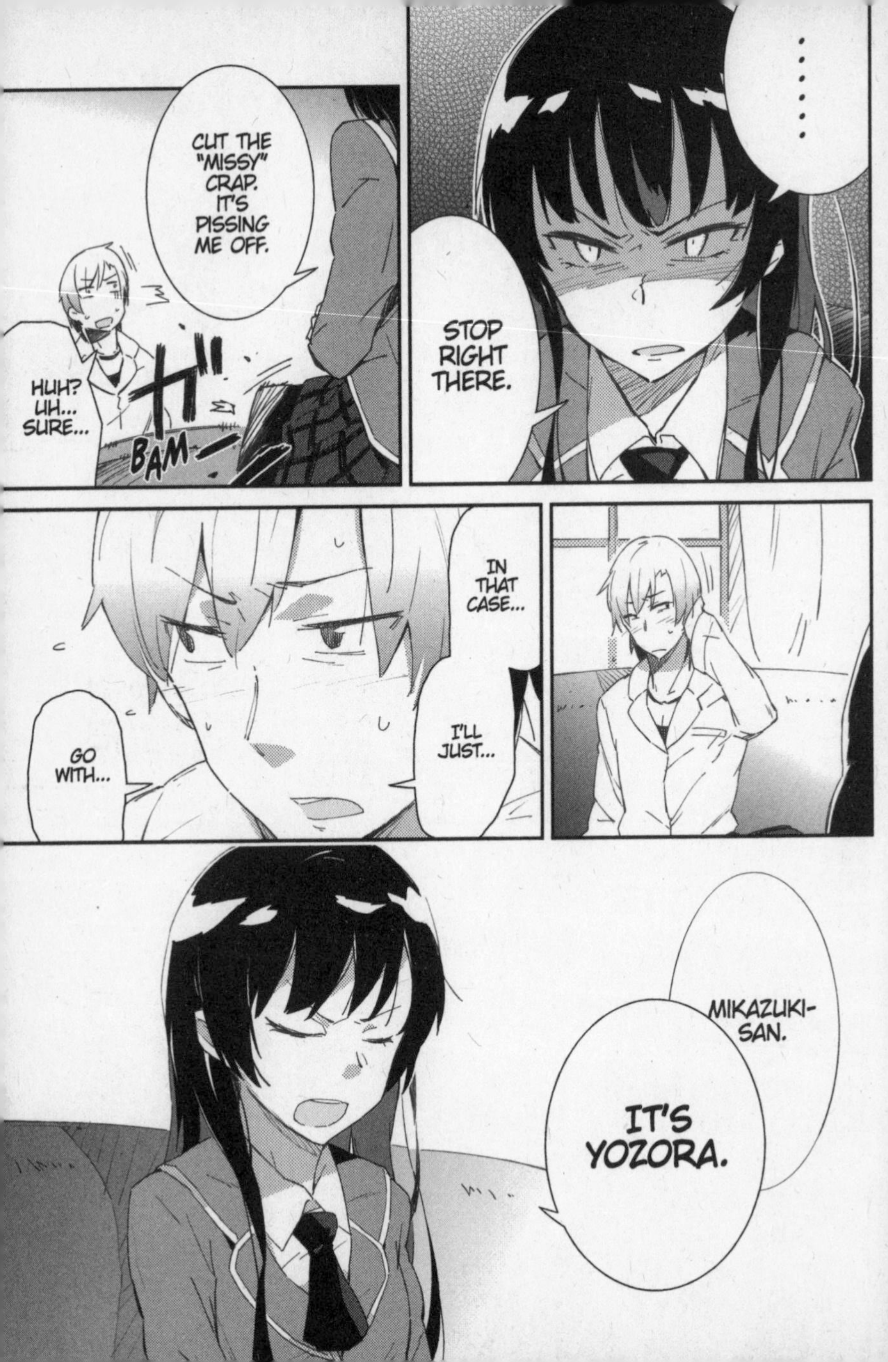
......
STOP RIGHT THERE.
CUT THE "MISSY" CRAP. IT'S PISSING ME OFF.
BAM
HUH? UH... SURE...
IN THAT CASE...
I'LL JUST...
GO WITH...
MIKAZUKI-SAN.
IT'S YOZORA.

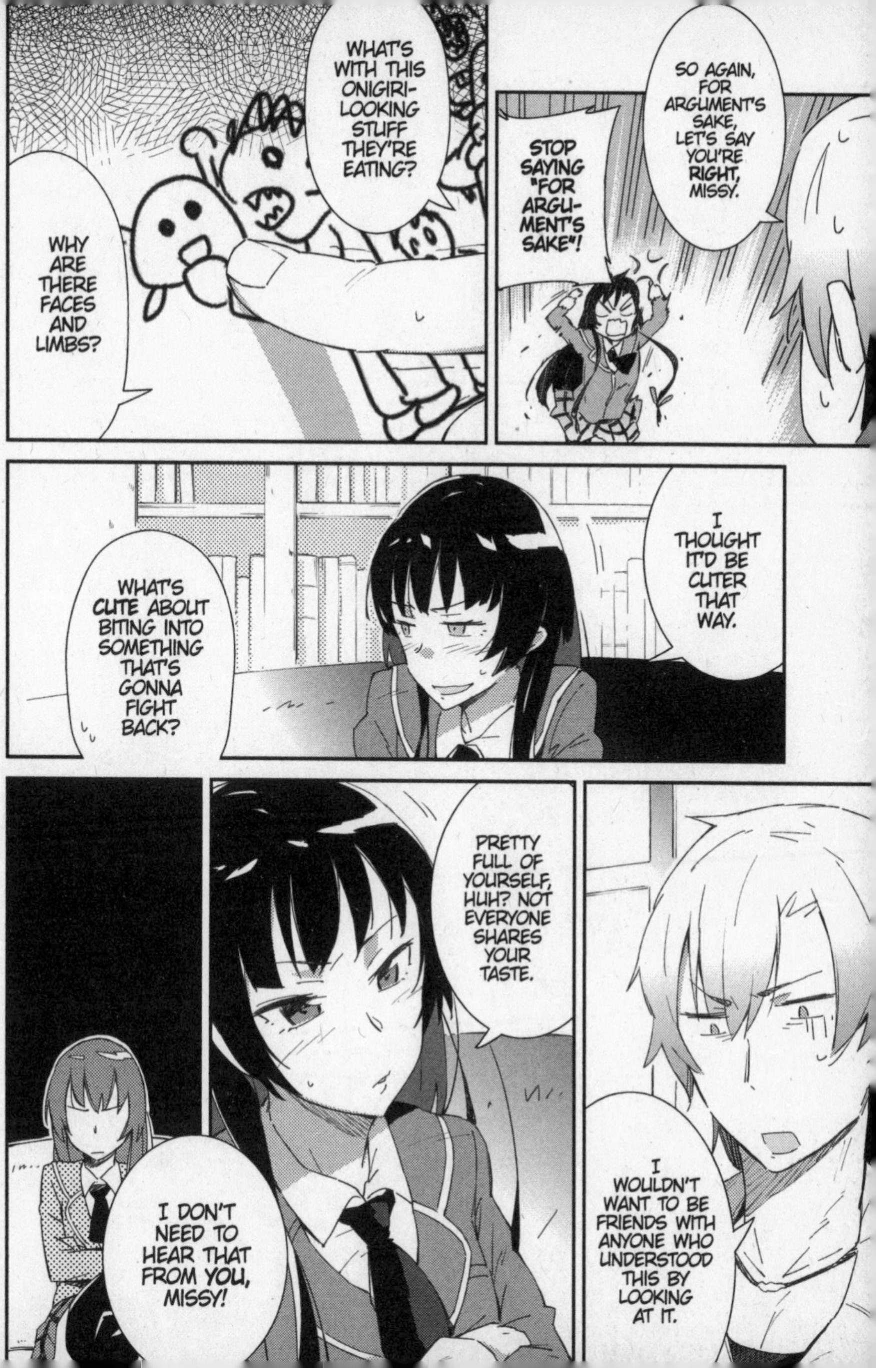
SO AGAIN, FOR ARGUMENT'S SAKE, LET'S SAY YOU'RE RIGHT, MISSY.
STOP SAYING "FOR ARGUMENT'S SAKE"!
WHAT'S WITH THIS ONIGIRI-LOOKING STUFF THEY'RE EATING?
WHY ARE THERE FACES AND LIMBS?
I THOUGHT IT'D BE CUTER THAT WAY.
WHAT'S CUTE ABOUT BITING INTO SOMETHING THAT'S GONNA FIGHT BACK?
I WOULDN'T WANT TO BE FRIENDS WITH ANYONE WHO UNDERSTOOD THIS BY LOOKING AT IT.
PRETTY FULL OF YOURSELF, HUH? NOT EVERYONE SHARES YOUR TASTE.
I DON'T NEED TO HEAR THAT FROM YOU, MISSY!

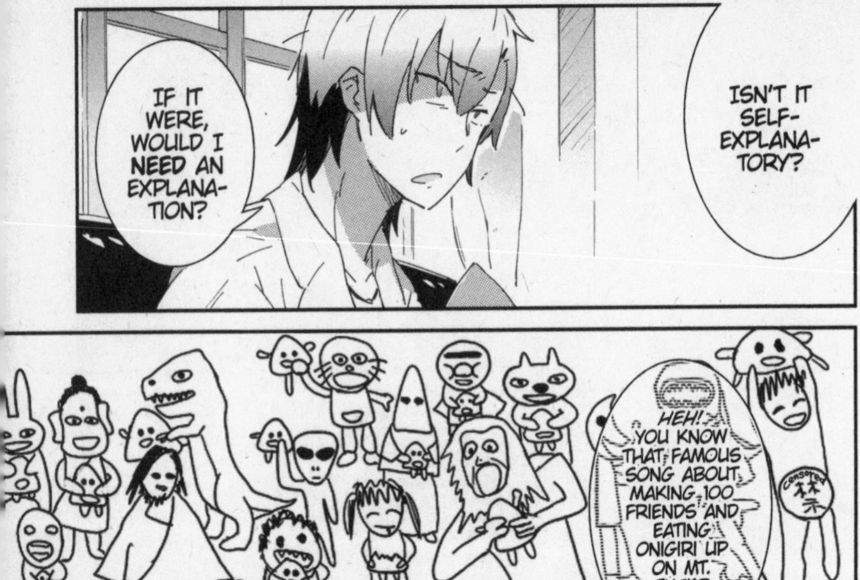
ISN'T IT SELF-EXPLANATORY?
IF IT WERE, WOULD I NEED AN EXPLANATION?
HEH! YOU KNOW THAT FAMOUS SONG ABOUT MAKING 100 FRIENDS AND EATING ONIGIRI UP ON MT. FUJI*?
I WAS INSPIRED TO DRAW THAT SCENE. IT'S A GOOD DEPICTION, HUH?
I... SEE...?
censored
MT. FUJI

*"Ichinensei ni Nattara," or "When I'm a first-grader."

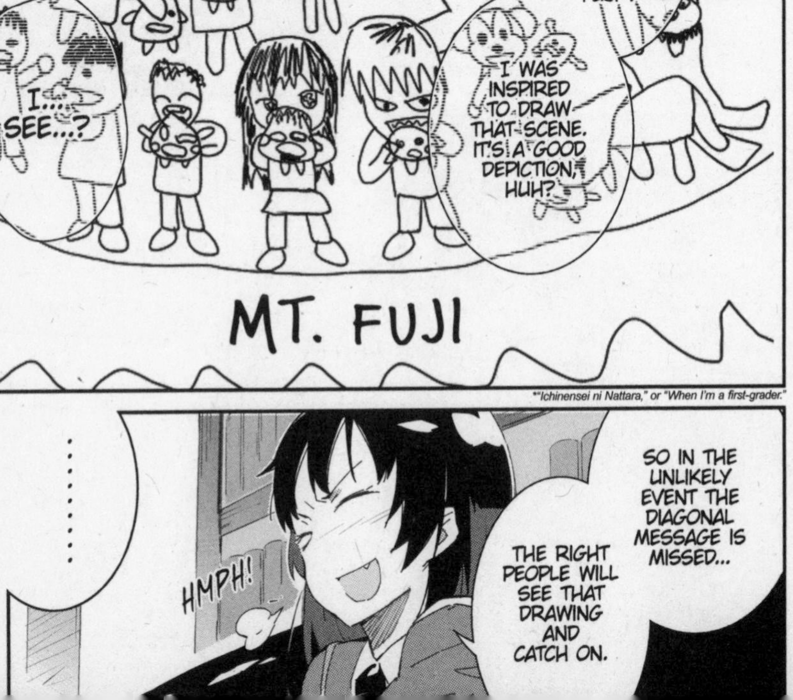
SO IN THE UNLIKELY EVENT THE DIAGONAL MESSAGE IS MISSED...
THE RIGHT PEOPLE WILL SEE THAT DRAWING AND CATCH ON.
HMPH!
......

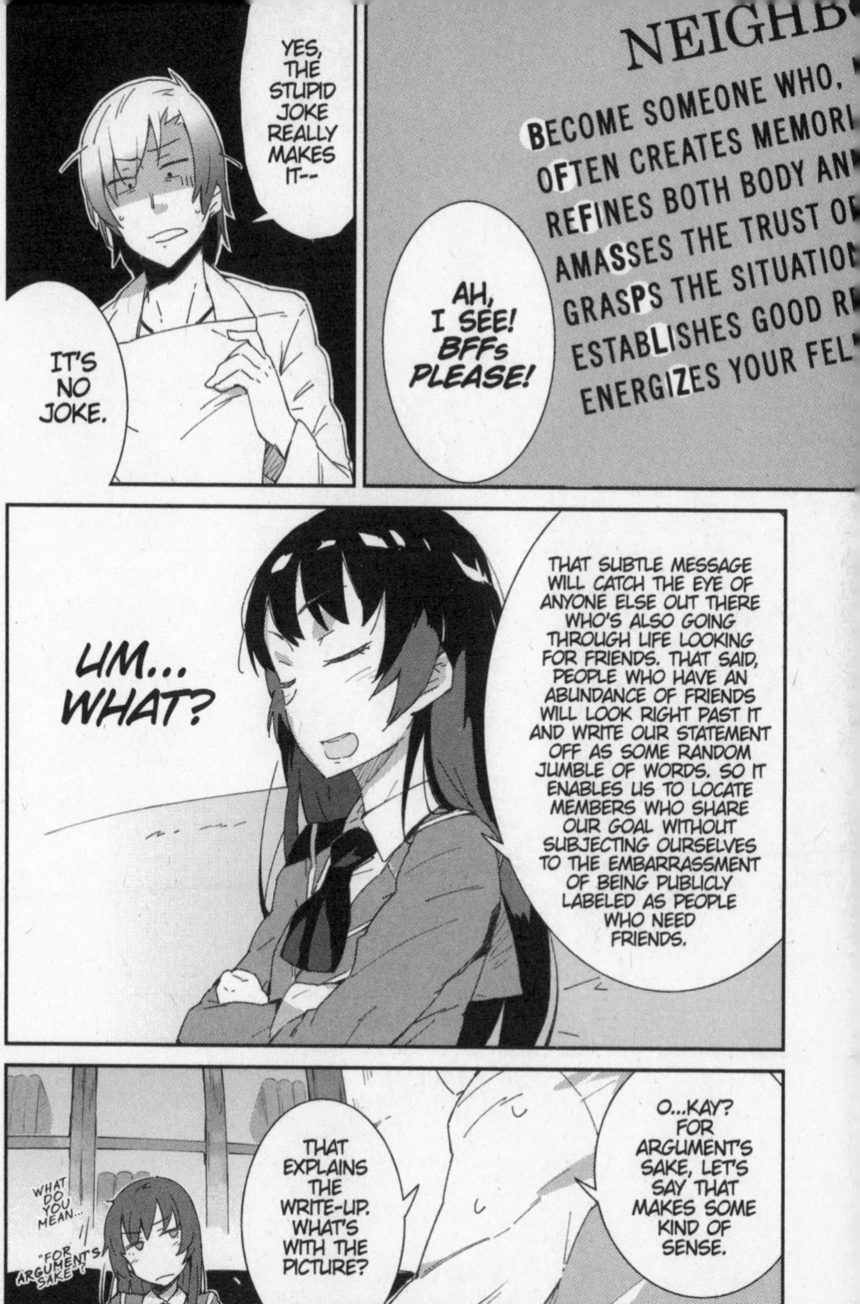
NEIGHB
BECOME SOMEONE WHO,
OFTEN CREATES MEMORI
REFINES BOTH BODY AN
AMASSES THE TRUST OF
GRASPS THE SITUATIO
ESTABLISHES GOOD R
ENERGIZES YOUR FEL
AH, I SEE! BFFs PLEASE!
YES, THE STUPID JOKE REALLY MAKES IT--
IT'S NO JOKE.
THAT SUBTLE MESSAGE WILL CATCH THE EYE OF ANYONE ELSE OUT THERE WHO'S ALSO GOING THROUGH LIFE LOOKING FOR FRIENDS. THAT SAID, PEOPLE WHO HAVE AN ABUNDANCE OF FRIENDS WILL LOOK RIGHT PAST IT AND WRITE OUR STATEMENT OFF AS SOME RANDOM JUMBLE OF WORDS. SO IT ENABLES US TO LOCATE MEMBERS WHO SHARE OUR GOAL WITHOUT SUBJECTING OURSELVES TO THE EMBARRASSMENT OF BEING PUBLICLY LABELED AS PEOPLE WHO NEED FRIENDS.
UM... WHAT?
O...KAY? FOR ARGUMENT'S SAKE, LET'S SAY THAT MAKES SOME KIND OF SENSE.
THAT EXPLAINS THE WRITE-UP. WHAT'S WITH THE PICTURE?
WHAT DO YOU MEAN... "FOR ARGUMENT'S SAKE"?

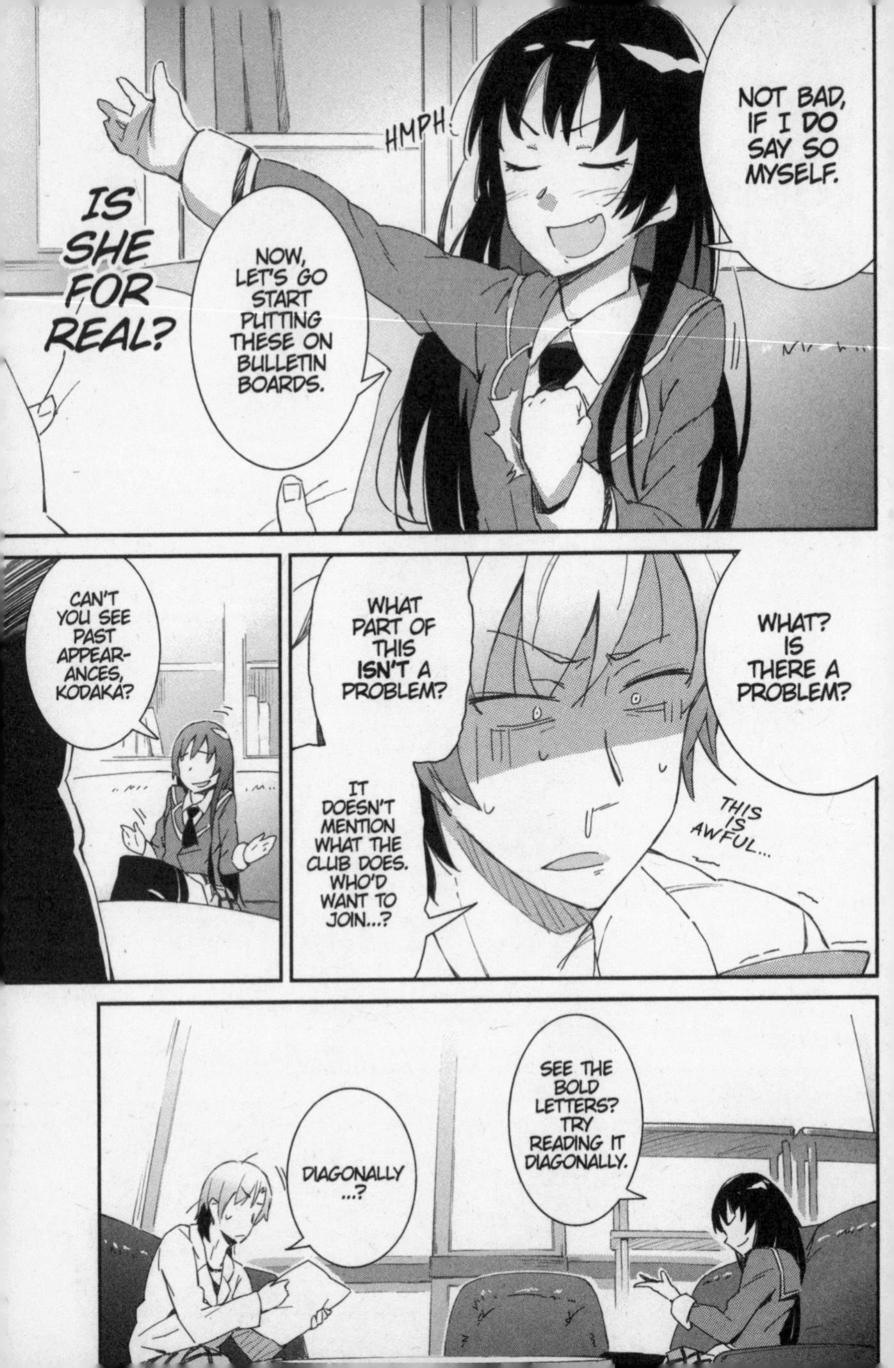
NOT BAD, IF I DO SAY SO MYSELF.
HMPH
NOW, LET'S GO START PUTTING THESE ON BULLETIN BOARDS.
IS SHE FOR REAL?
WHAT? IS THERE A PROBLEM?
THIS IS AWFUL...
WHAT PART OF THIS ISN'T A PROBLEM?
IT DOESN'T MENTION WHAT THE CLUB DOES. WHO'D WANT TO JOIN...?
CAN'T YOU SEE PAST APPEAR-ANCES, KODAKA?
SEE THE BOLD LETTERS? TRY READING IT DIAGONALLY.
DIAGONALLY ...?

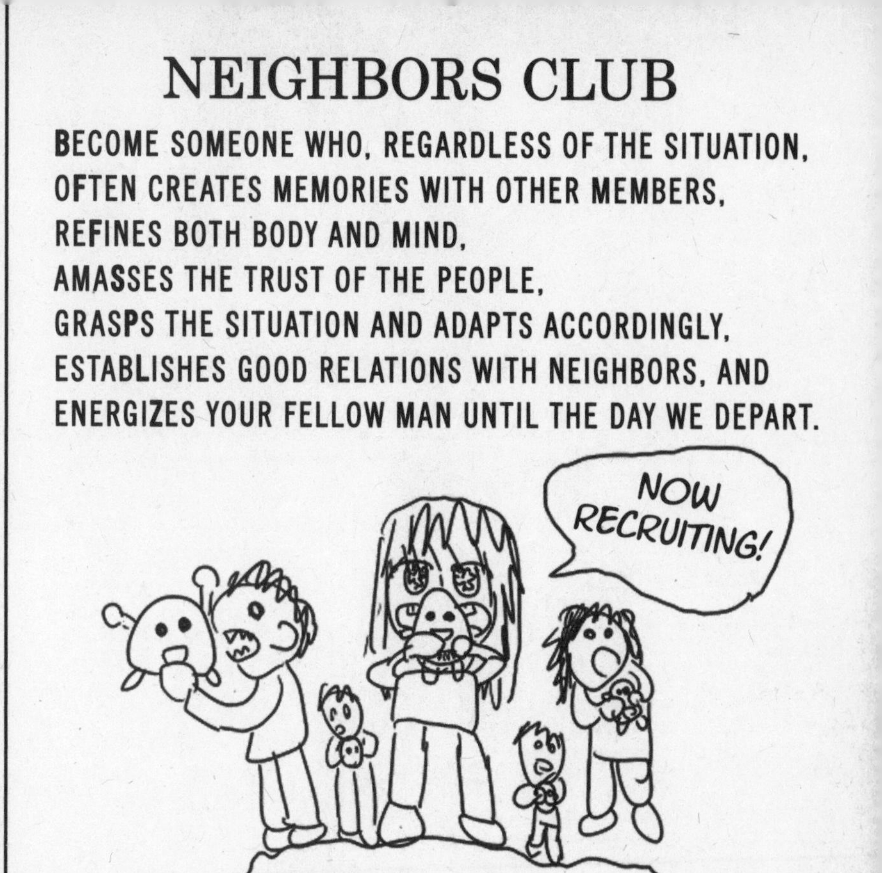
NEIGHBORS CLUB
BECOME SOMEONE WHO, REGARDLESS OF THE SITUATION,
OFTEN CREATES MEMORIES WITH OTHER MEMBERS,
REFINES BOTH BODY AND MIND,
AMASSES THE TRUST OF THE PEOPLE,
GRASPS THE SITUATION AND ADAPTS ACCORDINGLY,
ESTABLISHES GOOD RELATIONS WITH NEIGHBORS, AND
ENERGIZES YOUR FELLOW MAN UNTIL THE DAY WE DEPART.
NOW RECRUITING!
MEETING LOCATION: CHAPEL COMMON ROOM 4
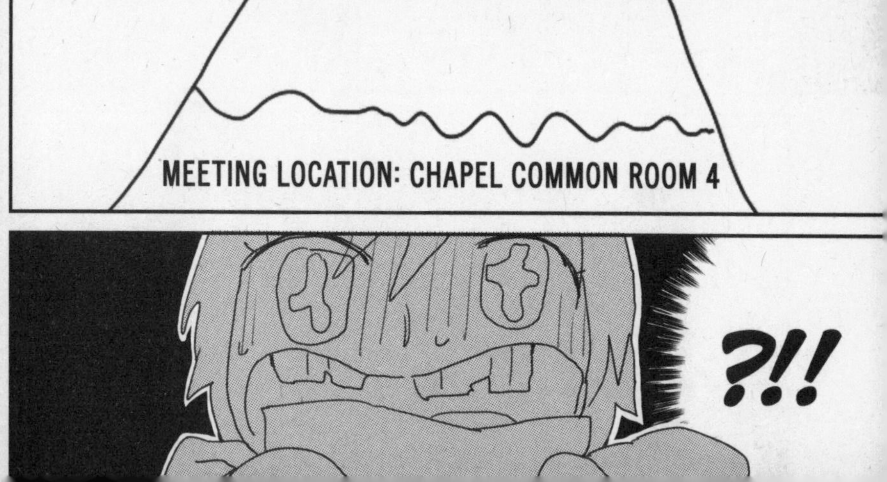
?!!

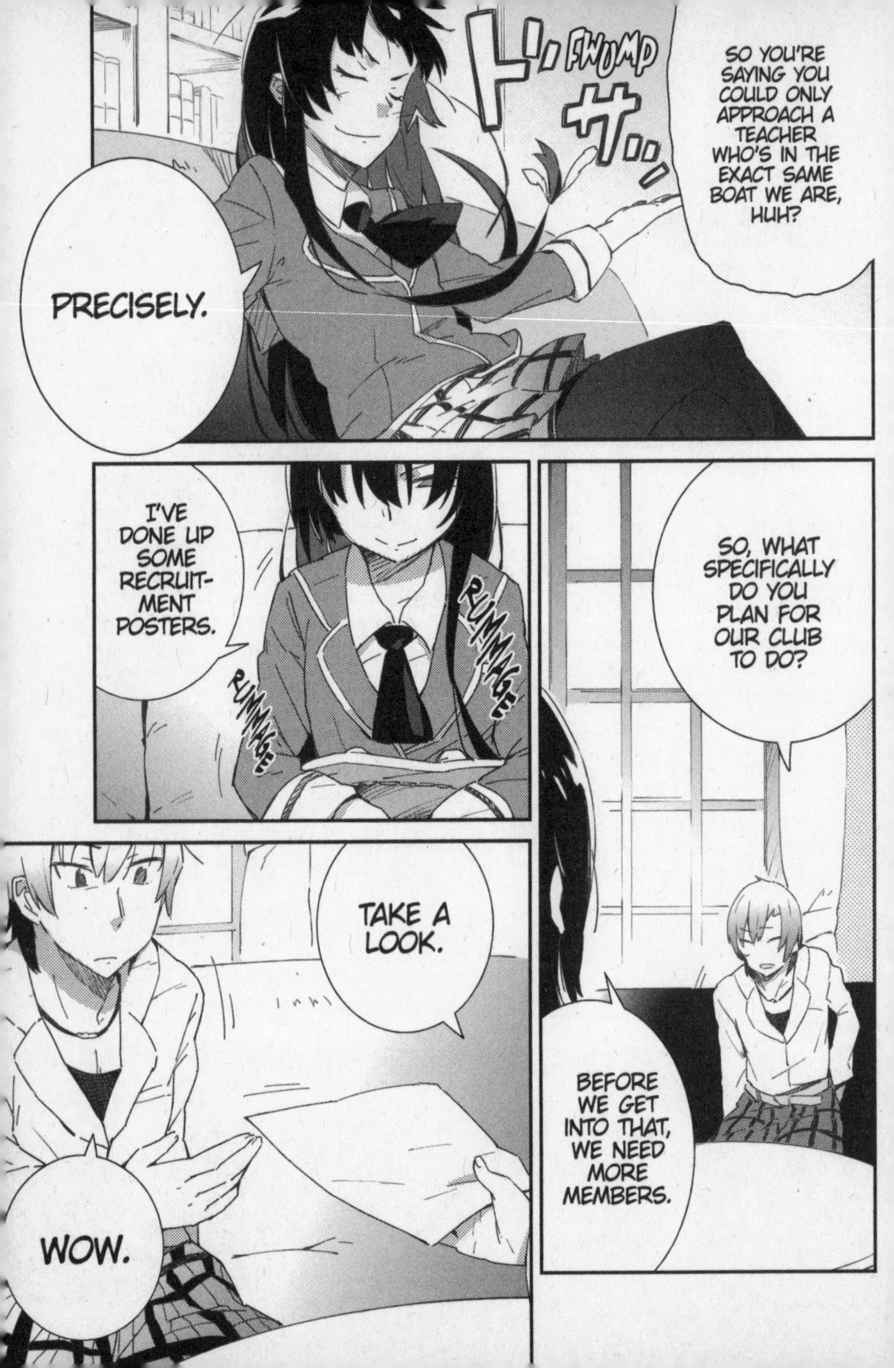
SO YOU'RE SAYING YOU COULD ONLY APPROACH A TEACHER WHO'S IN THE EXACT SAME BOAT WE ARE, HUH?
FWUMP
PRECISELY.
SO, WHAT SPECIFICALLY DO YOU PLAN FOR OUR CLUB TO DO?
BEFORE WE GET INTO THAT, WE NEED MORE MEMBERS.
I'VE DONE UP SOME RECRUIT-MENT POSTERS.
RUMMAGE
RUMMAGE
TAKE A LOOK.
WOW.

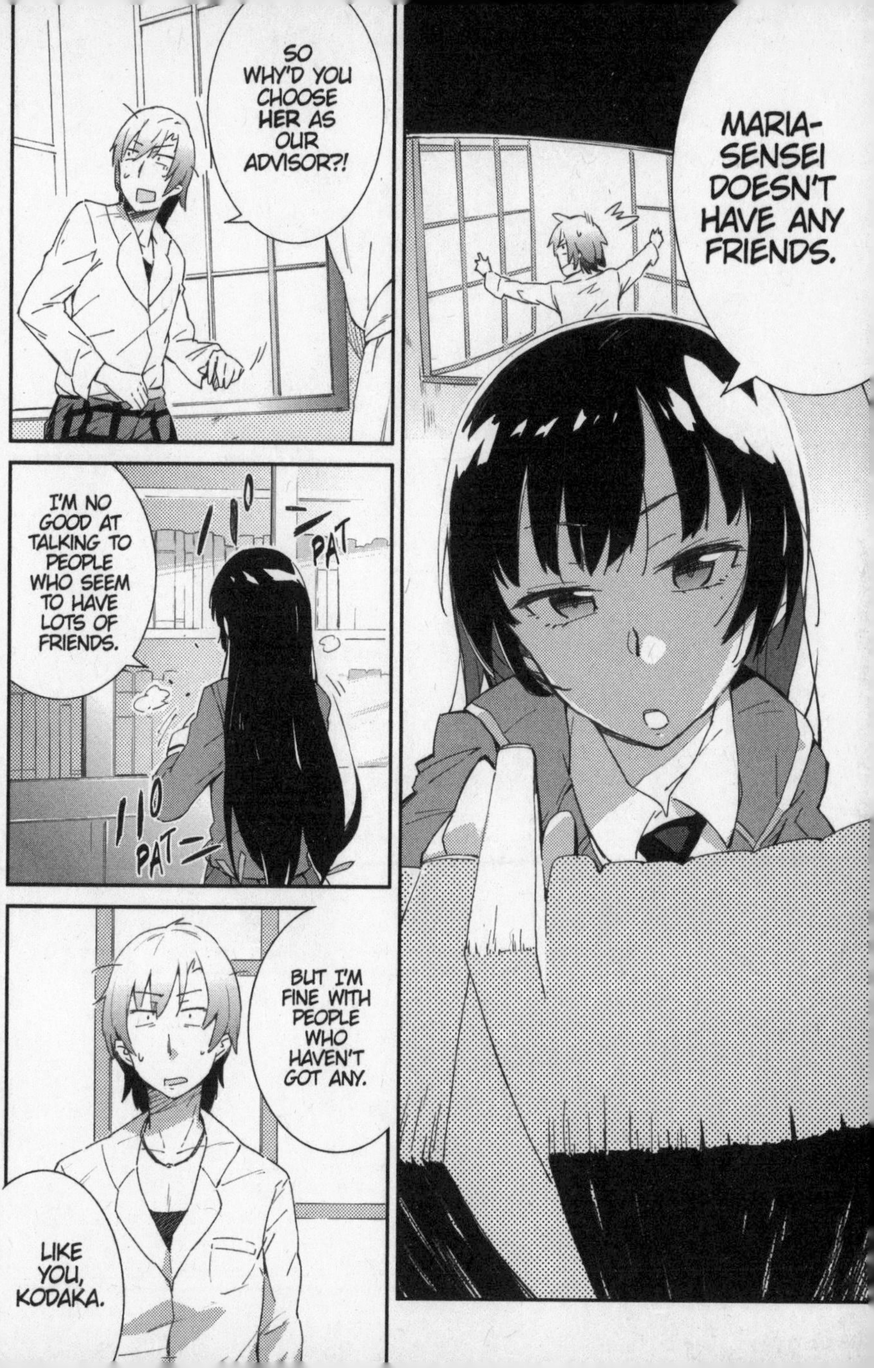
MARIA-SENSEI DOESN'T HAVE ANY FRIENDS.
SO WHY'D YOU CHOOSE HER AS OUR ADVISOR?!
I'M NO GOOD AT TALKING TO PEOPLE WHO SEEM TO HAVE LOTS OF FRIENDS.
PAT
PAT
BUT I'M FINE WITH PEOPLE WHO HAVEN'T GOT ANY.
LIKE YOU, KODAKA.

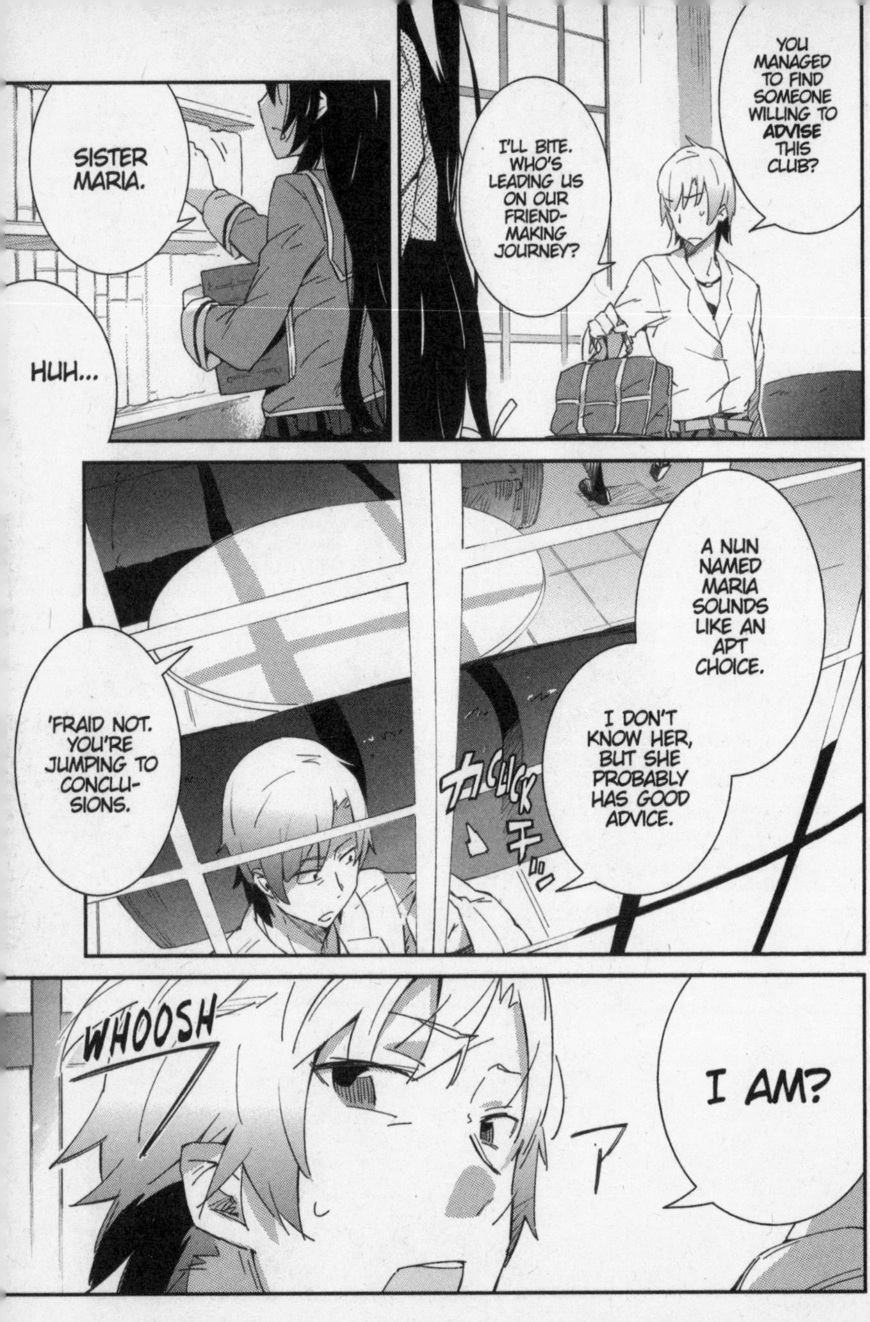
YOU MANAGED TO FIND SOMEONE WILLING TO ADVISE THIS CLUB?
I'LL BITE. WHO'S LEADING US ON OUR FRIEND-MAKING JOURNEY?
SISTER MARIA.
HUH...
A NUN NAMED MARIA SOUNDS LIKE AN APT CHOICE.
I DON'T KNOW HER, BUT SHE PROBABLY HAS GOOD ADVICE.
CLICK
'FRAID NOT. YOU'RE JUMPING TO CONCLUSIONS.
I AM?
WHOOSH

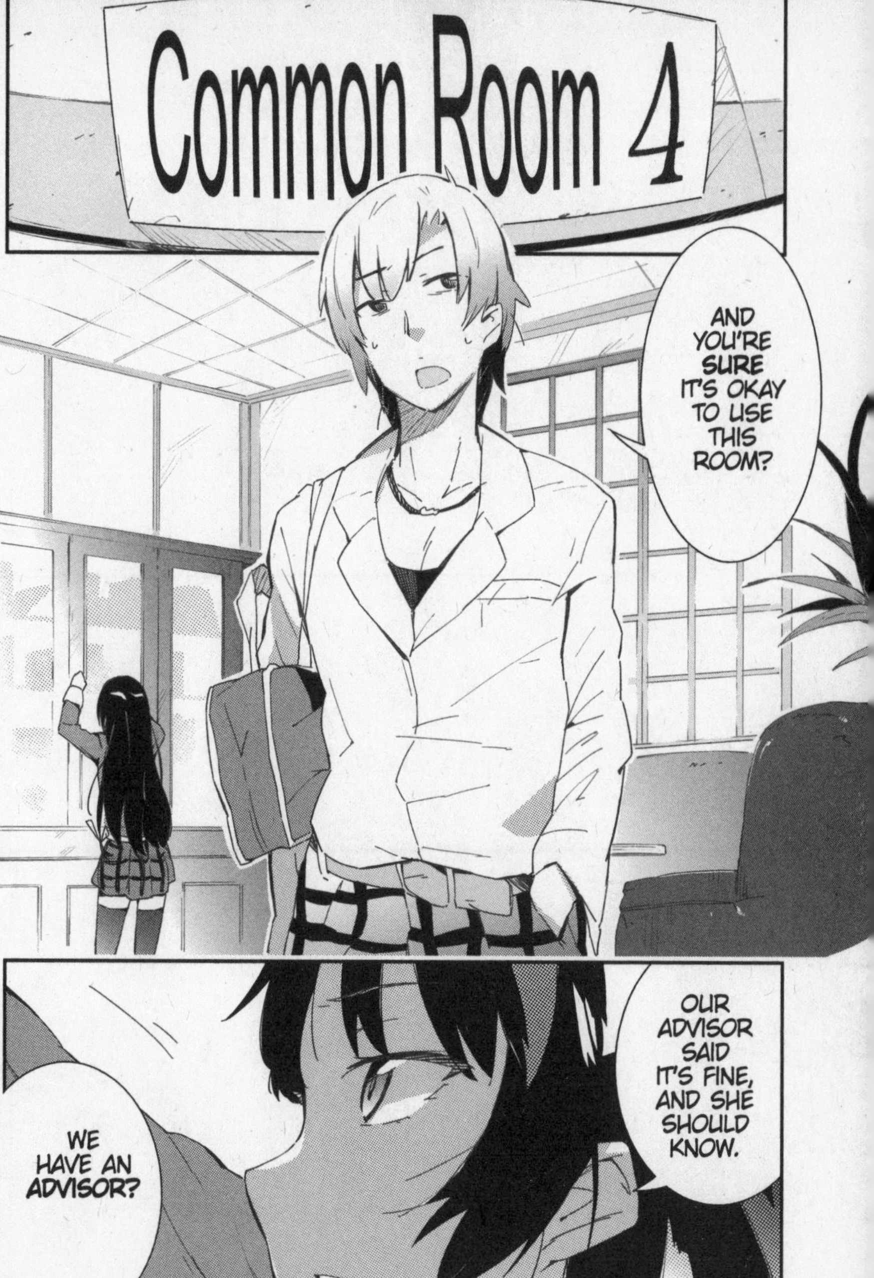
Common Room 4
AND YOU'RE SURE IT'S OKAY TO USE THIS ROOM?
OUR ADVISOR SAID IT'S FINE, AND SHE SHOULD KNOW.
WE HAVE AN ADVISOR?

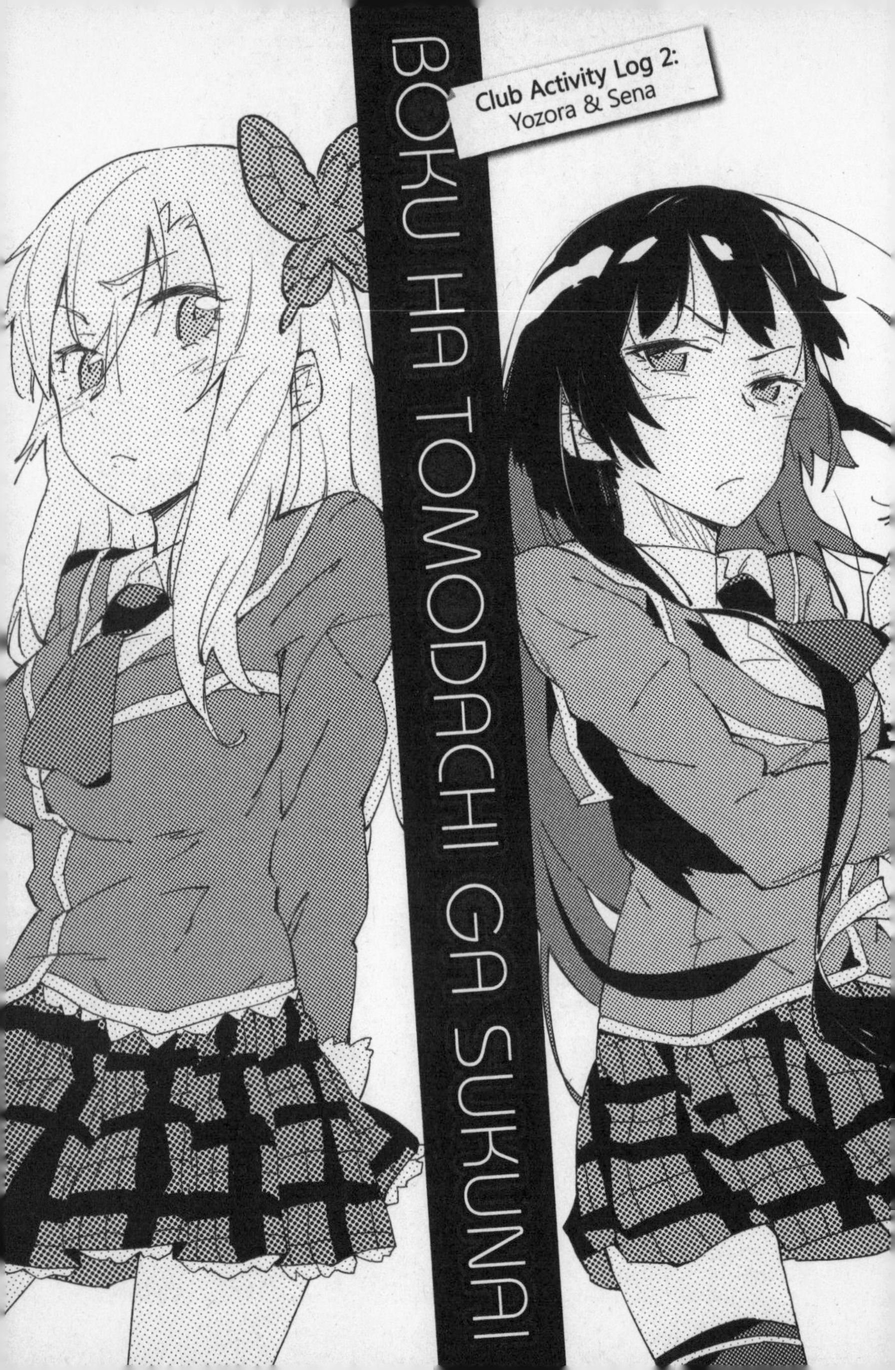
Club Activity Log 2:
Yozora & Sena
BOKU HA TOMODACHI GA SUKUNAI

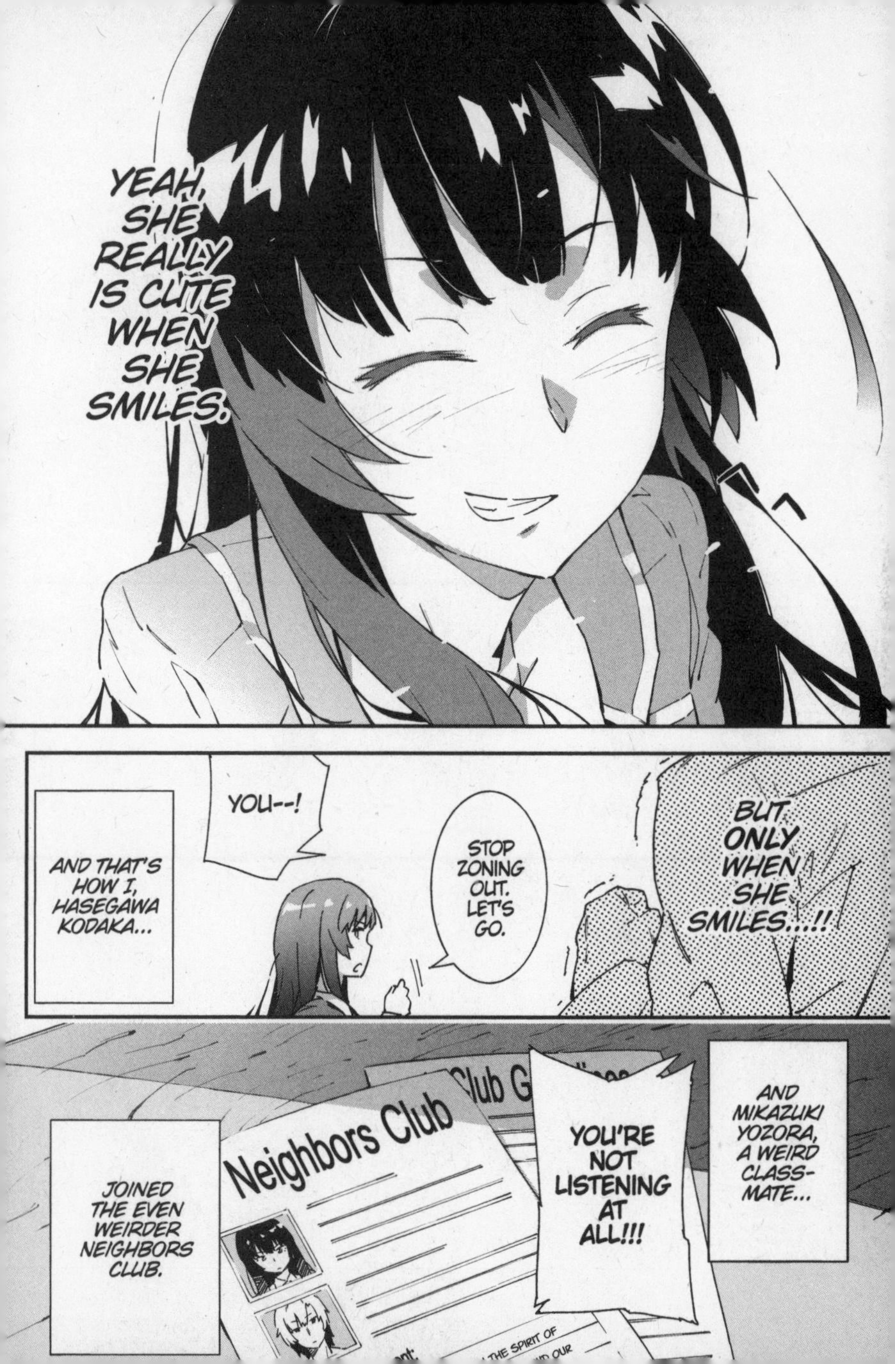
YEAH, SHE REALLY IS CUTE WHEN SHE SMILES.
BUT ONLY WHEN SHE SMILES...!!
STOP ZONING OUT. LET'S GO.
YOU--!
AND THAT'S HOW I, HASEGAWA KODAKA...
AND MIKAZUKI YOZORA, A WEIRD CLASSMATE...
YOU'RE NOT LISTENING AT ALL!!!
Neighbors Club
JOINED THE EVEN WEIRDER NEIGHBORS CLUB.

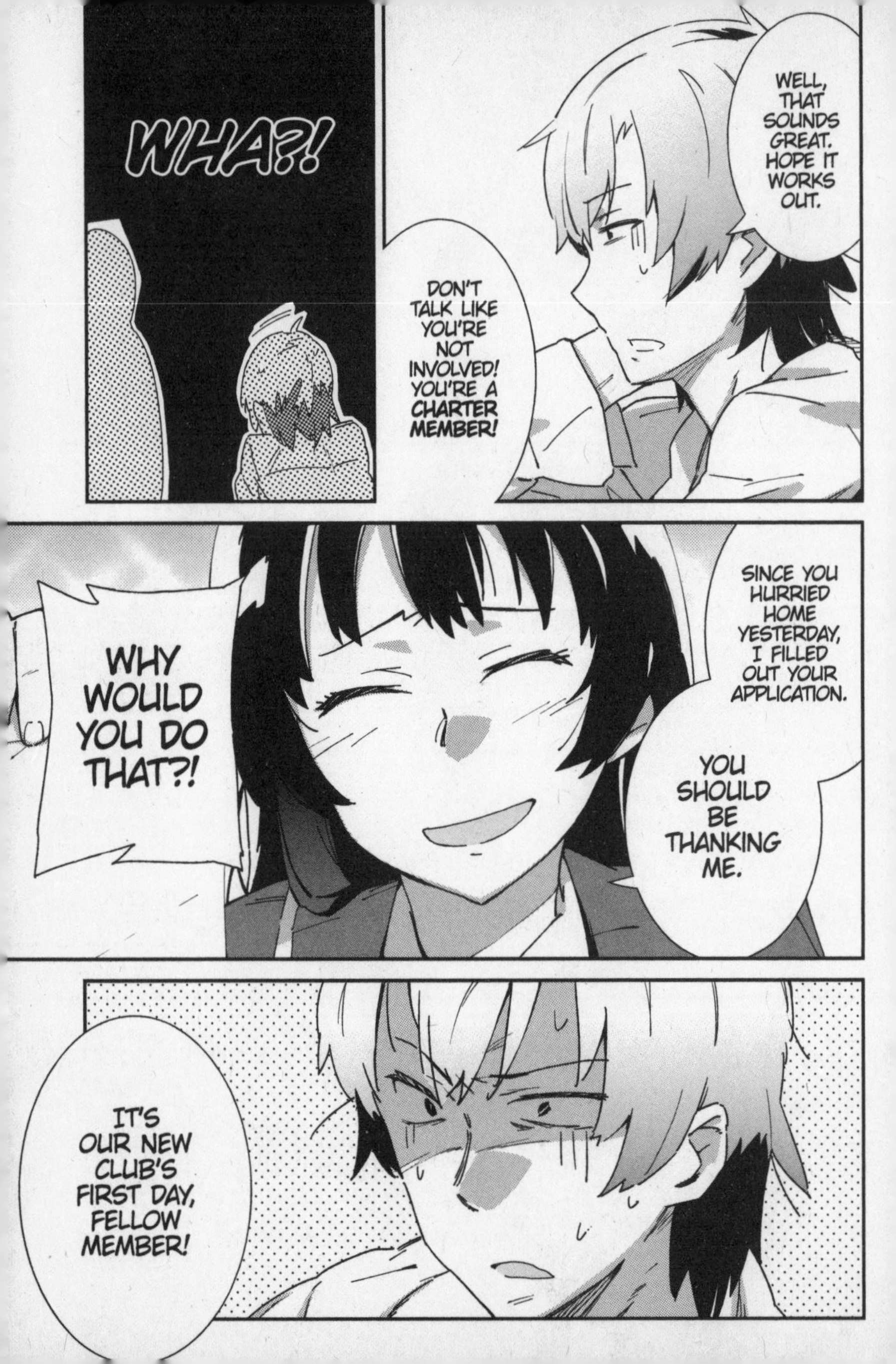
WELL, THAT SOUNDS GREAT. HOPE IT WORKS OUT.
DON'T TALK LIKE YOU'RE NOT INVOLVED! YOU'RE A CHARTER MEMBER!
WHA?!
SINCE YOU HURRIED HOME YESTERDAY, I FILLED OUT YOUR APPLICATION.
YOU SHOULD BE THANKING ME.
WHY WOULD YOU DO THAT?!
IT'S OUR NEW CLUB'S FIRST DAY, FELLOW MEMBER!

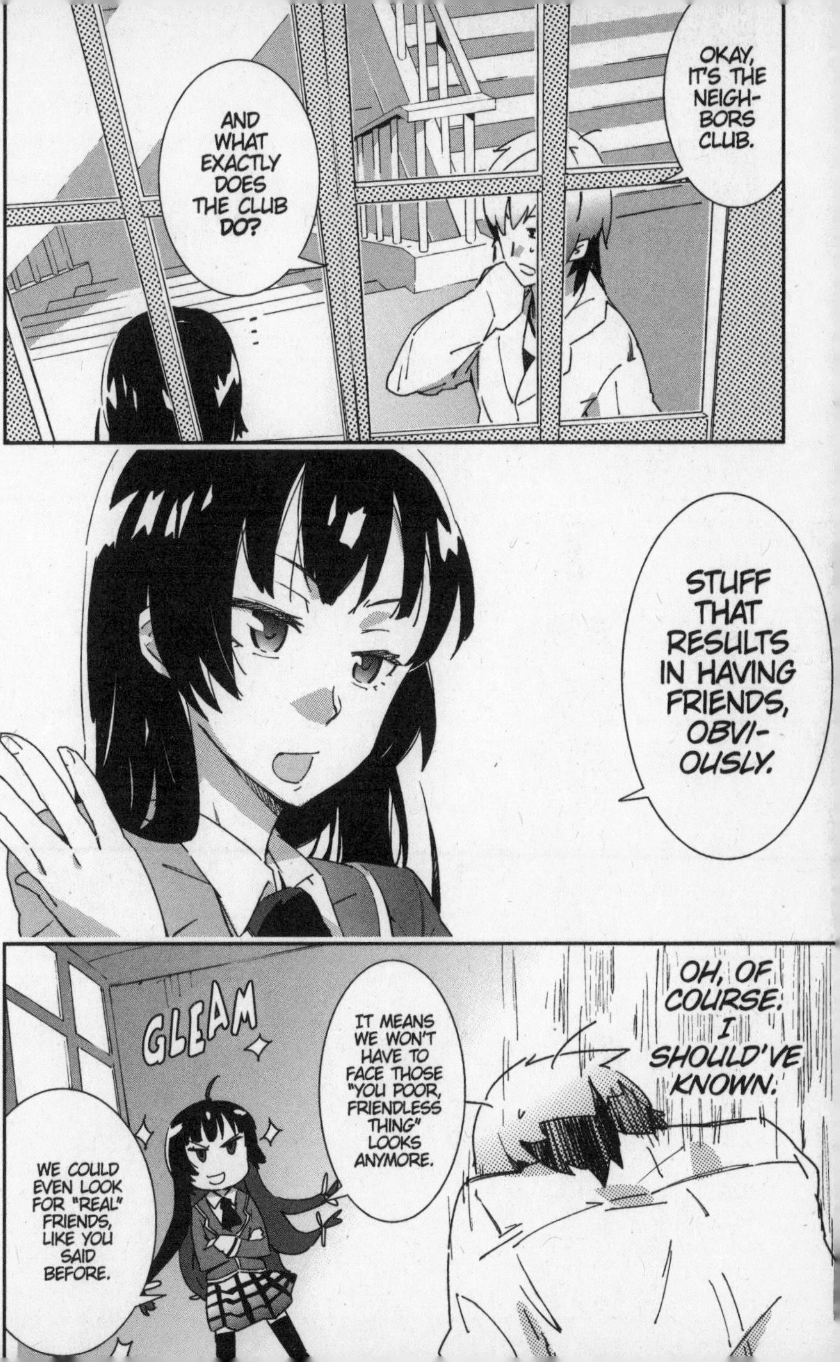
OKAY, IT'S THE NEIGHBORS CLUB.
AND WHAT EXACTLY DOES THE CLUB DO?
STUFF THAT RESULTS IN HAVING FRIENDS, OBVIOUSLY.
OH, OF COURSE. I SHOULD'VE KNOWN.
IT MEANS WE WON'T HAVE TO FACE THOSE "YOU POOR, FRIENDLESS THING" LOOKS ANYMORE.
GLEAM
WE COULD EVEN LOOK FOR "REAL" FRIENDS, LIKE YOU SAID BEFORE.

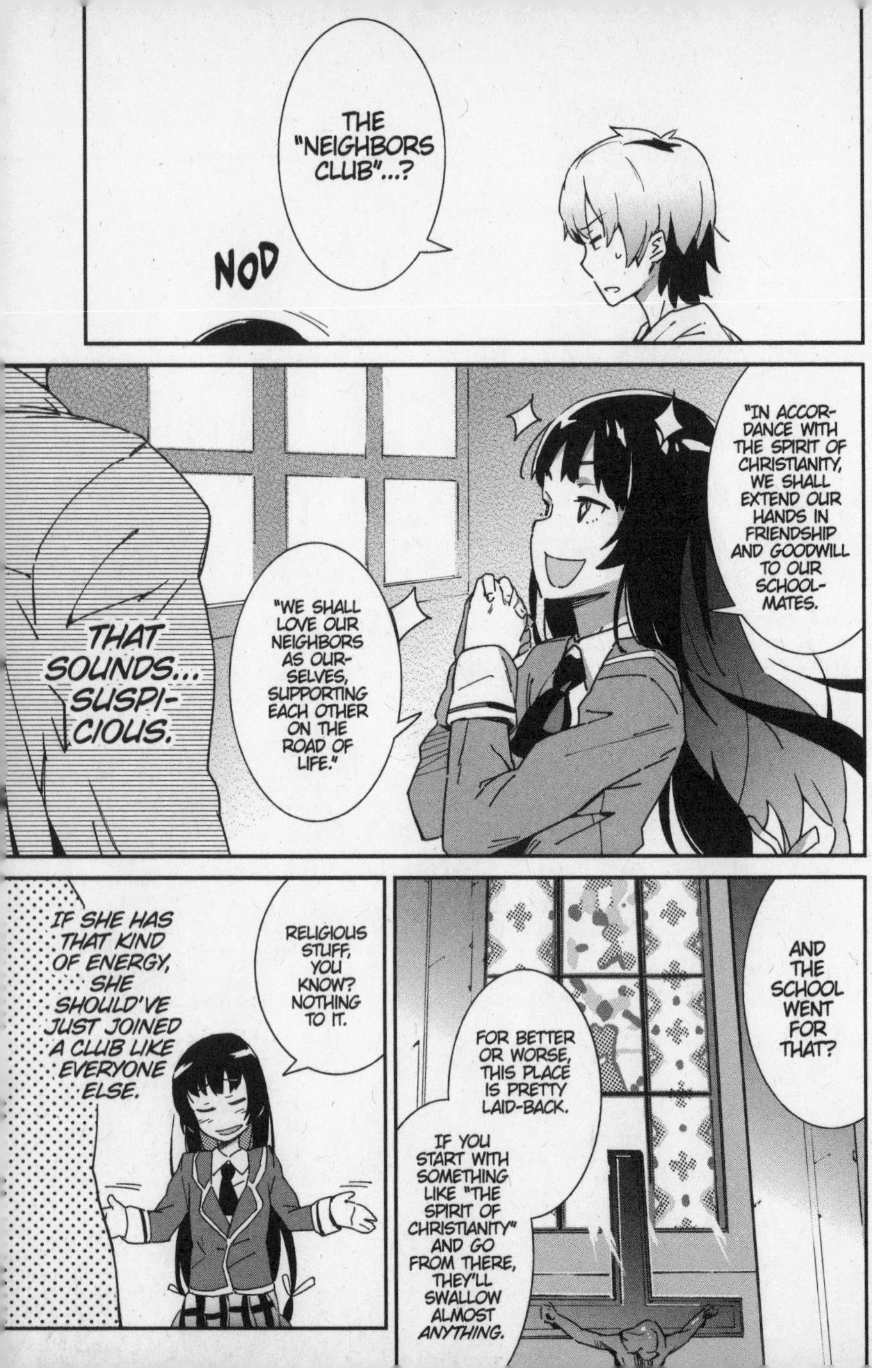
THE "NEIGHBORS CLUB"...?
NOD
"IN ACCORDANCE WITH THE SPIRIT OF CHRISTIANITY, WE SHALL EXTEND OUR HANDS IN FRIENDSHIP AND GOODWILL TO OUR SCHOOLMATES.
"WE SHALL LOVE OUR NEIGHBORS AS OURSELVES, SUPPORTING EACH OTHER ON THE ROAD OF LIFE."
THAT SOUNDS... SUSPICIOUS.
AND THE SCHOOL WENT FOR THAT?
FOR BETTER OR WORSE, THIS PLACE IS PRETTY LAID-BACK.
IF YOU START WITH SOMETHING LIKE "THE SPIRIT OF CHRISTIANITY" AND GO FROM THERE, THEY'LL SWALLOW ALMOST ANYTHING.
RELIGIOUS STUFF, YOU KNOW? NOTHING TO IT.
IF SHE HAS THAT KIND OF ENERGY, SHE SHOULD'VE JUST JOINED A CLUB LIKE EVERYONE ELSE.

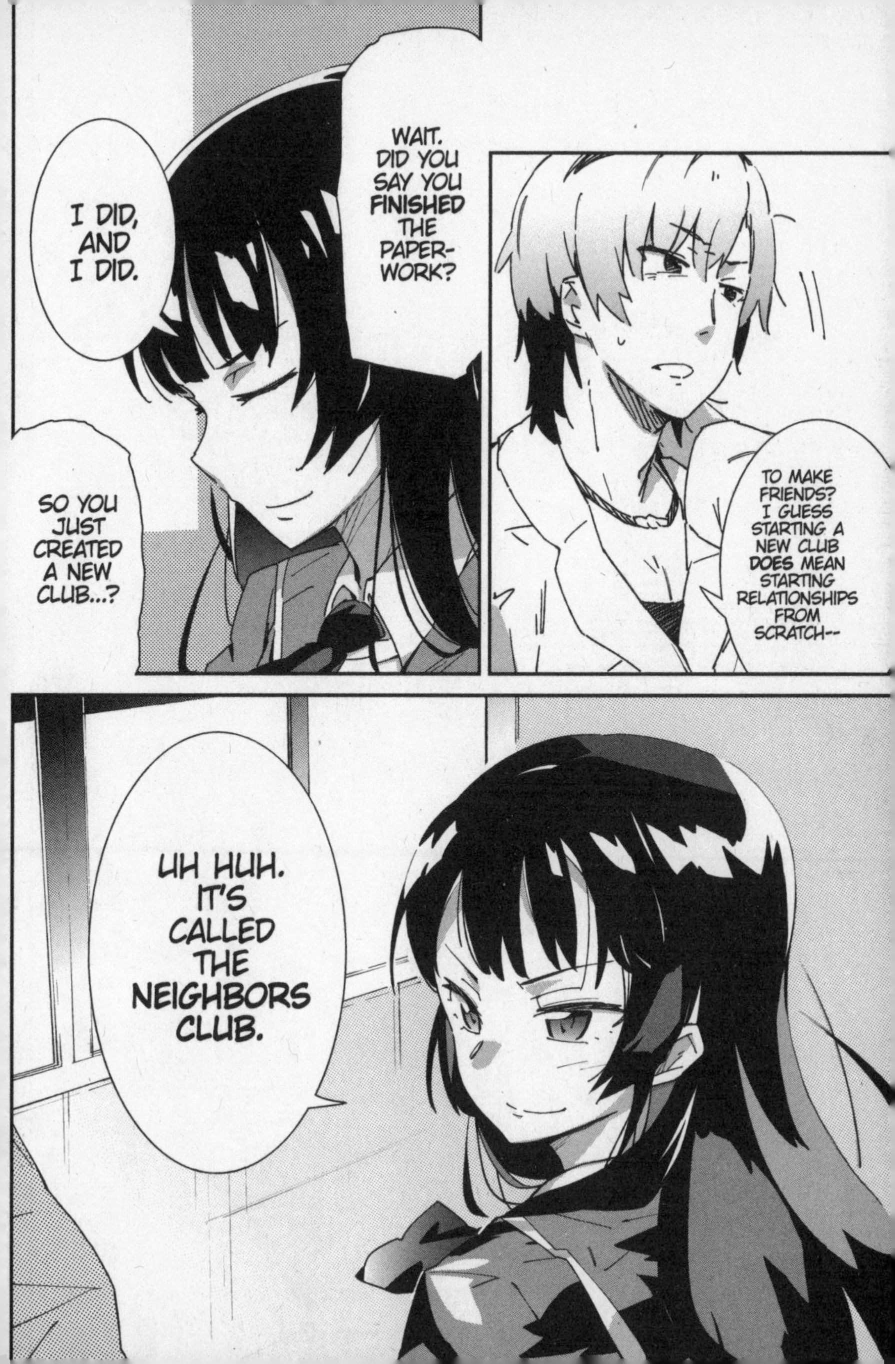
TO MAKE FRIENDS? I GUESS STARTING A NEW CLUB DOES MEAN STARTING RELATIONSHIPS FROM SCRATCH--
WAIT. DID YOU SAY YOU FINISHED THE PAPER-WORK?
I DID, AND I DID.
SO YOU JUST CREATED A NEW CLUB...?
UH HUH. IT'S CALLED THE NEIGHBORS CLUB.

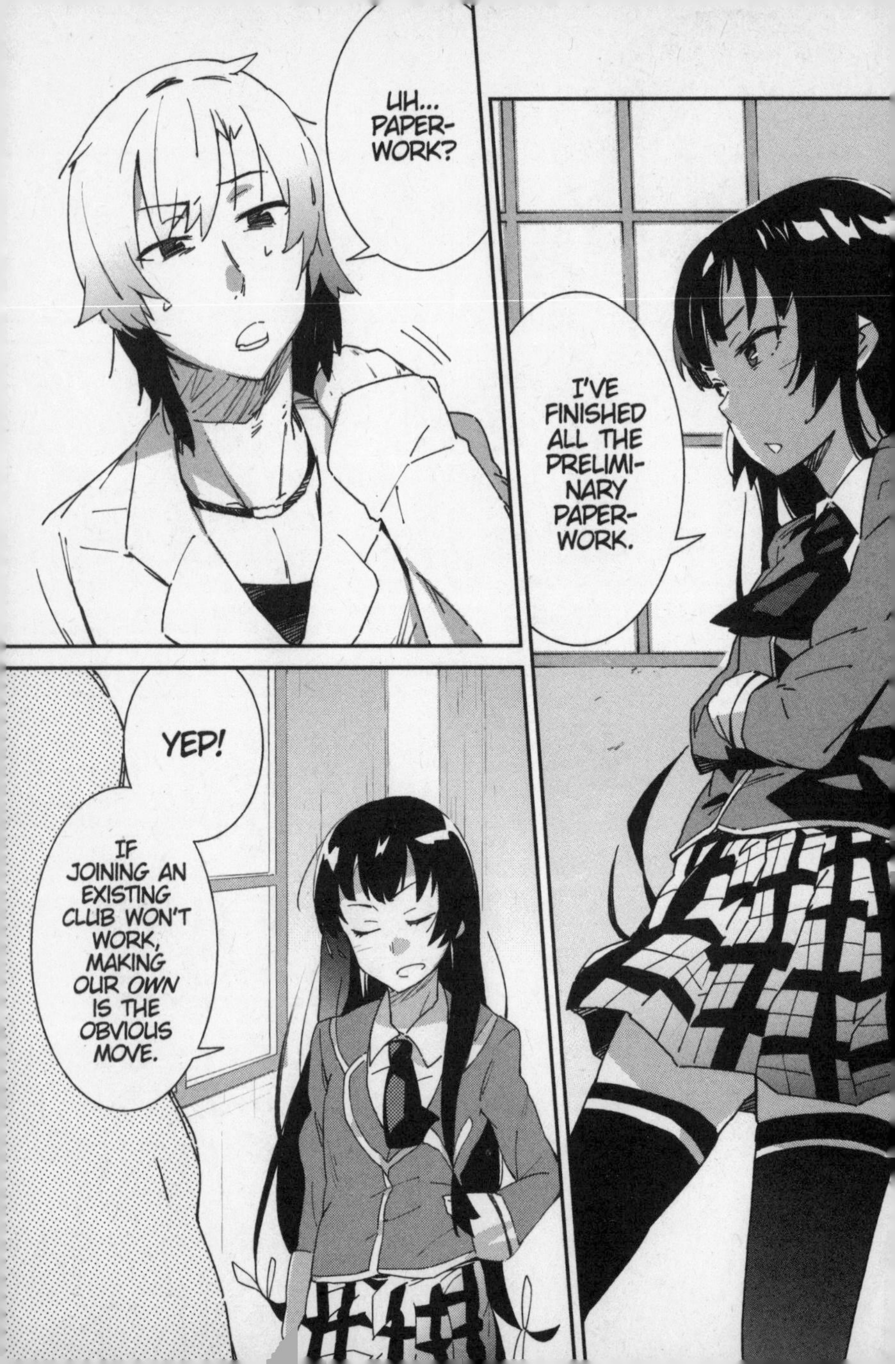

I'VE FINISHED ALL THE PRELIMINARY PAPERWORK.
UH... PAPERWORK?
YEP!
IF JOINING AN EXISTING CLUB WON'T WORK, MAKING OUR *OWN* IS THE OBVIOUS MOVE.

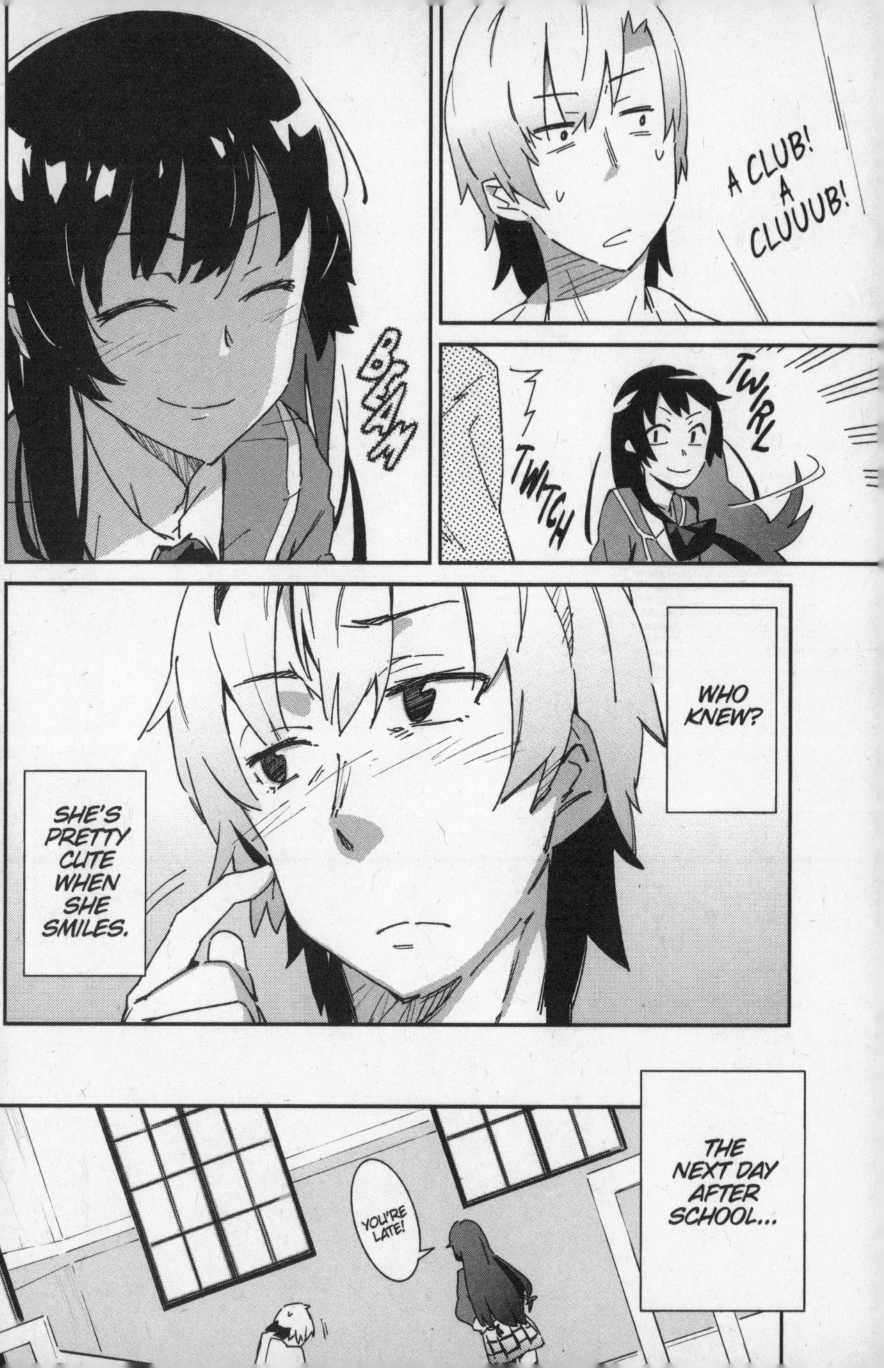
A CLUB! A CLUUUB!
TWIRL
TWITCH
BEAM
WHO KNEW?
SHE'S PRETTY CUTE WHEN SHE SMILES.
THE NEXT DAY AFTER SCHOOL...
YOU'RE LATE!

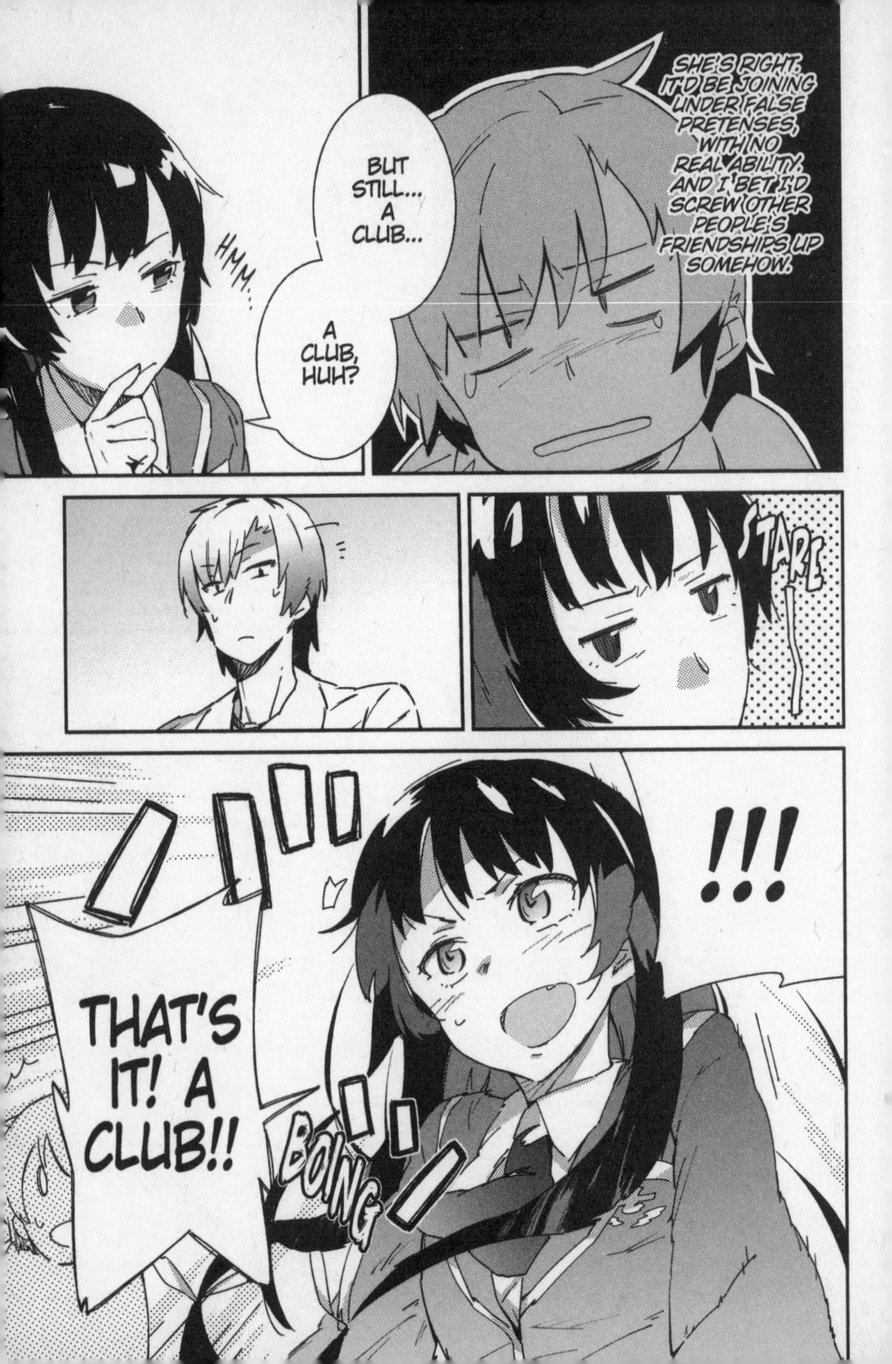
SHE'S RIGHT. IT'D BE JOINING UNDER FALSE PRETENSES, WITH NO REAL ABILITY. AND I BET I'D SCREW OTHER PEOPLE'S FRIENDSHIPS UP SOMEHOW.
BUT STILL... A CLUB...
A CLUB, HUH?
HMM...
STARE
!!!
THAT'S IT! A CLUB!!
BOING

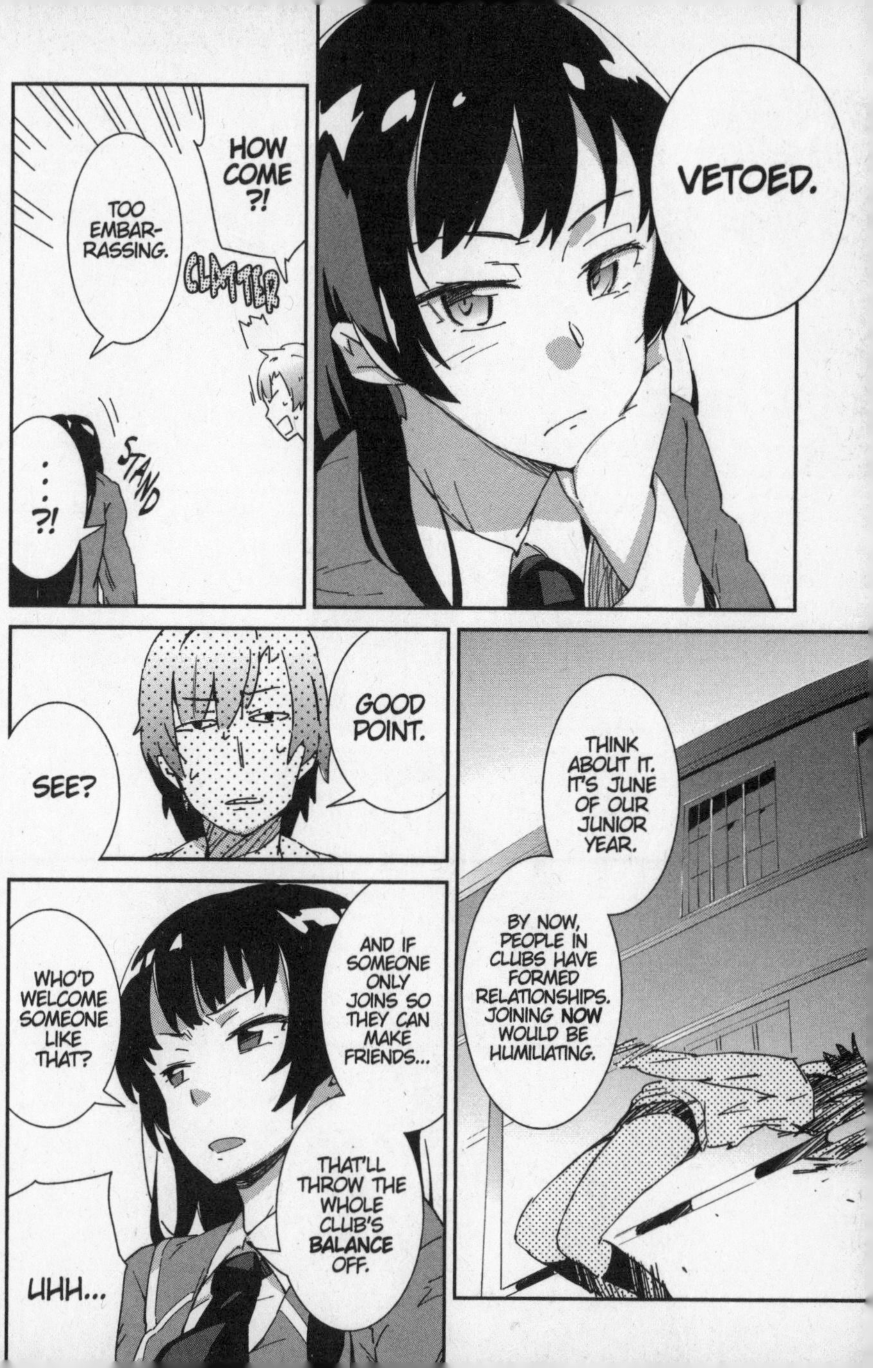
VETOED.
HOW COME ?!
CLATTER
TOO EMBAR-RASSING.
STAND
...?!
THINK ABOUT IT. IT'S JUNE OF OUR JUNIOR YEAR.
BY NOW, PEOPLE IN CLUBS HAVE FORMED RELATIONSHIPS. JOINING NOW WOULD BE HUMILIATING.
GOOD POINT.
SEE?
AND IF SOMEONE ONLY JOINS SO THEY CAN MAKE FRIENDS...
WHO'D WELCOME SOMEONE LIKE THAT?
THAT'LL THROW THE WHOLE CLUB'S BALANCE OFF.
UHH...

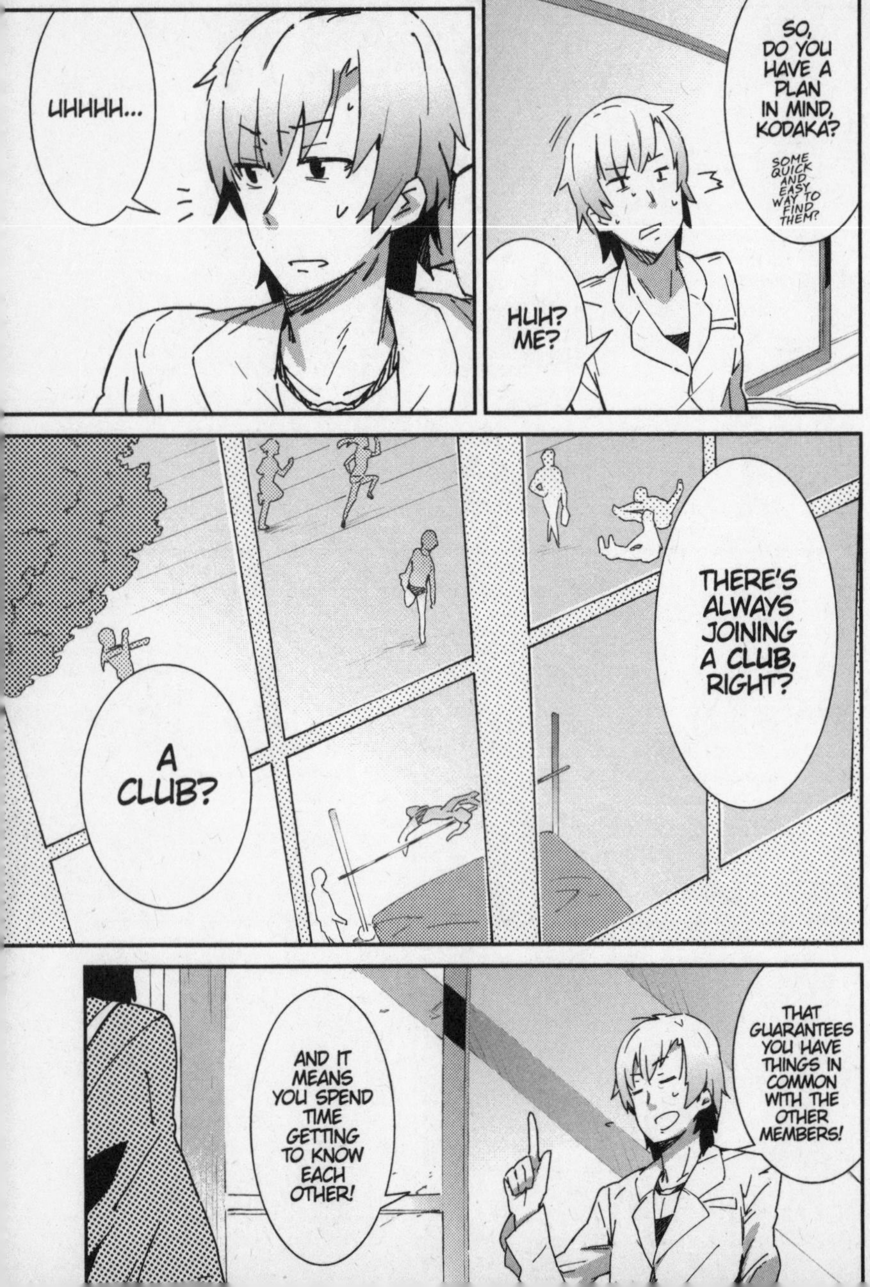
SO, DO YOU HAVE A PLAN IN MIND, KODAKA?
SOME QUICK AND EASY WAY TO FIND THEM?
HUH? ME?
UHHHH...
THERE'S ALWAYS JOINING A CLUB, RIGHT?
A CLUB?
THAT GUARANTEES YOU HAVE THINGS IN COMMON WITH THE OTHER MEMBERS!
AND IT MEANS YOU SPEND TIME GETTING TO KNOW EACH OTHER!

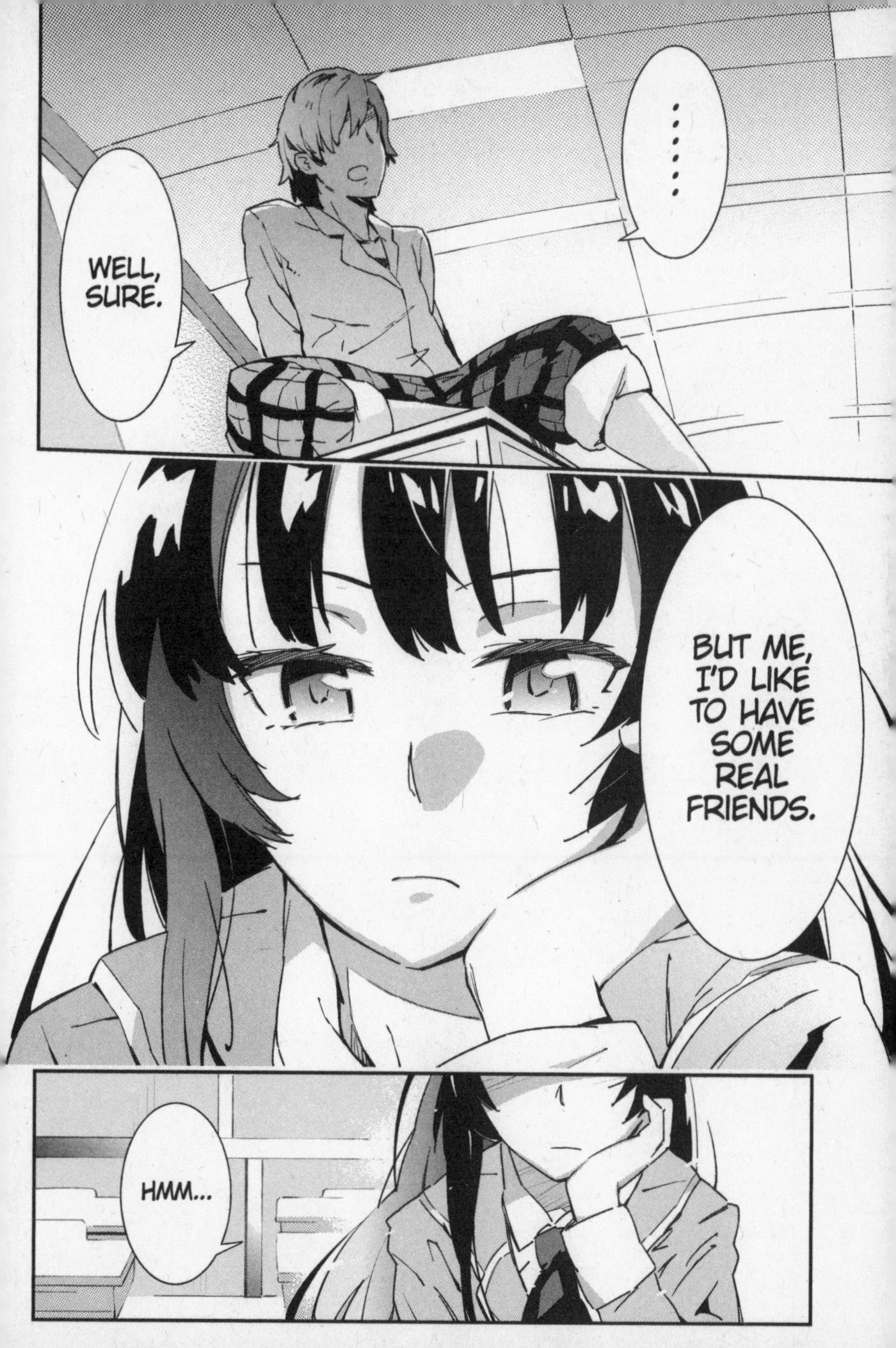

......
WELL, SURE.
BUT ME, I'D LIKE TO HAVE SOME REAL FRIENDS.
HMM...

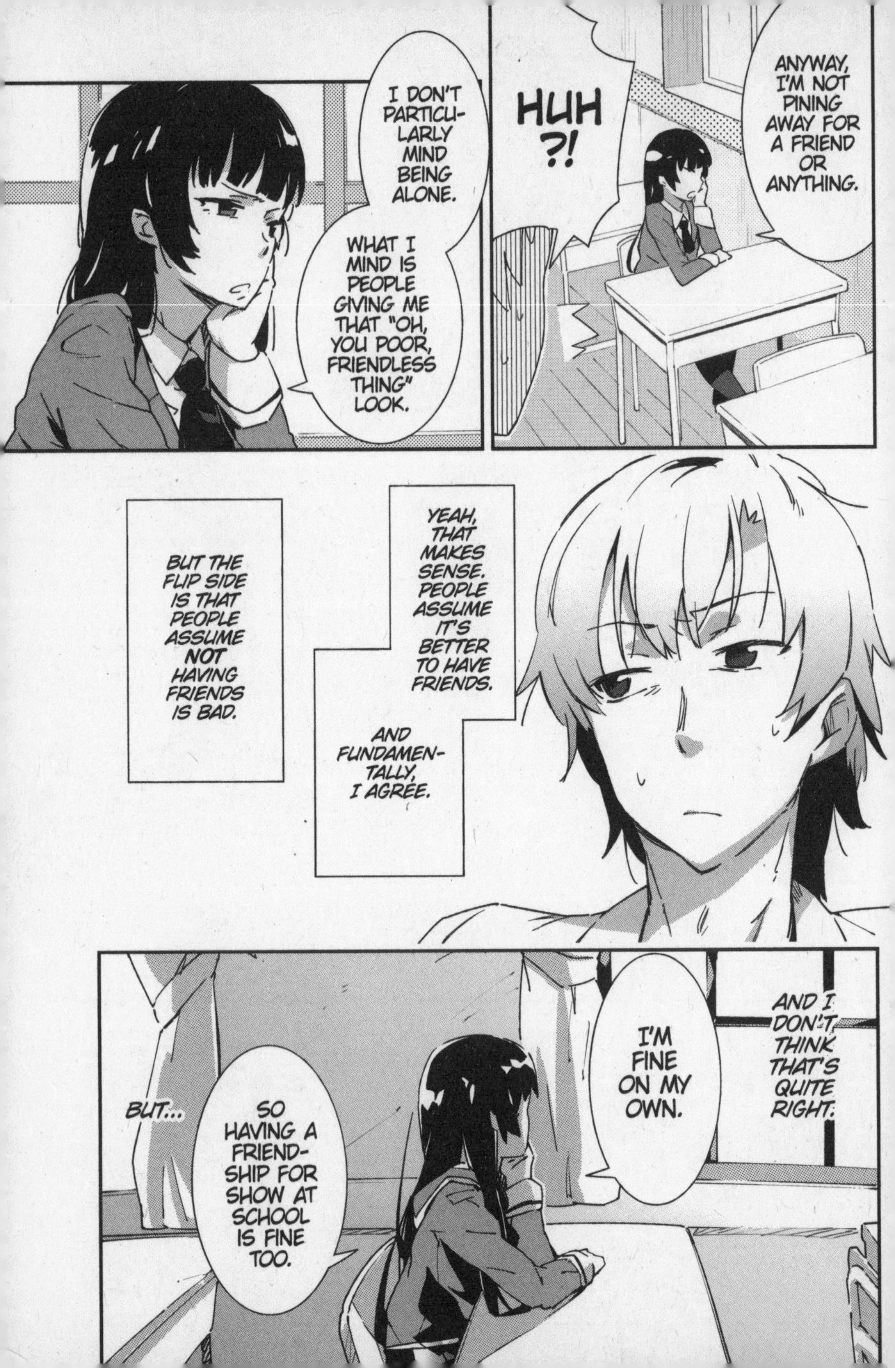
HUH ?!
ANYWAY, I'M NOT PINING AWAY FOR A FRIEND OR ANYTHING.
I DON'T PARTICULARLY MIND BEING ALONE.
WHAT I MIND IS PEOPLE GIVING ME THAT "OH, YOU POOR, FRIENDLESS THING" LOOK.
YEAH, THAT MAKES SENSE. PEOPLE ASSUME IT'S BETTER TO HAVE FRIENDS.
AND FUNDAMENTALLY, I AGREE.
BUT THE FLIP SIDE IS THAT PEOPLE ASSUME NOT HAVING FRIENDS IS BAD.
AND I DON'T THINK THAT'S QUITE RIGHT.
I'M FINE ON MY OWN.
SO HAVING A FRIENDSHIP FOR SHOW AT SCHOOL IS FINE TOO.
BUT...

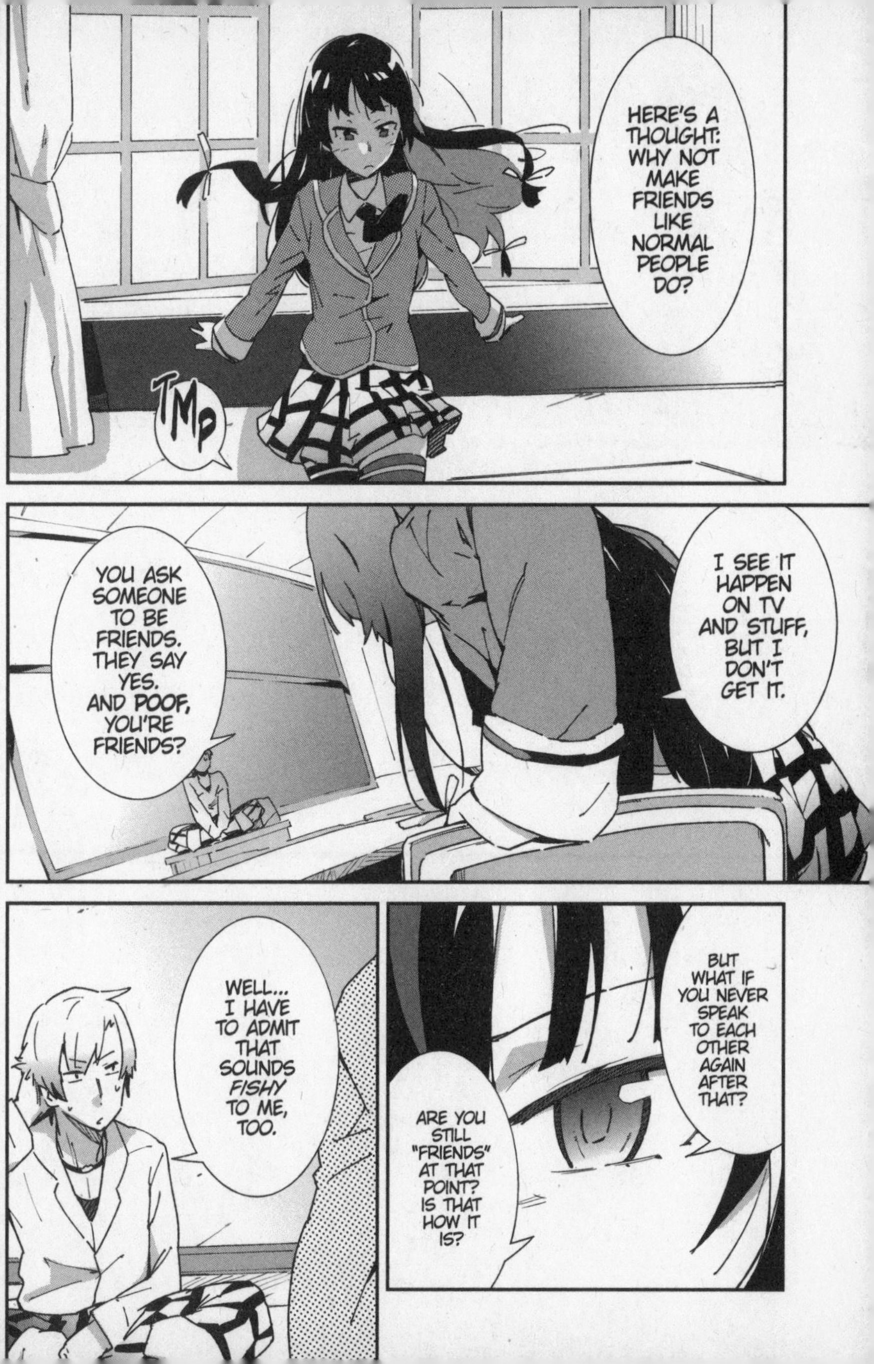
HERE'S A THOUGHT: WHY NOT MAKE FRIENDS LIKE NORMAL PEOPLE DO?
TMP
I SEE IT HAPPEN ON TV AND STUFF, BUT I DON'T GET IT.
YOU ASK SOMEONE TO BE FRIENDS. THEY SAY YES. AND POOF, YOU'RE FRIENDS?
BUT WHAT IF YOU NEVER SPEAK TO EACH OTHER AGAIN AFTER THAT?
ARE YOU STILL "FRIENDS" AT THAT POINT? IS THAT HOW IT IS?
WELL... I HAVE TO ADMIT THAT SOUNDS *FISHY* TO ME, TOO.

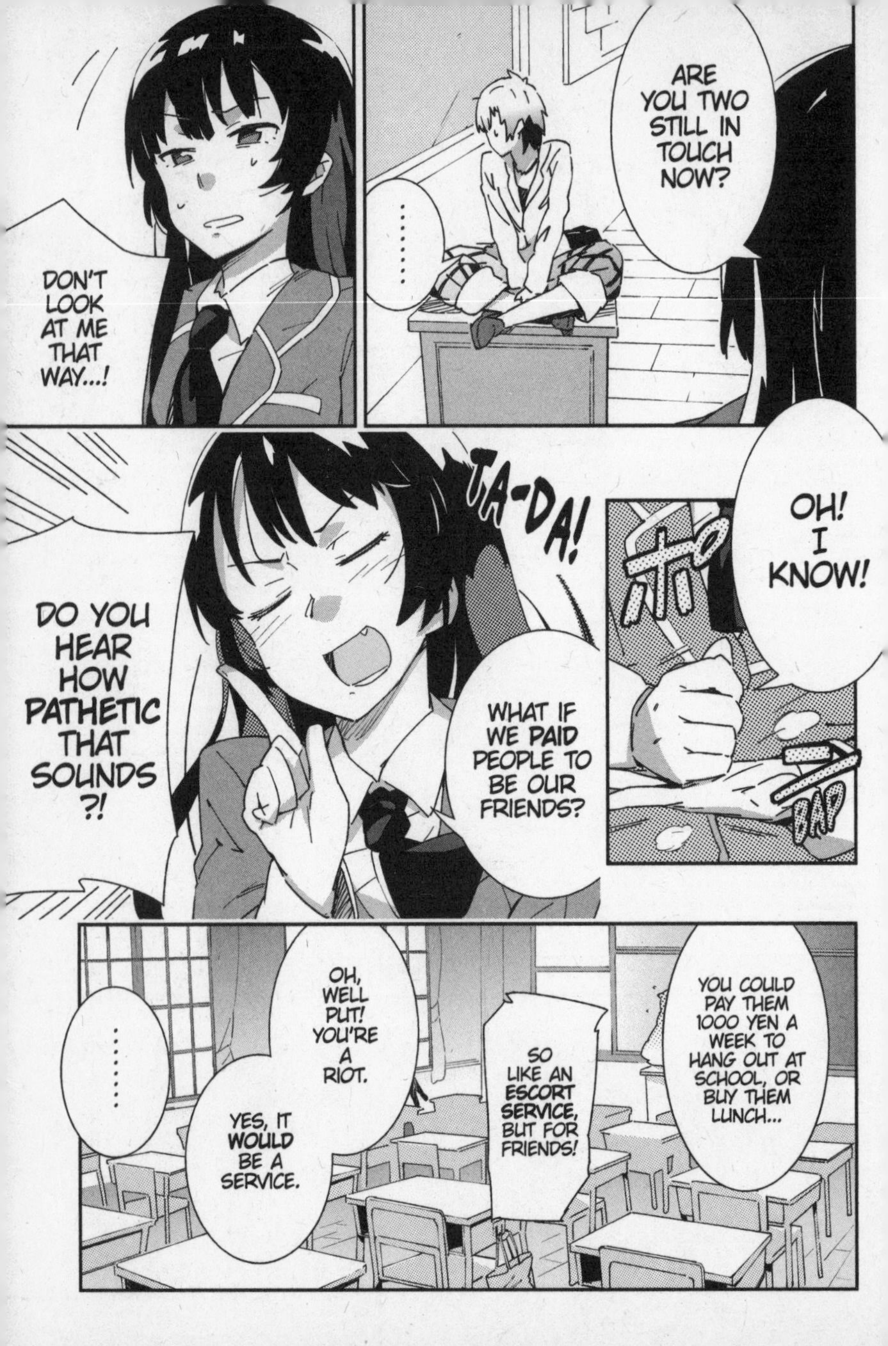
ARE YOU TWO STILL IN TOUCH NOW?
......
DON'T LOOK AT ME THAT WAY...!
OH! I KNOW!
BAP
TA-DA!
WHAT IF WE PAID PEOPLE TO BE OUR FRIENDS?
DO YOU HEAR HOW PATHETIC THAT SOUNDS ?!
YOU COULD PAY THEM 1000 YEN A WEEK TO HANG OUT AT SCHOOL, OR BUY THEM LUNCH...
SO LIKE AN ESCORT SERVICE, BUT FOR FRIENDS!
OH, WELL PUT! YOU'RE A RIOT.
YES, IT WOULD BE A SERVICE.
......

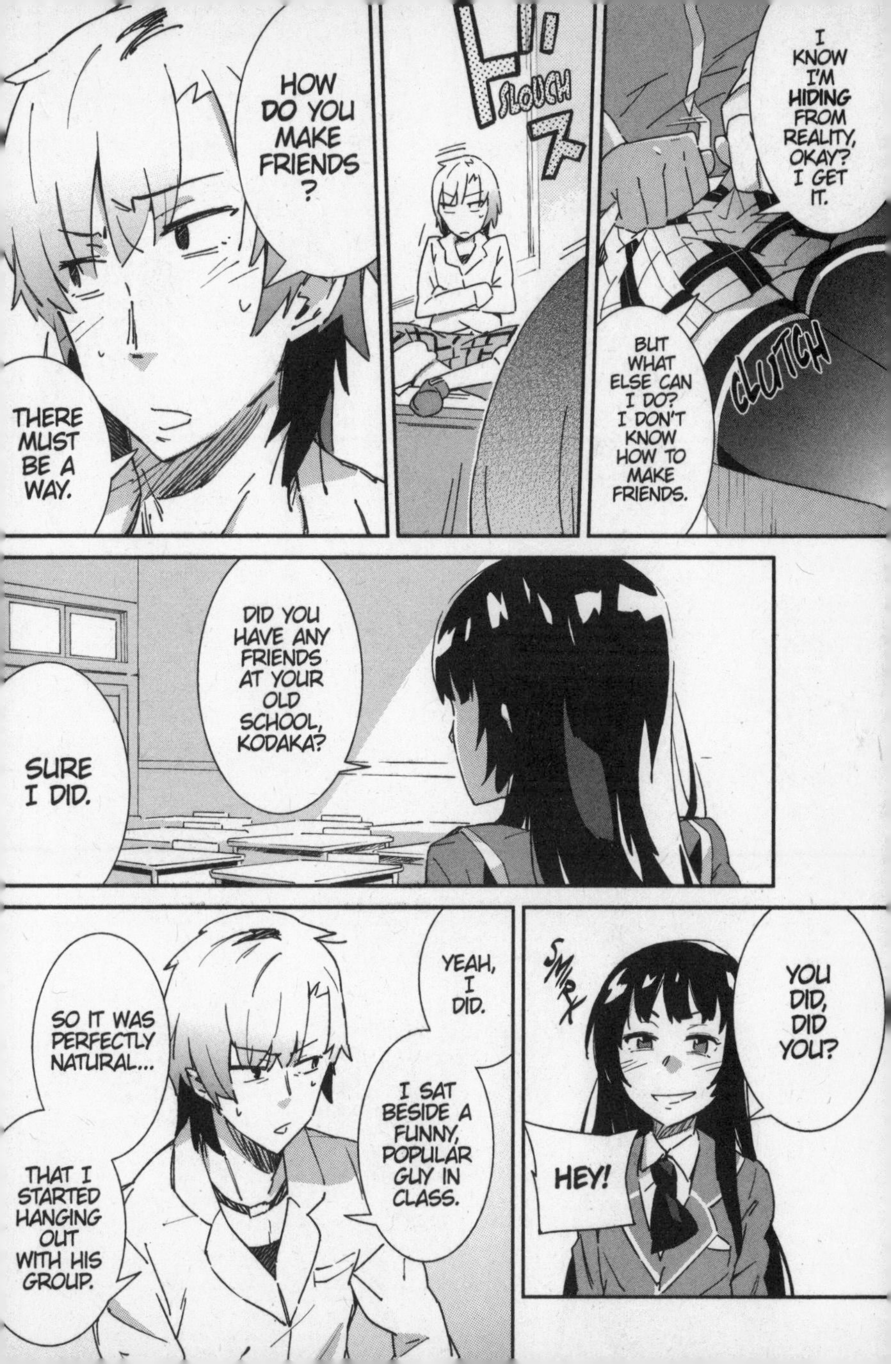
I KNOW I'M HIDING FROM REALITY, OKAY? I GET IT.
CLUTCH
BUT WHAT ELSE CAN I DO? I DON'T KNOW HOW TO MAKE FRIENDS.
SLOUCH
HOW DO YOU MAKE FRIENDS?
THERE MUST BE A WAY.
DID YOU HAVE ANY FRIENDS AT YOUR OLD SCHOOL, KODAKA?
SURE I DID.
SMIRK
YOU DID, DID YOU?
HEY!
YEAH, I DID.
I SAT BESIDE A FUNNY, POPULAR GUY IN CLASS.
SO IT WAS PERFECTLY NATURAL...
THAT I STARTED HANGING OUT WITH HIS GROUP.

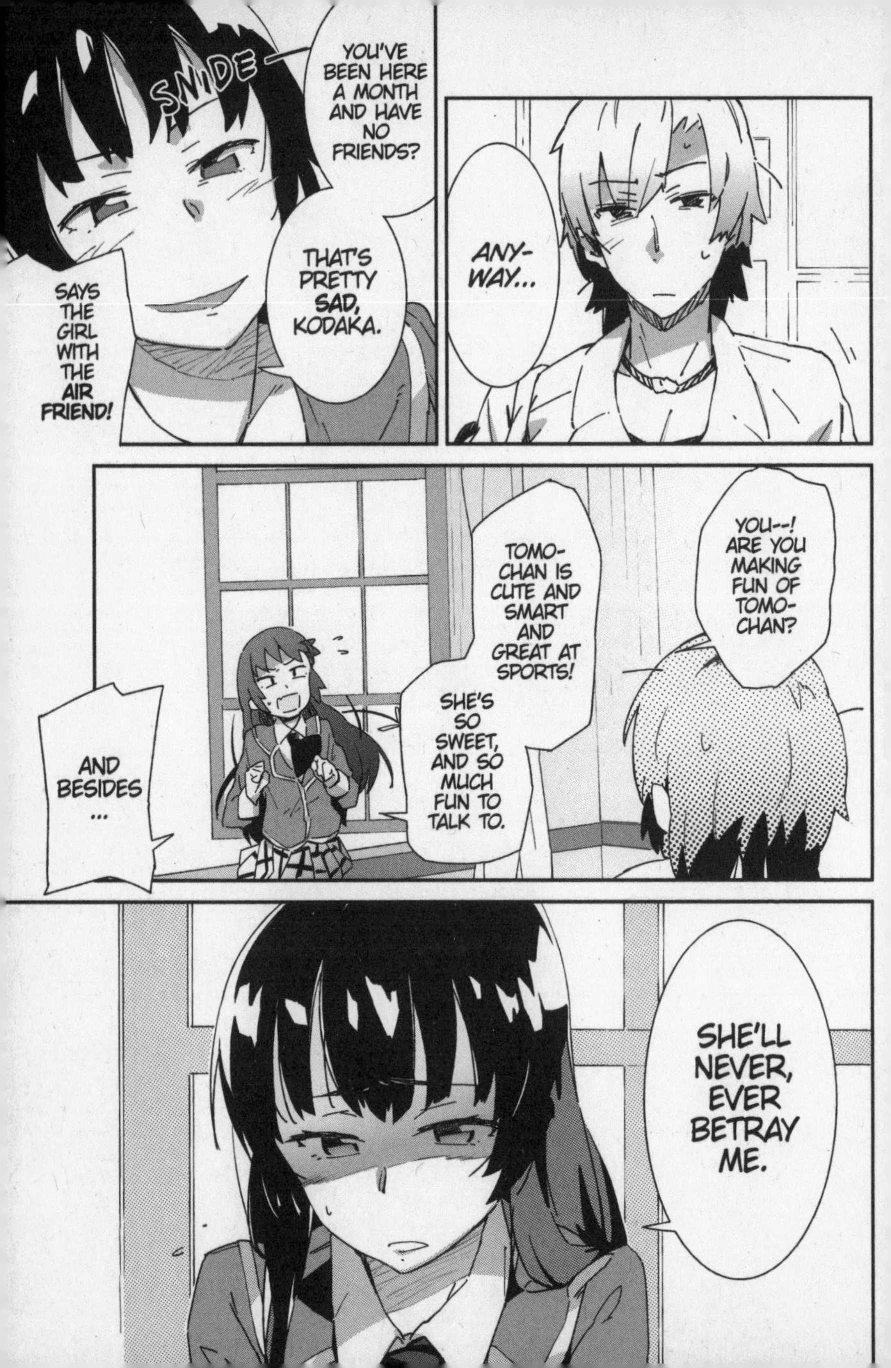
ANY-WAY...
YOU'VE BEEN HERE A MONTH AND HAVE NO FRIENDS?
SNIDE
THAT'S PRETTY SAD, KODAKA.
SAYS THE GIRL WITH THE AIR FRIEND!
YOU--! ARE YOU MAKING FUN OF TOMO-CHAN?
TOMO-CHAN IS CUTE AND SMART AND GREAT AT SPORTS!
SHE'S SO SWEET, AND SO MUCH FUN TO TALK TO.
AND BESIDES ...
SHE'LL NEVER, EVER BETRAY ME.

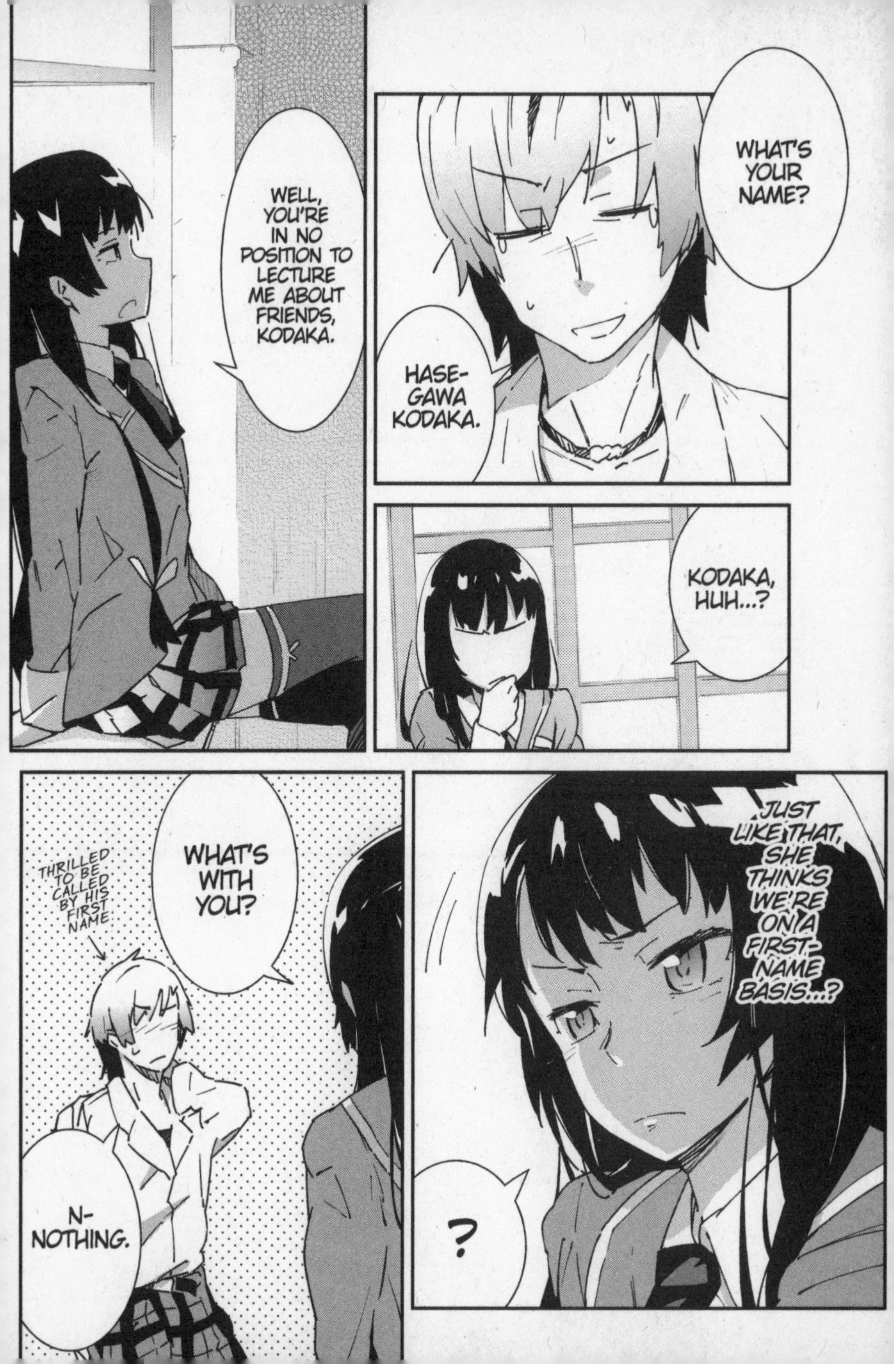
WHAT'S YOUR NAME?
HASE-GAWA KODAKA.
KODAKA, HUH...?
WELL, YOU'RE IN NO POSITION TO LECTURE ME ABOUT FRIENDS, KODAKA.
JUST LIKE THAT, SHE THINKS WE'RE ON A FIRST-NAME BASIS...?
?
WHAT'S WITH YOU?
THRILLED TO BE CALLED BY HIS FIRST NAME
N-NOTHING.

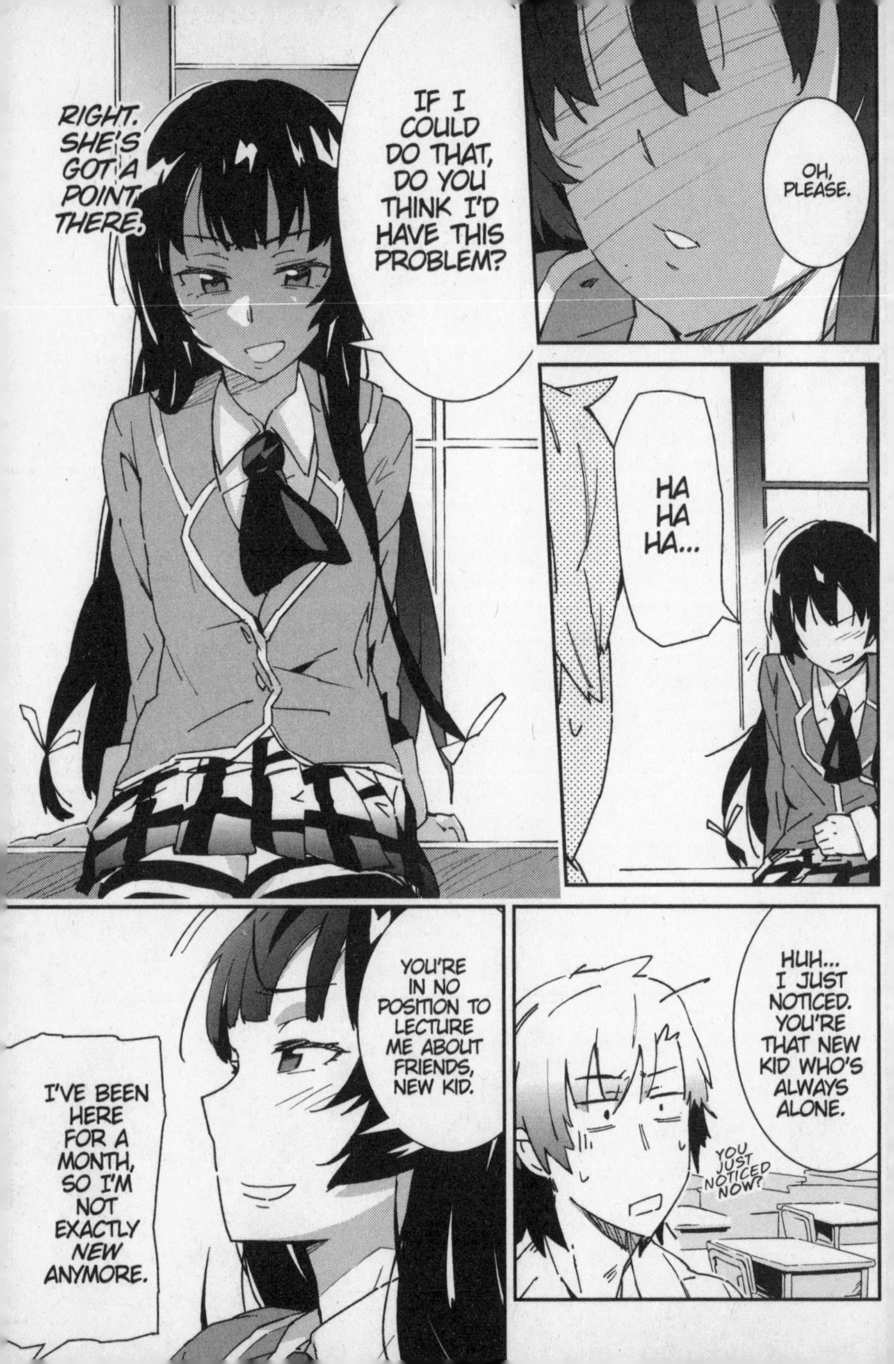
OH, PLEASE.
HA HA HA...
IF I COULD DO THAT, DO YOU THINK I'D HAVE THIS PROBLEM?
RIGHT. SHE'S GOT A POINT THERE.
HUH... I JUST NOTICED. YOU'RE THAT NEW KID WHO'S ALWAYS ALONE.
YOU JUST NOTICED NOW?
YOU'RE IN NO POSITION TO LECTURE ME ABOUT FRIENDS, NEW KID.
I'VE BEEN HERE FOR A MONTH, SO I'M NOT EXACTLY NEW ANYMORE.

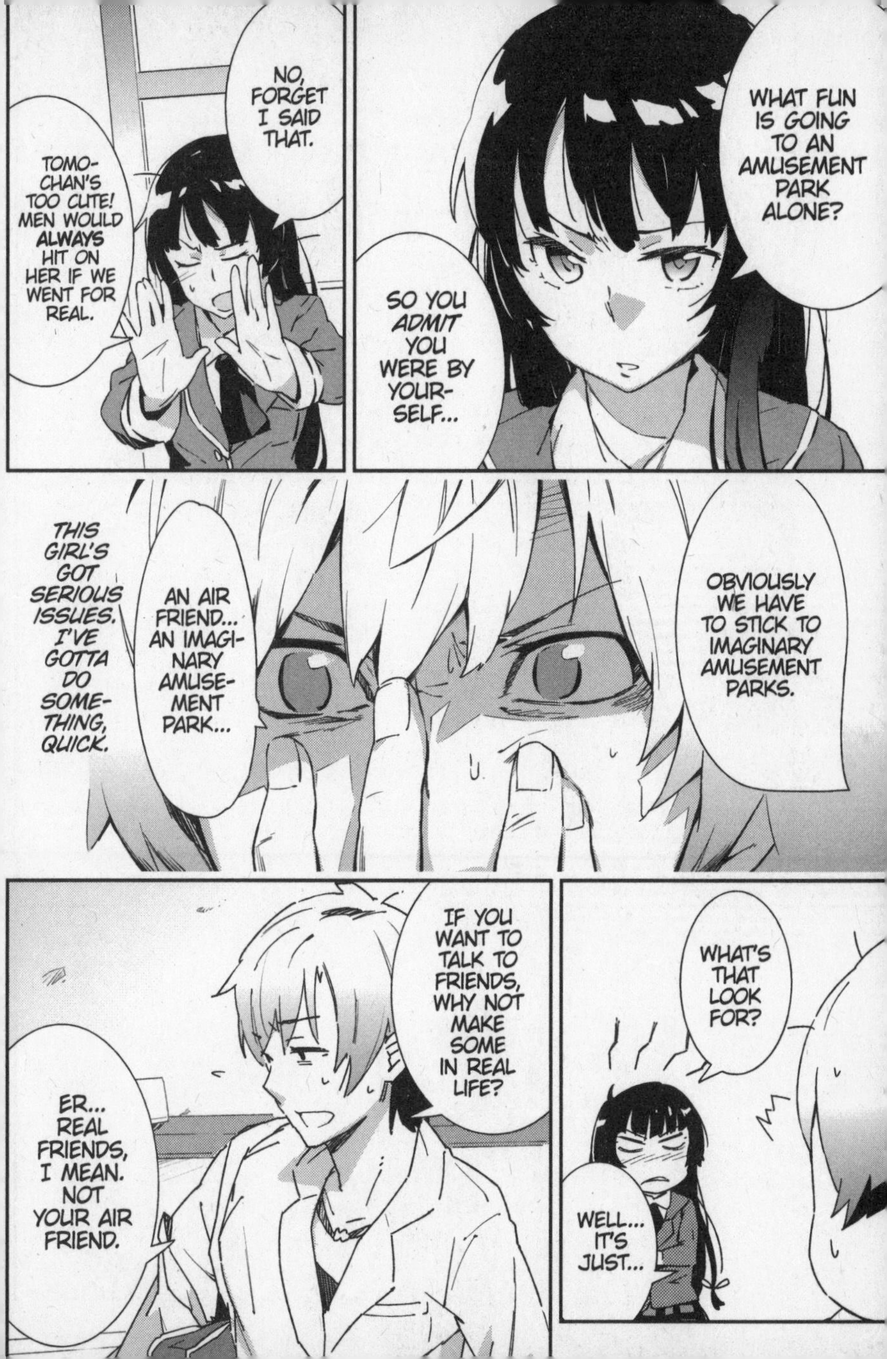
WHAT FUN IS GOING TO AN AMUSEMENT PARK ALONE?
SO YOU ADMIT YOU WERE BY YOURSELF...
NO, FORGET I SAID THAT.
TOMO-CHAN'S TOO CUTE! MEN WOULD ALWAYS HIT ON HER IF WE WENT FOR REAL.
OBVIOUSLY WE HAVE TO STICK TO IMAGINARY AMUSEMENT PARKS.
AN AIR FRIEND... AN IMAGINARY AMUSEMENT PARK...
THIS GIRL'S GOT SERIOUS ISSUES. I'VE GOTTA DO SOMETHING, QUICK.
WHAT'S THAT LOOK FOR?
WELL... IT'S JUST...
IF YOU WANT TO TALK TO FRIENDS, WHY NOT MAKE SOME IN REAL LIFE?
ER... REAL FRIENDS, I MEAN. NOT YOUR AIR FRIEND.

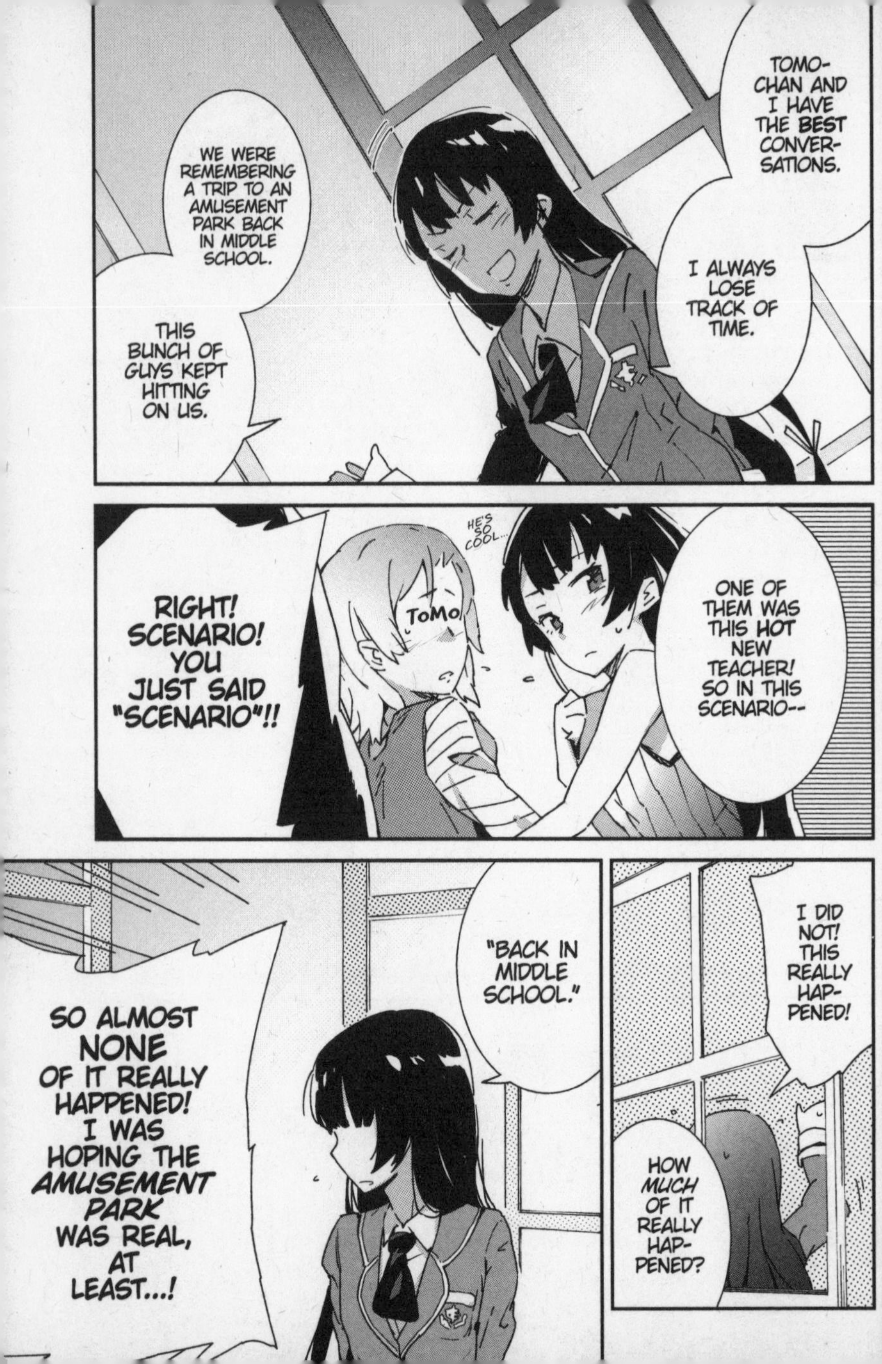
TOMO-CHAN AND I HAVE THE BEST CONVERSATIONS.
I ALWAYS LOSE TRACK OF TIME.
WE WERE REMEMBERING A TRIP TO AN AMUSEMENT PARK BACK IN MIDDLE SCHOOL.
THIS BUNCH OF GUYS KEPT HITTING ON US.
ONE OF THEM WAS THIS HOT NEW TEACHER! SO IN THIS SCENARIO--
HE'S SO COOL...
TOMO
RIGHT! SCENARIO! YOU JUST SAID "SCENARIO"!!
I DID NOT! THIS REALLY HAPPENED!
HOW MUCH OF IT REALLY HAPPENED?
"BACK IN MIDDLE SCHOOL."
SO ALMOST NONE OF IT REALLY HAPPENED! I WAS HOPING THE AMUSEMENT PARK WAS REAL, AT LEAST...!

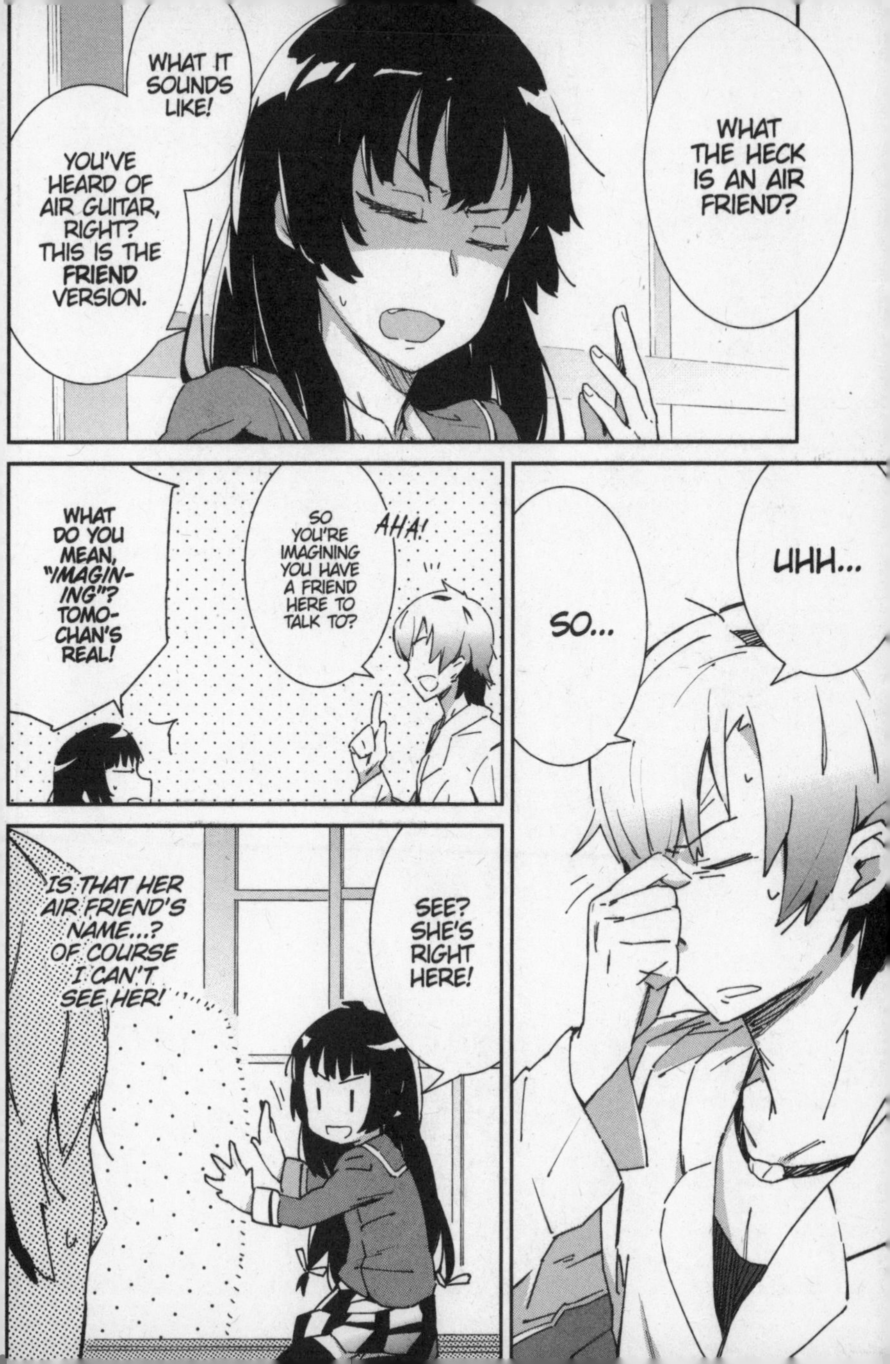
WHAT THE HECK IS AN AIR FRIEND?
WHAT IT SOUNDS LIKE!
YOU'VE HEARD OF AIR GUITAR, RIGHT? THIS IS THE FRIEND VERSION.
UHH...
SO...
AHA!
SO YOU'RE IMAGINING YOU HAVE A FRIEND HERE TO TALK TO?
WHAT DO YOU MEAN, "IMAGINING"? TOMO-CHAN'S REAL!
SEE? SHE'S RIGHT HERE!
IS THAT HER AIR FRIEND'S NAME...? OF COURSE I CAN'T SEE HER!

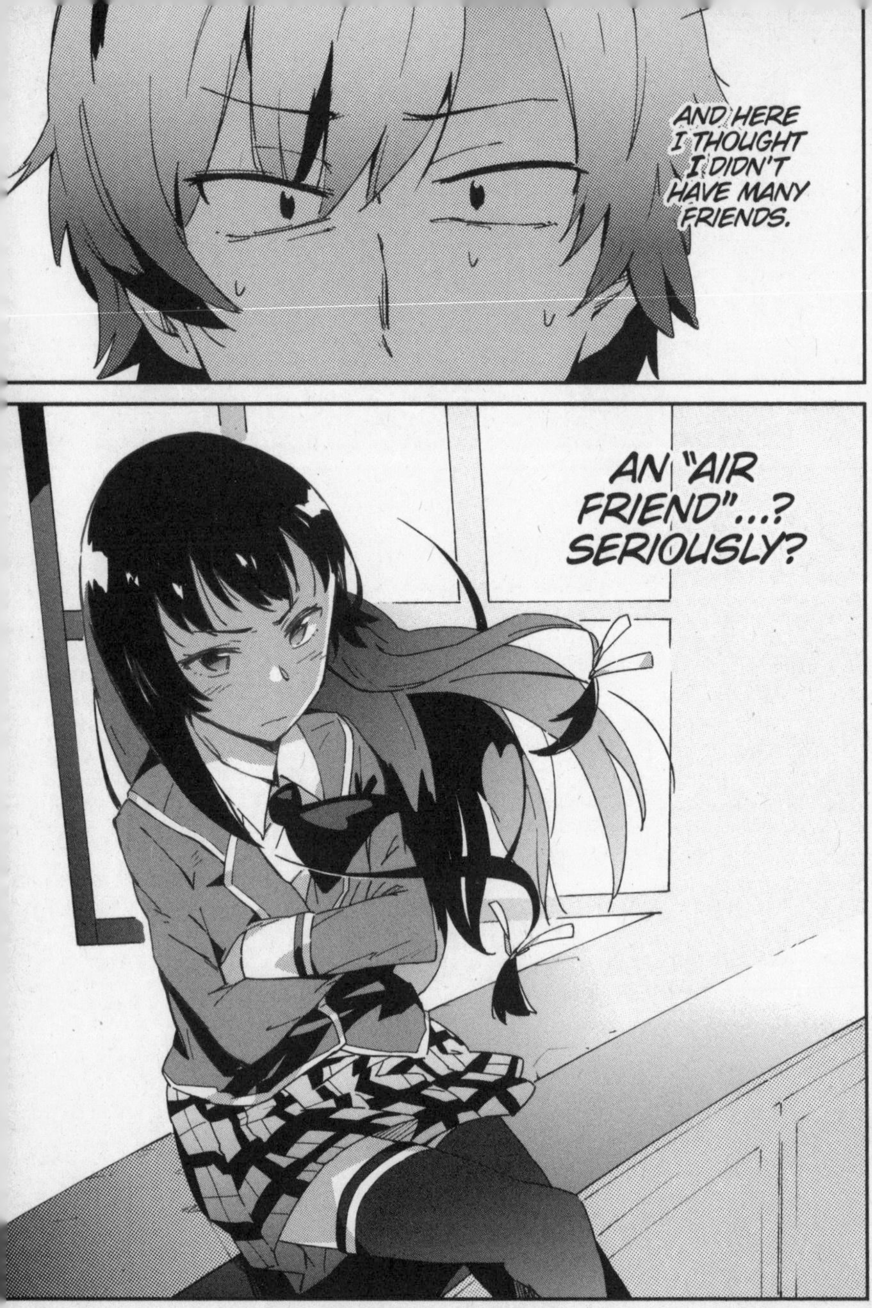
AND HERE I THOUGHT I DIDN'T HAVE MANY FRIENDS.
AN "AIR FRIEND"...? SERIOUSLY?

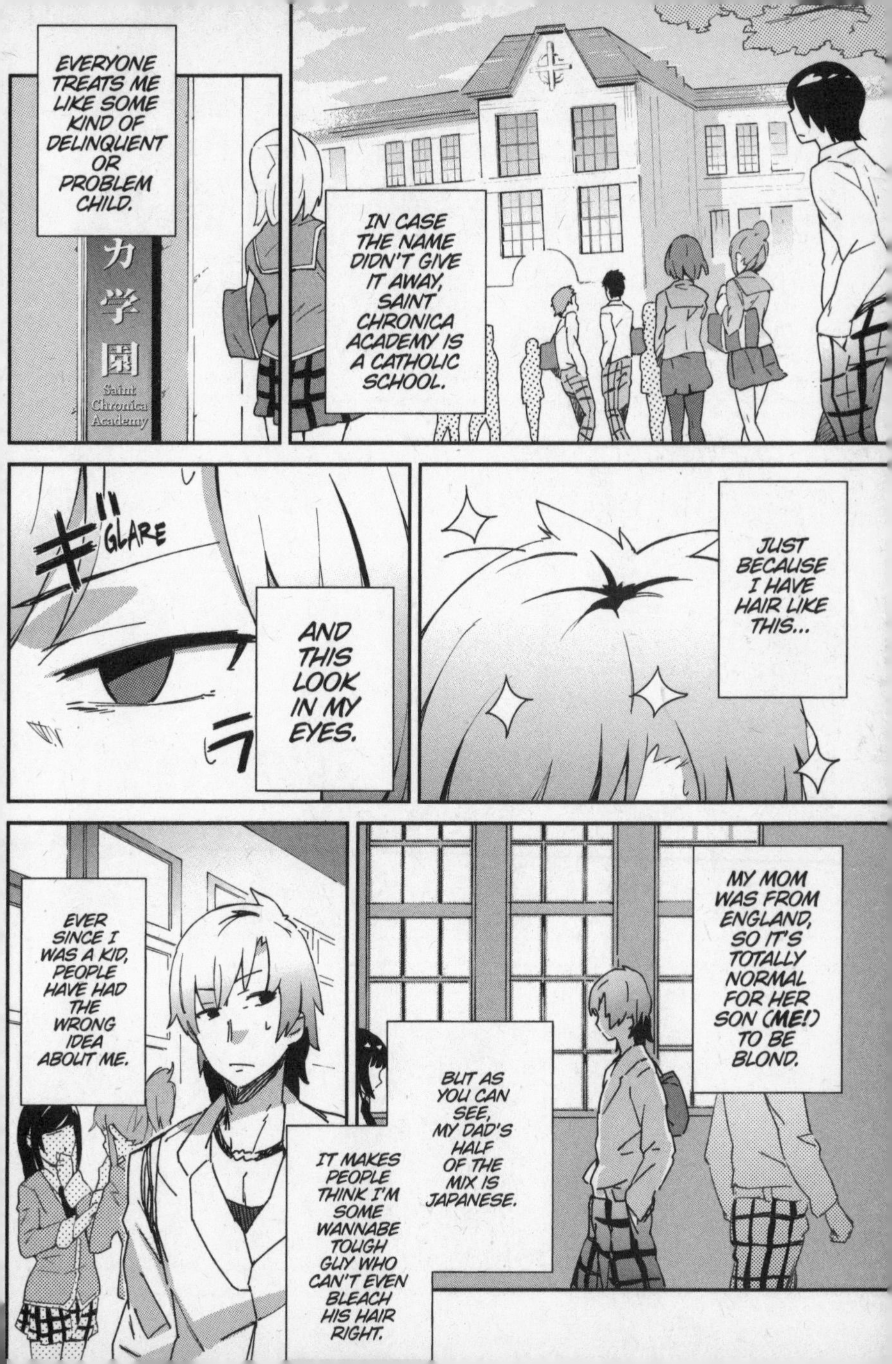
IN CASE THE NAME DIDN'T GIVE IT AWAY, SAINT CHRONICA ACADEMY IS A CATHOLIC SCHOOL.
EVERYONE TREATS ME LIKE SOME KIND OF DELINQUENT OR PROBLEM CHILD.
カ学園
Saint Chronica Academy
JUST BECAUSE I HAVE HAIR LIKE THIS...
GLARE
AND THIS LOOK IN MY EYES.
MY MOM WAS FROM ENGLAND, SO IT'S TOTALLY NORMAL FOR HER SON (ME!) TO BE BLOND.
BUT AS YOU CAN SEE, MY DAD'S HALF OF THE MIX IS JAPANESE.
EVER SINCE I WAS A KID, PEOPLE HAVE HAD THE WRONG IDEA ABOUT ME.
IT MAKES PEOPLE THINK I'M SOME WANNABE TOUGH GUY WHO CAN'T EVEN BLEACH HIS HAIR RIGHT.

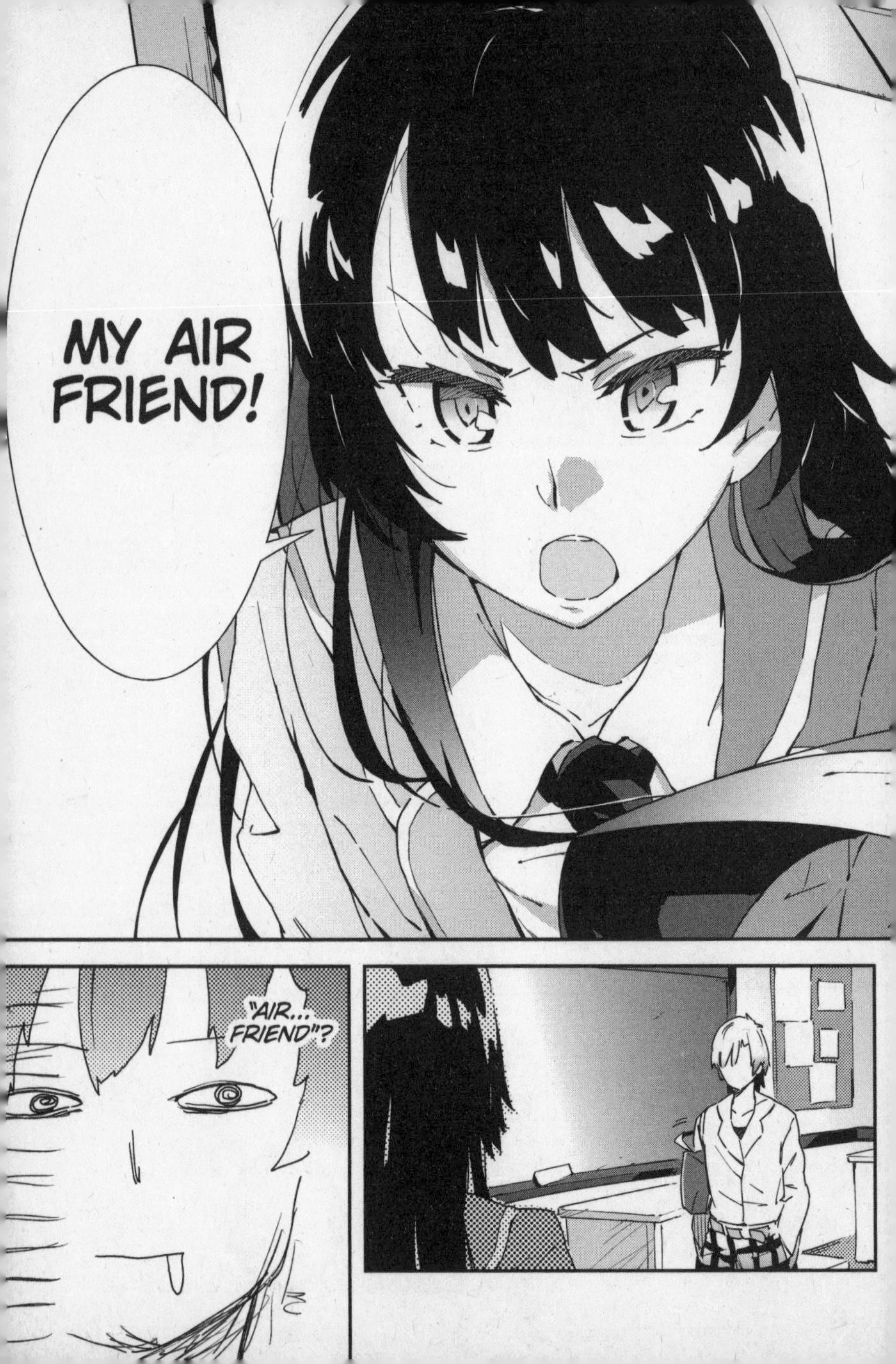
MY AIR FRIEND!
"AIR... FRIEND"?

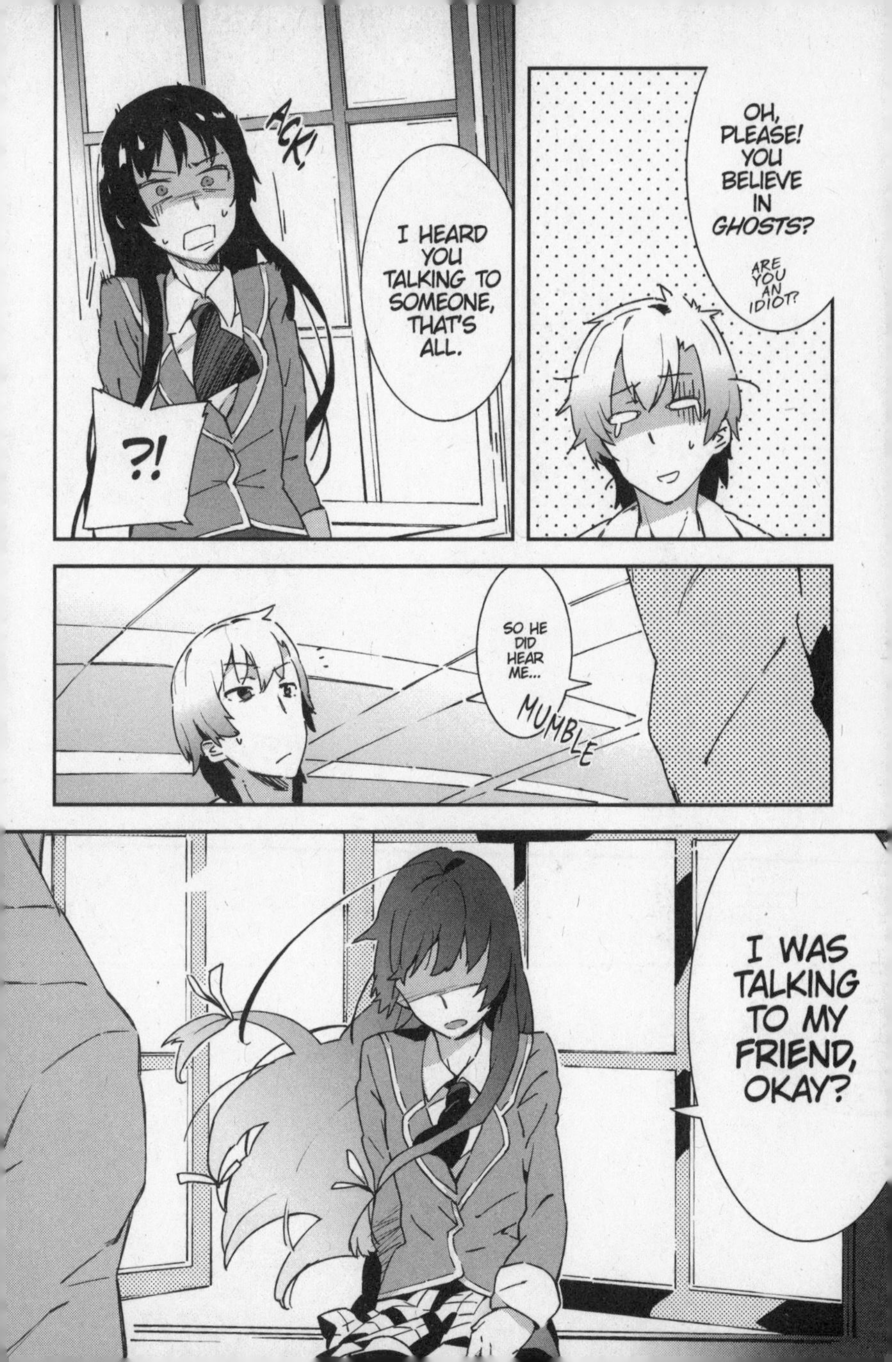
OH, PLEASE! YOU BELIEVE IN GHOSTS?
ARE YOU AN IDIOT?
I HEARD YOU TALKING TO SOMEONE, THAT'S ALL.
ACK!
?!
SO HE DID HEAR ME...
MUMBLE
I WAS TALKING TO MY FRIEND, OKAY?

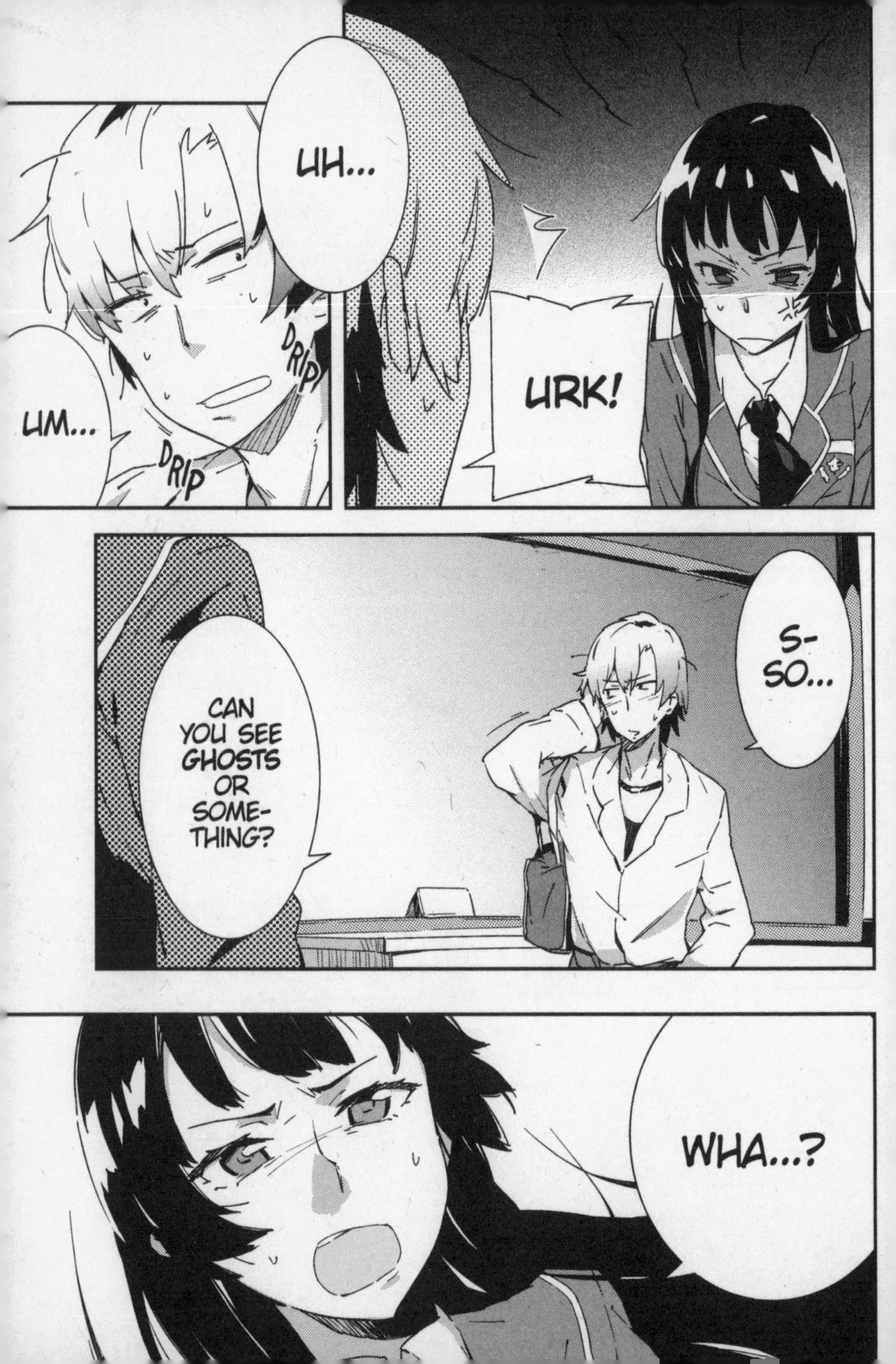
UH...
URK!
DRIP!
UM...
DRIP
S-SO...
CAN YOU SEE GHOSTS OR SOME-THING?
WHA...?

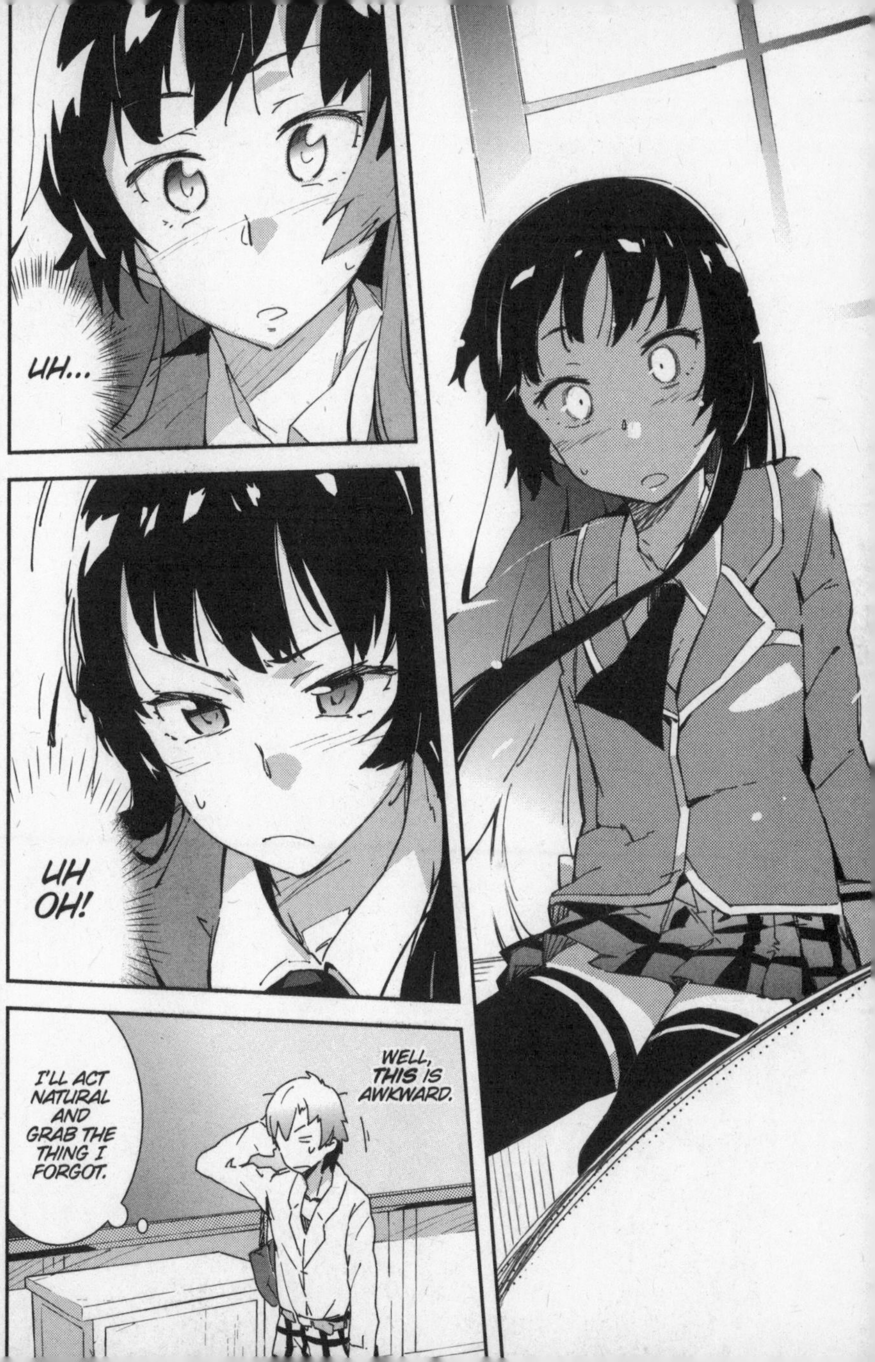
UH...
UH OH!
WELL, THIS IS AWKWARD.
I'LL ACT NATURAL AND GRAB THE THING I FORGOT.

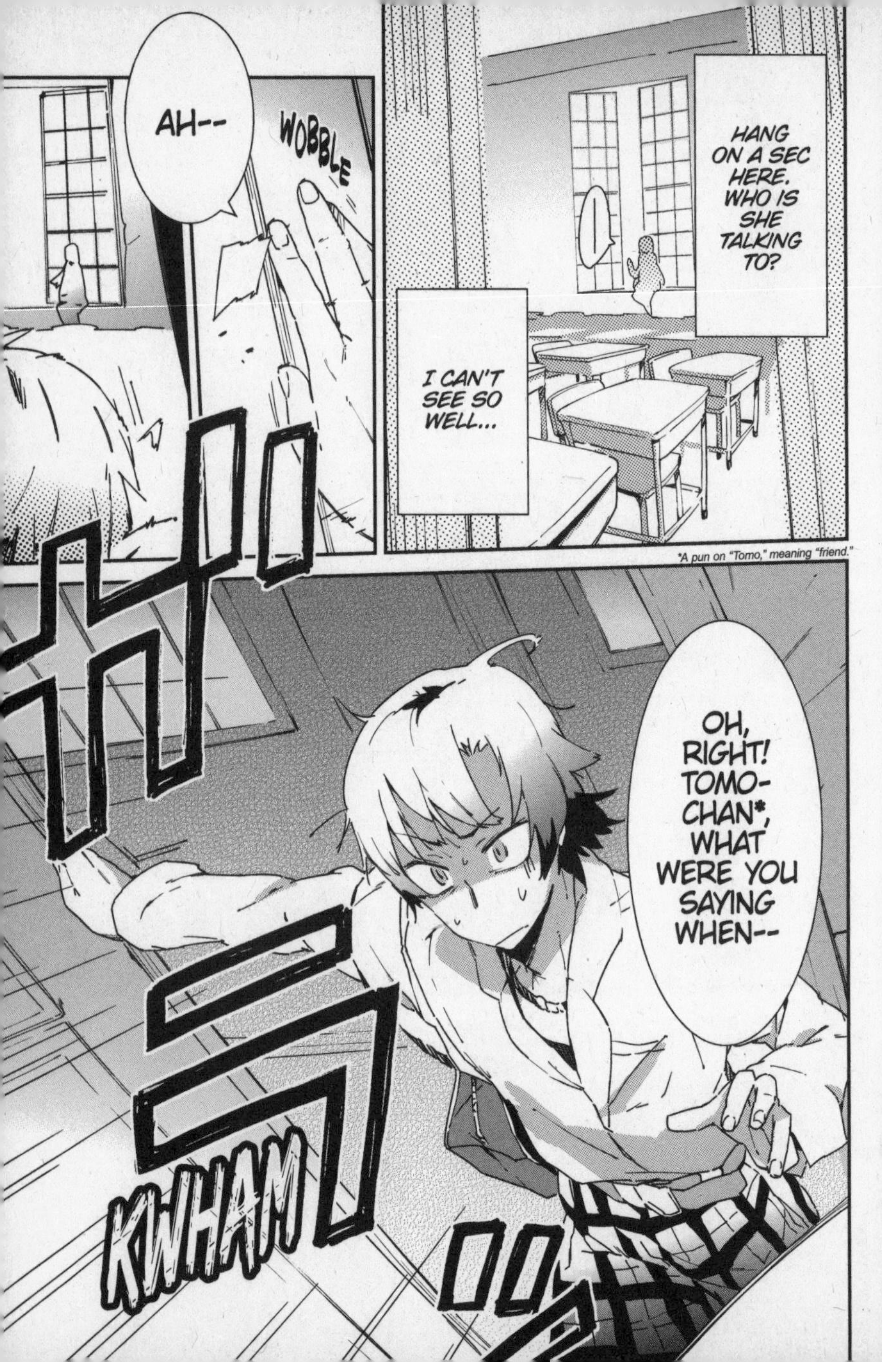
HANG ON A SEC HERE. WHO IS SHE TALKING TO?
I CAN'T SEE SO WELL...
AH--
WOBBLE
OH, RIGHT! TOMO-CHAN*, WHAT WERE YOU SAYING WHEN--
KWHAM

*A pun on "Tomo," meaning "friend."

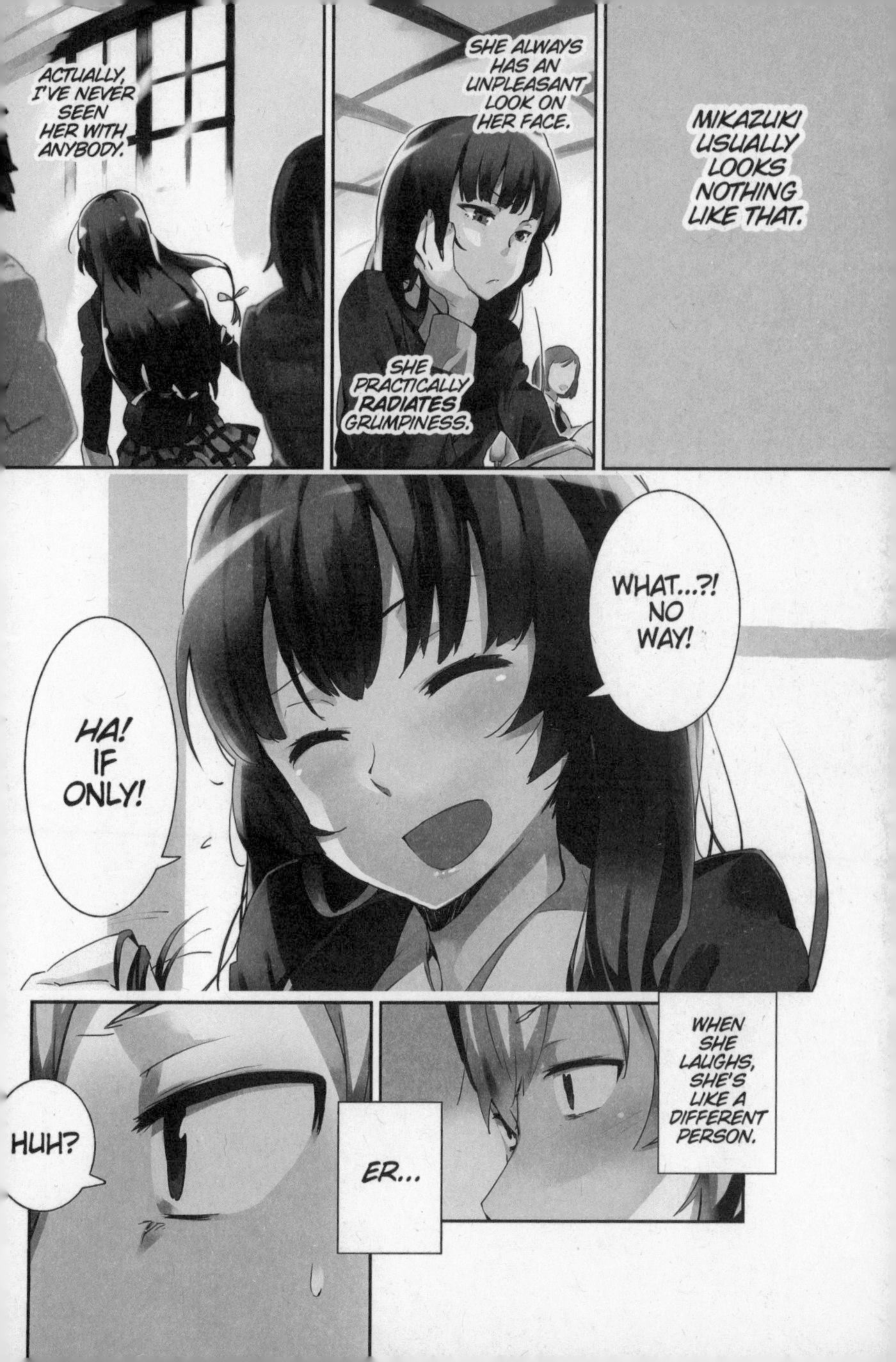
MIKAZUKI USUALLY LOOKS NOTHING LIKE THAT.
SHE ALWAYS HAS AN UNPLEASANT LOOK ON HER FACE.
SHE PRACTICALLY RADIATES GRUMPINESS.
ACTUALLY, I'VE NEVER SEEN HER WITH ANYBODY.
WHAT...?! NO WAY!
HA! IF ONLY!
WHEN SHE LAUGHS, SHE'S LIKE A DIFFERENT PERSON.
ER...
HUH?

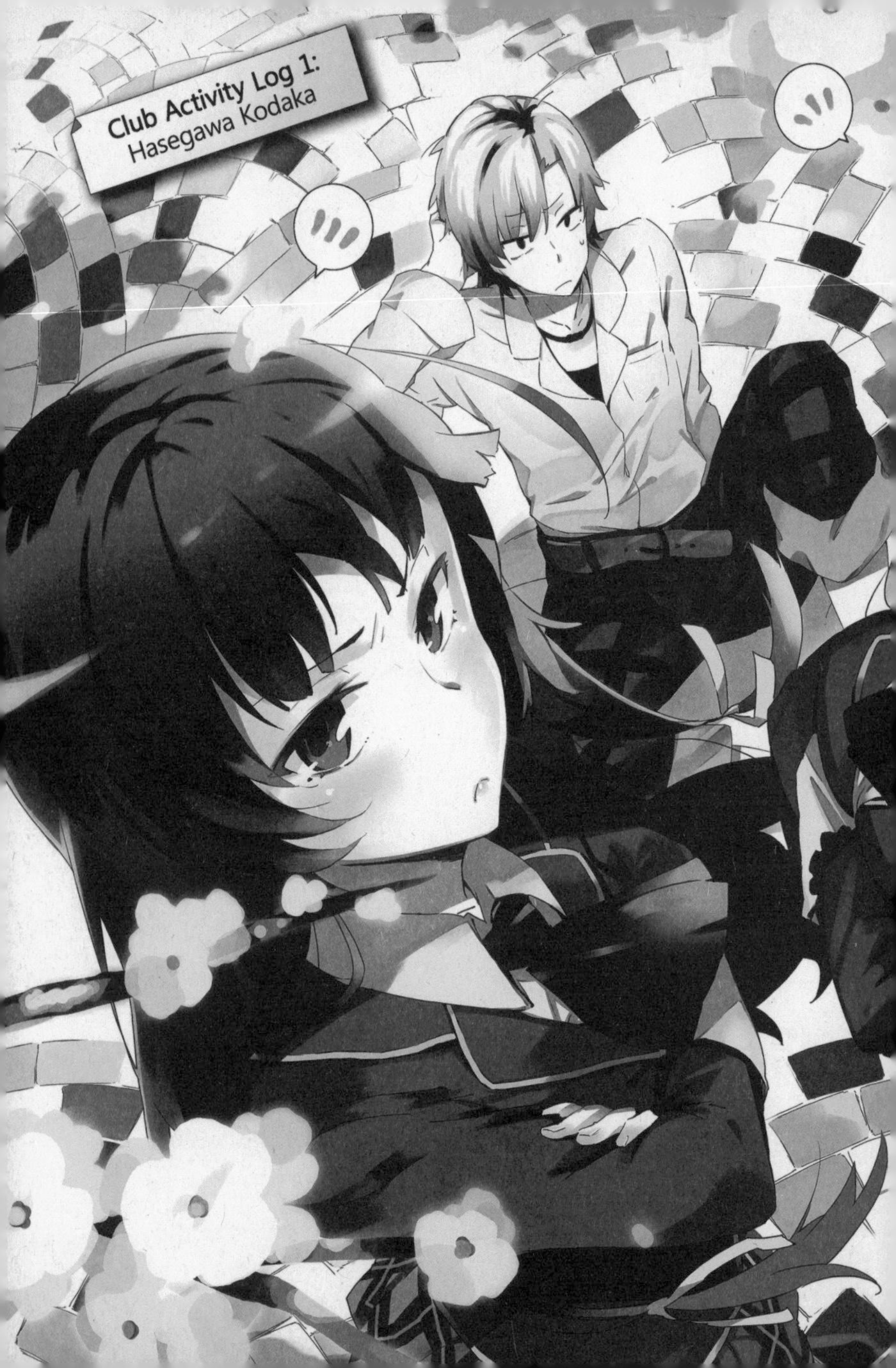
Club Activity Log 1:
Hasegawa Kodaka

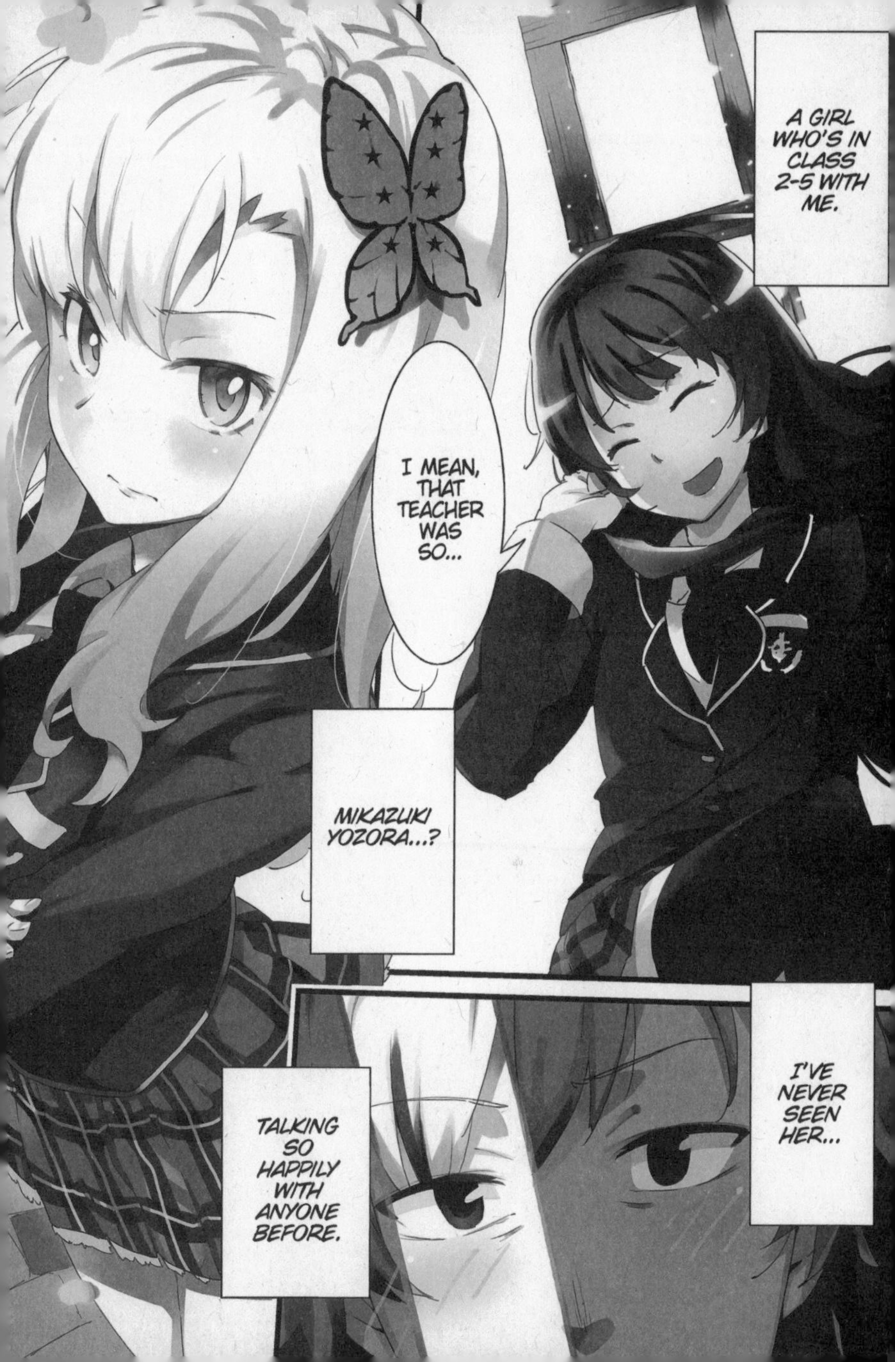
A GIRL WHO'S IN CLASS 2-5 WITH ME.
I MEAN, THAT TEACHER WAS SO...
MIKAZUKI YOZORA...?
I'VE NEVER SEEN HER...
TALKING SO HAPPILY WITH ANYONE BEFORE.

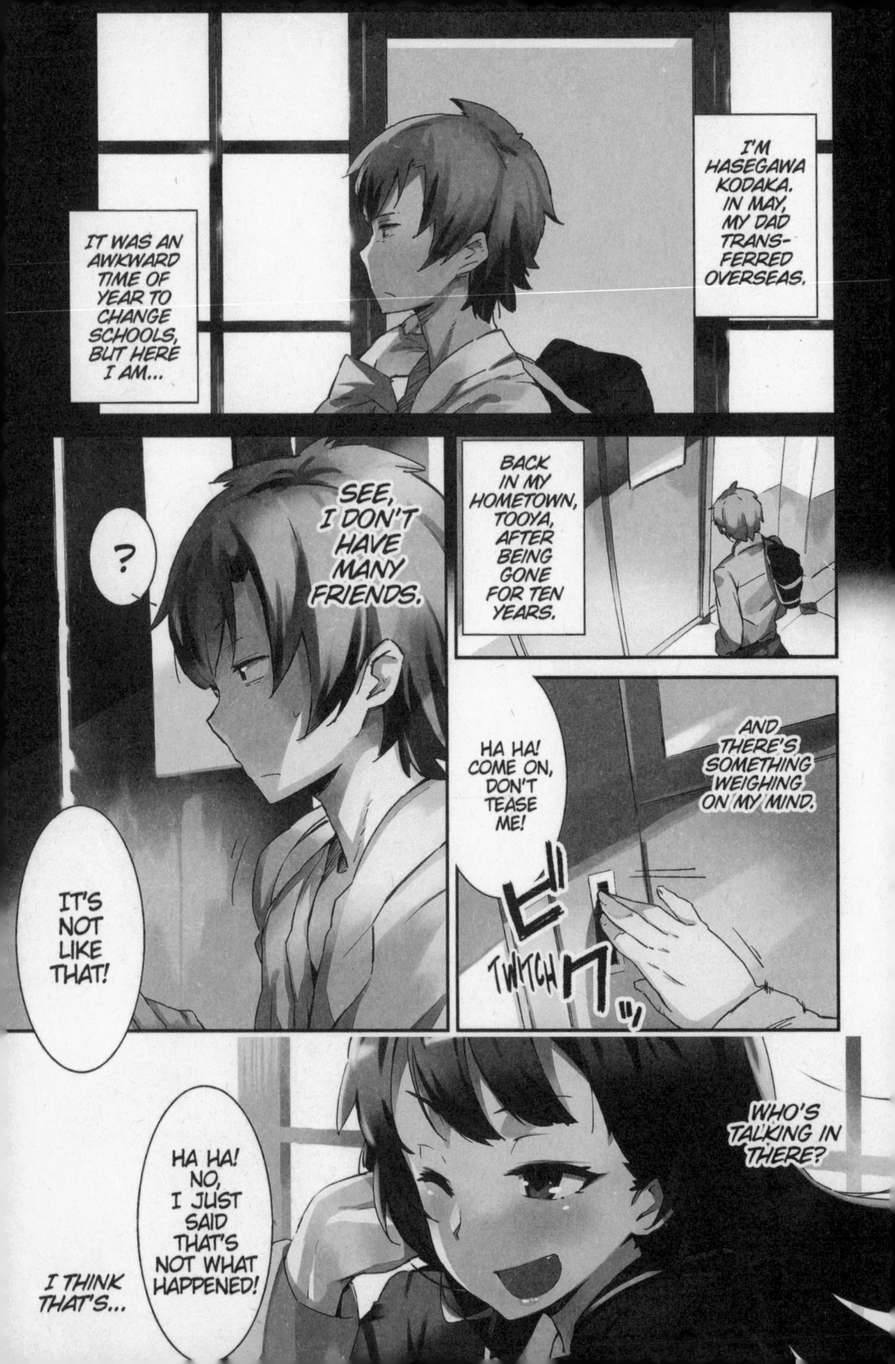
I'M HASEGAWA KODAKA. IN MAY, MY DAD TRANSFERRED OVERSEAS.
IT WAS AN AWKWARD TIME OF YEAR TO CHANGE SCHOOLS, BUT HERE I AM...
BACK IN MY HOMETOWN, TOOYA, AFTER BEING GONE FOR TEN YEARS.
AND THERE'S SOMETHING WEIGHING ON MY MIND.
HA HA! COME ON, DON'T TEASE ME!
TWITCH
SEE, I DON'T HAVE MANY FRIENDS.
?
IT'S NOT LIKE THAT!
WHO'S TALKING IN THERE?
HA HA! NO, I JUST SAID THAT'S NOT WHAT HAPPENED!
I THINK THAT'S...

Haganai

I don't have many friends

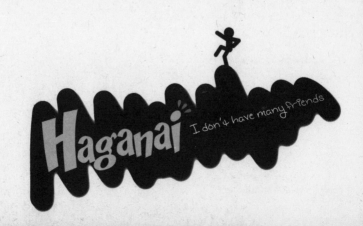

ONE HOUR
LATER...

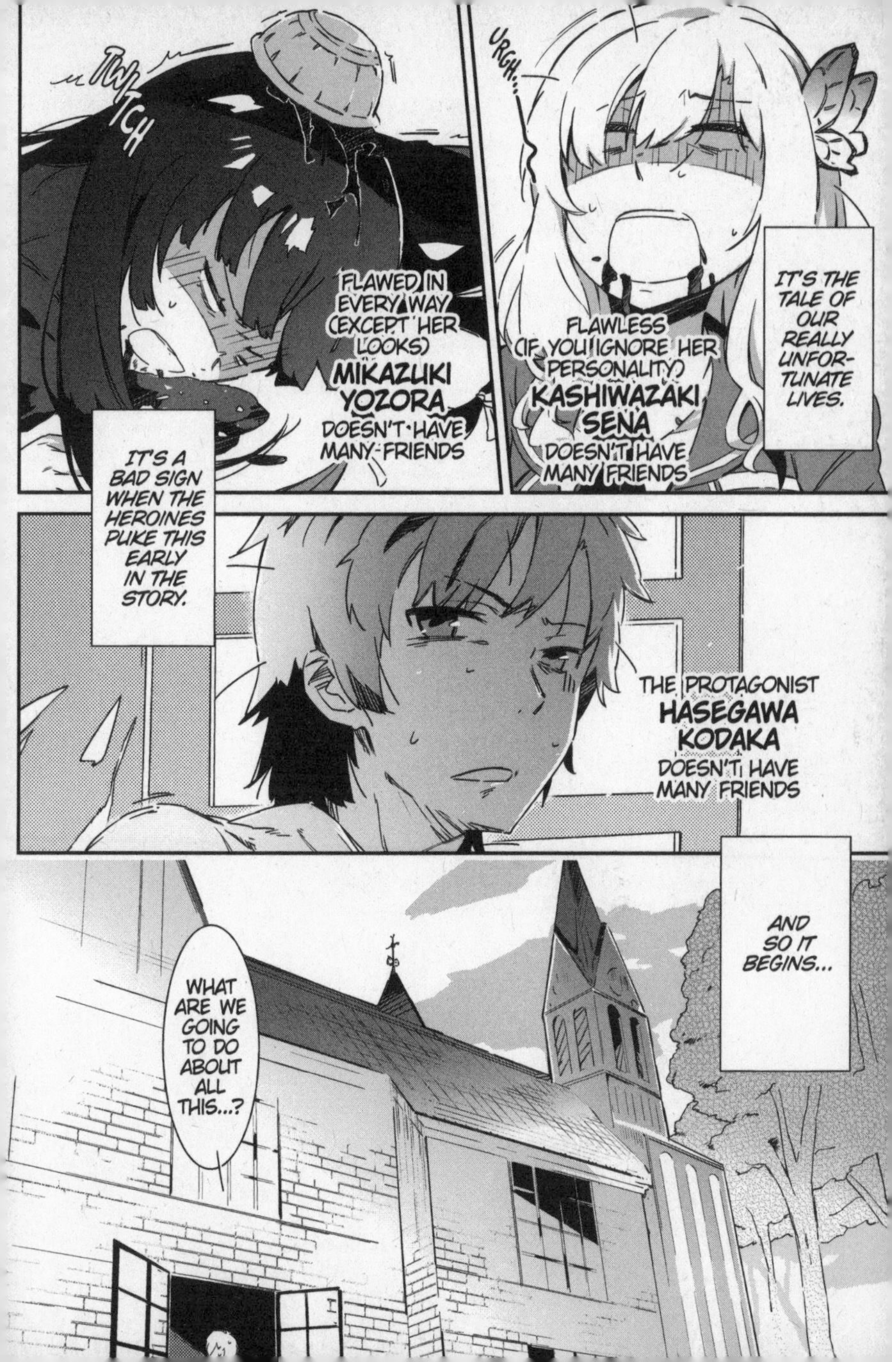
URGH...
IT'S THE TALE OF OUR REALLY UNFORTUNATE LIVES.
FLAWLESS (IF YOU IGNORE HER PERSONALITY) KASHIWAZAKI SENA DOESN'T HAVE MANY FRIENDS
TWITCH
FLAWED IN EVERY WAY (EXCEPT HER LOOKS) MIKAZUKI YOZORA DOESN'T HAVE MANY FRIENDS
IT'S A BAD SIGN WHEN THE HEROINES PUKE THIS EARLY IN THE STORY.
THE PROTAGONIST HASEGAWA KODAKA DOESN'T HAVE MANY FRIENDS
AND SO IT BEGINS...
WHAT ARE WE GOING TO DO ABOUT ALL THIS...?

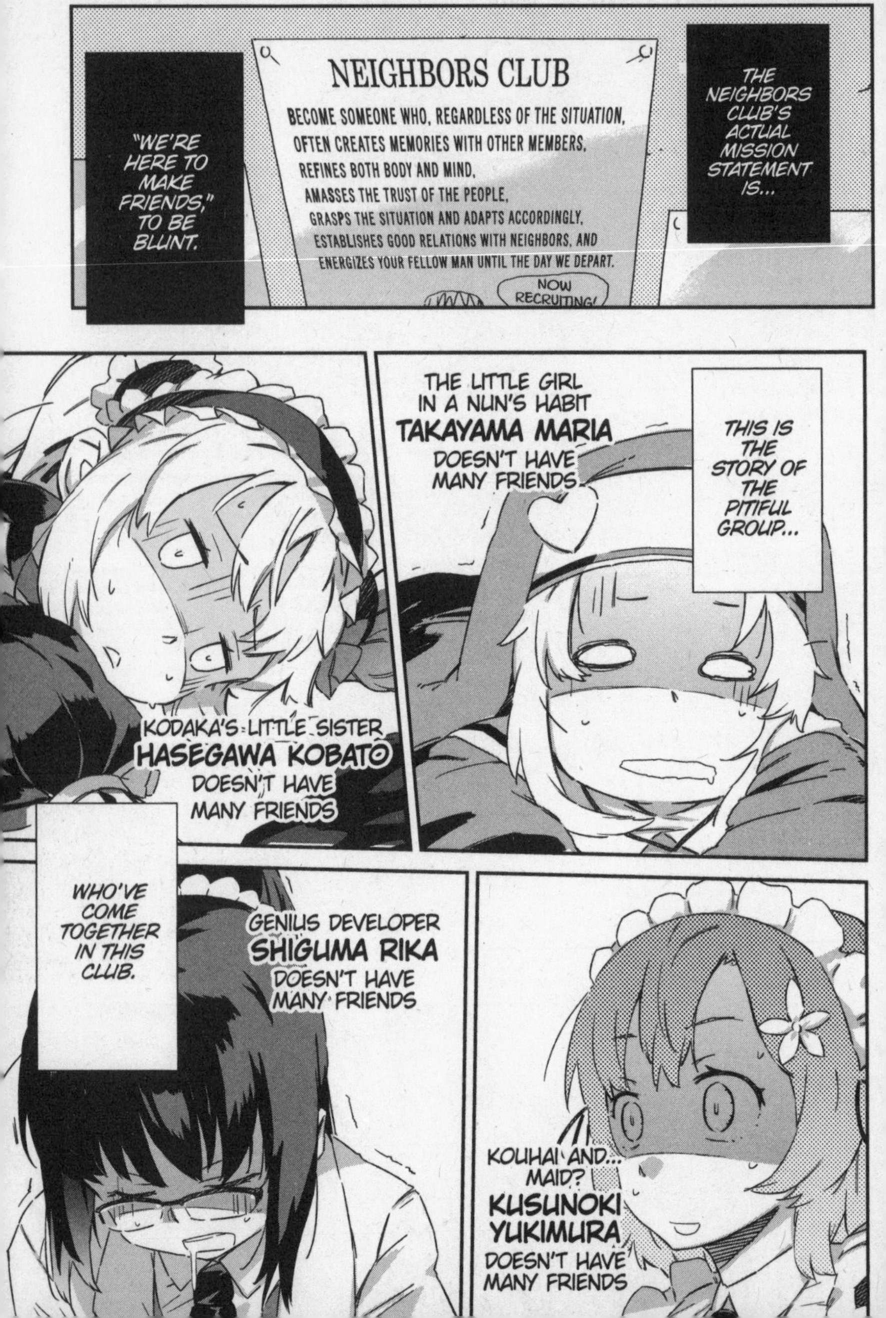

THE NEIGHBORS CLUB'S ACTUAL MISSION STATEMENT IS...
NEIGHBORS CLUB
BECOME SOMEONE WHO, REGARDLESS OF THE SITUATION,
OFTEN CREATES MEMORIES WITH OTHER MEMBERS,
REFINES BOTH BODY AND MIND,
AMASSES THE TRUST OF THE PEOPLE,
GRASPS THE SITUATION AND ADAPTS ACCORDINGLY,
ESTABLISHES GOOD RELATIONS WITH NEIGHBORS, AND
ENERGIZES YOUR FELLOW MAN UNTIL THE DAY WE DEPART.
NOW RECRUITING!
"WE'RE HERE TO MAKE FRIENDS," TO BE BLUNT.
THIS IS THE STORY OF THE PITIFUL GROUP...
THE LITTLE GIRL IN A NUN'S HABIT TAKAYAMA MARIA DOESN'T HAVE MANY FRIENDS
KODAKA'S LITTLE SISTER HASEGAWA KOBATO DOESN'T HAVE MANY FRIENDS
WHO'VE COME TOGETHER IN THIS CLUB.
KOUHAI AND... MAID? KUSUNOKI YUKIMURA DOESN'T HAVE MANY FRIENDS
GENIUS DEVELOPER SHIGUMA RIKA DOESN'T HAVE MANY FRIENDS

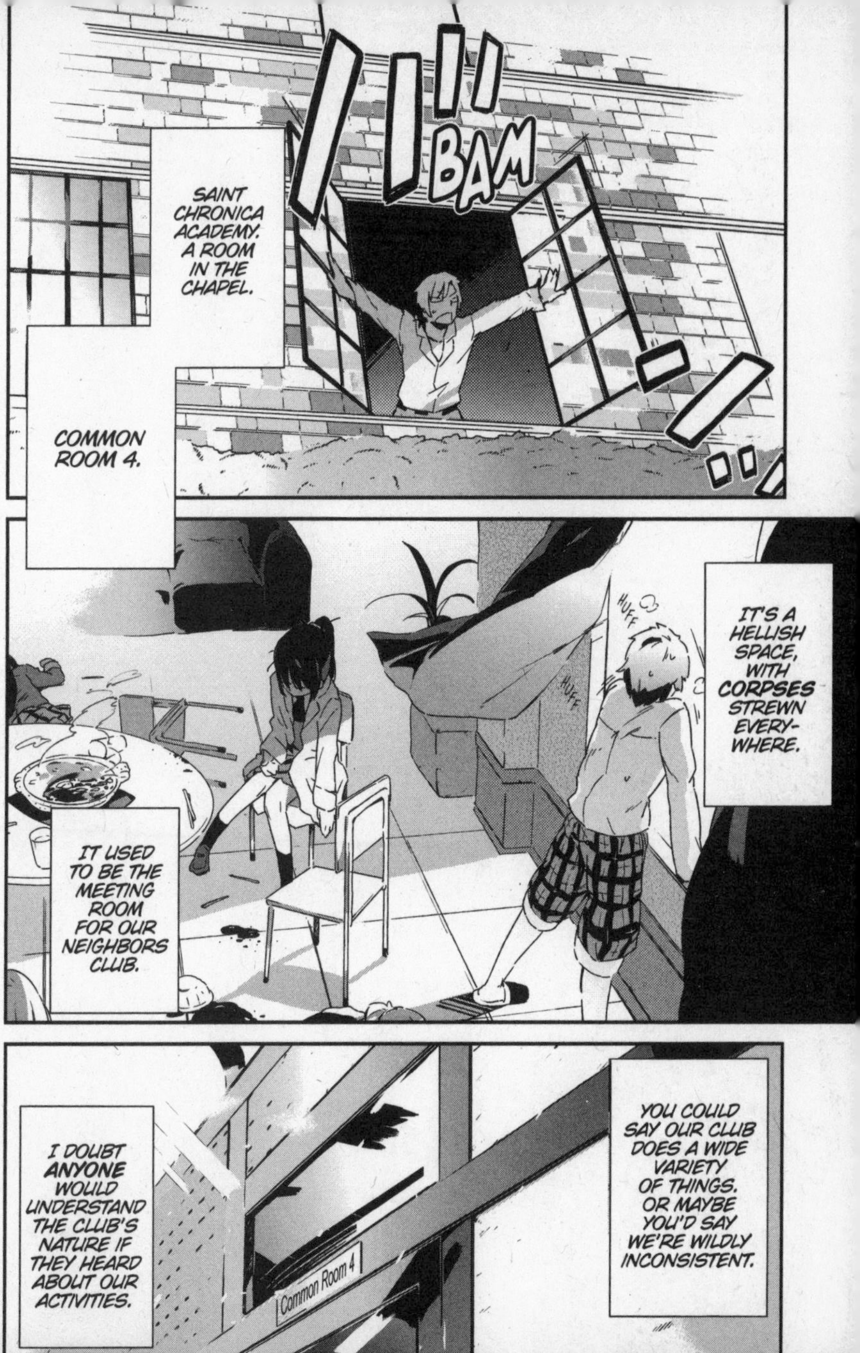
BAM
SAINT CHRONICA ACADEMY. A ROOM IN THE CHAPEL.
COMMON ROOM 4.
HUFF
HUFF
IT'S A HELLISH SPACE, WITH **CORPSES** STREWN EVERY-WHERE.
IT USED TO BE THE MEETING ROOM FOR OUR NEIGHBORS CLUB.
YOU COULD SAY OUR CLUB DOES A WIDE VARIETY OF THINGS. OR MAYBE YOU'D SAY WE'RE WILDLY INCONSISTENT.
Common Room 4
I DOUBT **ANYONE** WOULD UNDERSTAND THE CLUB'S NATURE IF THEY HEARD ABOUT OUR ACTIVITIES.

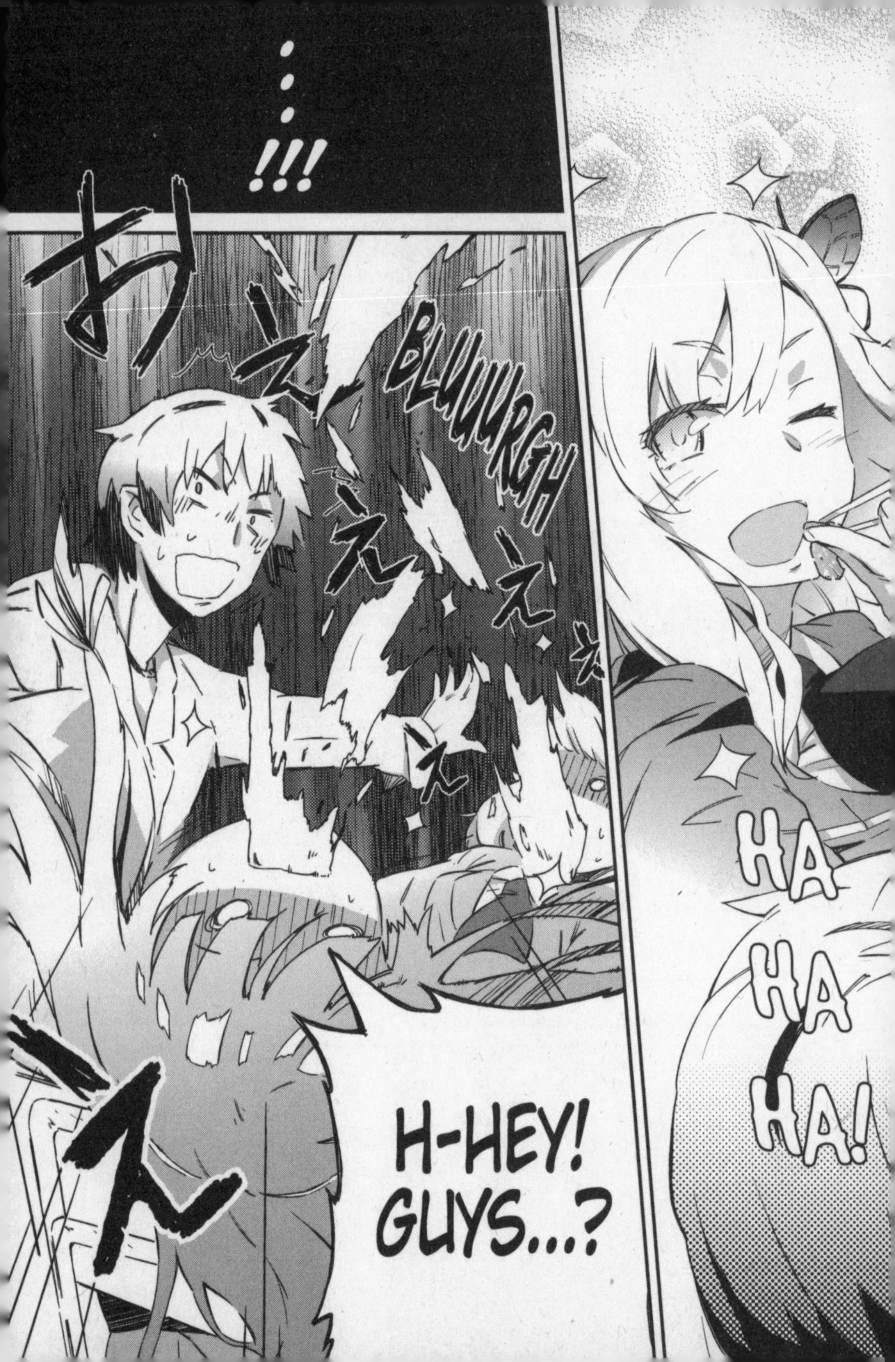
HA HA HA!
...!!!
BLUUURGH
H-HEY! GUYS...?

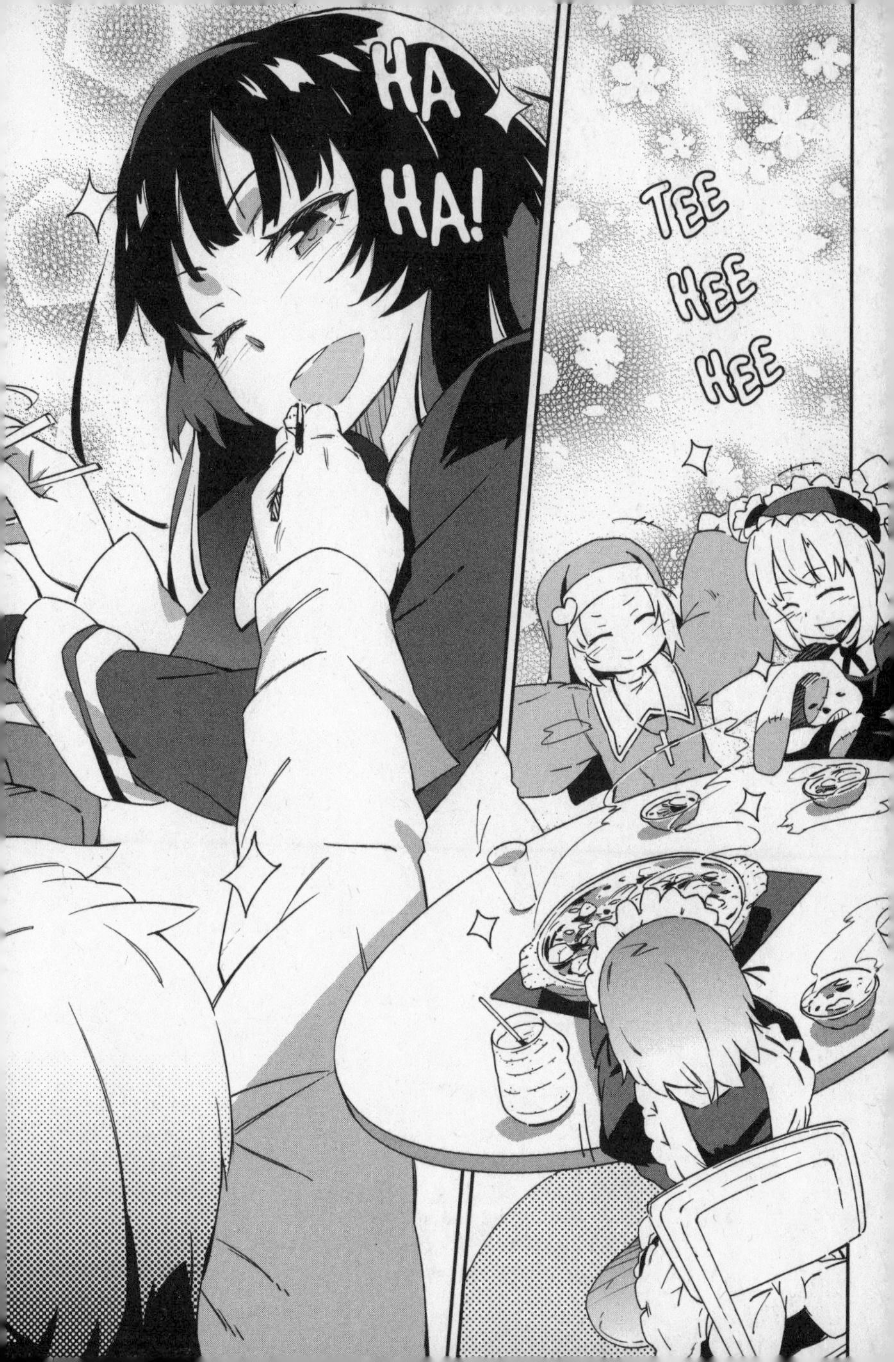
TEE HEE HEE
HA HA!

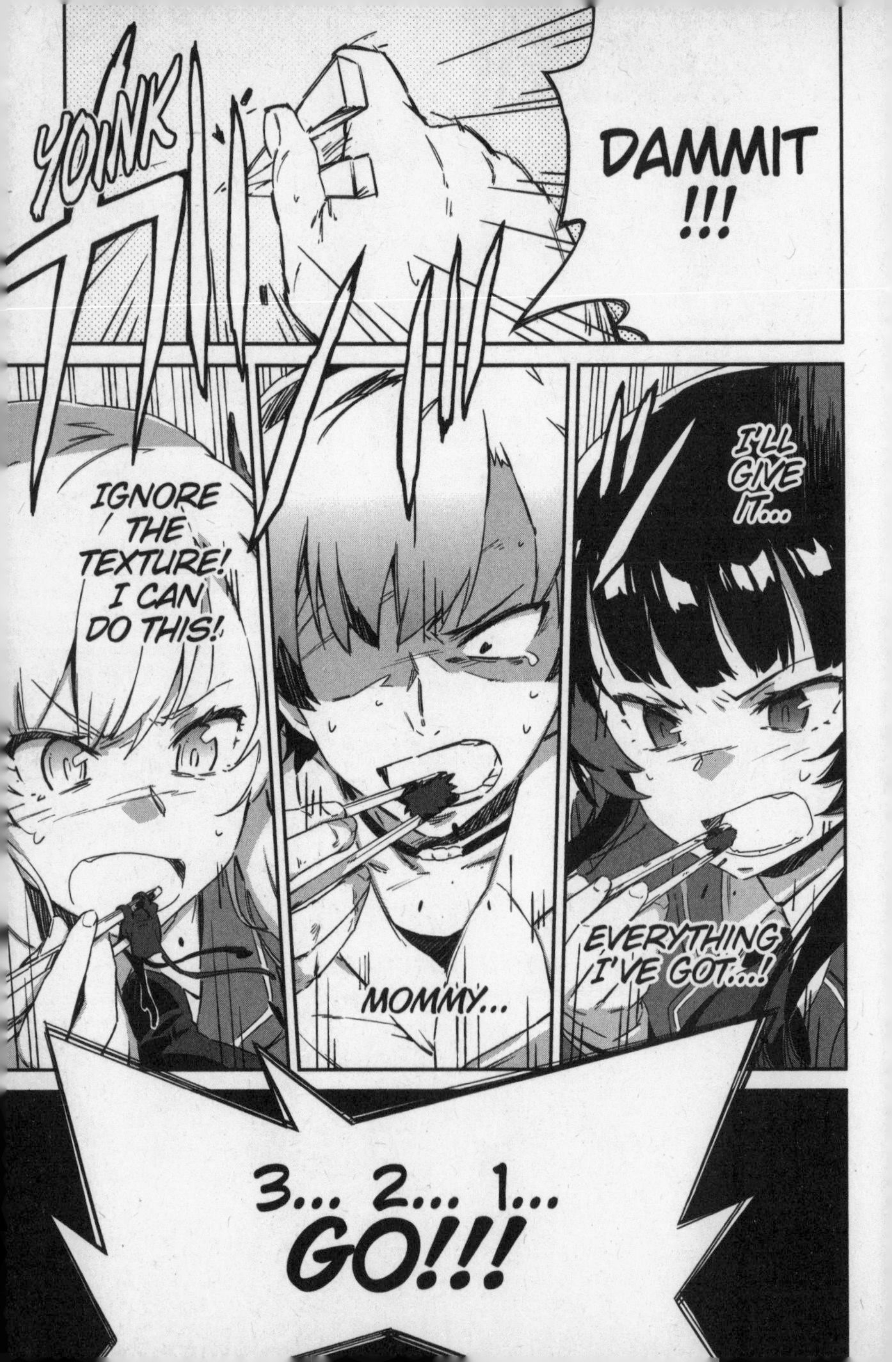
DAMMIT !!!
YOINK
I'LL GIVE IT...
EVERYTHING I'VE GOT...!
MOMMY...
IGNORE THE TEXTURE! I CAN DO THIS!
3... 2... 1... GO!!!

*Surströmming is a notoriously strong-smelling fermented herring from Sweden.
**Sticky rice cakes with a sweet filling.

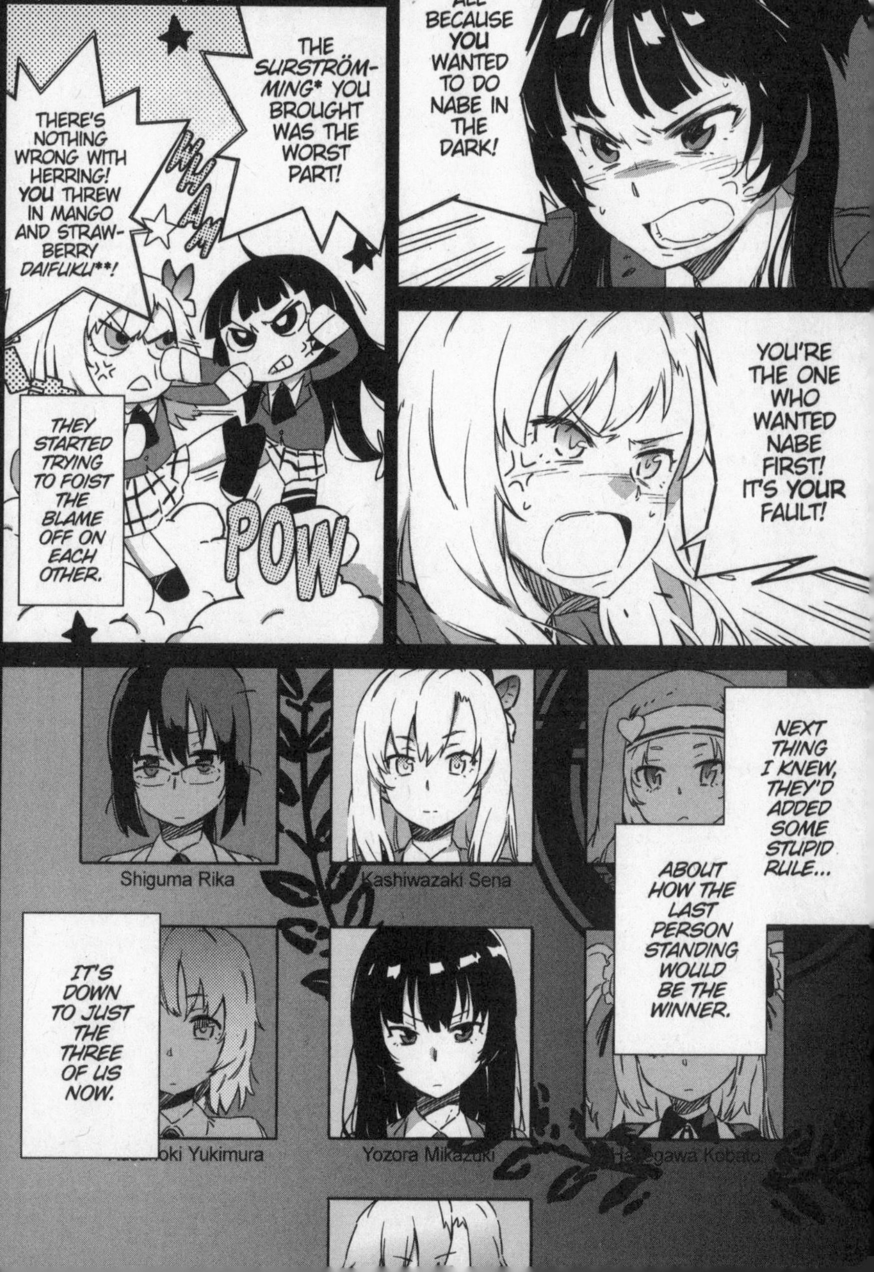

THIS IS ALL BECAUSE YOU WANTED TO DO NABE IN THE DARK!
YOU'RE THE ONE WHO WANTED NABE FIRST! IT'S YOUR FAULT!
THE SURSTRÖMMING* YOU BROUGHT WAS THE WORST PART!
THERE'S NOTHING WRONG WITH HERRING! YOU THREW IN MANGO AND STRAWBERRY DAIFUKU**!
WHAM
THEY STARTED TRYING TO FOIST THE BLAME OFF ON EACH OTHER.
POW
NEXT THING I KNEW, THEY'D ADDED SOME STUPID RULE...
ABOUT HOW THE LAST PERSON STANDING WOULD BE THE WINNER.
Kashiwazaki Sena
Shiguma Rika
Yozora Mikazuki
IT'S DOWN TO JUST THE THREE OF US NOW.

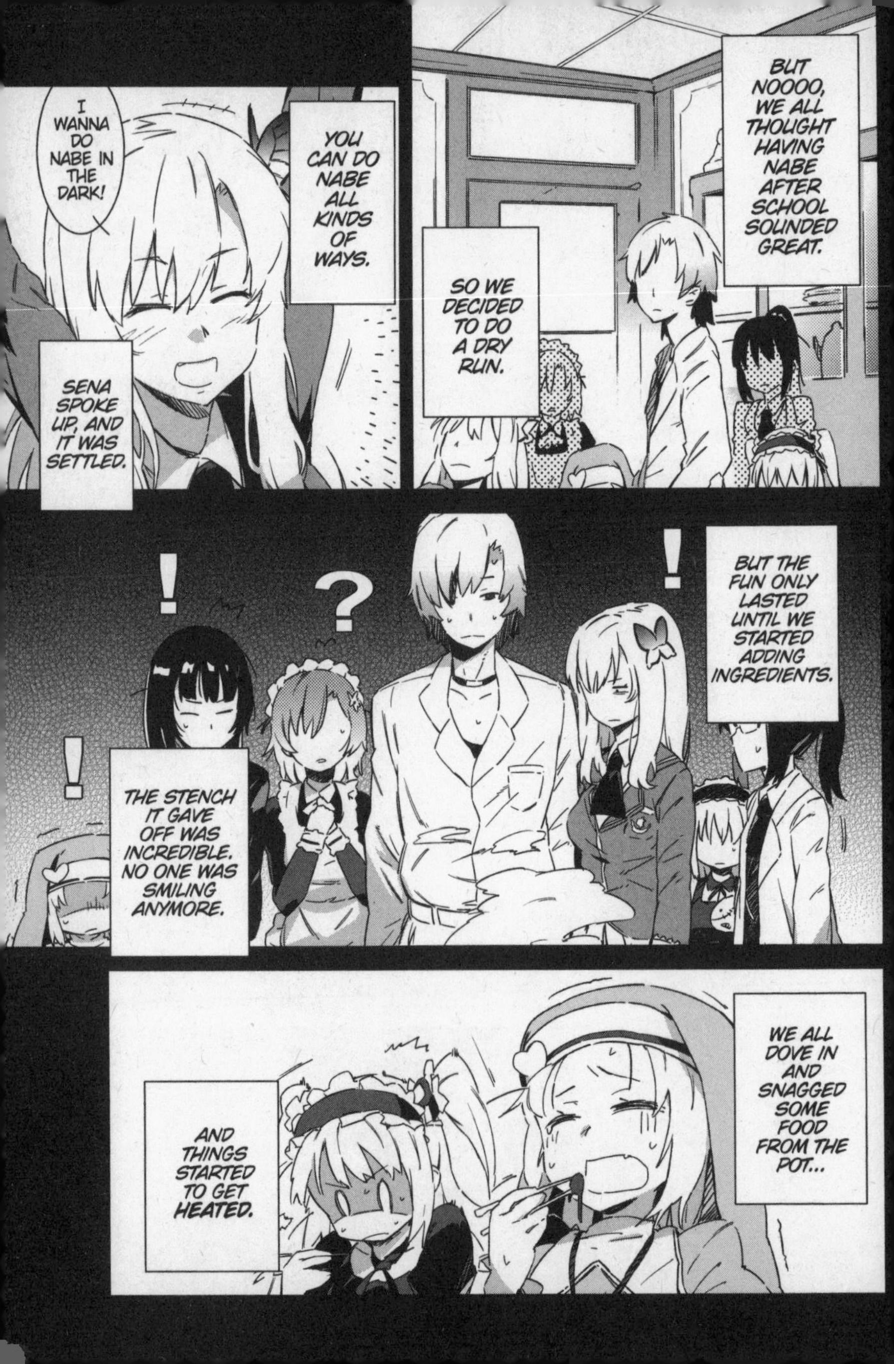
BUT NOOOO, WE ALL THOUGHT HAVING NABE AFTER SCHOOL SOUNDED GREAT.
SO WE DECIDED TO DO A DRY RUN.
YOU CAN DO NABE ALL KINDS OF WAYS.
I WANNA DO NABE IN THE DARK!
SENA SPOKE UP, AND IT WAS SETTLED.
BUT THE FUN ONLY LASTED UNTIL WE STARTED ADDING INGREDIENTS.
THE STENCH IT GAVE OFF WAS INCREDIBLE. NO ONE WAS SMILING ANYMORE.
WE ALL DOVE IN AND SNAGGED SOME FOOD FROM THE POT...
AND THINGS STARTED TO GET HEATED.

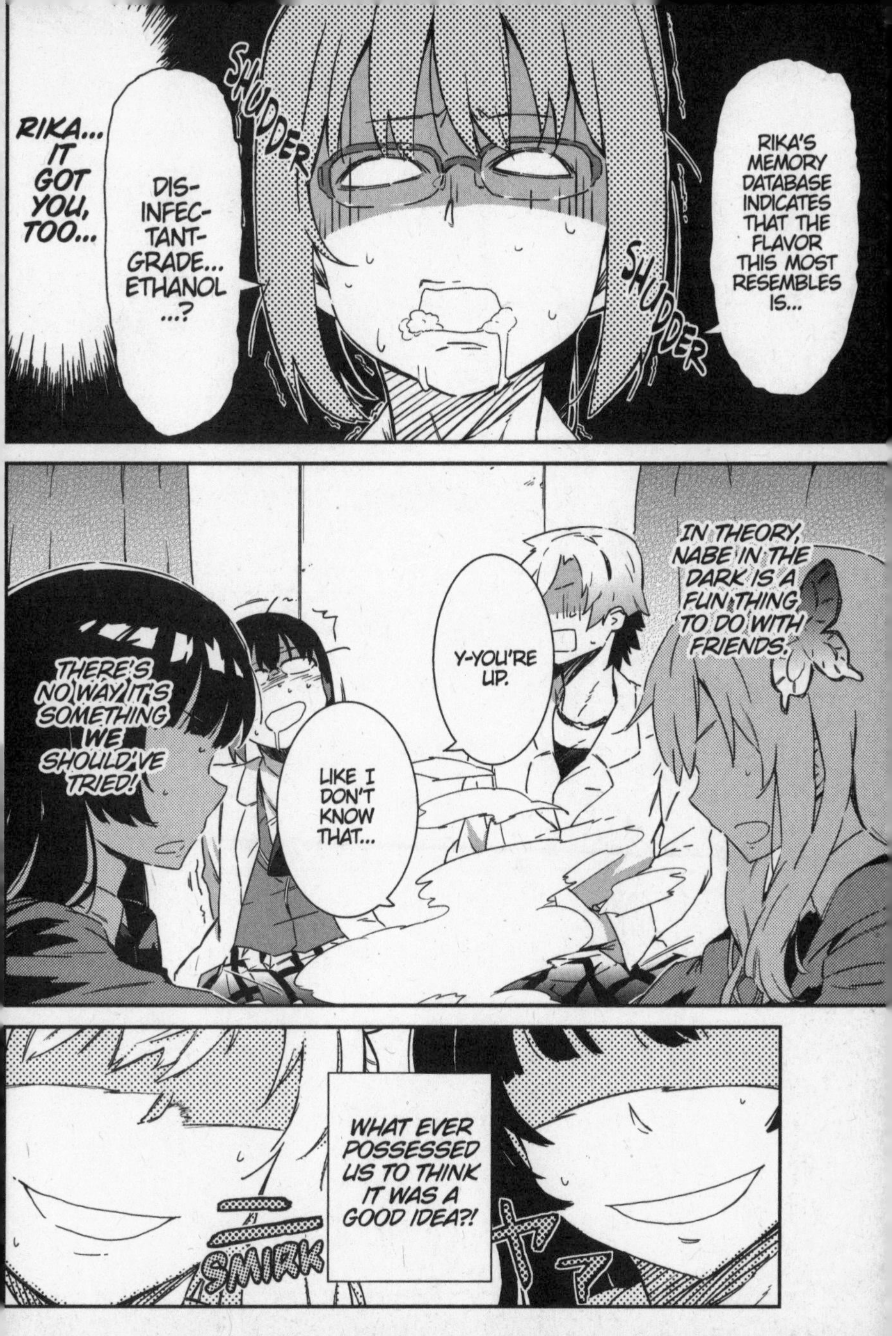
RIKA'S MEMORY DATABASE INDICATES THAT THE FLAVOR THIS MOST RESEMBLES IS...
SHUDDER
SHUDDER
DIS-INFECTANT-GRADE... ETHANOL...?
RIKA... IT GOT YOU, TOO...
IN THEORY, NABE IN THE DARK IS A FUN THING TO DO WITH FRIENDS.
Y-YOU'RE UP.
LIKE I DON'T KNOW THAT...
THERE'S NO WAY IT'S SOMETHING WE SHOULD'VE TRIED!
WHAT EVER POSSESSED US TO THINK IT WAS A GOOD IDEA?!
SMIRK

HIGHLY DUBIOUS...

SHALL WE...?

GULP

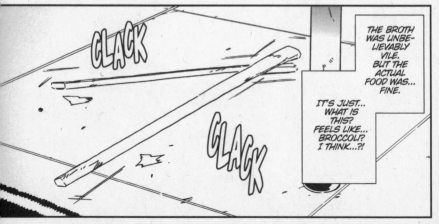

CLACK

CLACK

THE BROTH WAS UNBELIEVABLY VILE. BUT THE ACTUAL FOOD WAS... FINE.

IT'S JUST... WHAT IS THIS? FEELS LIKE... BROCCOLI? I THINK...?!

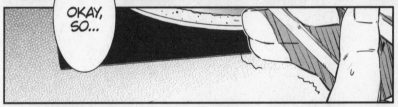

↑ In the dark, mystery ingredients are added to the pot and then fished out. The lights go on, and people eat...whatever they caught.

IT'S NABE IN THE DARK.
BUBBLE
BUBBLE
OKAY, SO...
WE'RE AT LEAST SURE THIS ISN'T POISONOUS, RIGHT?
THAT SHOULD BE CORRECT, KODAKA-SEMPAI.
RIKA'S POISON DETECTOR CAN IDENTIFY ANY KNOWN TOXINS.
IT'S PERFECT ...IN THEORY.

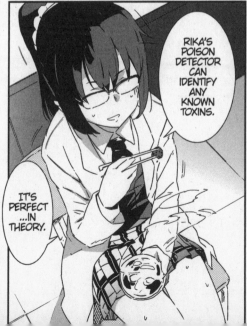

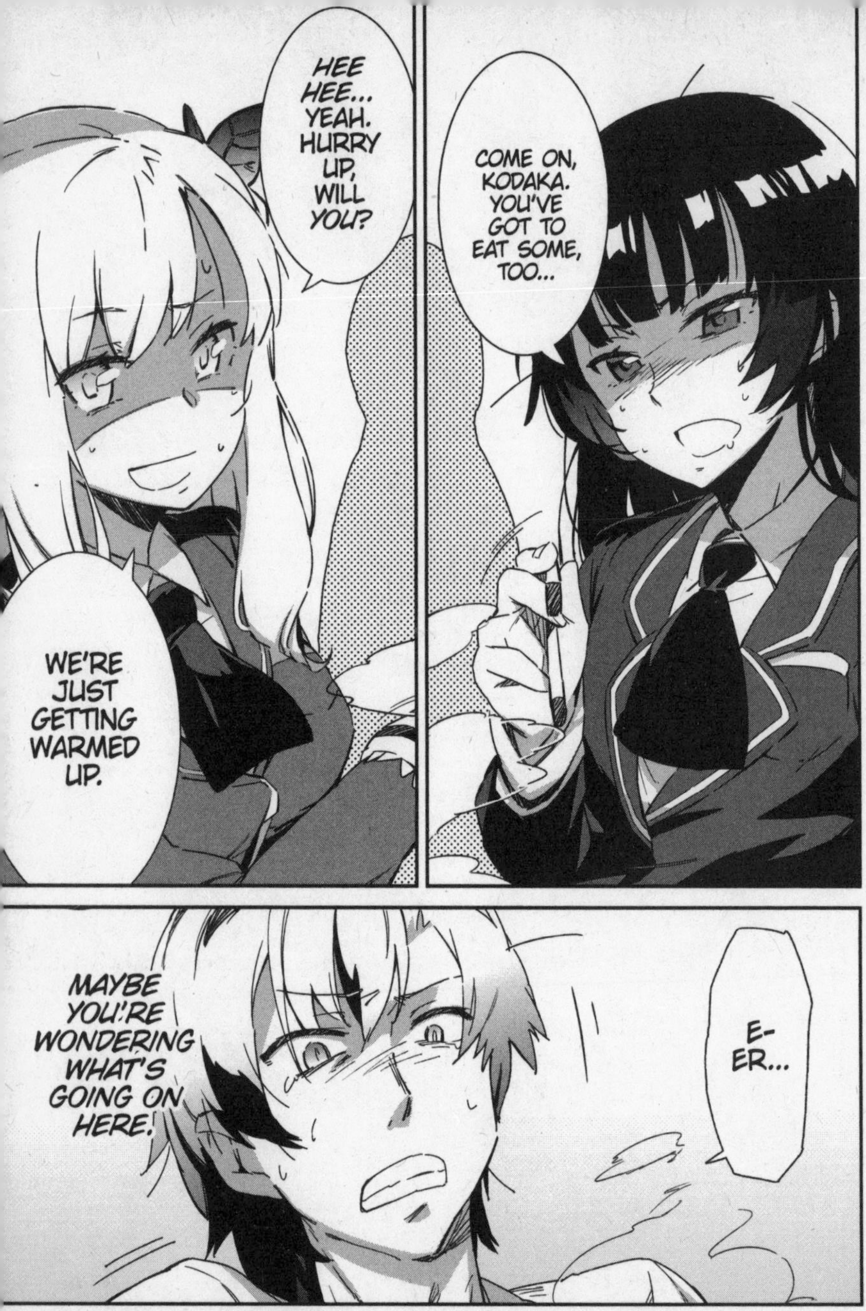
COME ON, KODAKA. YOU'VE GOT TO EAT SOME, TOO...
HEE HEE... YEAH. HURRY UP, WILL YOU?
WE'RE JUST GETTING WARMED UP.
E-ER...
MAYBE YOU'RE WONDERING WHAT'S GOING ON HERE!

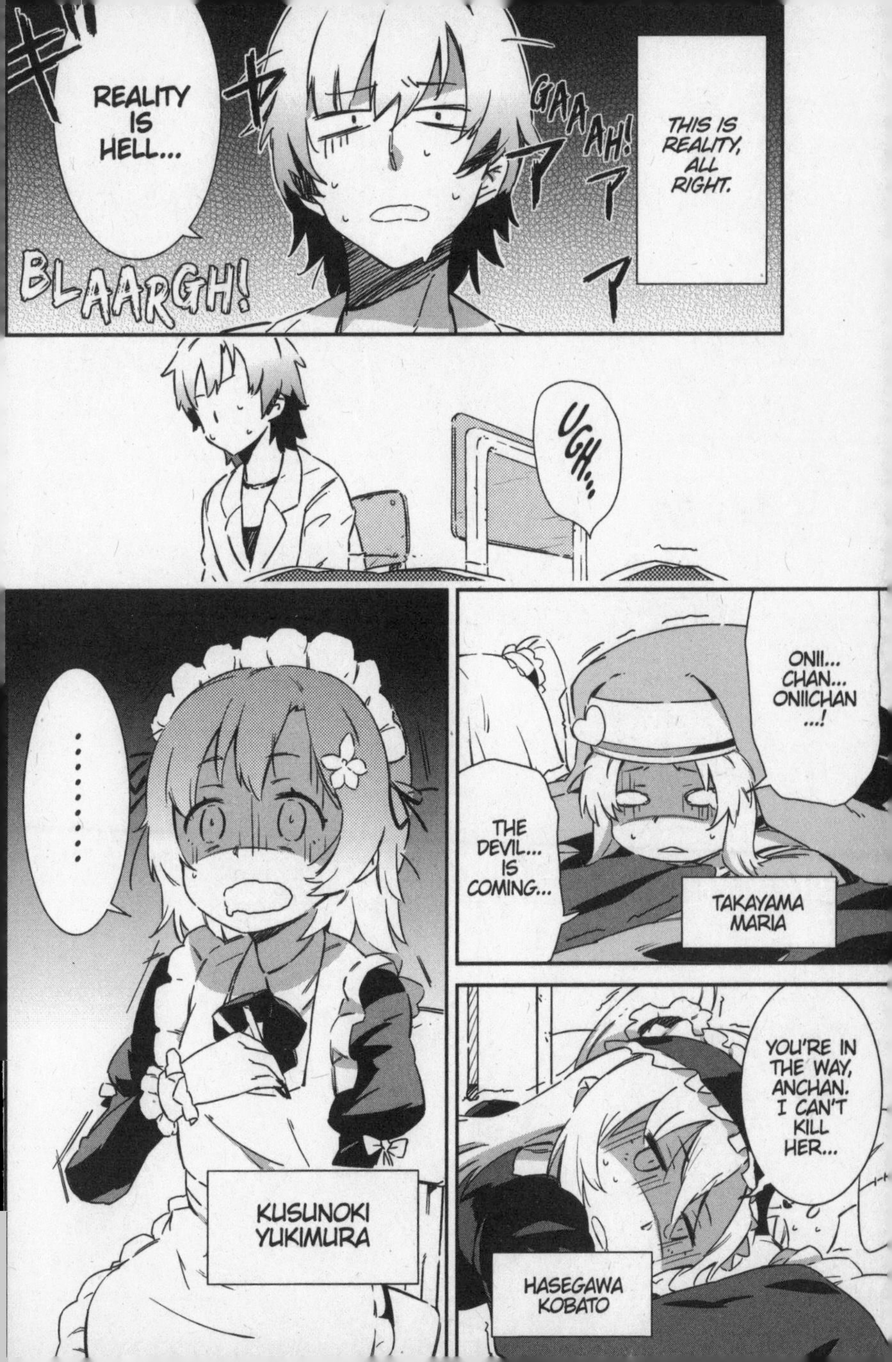
THIS IS REALITY, ALL RIGHT.
GAAAAH!
REALITY IS HELL...
BLAARGH!
UGH...
ONII... CHAN... ONIICHAN ...!
THE DEVIL... IS COMING...
TAKAYAMA MARIA
YOU'RE IN THE WAY, ANCHAN. I CAN'T KILL HER...
HASEGAWA KOBATO
....
KUSUNOKI YUKIMURA

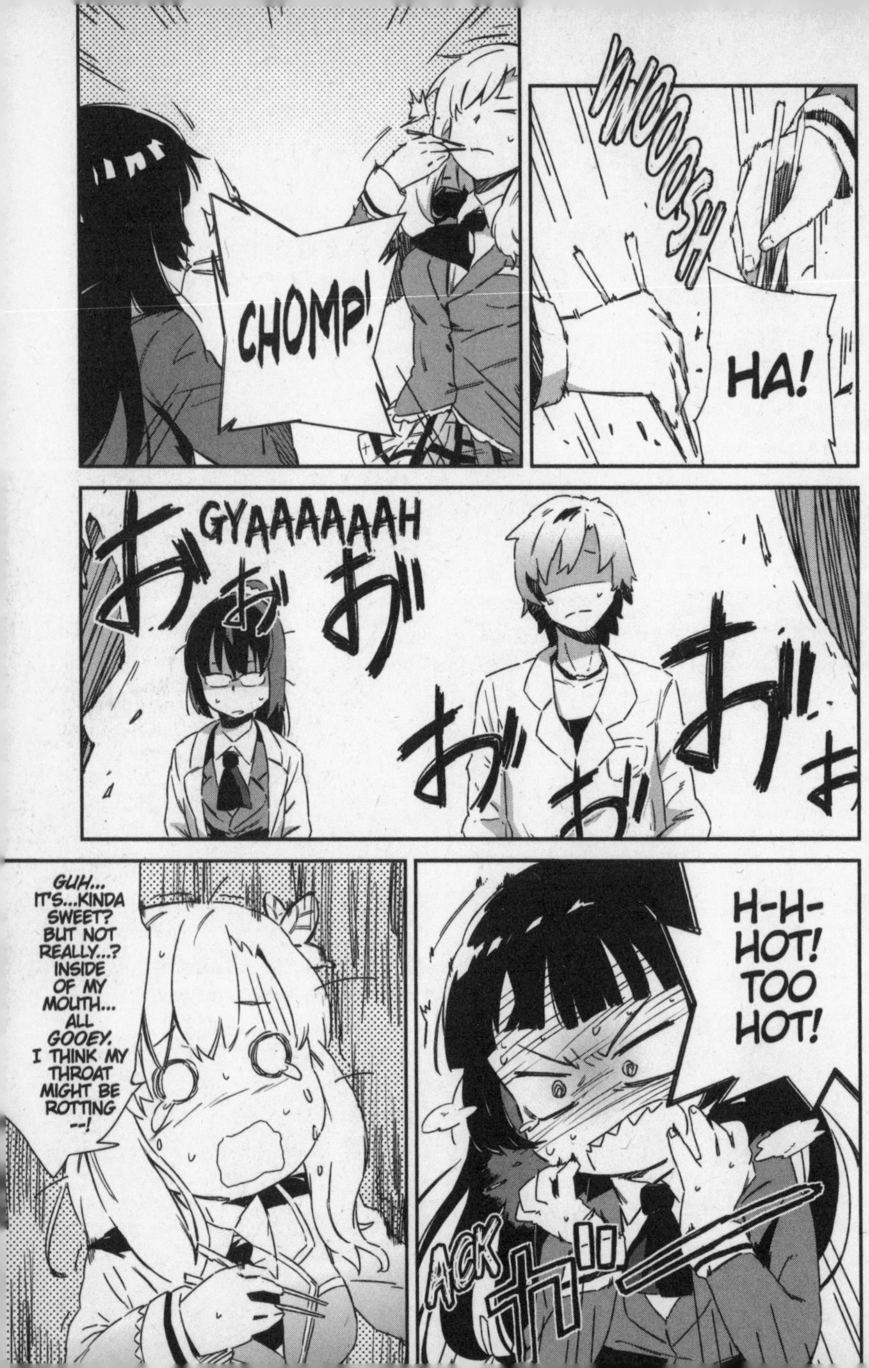
WHOOOSH
HA!
CHOMP!
GYAAAAAAH
H-H-HOT! TOO HOT!
ACK
GUH... IT'S...KINDA SWEET? BUT NOT REALLY...? INSIDE OF MY MOUTH... ALL GOOEY. I THINK MY THROAT MIGHT BE ROTTING--!

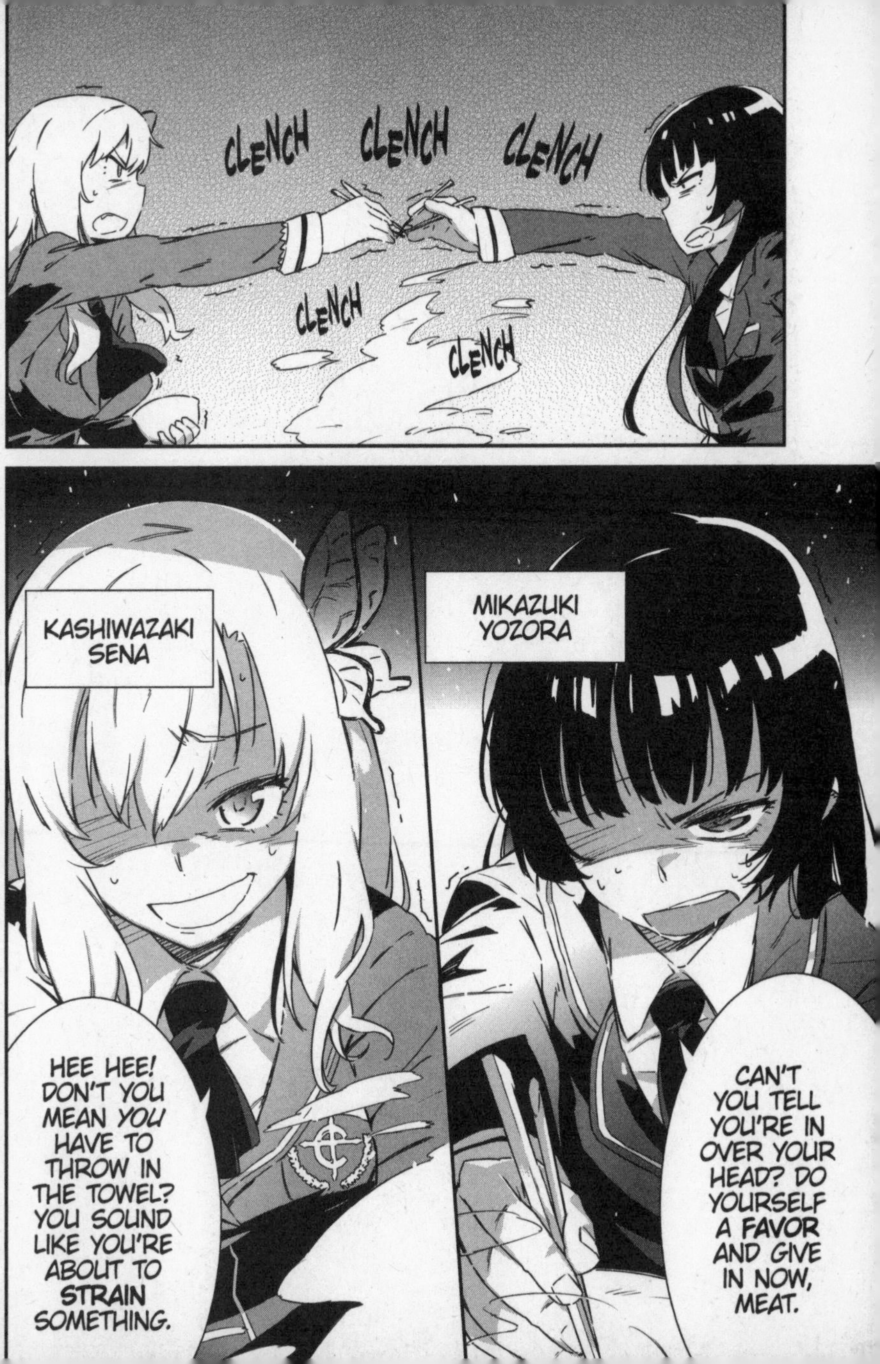
CLENCH
CLENCH
CLENCH
CLENCH
CLENCH
MIKAZUKI YOZORA
CAN'T YOU TELL YOU'RE IN OVER YOUR HEAD? DO YOURSELF A FAVOR AND GIVE IN NOW, MEAT.
KASHIWAZAKI SENA
HEE HEE! DON'T YOU MEAN *YOU* HAVE TO THROW IN THE TOWEL? YOU SOUND LIKE YOU'RE ABOUT TO **STRAIN** SOMETHING.

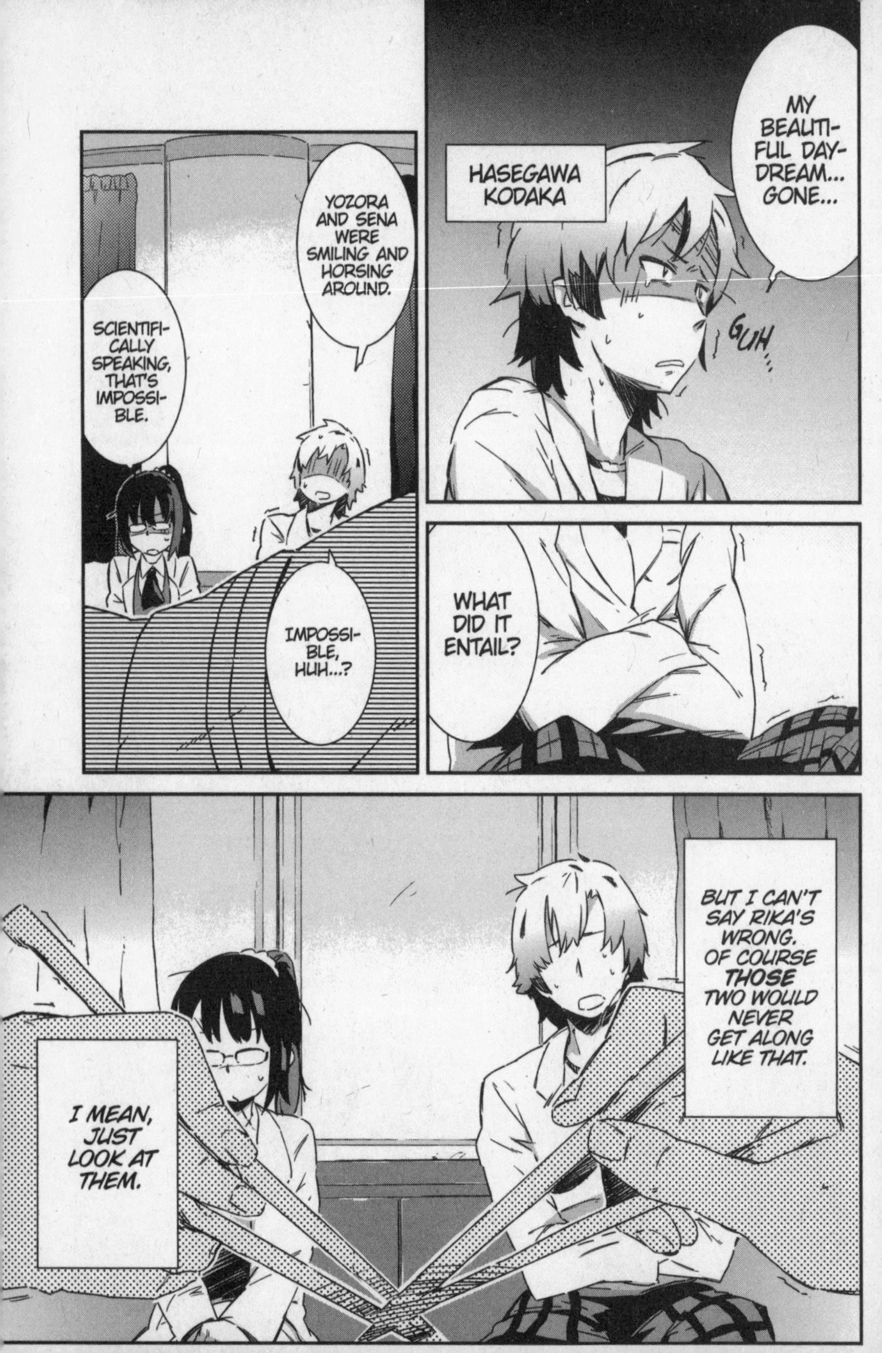

MY BEAUTI-FUL DAY-DREAM... GONE...
HASEGAWA KODAKA
GUH...
WHAT DID IT ENTAIL?
YOZORA AND SENA WERE SMILING AND HORSING AROUND.
SCIENTIFI-CALLY SPEAKING, THAT'S IMPOSSI-BLE.
IMPOSSI-BLE, HUH...?
BUT I CAN'T SAY RIKA'S WRONG. OF COURSE THOSE TWO WOULD NEVER GET ALONG LIKE THAT.
I MEAN, JUST LOOK AT THEM.

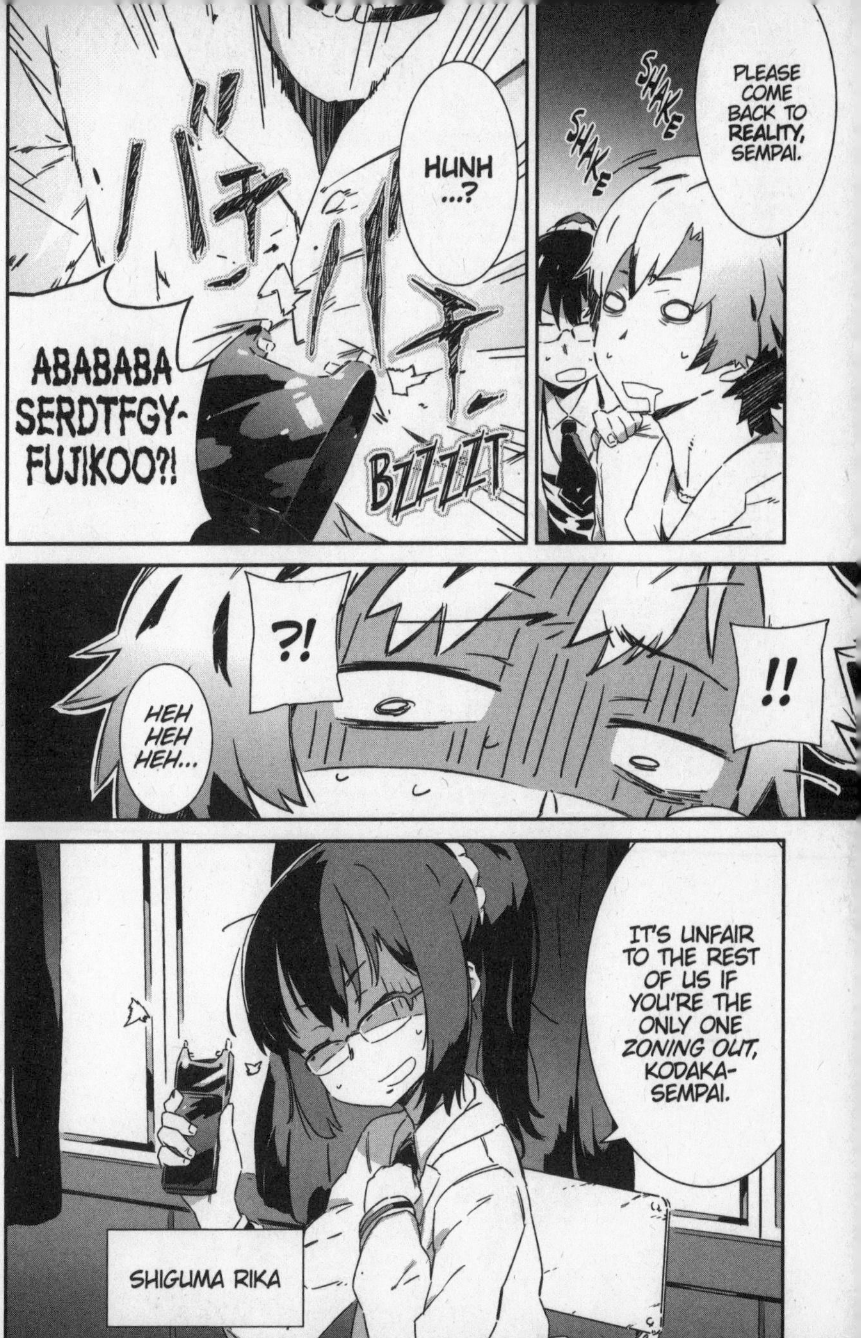
SHAKE
SHAKE
PLEASE COME BACK TO REALITY, SEMPAI.
HUNH ...?
ABABABA SERDTFGY-FUJIKOO?!
BZZZZT
!!
?!
HEH HEH HEH...
IT'S UNFAIR TO THE REST OF US IF YOU'RE THE ONLY ONE ZONING OUT, KODAKA-SEMPAI.
SHIGUMA RIKA

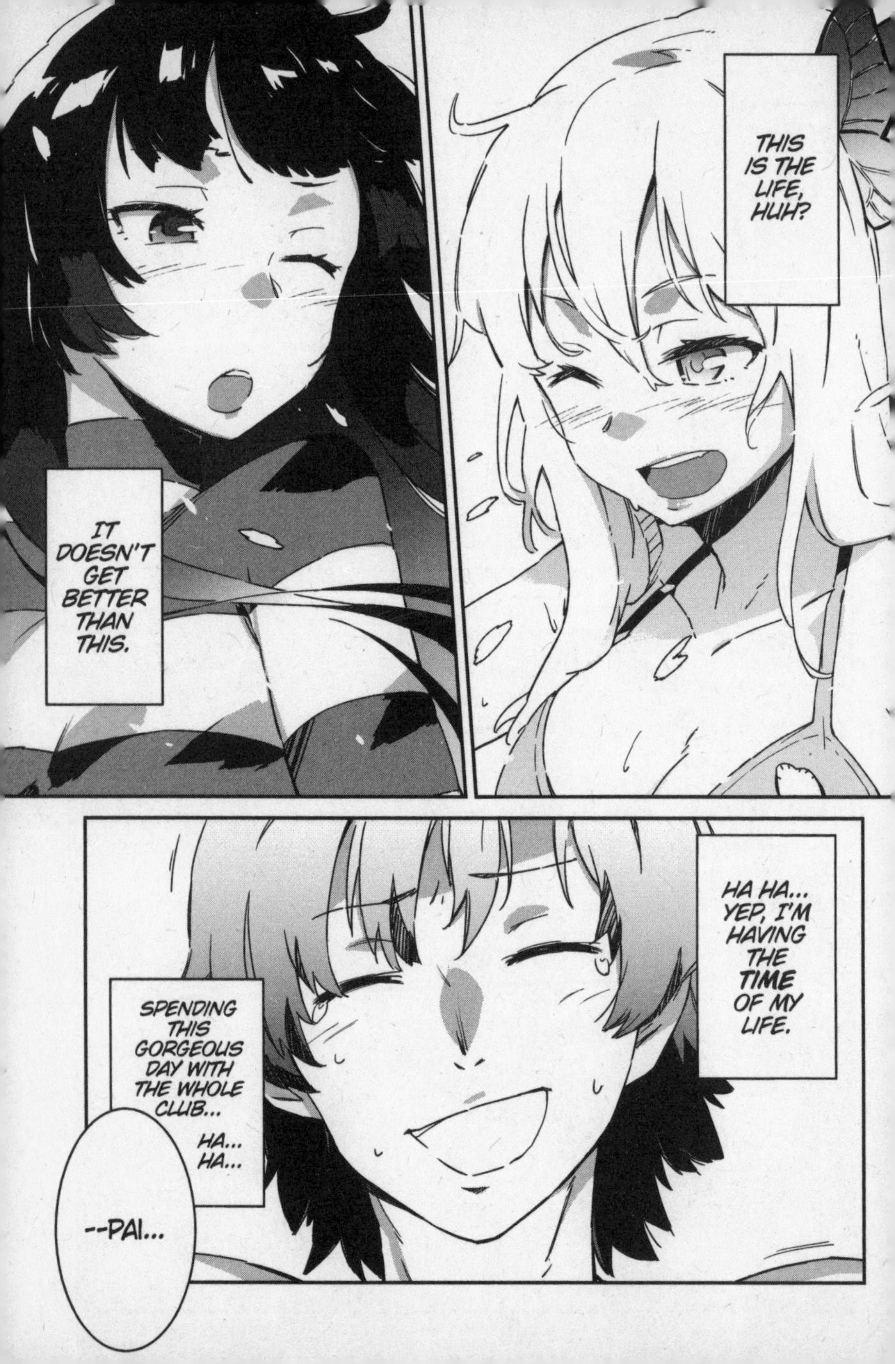
THIS IS THE LIFE, HUH?
IT DOESN'T GET BETTER THAN THIS.
HA HA... YEP, I'M HAVING THE TIME OF MY LIFE.
SPENDING THIS GORGEOUS DAY WITH THE WHOLE CLUB...
HA... HA...
--PAI...

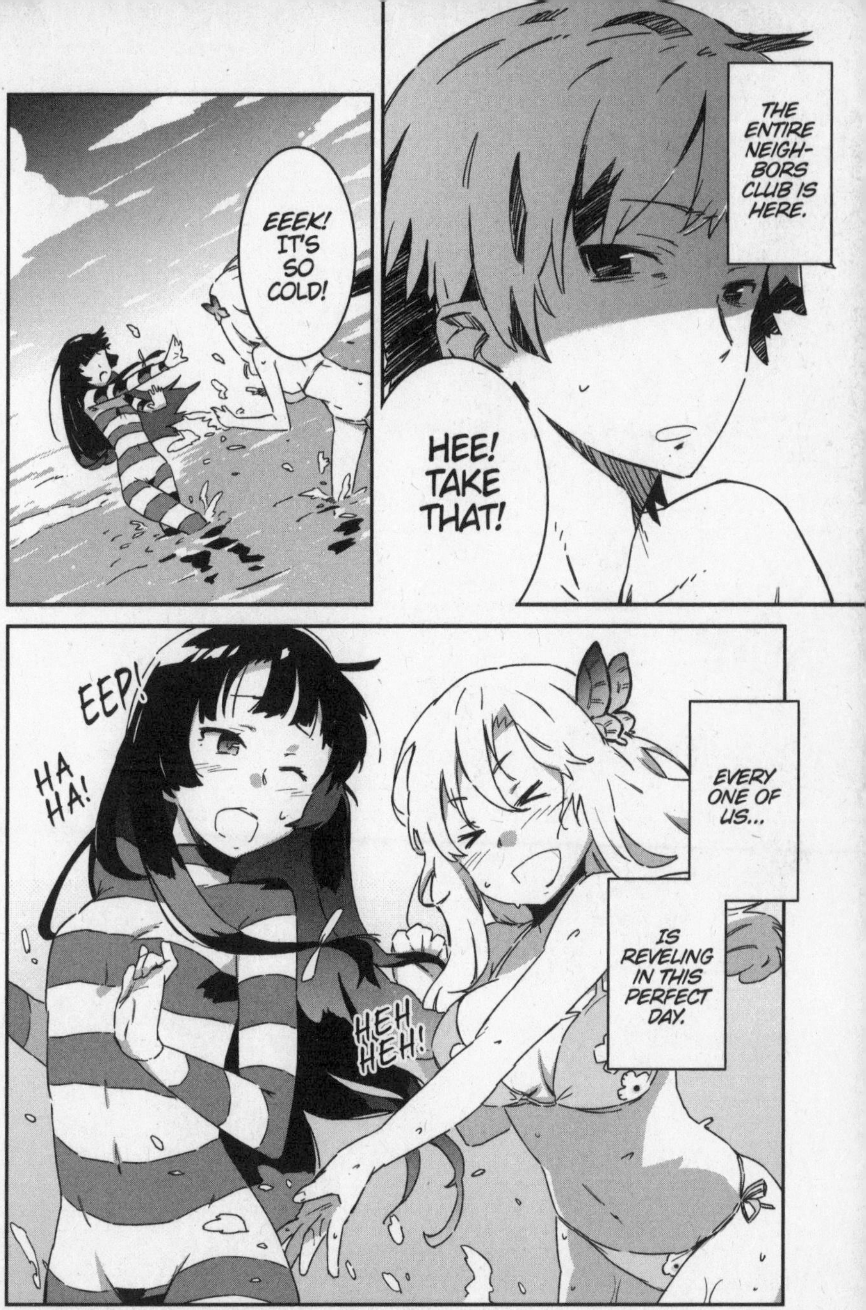
THE ENTIRE NEIGHBORS CLUB IS HERE.
HEE! TAKE THAT!
EEEK! IT'S SO COLD!
EVERY ONE OF US...
IS REVELING IN THIS PERFECT DAY.
EEP!
HA HA!
HEH HEH!

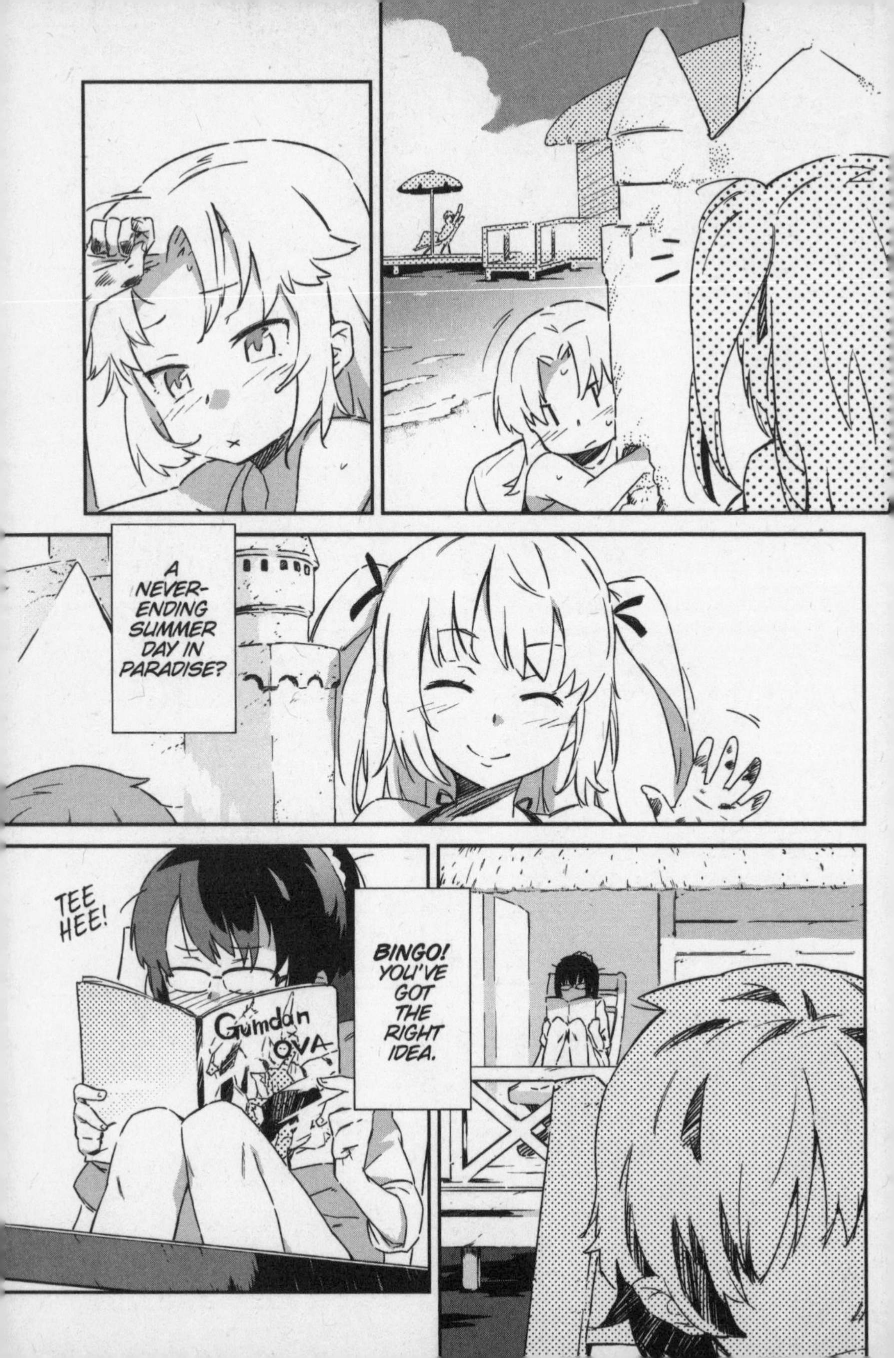
A NEVER-ENDING SUMMER DAY IN PARADISE?
BINGO! YOU'VE GOT THE RIGHT IDEA.
TEE HEE!
Gumdan OVA

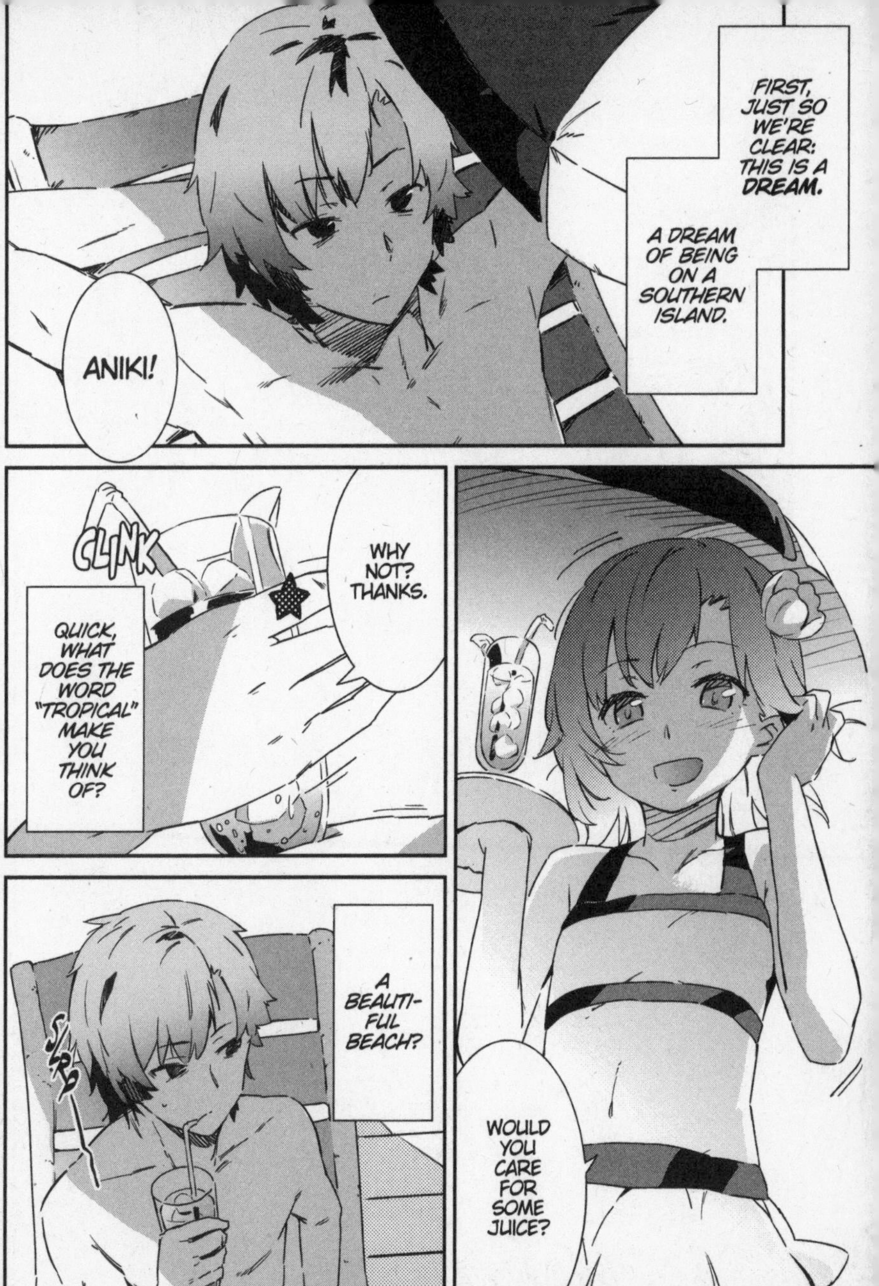
FIRST, JUST SO WE'RE CLEAR: THIS IS A **DREAM.**
A DREAM OF BEING ON A SOUTHERN ISLAND.
ANIKI!
WOULD YOU CARE FOR SOME JUICE?
WHY NOT? THANKS.
CLINK
QUICK, WHAT DOES THE WORD "TROPICAL" MAKE YOU THINK OF?
A BEAUTI-FUL BEACH?
SLRP

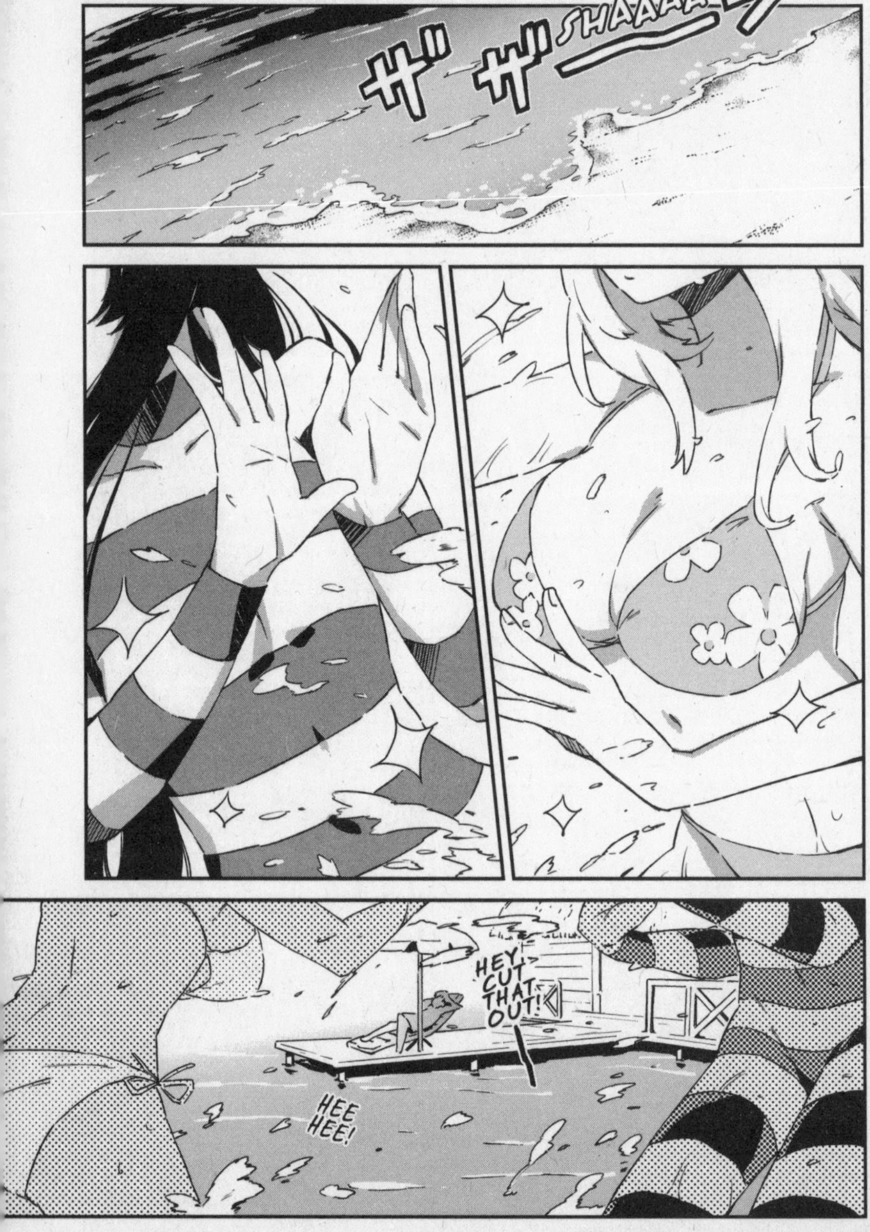
ザ ザ SHAAAA—!
HEY CUT THAT OUT!
HEE HEE!

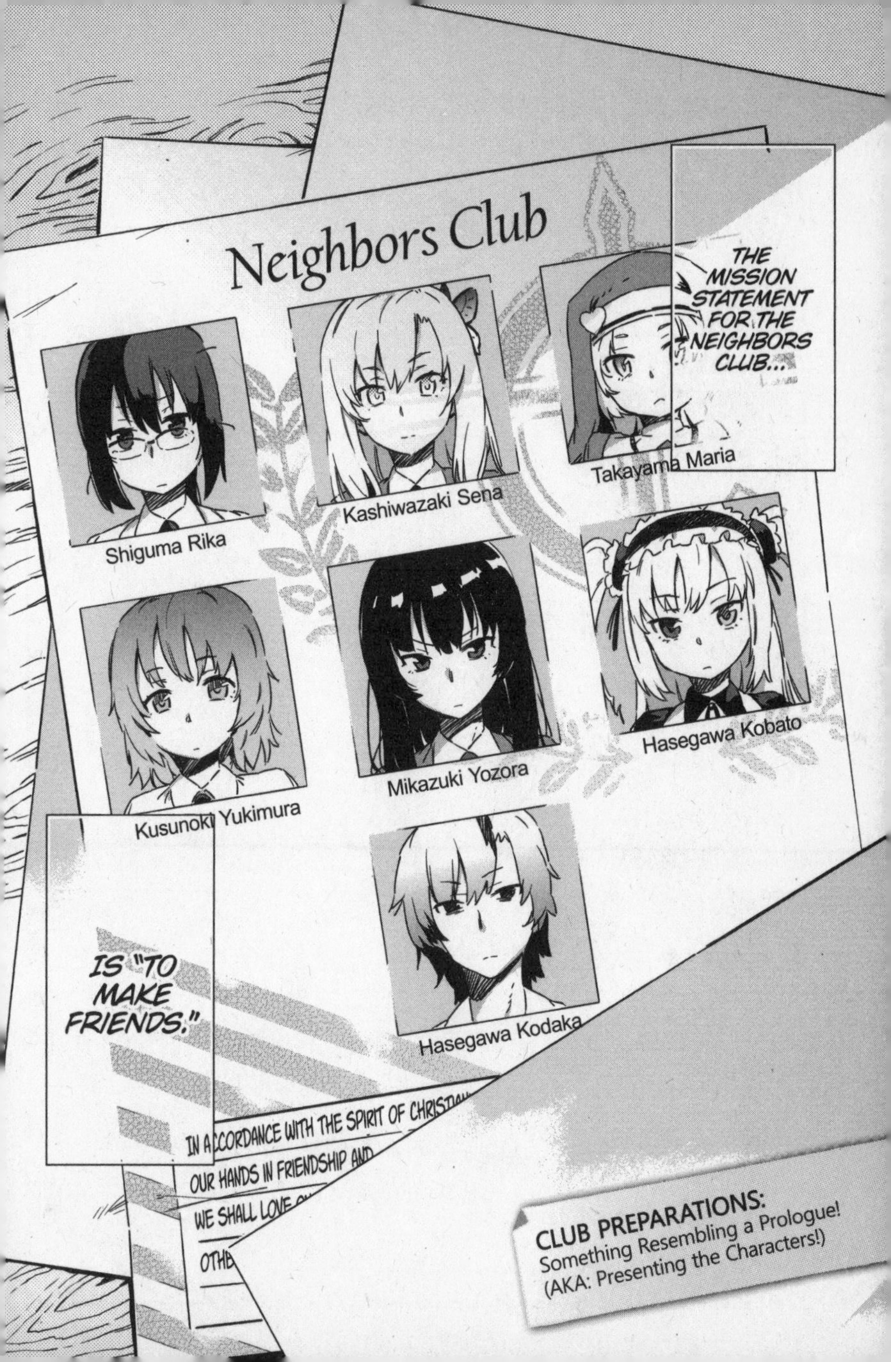
Neighbors Club
THE MISSION STATEMENT FOR THE NEIGHBORS CLUB...
Takayama Maria
Kashiwazaki Sena
Shiguma Rika
Hasegawa Kobato
Mikazuki Yozora
Kusunoki Yukimura
Hasegawa Kodaka
IS "TO MAKE FRIENDS."
IN ACCORDANCE WITH THE SPIRIT OF
OUR HANDS IN FRIENDSHIP AND
WE SHALL LOVE
CLUB PREPARATIONS:
Something Resembling a Prologue!
(AKA: Presenting the Characters!)

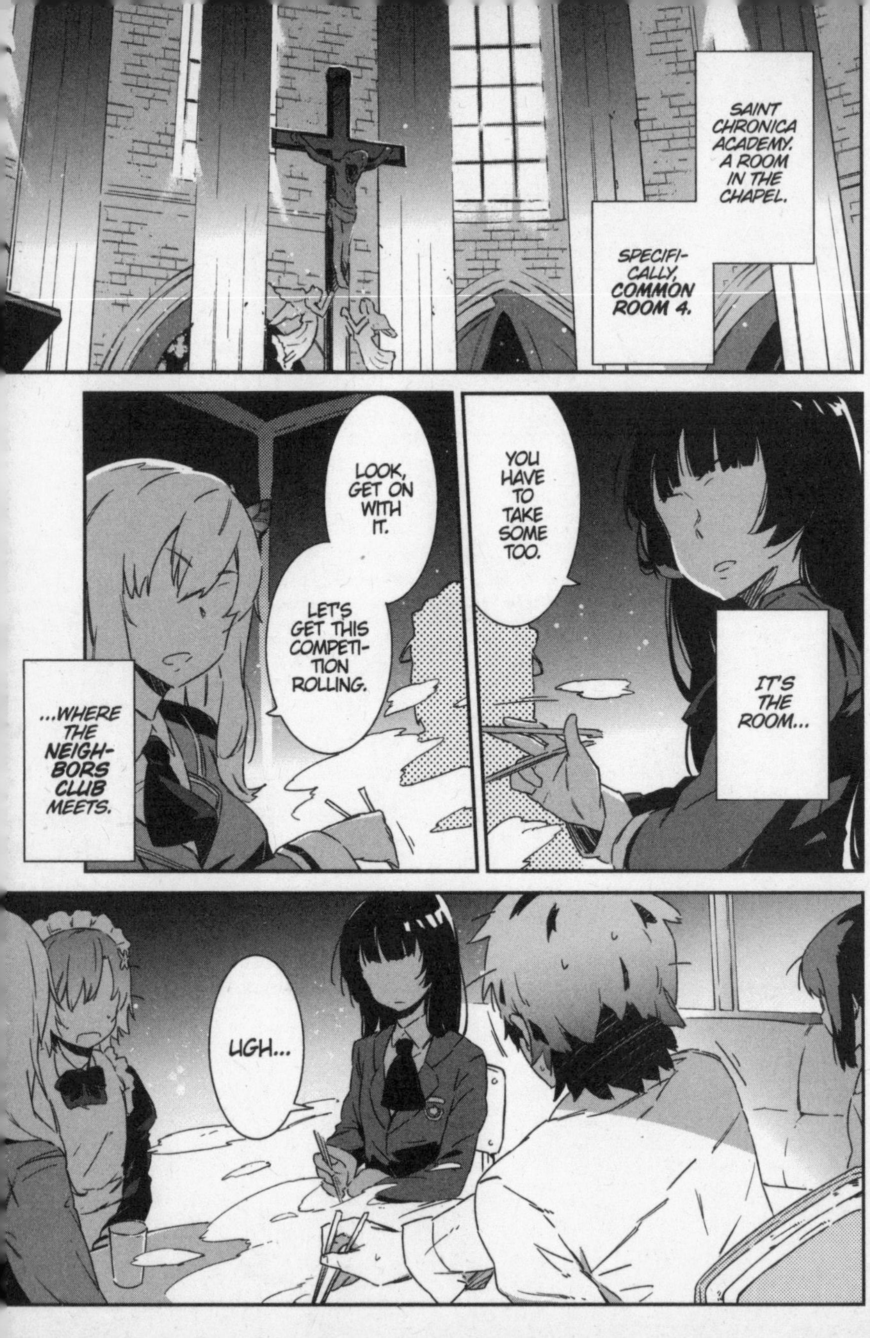
SAINT CHRONICA ACADEMY. A ROOM IN THE CHAPEL.
SPECIFICALLY, COMMON ROOM 4.
YOU HAVE TO TAKE SOME TOO.
IT'S THE ROOM...
LOOK, GET ON WITH IT.
LET'S GET THIS COMPETITION ROLLING.
...WHERE THE NEIGHBORS CLUB MEETS.
UGH...

MY AIR FRIEND!

volume 1

Haganai
I don't have many friends

僕は友達が少ない

BOKU HA
TOMODACHI GA
SUKU NA I

ART: ITACHI
STORY: YOMI HIRASAKA
CHARACTER DESIGN: BURIKI

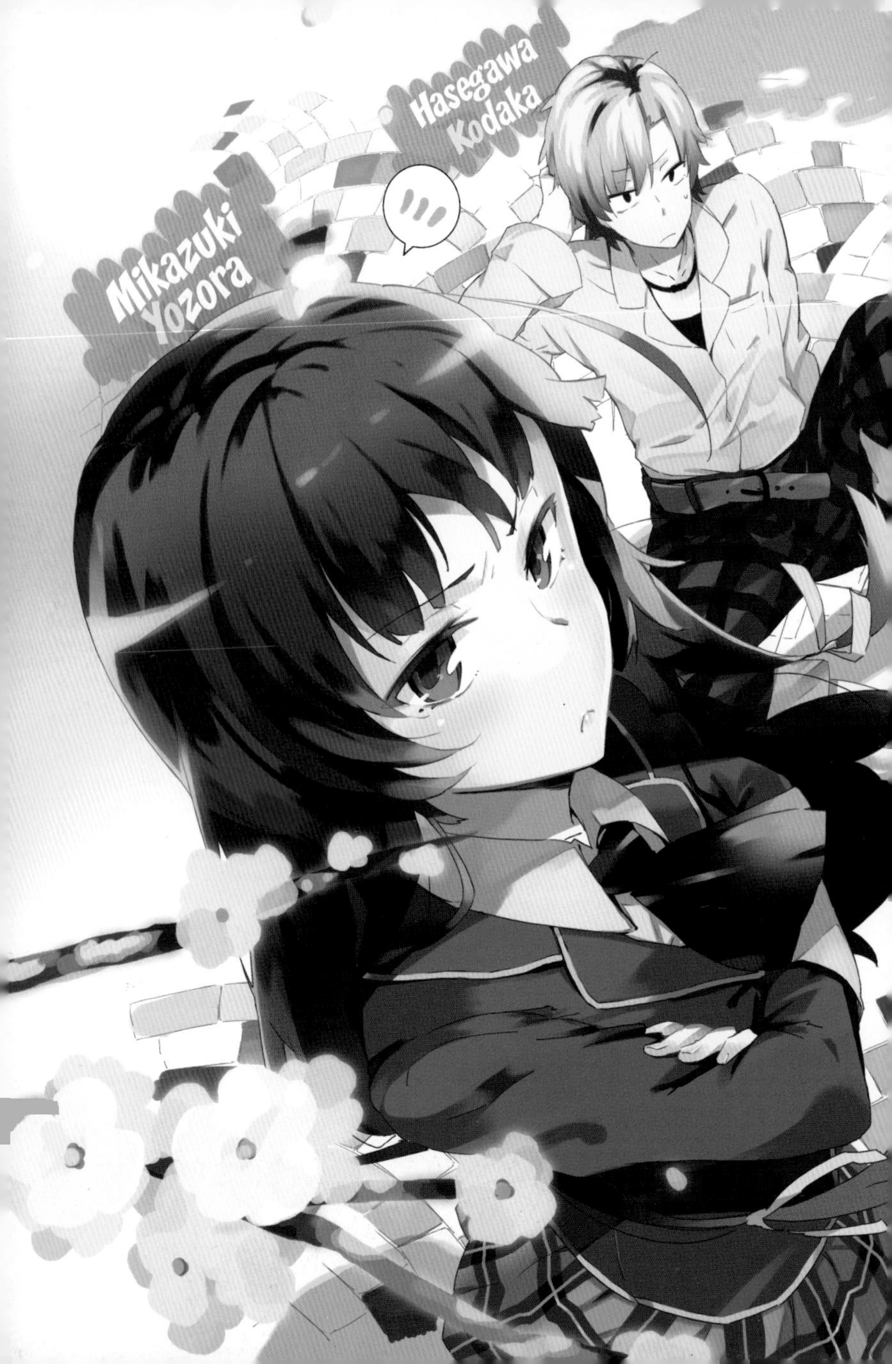
Hasegawa
Kodaka
!!
Mikazuki
Yozora